31243 00 536 1679
Lake Forest Library
W9-CIE-838

THE HANDBOOK FOR
Storytellers

ALA Editions purchases fund advocacy, awareness, and accreditation programs for library professionals worldwide.

THE HANDBOOK FOR Storytellers

JUDY FREEMAN *and* CAROLINE FELLER BAUER

An imprint of the American Library Association
CHICAGO 2015

Caroline Feller Bauer (1935–2013) was a public librarian, professor of children's literature, radio personality, international speaker and performer, author of nineteen children's books and professional books about children's literature for adults, and a tireless cheerleader for literacy and storytelling.

Judy Freeman is a former school librarian; an adjunct professor at Pratt Institute in New York City teaching courses in children's literature and storytelling; an international speaker and performer for children, teachers, librarians, and parents; a children's book reviewer; and the author of more than a dozen professional books about children's literature and storytelling. She continues to work closely with librarians, teachers, and hundreds of students at several elementary schools to test out new books, ideas, and ways to incorporate literature into children's lives.

Both have developed and performed thousands of programs and workshops incorporating children's literature, storytelling, music, poetry, and drama to tens of thousands of children and adults across the United States and abroad.

Printed in the United States of America

19 18 17 16 15 5 4 3 2 1

ISBN: 978-0-8389-1100-6 (paper).

Library of Congress Cataloging-in-Publication Data

Freeman, Judy.
The handbook for storytellers / Judy Freeman and Caroline Feller Bauer.
pages cm
Includes bibliographical references and index.
ISBN 978-0-8389-1100-6 (print : alk. paper) 1. Storytelling—Handbooks, manuals, etc. 2. Children's libraries—Activity programs—Handbooks, manuals, etc. I. Bauer, Caroline Feller. II. Title.
LB1042.F735 2015
372.67'7—dc23 2014027933

Book design by Kimberly Thornton in the Charis SIL and Tisa Sans Pro typefaces. Illustrations by Andere Andrea Petrlik/Shutterstock, Inc. Lettering by Nenilkime/Shutterstock, Inc.

♾ This paper meets the requirements of ANSI/NISO Z39.48–1992 (Permanence of Paper).

To Izzy Feldman, my right-hand man,
who graciously withstood five years of nonstop drama and stories

Contents

Acknowledgments

I'd like to thank the following people for their help and support:

Caroline Feller Bauer, whose books and ideas inspired a generation of creative storytellers

Richard Freeman, for expert close reading, corrections, and many odd facts

Ann Guthrie, for general sagacity, philosophies of teaching, and for allowing me to entertain her preschoolers at the Antioch School

Maren Vitali and Jennifer Fisher, two librarians extraordinaire, whose stream of clever ideas, projects, and book sense never failed to delight

Kristin Fontichiaro, for her contributions and know-how about technology

Sasha Kleinman, for her keyboard wizardry and research acumen, online and off

Jessica Schneider, for intrepid searching skills

Margaret and Sam Feldman, for harboring the writing girl through many deadlines

Sharron Freeman, for daily chats and respites

Caitlin Freeman, for instructing me on how to breathe correctly

Anita Silvey, for her exquisite taste in books and generosity in sharing it

Peggy Beck Haines, for general support and cheerleading

Michael Jeffers, for getting the ball rolling on this project

Jamie Santoro, acquisitions editor, for going to bat for this book series

Stephanie Zvirin, editor, for reading, reorganizing, and fine-tooth-combing every chapter
Johanna Rosenbohm, copyeditor, for ferreting out all those errors and knowing every weird formatting rule
Russ Damian, for wrestling with endless permissions
The whole publishing team at ALA Editions, for taking on this daunting project

Preface

By Judy Freeman

HERE'S HOW I FIRST MET THE WHIRLWIND THAT WAS CAROLINE Feller Bauer. Way back in the 1980s, when I was a young school librarian, my friend and librarian colleague, Alice Yucht, told me she had just gone to a workshop with the most amazing presenter she had ever seen, a book-crazed lady named Caroline Feller Bauer. Alice said, "She gave us so many ideas, my wrist got sore from taking notes! She wears costumes, brings puppets and all sorts of crazy props, and she's a total maniac." When Caroline rolled back into New Jersey the next year, I went with Alice to see her. In the hotel ballroom, we were more than a hundred strong, sitting in long rows of skinny tables at her seminar, sponsored by the speaker's bureau BER (Bureau of Education & Research). By the end of the day, we were all family.

In the morning session, Caroline blew us away with her hypercharged performance, a dazzling torrent of booktalks, storytelling, songs, wordplay, and creative drama. She pulled an endless assemblage of objects from her overflowing trunks, a veritable King Tut's tomb for book lovers, and bestowed upon us a staggering abundance of creative ways to turn kids into readers. She told the Eric Carle book, *The Very Hungry Caterpillar*, using a caterpillar glove puppet pulled over her arm; cracked jokes and recited poems; did magic tricks; and regaled us with her retelling of "Tikki Tikki Tembo," a nonsense tale about a boy whose great long name almost leads to his drowning in a cold, cold well.

Alice said, "Let's see if she wants to have lunch with us." Turns out, she did. "Nobody ever thinks to invite the presenter," Caroline said delightedly, and we ended up with about a dozen workshop folks at a long table in the hotel restaurant, having a raucous lunch where we laughed and told stories. I asked her if she knew a song I learned in summer camp called "Eddie Coochee Catchee Kama Tosa Neara Tosa Noka Sama Kama Wacky Brown." She didn't.

After lunch, Caroline caught me off guard when she announced to the audience, "And now Judy Freeman will come up and sing us another version of 'Tikki Tikki Tembo.'" Dumbfounded, I got up from my chair and did just that. As a performer, Caroline was always so generous with her audiences, learning as much from them as they did from her. How many of those fortunate enough to attend one of her sessions came out of it saying, "I want to be Caroline when I grow up!"? I know I did.

That day, I gave her my little business card, never thinking I'd hear from her again. I was wrong. Caroline sent postcards every now and then as she traveled the world. About once a year, I'd pick up the ringing phone to hear, "Hello, this is your friend, Caroline. I'm in the airport on the way to . . . (fill in the name of any city here)." It wasn't just me. Everywhere she went, Caroline talked with people and made friends. She was known to stand up on airplanes and give booktalks. Her lifelong job was to turn everyone in the world into a book and story lover. One time, I went into a restaurant with Caroline for brunch and watched her ask strangers on the buffet line what they were reading to their kids.

"Reading is a lifetime sport," she preached. "Books shouldn't be a luxury, a treat. They're a necessity, like toothpaste."

In the 1990s, I was asked to audition as a national speaker for BER. I had done plenty of speaking at workshops and conferences, and taught as an adjunct at Rutgers University for years, but working for BER was something I had always hoped I'd be able to do one day. Still, I was apprehensive. I called up Caroline and started whining. "This is a great opportunity, but I'm working as a school librarian full time and I'd have to find ten days for BER, if I even made the cut, and develop a whole big handbook and—"

She interrupted me and gave me an indispensable piece of advice I have used ever since as a mantra for my whole life. "Judy," she said firmly, "just shut up and do it." So I did.

Then there was the time she called and said, "I just found your business card that you gave me the first time I met you, decades ago. I was dumbfounded to see that you still live in the same house, in Highland Park, New Jersey. And my question to you is, 'Why?'"

I fell over laughing. Caroline always loved living in different places. She lived in Paris; Portland, Oregon; California; Miami Beach; Thailand; and Bangladesh. She relished learning about the different cultures in all the hundred-plus countries where she visited and/or gave her memorable book and storytelling programs. The notion that someone would stay in the same town year after year was utterly foreign to her.

When she called in 2008 and asked me to help update her now more than thirty-year-old book, I could not say no to my mentor. Caroline wrote *Handbook for Storytellers* in 1977, and then did a revised edition, *New Handbook for Storytellers*, in 1993. It has always been considered a classic in the field of storytelling and children's literature, so filled with original ideas, books, stories, and the author's insouciant personality.

Caroline said, "Judy, this will be easy. You can do it with one hand tied behind your back. Just update the booklists. Piece of cake."

I dove in and five years later finished a massive rewrite of the text and booklists, reflecting the rise of technology, the Common Core, the explosion in the number of children's books published each year, and an ongoing call for literacy through books and stories.

The stories and the passion for literature are one particular legacy of Caroline's. In 2000, she and her husband, Peter Bauer, moved to Chittagong, Bangladesh. Peter was working there, and for a while, Caroline continued to travel around the world presenting workshops and speeches. Then she homed in on Bangladesh, a country she particularly adored. She compiled and published *Bangladesh at Work*, a handsome book of her color photographs. And she opened a Play Park, "a facility dedicated to the entertainment and education of children in the village of Bhatiary," near Chittagong, serving five hundred children and their families. This was Caroline's baby. Her extraordinary undertaking now includes a three-story building with a library, open daily, with a collection of more than four thousand English and Bangla books; free classes for children in art, tae kwon do, English, computers, dance, embroidery, singing, crafts and cooking; a preschool; and a playground.

While I plugged away on the handbook, Caroline became gravely ill. She would call and say, "Are you working? Let's get this thing finished!" We both desperately wanted to publish this book sooner, but it refused to be rushed. Sadly, Caroline died in 2013 after a valiant battle with mesothelioma. (Her daughter, Hilary Wendel, is seeking to continue funding the Play Park, which costs about $20,000 a year to operate. If you'd like to contribute, go to www.gofundme.com/2lp9uk; for general information, see www.facebook.com/ThePlayParkBhatiary.)

It has been my honor to get to know and work with Caroline Feller Bauer. In this book, you'll still hear her irrepressible voice, exhorting you to tell more stories, read more stories, and share more stories with the children in your life.

Finally, an image and a story. When literature experts overanalyzed and deconstructed children's books, Caroline Feller Bauer remembered her grandmother's admonition, embroidered in needlepoint, which became her motto: "Those who live without folly are not so wise as they think."

Picture tiny, slender, elfin Caroline, dressed in a big, fat red tomato costume, waddling into a hotel ballroom filled with impassioned teachers and librarians. She makes her way to the front of the room, faces her wide-eyed, bemused audience, and starts to speak:

The Three Tomatoes

Retold by Caroline Bauer

A family of three tomatoes was walking in the woods one day. There was Papa Tomato, Mama Tomato, and Baby Tomato. Baby Tomato started dawdling and lagging behind. "Hurry up, dear," called Mama Tomato. But Baby Tomato walked even slower. "We're waiting for you!" Mama called again. Baby Tomato walked even slower. "Darling, walk faster," Mama cried.

Papa Tomato was very annoyed. He ran back to Baby Tomato. He stamped on Baby Tomato and hollered, "Baby Tomato, KETCHUP!" *(At which point, Caroline stamped her foot and held up a big bottle of . . . ketchup, of course.)*

Did you know that Uma Thurman told a version of that joke to John Travolta in the movie *Pulp Fiction*? Caroline's delivery was better.

Now you have a chance to sample some of the magic and the welcome folly that is Caroline Feller Bauer. May you find hundreds of stories, books, and delicious ways to use them in your life. What do we hope this newly revised book will help you to do? Ketchup!

Introduction

WHILE THIS BOOK (AND THE FORTHCOMING *THE HANDBOOK for Storytime Programs*) stands on its own, each complements and buttresses the other. The books contain scores of carefully compiled and annotated story lists, booklists, and website lists, plus hundreds of ideas and activities for using storytelling and literature with children.

When Caroline Feller Bauer's first *Handbook for Storytellers,* published by ALA, came out in 1977, there was nothing like it. Truth be told, there was no one like Caroline Feller Bauer in the library world back then—a book-mad sprite who not only advocated reading aloud and telling stories to children, but incorporated books, magic tricks, creative drama, readers' theater, puppetry, poetry, music, and technology in her books and presentations as part and parcel of what youth services librarians (both in schools and public libraries) and teachers could and should do with children. When she burst on the scene, she transformed the profession, giving us permission to fill our programs with delight and fun and joy. She revised her book in 1993, adding still more stories, poems, and songs, along with hundreds of new, useful, and innovative methods of storytelling and building a culture of reading with and for children.

Fast-forward a mere twenty-plus years and, at long last, we have revised, updated, reworked, rethought, and rebuilt Caroline's classic book—we've needed to break it into two large volumes to accommodate everything. Each book is filled to the brim with the best of Caroline's wonderful stories and ideas, plus an overflowing cornucopia of new stories, poems, songs, plays, and activities; a grand assembly of all-new annotated lists comprising thousands of the best stories, children's books, and professional titles; and a vast array of hundreds of related websites and technology tie-ins.

It's now an encyclopedic but very fun-to-read series of reference books that school and public librarians, teachers, and storytellers can use on a daily basis to support their programs and curriculums (tying in with the many education goals of the Common Core State Standards, with their focus on "reading, writing, speaking, listening, and language"), and to supplement and strengthen their story hours.

The thousands of titles and stories listed in this book are the most exemplary ones of the hundreds of thousands I have read over the course of my career as a librarian, storyteller, reviewer, writer, and speaker to tens of thousands of teachers, librarians, and children. Inspired by Caroline's masterwork, I have mined my own material and stretched my knowledge of children's literature and storytelling to add practical ideas and inspiration on every page.

Each book contains:

- An eclectic and wide-ranging mix of folklore and children's books to develop innovative connections between storytelling and literature
- Practical, surefire suggestions for using storytelling and children's books together to create a literature-based and story-infused environment in schools and libraries
- Easy-to-learn storytelling techniques and read-aloud strategies to make each storytime session an enthralling experience for tellers and listeners
- The full texts of many dozens of stories just right for telling
- Scores of stories, poems, songs, chants, jokes, crafts, story scripts, magic tricks, and other literary delights to share with children
- Ideas, ideas, ideas, everywhere! The plethora of successful and invigorating ideas and activities can be used immediately in story hours, programs, booktalks, and lessons across the curriculum.
- Hundreds of painstakingly selected and annotated folktale, children's book, professional book, and website bibliographies, all of which are the most up to date and comprehensive in scope in a storytelling and literature guide
- Comprehensive indexes by author, title, and subject

Here's what you'll find in *The Handbook for Storytellers.*

The first half of the book, "Part One: Getting Started with Storytelling," provides:

- Practical information on how to publicize and promote your storytelling programs
- Basic techniques for pulling together a story hour
- Detailed step-by-step instructions on how to select, learn, prepare, and tell stories

The second half of the book, "Part Two: Sources for Storytelling," contains these features:

- Inspiration, hands-on instruction, and practical, easy-to-follow suggestions for success, especially for the novice teller, nervous about learning stories to tell
- An overview of the major types of folk and fairy tales, including many sample stories and annotated booklists. Types include: cumulative, repetitive, and swallowing stories; trickster tales; drolls and humorous stories; pourquoi (how-and-why) tales; jump tales, scary stories, and urban legends; fairy tales; fables, myths, legends, and epics.
- A history and virtual tour of folktales told on six of the seven continents (the penguins in Antarctica don't tell stories) that illuminates how people in other parts of the world are not so different after all
- Other literature-based sources for storytelling, including: parodies, literary tales and short stories, picture books and beginning readers, informational books and biographies, and family stories
- "Favorite Stories to Tell," an extensive annotated list of more than five hundred of Caroline and Judy's personal favorites, arranged by subject/theme, from which tellers can find the perfect stories to fit every occasion and begin to build their own repertoire of wonderful tales to tell

In this book and its companion, *The Handbook for Storytime Programs* (2015), you'll find countless stories to tell as well as songs, poems, jokes, crafts, puppets, and magic tricks to use in your story hour programming; and ways to use them with children. So many gorgeous and enticing children's books are published every year, and we have included our recommendations of more than a thousand irresistible titles to read aloud, tell, and share. There's a spectacular mix of brand-new and tried-and-true, all books we have read, adored, and, in more cases than not, used with the people for whom they are intended: actual kids.

On a practical note, many of the marvelous books Caroline originally recommended for reading and/or telling a quarter of a century ago are long out of print. In this new book and in *The Handbook for Storytime Programs,* we've omitted the ones that will be far too hard to locate, though we've kept a small number of ones we couldn't bear to toss.

When we list an older book in the many booklists you'll find within, we've used the original publisher and copyright date, even if the book has changed publishers or the publisher had merged with another house or gone out of business. One can't keep up with all the merges and purges of the publishing world. Assume, if it's an old book or an unfamiliar publisher, that the book is still in print in one edition or another. If it's out of print, chances are good that you can still find a remaindered or used copy to buy online. For any title you seek online, there might be one or more hardcover or paperback versions, an e-book, a DVD, and/or an audiobook. Sometimes the choices of formats are downright dizzying.

Here's something that's going to startle and vex book lovers, especially if you're a librarian trying to replace worn-out or lost treasures: the number of books no longer available in hardcover editions. Publishers are putting their older hardcovers—even popular ones that are still read and loved—out of commission in favor of paperbacks and e-books. This is the case with every genre in children's literature, from picture books to fiction. Unless it's a runaway and perennial hit, expect a huge percentage of hardbacks more than five years old to be no longer in print, including many big award winners.

Libraries can turn to companies like Perma-Bound (www.perma-bound.com) that take paperback books and rebind them inside a laminated book cover, or the prebinder Bound to Stay Bound (www.BTSB.com), which use the interiors of hardcover books and add a pretty much indestructible cover and binding so they'll last through one hundred circulations. (The tradeoff is that there is no dust jacket, though the cover is imprinted with the hardcover book's original artwork.) They also might have in stock those books that are no longer available from the publisher in hardcover.

Along with boundless annotated bibliographies of children's and professional books, look for annotated website lists in each chapter, but please forgive us for dead links. The Web is evanescent—websites go viral, then collapse and disappear in a trice, like stars into black holes.

Where does storytelling fit in our high-tech whirlwind? Will it become obsolete? Even in today's testing-obsessed educational climate, my personal prediction is that we will never stop needing to hear and read stories. The caring, sharing, eye contact, and sheer love that are passed from teller to listener, parent to child, teacher to student, librarian to child, are part of our shared humanity. You can appreciate the technology and use it to make your curriculum or your teaching more cutting edge, but the stories we tell and read will continue to fill our hearts and make us all—tellers and listeners—kinder, better people.

part 1

GETTING STARTED WITH STORYTELLING

Why the World Has Stories

Retold by Caroline Feller Bauer

In the beginning of time, when the world was so new and all, the animals did not work for Man.

The rooster refused to crow. "Why should I get up at first light and wake the world? I'm going back to sleep."

The dog refused to fetch and carry. "I don't want to go and get the newspaper. I don't even know how to read."

The sheep didn't want to give wool. "Sorry, I don't want to stand here in the freezing cold. I'm keeping my wool."

The cow refused to give milk. "I don't enjoy being tugged on every evening. My milk will stay where it is."

The cat was too lazy to chase mice. "I'm exhausted just thinking about stalking mice. I'm taking a nap."

The horse refused to pull the cart. "I don't want to pull a heavy load. I'd rather eat grass."

The man, who was trying to keep a tidy world, was outraged. "If you don't crow, fetch and carry, give me wool, give me milk, catch mice, or pull, I won't read you a bedtime story."

"I'll crow," said the rooster.

"I'll fetch and carry," said the dog.

"I'll give you wool," said the sheep.

"I'll chase mice," said the cat.

"I'll pull the cart," said the horse.

And the man said, "*Once upon a time . . .*"

And today, stories are told and animals work . . . including my ferret, whose job it is to look cute.

You've just read a story that you loved, and you can't wait to share it with someone. You start talking about it, and before you know it, you're telling the whole thing. Your listeners are enthralled. It's such a satisfying experience that you decide you'd like to learn about storytelling and even hold story hours. But how do you get started? What story should you learn first?

Perhaps you should start learning something tried and true, like "Little Red Riding Hood." Or a contemporary version of the classic—maybe Niki Daly's *Pretty Salma: A Little Red Riding Hood Story from Africa*, in which bad Mr. Dog tricks young Salma out of her basket, her clothes, and even her song. Or a more comical version like *Tortuga in Trouble*, by Ann Whitford Paul, where tortoise Tortuga runs into that bad actor Coyote while taking a basket of *ensalada*, tamales, and flan to Abuela's house. Or, wait! Maybe you want to learn all three.

If you are a beginning storyteller, welcome! This book is especially for you. It will help you to answer fundamental questions about storytelling and start you off with a wonderful selection of tales to tell and resources where you can find more. If you are a more experienced storyteller, think of this book as a refresher course. Browse through the chapters and see if you can find a creative promotion tip you haven't tried, or a new story to learn and tell. There's something for everyone.

Welcome to Storytelling

It takes a thousand voices to tell a single story.

—NATIVE AMERICAN PROVERB

WHY SHOULD YOU TELL STORIES WHEN THERE ARE PERfectly wonderful books out there that you can read aloud and share with kids? Or book apps or websites where kids can hear someone else read to them? Isn't that enough? We're not saying that reading aloud isn't vital. We just happen to think that storytelling is a senior partner to all the literary print and technological activities you share with your children.

We can think of many reasons to tell stories to children. For parents and grandparents, it's a way to induce wonder in your kids. Children will be amazed that grown-ups they know can make up such marvelous stories and will start wondering if they can make up and tell stories of their own.

Pragmatically speaking, storytelling is all about language. When children listen and focus on a story told to them, they are developing listening, comprehension, and analytical skills. In terms of higher-level thinking skills, storytelling helps children recall details, summarize a plot sequence, and visualize and describe settings and scenes. They can speculate on what will happen next in the story, and afterwards, cite clues that supported their predictions. They can analyze the story structure; discuss plot elements; and evaluate, debate, and make their own judgments about why the characters behaved the way they did. They can compare and contrast other similar stories. Finally, they can synthesize the experience in a creative way, perhaps acting out the story, writing a new story using the same structure, or retelling the story from another character's point of view. All the strategies that we use to analyze and evaluate other texts, both fiction and nonfiction, work just as well—if not better—when a story is told.

Hearing stories also makes a child want to read more of them. Storytelling helps turn kids into readers.

To Whom Should We Tell Stories?

One of the first things to think about is the age of your target audience. Here are some simple ideas that may help you along.

BABIES AND TODDLERS

Babies and toddlers will go gaga over lap-sit storytimes planned just for them, which are now standard at most public libraries. Keep in mind that the children will be accompanied by adults, so the programs you present will be for the caregivers as much as their charges. Brief stories, simple books, fingerplays, songs, and a rhyme or two will begin a toddler's introduction to the treasures of the library. If you're meeting with the same group every week, revisit activities from previous programs. Small children delight in repeated stories, songs, chants, and fingerplays.

One of Judy's favorite stories for this age group is the silly and infectious "Little Bunny Foo Foo," sung to the approximate tune of "The Eensy-Weensy Spider." Many preschool teachers know a version of it. Here's the way Judy likes to tell and sing it.

Little Bunny Foo Foo

Retold by Judy Freeman

(*Sung*) Little Bunny Foo Foo, hopping through the forest,

Scooping up the field mice and bopping them on the head.

(*Spoken*) Along came his Fairy Godmother, and she said:

(*Sung*) "Little Bunny Foo Foo, I don't want to see you
(*wag finger reprovingly*)

Scooping up the field mice and bopping them on the head.
(*Spoken*) I'm going to give you three chances to be a good little rabbit,
And if you won't, I'm going to turn you into a GOON!"

Little Bunny Foo Foo, hopping through the forest,
Scooping up the field mice and bopping them on the head.
Along came his Fairy Godmother, and she said:
"Little Bunny Foo Foo, I don't want to see you
Scooping up the field mice and bopping them on the head.
I'm going to give you two more chances to be a good little rabbit,
And if you won't, I'm going to turn you into a GOON!"

Little Bunny Foo Foo, hopping through the forest,
Scooping up the field mice and bopping them on the head.
Along came his Fairy Godmother, and she said:
"Little Bunny Foo Foo, I don't want to see you
Scooping up the field mice and bopping them on the head.
I'm going to give you one more chance to be a good little rabbit,
And if you won't, I'm going to turn you into a GOON!"

Little Bunny Foo Foo, hopping through the forest,
Scooping up the field mice and bopping them on the head.
Along came his Fairy Godmother, and she said:
"Little Bunny Foo Foo, I don't want to see you
Scooping up the field mice and bopping them on the head.
I gave you three chances to be a good little rabbit, and
you goofed.
So now, I'm going to turn you into a GOON!"

POOF!

And the moral of the story?

HARE TODAY, GOON TOMORROW.

As you sing the song part, make a fist, stick up two fingers to make bunny ears, and have your "bunny" hop along to the song. For the scooping and bopping parts, scoop with one hand and then bop your other fist.

When you tell this story to preschoolers, they may think the final line is, "I'm going to turn you into a GOOF," which is pretty hilarious. You can simply tell them a goon is "a very silly rabbit." Paul Brett Johnson wrote and illustrated a sweet picture-book version, *Little Bunny Foo Foo*, with which you may want to follow up.

PRESCHOOL AND PRIMARY SCHOOL CHILDREN

Your preschool program (which may include children from infancy to age five) will usually feature simple stories, songs, and picture books. If the children are enrolled in day care or nursery school, they may not attend full time, but they are still an eager audience for any organized entertainment. Programming for this age group is usually strongly supported by parents who are looking for book-oriented activities outside the home. If you are a teacher of preschool or primary children, storytime is undoubtedly a daily activity in your classroom. It is through stories, poems, and songs that children acquire information, work on listening and group social skills, and develop a love for words and fine illustrations.

In the spring, parents register their children for the preschool or kindergarten in their local elementary schools. Often, the children come to school for a few hours to meet the staff and get a brief orientation to the school. This is a grand opportunity for the school librarian to initiate a free story hour, once a week for anywhere from two to six weeks, for parents and about-to-be new students. Hand out a flyer to prospective parents and encourage them to sign up.

At these programs, you can tell and read stories, use puppets, do simple crafts activities, and help children and their parents get comfortable with the school library. Encourage parents to borrow books with their kids after each program. As part of each session, take the group on a school walk to see where the different rooms are—the art room, music room, gym, auditorium, nurse's office, and office, for starters—and to help the incoming students acclimate to their new environment. Arrange for staff members to introduce themselves and lead the children around their rooms. Meeting the principal, nurse, special-area teachers, and custodian will make the kids feel they're part of their new school family. When they come back to school in September, they will consider themselves old-timers, and you will probably gain a whole new set of parents who support your library program and even sign on as weekly volunteers.

Children in the primary grades—kindergarten through second grade—are also active listeners. They will hang on every story you tell. The classroom is a perfect place to hold story hours for these youngsters. If you are a public librarian or church-group leader, you may be tempted to include both preschool and primary children in one story hour, especially if the groups can be kept small. Keep in mind, however, that many primary-grade children are able to listen longer and understand on a higher level than preschool children, though they also love group participation stories and humorous folktales.

One of the objectives of your program will be to teach your audience to listen to stories that are more complex. This comes about as children become more accustomed to listening.

CHILDREN IN GRADES 3 THROUGH 6

Children in grades 3 through 6 simply love book-and-storytelling programs, and they are old enough to appreciate longer folktales, more complex fairy tales, and myths. Children in this age group are likely to belong to clubs (Boy Scouts, Girl Scouts, and other youth organizations) that can provide you with a ready-made audience. Once the hormones kick in around fifth and sixth grade, children may make a show of rolling their eyes and being "above all that," but they still appreciate suspenseful, compelling stories and booktalks that don't treat them like their younger brothers and sisters. Programs for these kids offer the storyteller an added opportunity to experiment with multimedia programs and theater-based follow-ups, such as making podcasts or story trailers, or writing and acting out readers' theater scripts. They can also learn stories to tell to each other and to younger children.

MIDDLE SCHOOL CHILDREN AND YOUNG ADULTS

Pull together stories from folklore, classic literature, poetry, and excerpts from contemporary fiction when considering programs for this audience. Booktalks, which combine storytelling with reading aloud, are popular, as young people enjoy the language of good literature. These children are digital natives and will be game for taping book trailers, poetry slams, and music videos. They may be reached in the classroom, in the library, or through special-interest clubs. They can be a challenging audience, but ultimately a satisfying one.

Where to Tell Stories

It was raining. No, it was pouring. The promised picnic was definitely out of the question. Clearly the children were disappointed, and Caroline felt bad. After all, she had promised her daughter, Hilary, and her friend, Holly, a picnic. They had a picnic anyway—on a make-believe beach, under a dining room table, with a blanket tent cover to provide privacy and a sense of mystery. With the rain drumming on the roof, the blanket tent turned out to be the perfect place to tell and listen to ghost stories. Even Caroline's husband, Peter, crawled into the tent and told about a snowbound ski trip in Vermont. That memory remains a special one for Hilary, now long grown and with children of her own.

The importance of the physical setup for storytelling cannot be underestimated. It will determine whether your listeners truly feel part of the presentation. But how can you make that space your own? In a library or school, you might be telling stories in a classroom, a meeting room, a cafeteria, or even in an auditorium with a stage. Do your best to be adaptable. Survey each new space to figure out how to make the most of it for your intended audience, whether you are expecting ten preschoolers and their caregivers in a library story room or one hundred rowdy teens on bleachers in a school gym. Move chairs when needed. When she knew she would be speaking in a large auditorium, Caroline would bring yarn with her to close off the back rows. Sometimes—particularly when you are a visiting storyteller—your heart will drop as you enter a proposed storytelling site, but the experience can still turn out well for you and your audience.

When Caroline was a branch librarian in the New York Public Library system, story hours were held in a dusty attic piled high with broken, unused furniture. At first, from her adult point of view, it seemed an entirely unattractive place; but when she saw the children's reactions of awe and delight, she realized what a splendid story room it really was. Not many of the apartment-dwelling children who came to her story hour had ever seen a real attic, let alone spent time in one. She says, "I'm certain that those stories were long remembered in part because of the magical atmosphere in which they were told."

SCHOOLS

If you are a classroom teacher or a school librarian, think about how you can best situate your classes for storytelling and book-and-story-sharing sessions. Having kids stay at their desks or at library tables will not foster the camaraderie of sitting together on the floor or on a "story rug." Irving Primary School in Highland Park, New Jersey, has a large, lovely, oval-shaped dragon rug that fits a class nicely. The children love sitting on it for storytime. You can find some beautiful, kid-friendly, stain-protected rugs at www.schooloutfitters.com and www.demco.com. (You can even find a dragon rug, if you now think you need one, too.)

If you don't have a designated story area, think about creating one. It doesn't take long for students to move desks and tables to make a temporary spot. Work out a procedure for clearing the floor, and practice it with your group. It will soon be just like any other routine.

ASSEMBLIES

Although storytelling might seem best suited to a family sitting around a peat fire in Ireland, the most prevalent contemporary setting may be the school assembly. Although the optimum number of children at an assembly is under two hundred, larger schools will have five hundred or more children. Try telling participation stories and stories that bring overt responses (such as a good laugh!) to groups like these. The trickiest programs are the ones where children sit at long lunchroom tables, on long, hard benches. That can mean trouble, since half of the children have to turn around to sit with the tables at their backs. There can be squirming, kicking, and, thanks to the environment, a yearning for lunch. It is more difficult to capture their attention and to weave a spell with stories when your group is physically uncomfortable.

When Judy gives a school assembly program, she likes to have the children sit in rows on the floor of the all-purpose room/gym/cafetorium. She keeps a center aisle free so she can walk to the back of the room during her presentation and make eye contact with the kids in the last rows. Can children sit on the hard floor for an hour? Listening to and participating in good stories and songs make an hour fly. The rule of thumb is to arrange the room and your group to create an environment that works best for all. Even if that's not possible, put on a big smile, make the best of what you have, and persevere. You'll do just fine.

THE PUBLIC LIBRARY

A typical storytelling program in a public library features the children's librarian telling stories, doing fingerplays, singing songs, and reading children's books on a given theme, followed by games or crafts related to the stories. Sometimes there is a separate story room; usually there is simply a corner or section of the room devoted to storytime where children sit on the carpet or on chairs and then move to tables afterwards.

Judy was privileged to be a visiting storyteller and give a program of her songs and stories for children and parents at the Palmer Public Library in Palmer, Alaska. When she finished her presentation, one little girl said, pointedly, “We’re ready for our craft now.” Kids do love those hands-on craft activities. Often, the public library is the only place, besides summer camp, and—if the arts haven’t been slashed from the school budget—art class at school where they get to make cool stuff.

STORES AND OTHER PUBLIC SPACES

And then there is the bookstore. Although the advent of e-books and Amazon.com has changed things, megabookstores and box stores with huge children’s departments still exist, and they often offer book, activity, and author programs (something indie bookstores have always done). You may find these large stores receptive to the offer of a story hour, but be forewarned. As a consultant for a large bookstore chain, Caroline gave book programs around the United States. Undisciplined little darlings would pick up her puppets and props, throw temper tantrums, and generally misbehave while their parents looked on benevolently. The storekeepers were loath to offend their customers and, as a visitor performer/storyteller, Caroline felt it was hardly her job to discipline the children. In situations like this, the rule of thumb is simply to do the best you can.

Storytellers at the Hans Christian Andersen statue in New York City’s Central Park must work especially hard to capture the attention and imagination of their audience. In addition to wiggly, noisy kids, they have to contend with the often deafening roar of passing traffic and the distractions of loud passersby. Famed storyteller Diane Wolkstein, who died in 2013, began this Central Park tradition in 1967 as the only teller. The storytelling turned into a weekly event for more than twenty presenters each season, from June through September, featuring some of the leading performers in the storytelling community. As Diane said, “Often I meet adults who are bringing their own children to hear stories that they heard twenty-five years before.” Now under the leadership of Laura Simms, the summer programs have continued. Each session includes at least one Hans Christian Andersen story. Though it is recommended for ages six and up, the audience can range from babies in strollers to seniors sitting on the benches, basking in tales well-told. For information and program schedules, go to www.hcastory center.org.

Today many parks and performance spaces like town squares, playgrounds, and mini-stages at town street festivals sponsor storytellers and other presenters, usually in the summer months.

Here are some other possible venues:

- School buses during field trips
- Afterschool programs
- At home or at someone else's home
- Backyards
- Neighborhood garage sales
- Scout troop meetings
- Summer camps
- Holiday and family dinners
- Birthday parties, graduations, and other occasions
- Weddings
- Child-care centers
- Hospitals
- Senior citizens' clubs and retirement homes
- Police stations and firehouses
- Detention centers and prisons
- Shopping malls
- Community events
- County fairs and street festivals
- Book fairs
- Open-air markets and craft fairs
- Bookstores and toy stores
- Houses of worship
- Campfires
- The beach, the woods, and during a hike
- Any form of transportation where people look like they could use a pick-me-up

Who Can Be a Storyteller?

Who will actually tell the stories at your story program? You. Yes, you should be your first choice. Why shouldn't you be the person to get that wonderful feeling that comes with telling a good tale to an audience of enthralled listeners? Watch their eyes get wide and glazed as they fall into your story and their imaginations start to whir. Who are you? Are you a school librarian? A public librarian? A classroom teacher? A volunteer? A student? A parent, grandparent, or doting relative? All kinds of people love to tell stories, and you don't have to be a professional to do it.

THE SCHOOL LIBRARIAN

These days, many school librarians teach research and information skills; effective searching skills, starting with the library's computer catalog; and literature appreciation. In the elementary school, they may have a structured schedule, or a flexible one where teachers sign up their classes as needed.

If you are a librarian with a structured schedule, you have a built-in weekly audience and can probably slot in storytelling on a regular basis. With a flexible schedule, you will need to approach your teachers and ask if they have a time you could see their students for storytelling, especially a session that ties into a curricular area. If a social studies class is studying Native Americans, explorers, or the fifty states, offer to tell stories relating to those subjects. If students are learning about astronomy, animals, or weather in science, offer to do a program of pourquoi tales that give listeners a very different explanation of scientific phenomena.

If you are a librarian in a middle or high school, you may not see classes on a weekly basis, but you can still collaborate with subject-area teachers when students are working on projects, research, or papers. Keep track of who's studying what when, and offer to tie that subject matter into a related program that will also familiarize students with library resources. When a class comes in to do research on the presidents, as a part of your instructions on where and how to look for information, slip in the story of how Washington crossed the Delaware on Christmas Eve, 1776, and turned the tide of the Revolution, which you read about in a biography of George Washington. History, after all, is just a collection of stories.

Look for times when the teachers can use a breather and offer to take their students for a class period or even ten minutes. Right before a holiday or during standardized testing, when the kids are desperate to have a bit of fun, invite several classes to the library and knock their socks off with a couple of well-placed stories, songs, poems, and booktalks. You'll need to be proactive, but once you've established a reputation as someone who can tell a mean story, the word will spread.

THE PUBLIC LIBRARIAN

Historically, public librarians have done more to introduce children to storytelling than anyone. They routinely hold weekly programs of songs, stories, crafts, and activities for babies through teens. Often these programs are dependent on reading aloud, not storytelling, but you can easily integrate storytelling into a weekly session. Sometimes you'll find you've read a book aloud so many times, you already know the story. Try telling the story without the book and see how it goes. You will get hooked on telling.

It's tricky sometimes to get older children to come to the library for scheduled programs, so you'll need to be inventive, maybe offering irresistible incentives. If you're showing a movie, tell a story or two beforehand. Invite older kids to a book party, a pizza night, or a games night, and they'll come back for more once they hear the stories you tell.

Public librarians were expected to tell stories to children, back in the days of iconic public librarians like Pura Belpre (1903–1982), the first Hispanic public librarian in New York City, and Augusta Baker (1911–1998), first African American public librarian in the same system. The first library in the United States to establish a weekly story hour for children was the Carnegie Library of Pittsburgh, Pennsylvania. Until recently, New York City public youth services librarians were trained within the system to tell stories, but with budget cuts and more budget cuts, that training went by the wayside. What a loss to the children.

If your library system has no formal classes or workshops in storytelling, you can train yourself by reading books like this one and taking a leap. Take a class in storytelling or get together with other librarian and teacher friends and form a storyteller's league to practice new material on each other.

TEACHERS

Each year, classroom teachers are expected to cover more and more curriculum. At the same time, they are expected to be social workers, psychologists, coaches, medical advisors, and surrogate parents, and, above all, miracle workers, transforming children each year into eager, industrious, and successful learners. On top of that, they should be storytellers? Sure. What's one more thing?

Whether you're a subject area teacher, a self-contained classroom teacher, a special-area teacher, a resource-room teacher, an aide, or a substitute, it can never hurt to have some stories in your bag of tricks. You don't need to know a hundred—a handful to pull out when the time is right will do. Your kids will forget the spelling tests, the worksheets, the textbook chapters, but they won't forget the books you read aloud, the songs you sing, and, especially, the stories you tell.

FAMILY MEMBERS AND OTHER CAREGIVERS

Are you one of those parents who tells stories to your kids at bedtime? Maybe you start a story about a blue whale or a princess or your child as a superhero, and each night you continue the saga or make up a new adventure. You probably never thought of yourself as a real storyteller, but, of course, you are. Your kids remember your stories and wait for each new installment, which is why you started telling stories in the first place.

Middle school English teacher Rick Riordan had published several adult mysteries before making his first foray into children's fiction. The book came about because of bedtime stories about Greek gods and heroes he told his second-grade son, Haley, who was having reading difficulties. When Rick ran out of stories about the gods and heroes, Haley asked him to make up a new story about them, so Rick created the character of Percy Jackson, an American kid with ADHD and dyslexia, whose father is a Greek god. When he finished his story, Haley told him he should turn it into a book. The story became *The Lightning Thief*, and Riordan is now a huge favorite among readers, especially reluctant ones who identify with Percy.

Does this mean the stories you tell your kids will turn into best sellers? Probably not, but you can still tell stories at bedtime, birthday parties, in the park. Maybe you're a grandparent or devoted aunt or uncle who tells the kids about what life was like in the olden days. Any story you share will be a hit with your kids, who will grow up and tell stories to their kids. What better legacy can a parent or grandparent leave?

Start a family storytelling tradition. Choose a night to relax, stay home, and enjoy stories or read aloud as a family affair. Don't limit these staycation sessions to the preschoolers at home, either. Your entire family will delight in a good story well told. As your children grow up, they can tell stories of their own or take turns at reading alternate book chapters aloud. Why not record each other telling stories on video? Your kids will watch it again and again.

Now think in terms of families in your neighborhood, or where you work or worship. Why not plan a joint family program in someone's home or even in a public place—at your school or library or park—where parents can share their stories with everyone's kids? Afterwards, serve lemonade and cookies. If you're at the library, everyone can then check out an armload of books to continue the fun at home.

STUDENTS

You may discover that some of the older children and young adults who have been coming to story hours at your library, school, place of worship, or club are as interested in learning and telling stories as you are. Consider organizing a storytelling class for them. Keep the group small, between three and ten; that way the members will be assured of your personal attention.

Begin the training by having members perform informally, telling jokes, describing their families, or relating school experiences. Tell them a story or anecdote yourself, or perhaps invite a guest to tell a story. Explain that there are different types of stories, such as folktales, fairy tales, pourquoi tales, fables, myths, epics, and modern short stories. Help your students select appropriate stories by providing them with a list of tales particularly suited to beginners. *Twenty Tellable Tales: Audience Participation Tales for the Beginning Storytellers* is just one of many easy-to-tell collections by master storyteller and collector Margaret Read McDonald. Anne Pellowski's *The Story Vine: A Source Book of Unusual and Easy-to-Tell Stories from Around the World* is another good source for beginners.

Encourage students to practice on each other to develop their proficiency and gain self-confidence. Permit the student who is ready to perform to tell his or her story all the way through. Don't interrupt to make suggestions. Take notes as you listen, but be responsive. Afterwards, be sure to say something positive. Gently point out any common faults, and do not permit a situation to develop in which everyone acrimoniously criticizes a performance. To pinpoint and correct particular faults, talk privately with each child.

If students are willing, record their stories on video so they can see themselves as others see them. (Watching the playback afterwards will help them shed undesirable traits, like swaying back and forth or saying "You know" every other sentence.) You can also build a performance library that others can watch and enjoy. Encourage each student to try a variety of stories in the shelter of the group. You'll be astonished at how quickly they master their selections—learning new stories is child's play for them.

To whom can the students tell stories? Everyone. Fifth graders can tell them to third graders, seventh graders to fourth graders, and so on. If administrators and teachers are reluctant to take time away from other activities to permit your group to tell stories, explain that learning and telling stories enriches sequence, comprehension, and public-speaking skills, helps students develop self-confidence, and raises test scores. (Okay, we don't have any hard data on the last one, but it wouldn't surprise us one bit if it were true.)

A storytelling club in elementary school or a storytelling elective in middle school can encompass literature, folklore, theater, and child-care activities all in one. Send out teams of storytellers. Anyplace an adult can tell stories, your student group should be welcome, too: hospital wards, the public library, day-care centers, day camps, and playgrounds. Keep the program brief. Twenty minutes is more than enough. It's not necessary to coordinate the program around a theme, for each storyteller can tell his or her story in turn, introducing it with the title and its place of origin. Student tellers will take comfort in each other's presence, and half the fun is discussing the experience later. You might want to record the performance on video and edit it down to small snippets of each teller to justify your program. You could put it on the school's website for some good publicity.

For more about student storytelling, visit author-librarian-blogger Esme Raji Codell's idea-packed lesson plan at www.planetesme.com/storytelling.html.

GUEST STORYTELLERS

A guest storyteller may provide a welcome change of pace for you and your audience. If you are planning a storytelling program and don't have enough money for a fee or expenses, don't be discouraged. A guest might want to pitch in for reasons other than a paycheck. Perhaps he or she wants to become better known in the community, publicize a personal event, do a public service, or just have fun. It never hurts to ask. You may find possible guests almost anywhere. Perhaps the local radio announcer, aspiring children's book author, or amateur magician you meet casually may find the prospect of storytelling intriguing. Look for storytelling talent in your local high school, college theater department, or amateur theater group, or among retired teachers and librarians in your community.

Is there a graduate school of library science or education in your area? Most will offer courses in children's literature and, sometimes, storytelling. Those students usually need a practice venue, and you might be the answer to their prayers. Contact the professor to offer your audience as willing guinea pigs.

How do you determine whether a guest will be a smash hit or a flop? Before you delegate the responsibility of a program to an untried performer, you can arrange an audition, but it may be better to take a chance and risk being disappointed than to lose volunteer talent by default.

In your initial contact with a potential guest, be specific about what you want. Discuss where the program will take place, describe the audience, set the program length, and explain post-telling expectations, such as a dinner or an autograph session. Be clear about financial arrangements. Will you pay for transportation and/or meals, arrange for a hotel room, and pay an honorarium or speaker's fee? This information will help the individual decide whether to accept your invitation. It may be that the presenter has his or her own contract with all the details included.

The Professional Storyteller

The information above also applies to hosting a professional storyteller. There are many folks out there who have devoted their professional lives to storytelling, making their living traveling the world giving performances. You can find several hundred professional storytellers listed at www.story teller.net/tellers, and, on the National Storytelling Network's Directory at www.storynet.org, more than six hundred storytellers from the United States. Both sites are searchable by a storyteller's name, state, and region, and provide contact information and links to their websites.

Children's book authors, illustrators, poets, magicians, singers, and other performance artists are also storytellers. Many authors and illustrators relish the opportunity to leave their computers and deadlines and meet with their fans or potential readers. Many will visit schools, libraries, and small theaters to speak to children and young adults. Not every speaker is an outstanding presenter for young people, naturally, so choose carefully. Ask your friends and colleagues, including listserv members on LM_Net (for school librarians) and PUBYAC (for youth services public librarians) for recommendations of good storytellers whom they have seen who can connect with and hold the attention of large groups of children and deliver content that is entertaining, inspiring, and worthwhile.

Because honorariums for professionals can range from hundreds to thousands of dollars, discuss fees directly with the speaker or agent. If you ask a newly published author or illustrator to speak, they will often charge far less than the hot-ticket best-selling star. If they start winning major awards, expect their fees to rise proportionately, and for good reason. If you are strapped for funds, ask if fees are negotiable. However, realize that this person often makes a living from speaking and will work hard to exceed the expectations of you and your audience. A top performer may be pricey, but it will usually be worth it, even if you have to write a grant or hold a fundraiser to pull together the needed funds. More cost-effective might be a Skype session, where you ask a guest to spend a short time talking with your group or telling tales via computer. This is an excellent way to get to host someone who lives too far away to visit.

GUESTMANSHIP

One person should be in charge as “the minder” of a visiting performer. If that person is you, there are niceties you should consider in the care and feeding of your esteemed guest. After your speaker has agreed to come, make certain that you follow up with a written reminder of the date, time, and place well before the day of the event. By doing this you not only inform your guest when and where he or she is expected but also avoid disappointing your audience and yourself should there be any misunderstanding. Be sure you trade cell phone numbers in case of emergencies.

If the speaker will be driving, check out the directions in case there are any changes, road closings, or best routes to take. Online map services are a godsend, but they’re not always accurate. Navigation devices can get it wrong, too. On Judy’s way to one school program, the GPS led her to a dead end overlooking a cliff, and said, “You have arrived.” Whoops.

If your speaker is coming from out of town and staying overnight or for a meal, arrange to meet him at the airport, train, or bus station and take him to his hotel. Arrange for meals at private homes or a good local restaurant. However, always check with the guest beforehand. He or she may prefer room service at the hotel and an early-to-bed evening.

Judy says, “In some places I’ve spoken, no one seemed to be in charge of the program; in others, there have been festive banners around the school welcoming me, and kids who cheer and make me feel like a rock star. Sometimes I’ll be asked if I want to eat lunch with kids who have entered in a lottery to win a place at the table. This can be an entertaining adventure, a window into the lives of children, and often, a source of good stories, jokes, and string games.”

What should you, as a presenter, hope for? Ideally, the minder greets you in a friendly way, asks you what you need, and takes you to the speaking room. You should expect someone to know how to work the sound system and someone to prime your audience for the visit. Someone should introduce you and remind the audience to behave (“I know you will be an excellent audience of wonderful listeners. Don’t forget to use your very best manners and make us proud of the way you listen to and treat our special guest.”). You should expect your minder to stay in the room during the presentation, just in case the microphone dies, a child has an emergency, or something weird happens. And at the close of the program, there should be someone available to give you (and the audience) clear instructions on what to do next. As a host, be sure to send a follow-up thank-you to the guest. Mention some of the favorable comments you heard. Sometimes teachers have children write and illustrate thank-you notes. This is always appreciated! And if you are a guest presenter, don't forget to send your nicelies to the person who sponsored you, expressing appreciation for all the time and effort it took to organize your visit. Both of you will have worked hard to make your visit a smash.

Sources for Stories and Storytelling

STORYTELLING FESTIVALS

A good venue for storytellers is a storytelling festival. Festivals are planned for adults only, for children only, or for a mixed-age group, and they are held in hotel ballrooms, auditoriums, school gyms, classrooms, outside, or under a big tent. A festival can feature stories from a particular country or region or stories centered on a single theme or subject. Sometimes there's a story swap or open-mic session, where adults and/or kids volunteer to come up and tell a story. You don't have to be famous to share a rattling good tale.

The National Storytelling Network (www.storytellingcenter.net) holds the oldest—and probably the biggest—yearly storytelling festival in the United States. It started in 1973, in the pretty little town of Jonesborough, Tennessee, the oldest town in Tennessee (population 3,000), with a small group of storytellers and listeners. What a difference a renaissance can make. The now three-day festival, held the first full weekend in October, is billed as one of the "Top 100 Events in North America." It draws ten thousand folks to half a dozen big-circus tents where storytelling sessions feature dozens of nationally known performers. (The "family tent" hosts kid-friendly stories if you bring the young'uns.)

On the National Storytelling Network's website, you will find a calendar listing details of hundreds of other storytelling fests, conferences, meetings, concerts, and get-togethers across the United States (www.storynet.org/events/calendar.php?). Surely you'll be able to find something near your neck of the woods.

Want to get together online with hundreds of other storytellers and talk shop? Join the listserv Storytell (lists.storynet.org/lists/info/storytell), sponsored by the National Storytelling Network. It's described as "a forum of more than 500 subscribers worldwide for discussion about storytelling. All persons interested in storytelling are invited to participate. The group reflects viewpoints from around the world of issues and topics concerning the storytelling community. Storytell serves as a source of information on conferences, workshops and events as well as a place to ask (and answer) questions about the origins and variations of stories, the business of story-telling, or organization of storytelling events."

STORYTELLING GUILDS

A storytelling guild is a company of volunteers who create programs that bring children and books together. A successful storytelling program doesn't just happen, as the members of the Storytelling Guild of Medford, Oregon, can tell you. It takes organization and hard work. According to their website, the Storytelling Guild is "a group of volunteers dedicated to serving the community by providing opportunities for children to be exposed to the magic of books and the joy of reading."

The Medford program began in the 1970s, when Myra Getchell, the children's librarian at the public library, gathered together five interested women to help plan and contribute to the library story hours. Originally, the volunteers limited their efforts to the central county library and a school or two. When they discovered that there were lots of neighborhood children who were unaware of the library's story hours, they recruited and trained other volunteers and organized mobile storytelling units.

Today, all these years later, the guild continues to run innovative and kid-friendly programs, such as a "Pass the Book Program" that collects and distributes children's books to organizations that support early literacy, and hosts a spectacular three-day Children's Festival each July. The first year, 1967, the festival drew five hundred children over two days. The $50 it cost to run it was repaid from the 25-cent admission fee. The second year drew two thousand over two days.

After all these decades, the now three-day festival each July continues to pull in between eight thousand and ten thousand attendees, thanks to the efforts of two thousand dedicated and supportive community members who volunteer each year. With inflation, the entry fee has gone way up to a whopping $3 a head. Children and their parents can participate in more than thirty hands-on art, craft, and science projects including candle making, weaving, pottery, wood-working, puppet-making, sand and easel art, murals, and face painting. Child-focused stage performances include an array of storytellers, dancers, singers, and musicians.

To see what their festival is all about, go to www.storytellingguild.org/childrens-festival.html and click the link to the Children's Festival video. Obviously, the activities of such an ambitious group take an enormous amount of planning and volunteers. If you want to begin your own volunteer program, start with a few friends or colleagues. Organizations such as Friends of the Library or the PTA could be excellent sources of "storytelling power." Don't be discouraged if some of your recruits are not natural storytellers. They may have other talents—perhaps they can help with publicity, arrange for transportation, or make props. Plan your volunteer program with care and creativity and you will be rewarded with a popular, smoothly run storytime.

DIAL-A-STORY

Preschoolers delight in playing with the telephone, but ordinarily they have no one to call. One way to capitalize on this preoccupation and introduce children to stories at the same time might be a Dial-a-Story program. The San Francisco Public Library (http://sfpl.org) has sponsored a free Children's Story Line program for more than twenty years. Young children are encouraged to call a designated telephone number to hear a choice of songs and rhymes or a three-minute story that is changed each week. The service is available twenty-four hours a day, in English, Spanish, and Chinese. Thousands of libraries across the United States have Dial-a-Story programs for those times when parents need a quick breather and their little ones need a story. Google *dial-a-story* and you will be amazed at the array.

If your organization decides to implement a Dial-a-Story service, you will need a dedicated phone line. You can be low-tech about it, recording stories on the same voice-messaging system you use to have callers leave phone messages. Some libraries purchase already-recorded stories; others have the staff or volunteers select and record new stories each week. When patrons call the library, they pick "hear a story" on the voice-mail menu to hear that week's prerecorded story. Libraries also download stories to their websites' Kids Pages.

If you tape children's stories, do you need to get permission to use them? This question is not easily resolved. Works created and published before 1923 are considered part of the public domain, so you can usually reproduce them without fear of violating copyright, though it's always wise to check. If you find a story on Project Gutenberg (www.gutenberg.org), know it's fine to use and will not require permission.

If you want to record a story published more recently, must you get permission from the publisher? Is it permissible—fair use—to record newer stories for children to listen to one-on-one? After all, it's fine to read stories aloud to groups of children; why would recording them be a problem? It's a gray area, but if you are planning to record stories for children to hear online or over the phone, it's probably smart to search out stories in the public domain or contact the publisher and ask for permission. You might want to contact the children's book authors who live in your area and ask if you can use one of their stories. Perhaps they will agree to record the story for you—it's great publicity for them, too.

INTERNATIONAL CHILDREN'S DIGITAL LIBRARY FOUNDATION

The International Children's Digital Library Foundation (http://en.childrenslibrary.org) identifies itself as "A Library for the World's Children." Its goal is "To create a collection of more than 10,000 books in at least 100 languages that is freely available to children, teachers, librarians, parents, and scholars throughout the world via the Internet." So far, the foundation offers free access to books from more than forty-two countries and in scores of languages. English is the most prevalent by far, but there are also stories in languages including Greek, Swahili, Yiddish, Mongolian, and Farsi.

THE MOTH

Ready to go national with your life stories? That's what The Moth Radio Hour is all about. The Peabody Award–winning program was founded by author and poet George Dawes Green in 1977. Here's how they describe themselves: "A celebration of both the raconteur, who breathes fire into true tales of ordinary life, and the storytelling novice, who has lived through something extraordinary and yearns to share it."

Go to http://themoth.org, where you'll see sample videos of people performing their original stories and find a link to its PRX (Public Radio Exchange) podcasts on NPR stations across the United States. People perform live at The Moth Mainstage in New York City, "which has featured stories by Malcolm Gladwell, Ethan Hawke, Annie Proulx, Salman Rushdie, as well as an astronaut, a pickpocket, a hot-dog eating champion, and hundreds more." The Moth on the Road brings performers and their stories across the country. The Moth StorySLAM is a popular open-mic storytelling competition in many cities.

PUBLIC-ACCESS TV

There are more than one thousand local public-access cable channels in the United States. PEG (public, educational, and governmental) channels are noncommercial and provide airtime for programs that meet a community's needs, such as city council and board of education meetings. Who's to say your local PEG channel wouldn't jump at the chance to offer a program that would appeal to children and their parents? Just call the public-access channel of your local cable system to find out if they would be interested in filming a live story hour each month or in having you tape a weekly ten-minute story for the cameras. Often these stations will provide workshops on studio production, field production, editing, and other digital-media skills you need to know, if you want to get into the production as well as the talent end of things. If your town does not have a public-access channel, try contacting other nearby cable systems. For a fairly comprehensive list of public-access TV stations in the United States, see http://en.wikipedia.org/wiki/List_of_public_access_TV_stations_in_the_United_States.

WEBSITES FOR STORYTELLERS AND STORYTELLING

Storytelling has migrated to the web. Below you'll find a variety of sites that can help you learn more about stories and the storyteller's craft.

Bookflix *http://teacher.scholastic.com/products/bookflixfreetrial*
On this site Scholastic pairs classic video storybooks from Weston Woods and related nonfiction e-books from Scholastic.

Día! Diversity in Action *http://dia.ala.org*
Information about El día de los niños/El día de los libros (Day of the Child/Day of the Book), an annual book and literacy celebration.

Google Books Library Project *www.books.google.com*
Search millions of books for previewing or reading for free. You can download full texts of books in the public domain, which can be printed. This is ideal when you need a hard copy of an old story to carry around while you are learning it.

Holiday Insights *www.holidayinsights.com/moreholidays*
A listing with descriptions and ideas on how to celebrate hundreds of the current year's "Bizarre, Wacky and Unique Holidays."

International Children's Digital Library *http://en.childrenslibrary.org*
A site dedicated "to excite and inspire the world's children to become members of the global community" by offering children's literature online, free

of charge. So far, they offer free access to books from more than forty-two countries and in scores of languages, with English the most prevalent by far, but also including stories in Greek, Swahili, Yiddish, Mongolian, and Farsi.

International Children's Storytelling Center *www.storytellingcenter.net*
"Dedicated to building a better world through the power of storytelling," the center is a sponsor of the National Storytelling Festival.

Myths and Legends *http://myths.e2bn.org/mythsandlegends*
Lovers of myths and legends can listen to their heart's content on this site, which offers dozens of animated and narrated tales from the British Isles. Click on "Create Your Own" for Story Creator 2, a feature where children can record themselves telling a story and add text, illustrations, speech bubbles, and even sound effects.

Planet Esme *www.planetesme.com/storytelling.html*
Librarian, blogger, and author Esme Raji Codell gives an overview of how to teach children to be storytellers.

Storyline Online *www.storylineonline.net*
Want to see, read, and hear some great picture books read aloud by actors and other famous people? Go to this spiffy site sponsored by the Screen Actors Guild Foundation. Simultaneously, children can read and listen to an assortment of well-known children's books, read expressively by the likes of James Earl Jones, Hector Elizondo, Betty White, and Elijah Wood. In each video, the famous reader, sitting in a chair, introduces himself or herself and shows the book he or she is about to read. A facsimile of the book then opens on the screen so children can follow the text at the bottom and examine the illustrations. You can also download an activity guide for each book.

Storynet *www.storynet.org*
The website of the National Storytelling Network provides a US calendar of events and links to resources for storytelling, including an extensive Directory of Storytellers with a profile, photo, and contact info for each teller. Join their listserv, Storytell, at: lists.storynet.org/lists/info/storytell.

Storynory *www.storynory.com*
Listen to the stories of the Brothers Grimm, Hans Christian Andersen, Charles Perrault, Aesop, Oscar Wilde, and more on this splendid British site. Storynory has published a new audio story every week since November 2005. Children can listen to the story as they follow along on the text, which promotes reading fluency and helps English language learners. As they say, "Our stories have brought harmony in place of strife on the back seats of cars all over the world."

Storyteller.net *www.storyteller.net/stories/audio*

Here you'll find podcasts of more than a hundred short, delightful tales, told by different storytellers, which can be listened to on a computer.

Tumblebooks *www.tumblebooks.com*

An e-book subscription service offering scores of animated picture books online.

YouTube *www.youtube.com*

On this well-known site there are numerous short videos of storytellers strutting their stuff, including, if you type *"Barefoot Books Storytelling"* in the search bar, tales told by children. One storyteller from Oregon, Leslie Snape, has uploaded dozens of short videos of herself telling stories. You could do this, too! With the explosion of fit-in-your-palm video cameras and smartphones, everyone can be a filmmaker with minimal training or fuss. It's ridiculously simple to make a little video recording and post it here. On the home page you'll find links to instructions on how to upload your video; each can be up to ten minutes long, plenty of time to tell a good story. Of course, you'll need to make sure to pick stories in the public domain, and not something like Maurice Sendak's *Where the Wild Things Are*, which would be a violation of copyright. Post a link to your video on your school or library's website, and watch your audience grow. If you don't want to put your videos on YouTube, you can simply upload them to your library's website for children and parents to watch at home.

Zinger Tales *www.plcmc.org/bookhive/zingertales/zingertales.asp*

At the Public Library of Charlotte and Mecklenburg County in North Carolina, you'll find Zinger Tales, a video collection of dozens of stories told by master storytellers, including Doc McConnell, the late Jackie Torrence, Tony Tallent, Donna Washington, and the Frontline Storytellers, a group of librarians from that library.

Promoting Your Program

If you don't know the trees, you may be lost in the forest;
but if you don't know the stories, you may be lost in life.

—SIBERIAN PROVERB

Promoting Yourself

STORYTELLERS LOVE TWO THINGS: STORIES AND SHARING. HOW CAN AUDIences find you to hear your tales? Having an online presence can help. People will use it to explore your work and share in your experiences. Whether you're naturally gregarious or naturally shy except onstage, there are some things to consider:

WEB PAGES

You'll want to have a web page that talks about you, your stories, and your upcoming engagements. You can hire a designer to host and build a custom site for you, but you can build one pretty easily on your own for free using the following website builders. You'll find lots of tutorials on www.youtube.com if you need tech support.

- Google Sites (www.sites.google.com): Offers free web pages for anyone. With a variety of attractive templates to choose from, you can begin building pages in minutes as easily as typing in a word-processing program.

- Weebly.com: Weebly uses drag-and-drop modules to help you construct a page, though some users find using modules more difficult than merely typing in content. Like Google Sites, you'll have many attractive templates from which to choose.
- Moonfruit.com: The name is definitely a conversation starter. Sites are free, and the templates feature intense colors and gorgeous layouts. It's more time consuming to learn than Google Sites, but the attractive results might be worth it.

BLOGGING

Some folks prefer blogging, or keeping an online journal, either in addition to or instead of a web page. Blogging helps your fans keep in touch with the events you participate in and also allows you talk about them. Try these easy-to-use blogging sites:

- Blogger.com: Google's free blogging tool is the easiest to use, and you can embed many kinds of digital content (except podcasts) right into your site.
- WordPress.com: WordPress has a few more bells and whistles. One of the best features is the ability to adjust the date and time of day when a post will be published. You can download the software at www.wordpress.com and host your blog on your own site, or self-host it at www.wordpress.org.
- Tumblr.com: Tumblr streamlines and simplifies blogging and helps you connect with other Tumblr users. Luscious, easy-to-use templates have made Tumblr explode.

FACEBOOK

If you're like most Americans, you already have a personal Facebook page, but you may not want members of your storytelling audiences to friend you there. Set up a fan page on Facebook where people can connect with you as a storyteller and see images from your shows. It's free.

PINTEREST

Pinterest.com is "a tool for collecting and organizing the things that inspire you." When you log on to Pinterest (it's free), you can pin images and videos you find on the Internet, and repin other folks' interesting pins from their boards. Set up as many different boards as you like, organized by topic. Your boards can be secret or public. Warning: When you start pinning, you may have to give up on sleeping, because there's more information available than any human has time to absorb in a day.

For instance, take a look at www.pinterest.com/valeriebyrdfort/teacher-librarian-things, the Pinterest site of school librarian Valerie Fort (whose website, www.valeriebyrdfort.com, has as its heading "Library Goddess"). You'll be galvanized by all of the worksheets, ideas, videos, author links, and other cool stuff she has on her endless Pinterest boards.

TWITTER

Twitter.com, like Facebook, is a quick way to send out announcements about upcoming events, keep up with what peer storytellers are doing, and talk with fans. With each announcement limited to just 140 characters, it's an easy, quick way to stay in touch. Having separate personal and professional accounts is worth considering—be thoughtful about what your fans want to hear about you and what you want to share with them.

LINKEDIN

If Twitter and Facebook feel too vulnerable for you, consider setting up a no-cost profile on this professional networking site. If you're feeling adventurous, you can link your Facebook and Twitter feeds to your LinkedIn presence.

FLICKR

You may wish to post photos from your events online, and a free or low-cost Pro account on Flickr, an enormous photo-sharing site, might be just what the doctor ordered. You can use tags, or descriptive words like Omaha, StoryFest '13, or Edgar Allen Poe to help users discover your content. Take care, however, with posting photos of minors without parental permission.

VIDEO

Money is tight in schools and libraries, the two venues most likely to hire a storyteller. As a result, many educators and librarians want to preview your style before hiring you. In addition, if you teach or lead workshops, you may wish to have a sample of your teaching style. There are numerous sites that will host your videos at no cost and let you embed (or place) that video on your web page. Hosting your videos on these public sites increases the possibility that others will find your content. Consider these options:

- Vimeo.com: This site is less likely to be blocked in K–12 settings. A free basic account will be adequate for most storytellers. Embedding is available, and Vimeo allows you to upload videos of more than an hour in length. That's a big advantage.
- YouTube.com: The most popular free option, YouTube lets you host short videos and create a "channel." Your fans can subscribe to your channel and receive an e-mail whenever new videos are updated. Videos can be embedded (placed) onto your blog, web page, and more. Because YouTube is blocked in many K–12 schools, however, consider duplicating your content elsewhere.
- Flickr.com: The photo-sharing site also lets you upload video clips.

Promoting Your Program

You're probably saying to yourself, "You mean I have to plan a program, learn the stories, present them, *and* publicize it?" In many communities, if you whisper, a crowd appears. In others, after advertising the first few story sessions, you may not need to do another thing. Part of planning and producing an event is thinking and doing something about publicity, and that's almost as important as planning the program itself. Keep in mind that publicity may involve spending some money, but there are many ways of achieving effective, low-cost publicity. Your promotional efforts can range from informal notices posted on real or online bulletin boards to paid commercial advertising.

We do need to make a distinction between teachers and school librarians and public librarians and other storytellers. Teachers and school librarians are fortunate, of course, because they essentially have captive audiences. If you are a second-grade teacher, for instance, you can simply declare that Tuesdays at 2 p.m. are reserved for storytelling, and you will have instantly created an audience of twenty-five six- and seven-year-olds for yourself. Public librarians and professional librarians need to drum up their audiences each time.

Nevertheless, all of us need to bang the drum for library programs. On an ongoing basis, let people know not only what you are doing but also why it is so vital. The news is filled with stories of school and public library closings and slashed hours, staff, materials budgets, and programs. Across the United States, librarians are being let go and replaced with aides or volunteers. Libraries are perceived as being too acquiescent to fight back. Your programs can help support them and the work they are doing.

One library system in Virginia didn't take this sort of thing lying down. In 2010, when faced with dire cutbacks, the entire staff of the eight branches of the Central Rappahannock Regional Library in and around Fredericksburg, Virginia, got dramatic. To reassure their patrons that the library would survive budget cuts and that they would still be there for them, they made a video and posted it on YouTube. To the tune of the disco hit, "I Will Survive," they wrote new lyrics and filmed a video about the glories of their library, with staffers lip-syncing the words. A real charmer, the video garnered more than 150,000 views, and even got TV coverage. Look up "Libraries Will Survive" on YouTube, then watch and be inspired to be a better advocate for your situation—and publicize every wonderful thing that you are doing.

WEBSITES AND SOCIAL MEDIA

Today almost every public library and school has a website (not to mention a Facebook page, Twitter feed, and blog), with a calendar of events, a description of programs, photographs, links to further information, and contact numbers. Many children's departments have their own page on the site, which lists events and programs; has booklists, photos and links to games; and provides online activities. Registration for children's programs can usually be done online, which is a welcome convenience for busy parents.

The library's website and Twitter feed are your easiest and best advertisements. Write compelling descriptions for the website, add photos or videos of prior programs, and pay attention to design, composition, and visual appeal. Then use your library's Twitter feed to post pithy messages, quotes from authors, and ads for upcoming programs. Do you have a blog and/or a Pinterest page and/or a Facebook page with photos and programming ideas, posters, and interesting links? Do you post YouTube videos of your programs? Do you send e-newsletters? Post information about each event after it's done? If you do all of these things, your program attendance will soar (though you may not have time to sleep anymore).

POSTERS, FLYERS, AND NEWSLETTERS

It may seem obvious, but be sure that the posters and flyers—whether printed or virtual—clearly spell out the name of the event, the time, the date, and the place. You should also include names of performers, a phone number, and a website address for additional details. Eye-catching graphics are a must. Make your poster different by trying a new shape or using jazzy colors, but don't be so clever that the message becomes lost in the design.

The most important elements in poster and flyer composition are clear lettering, uncluttered design, and plainly stated information. When you are designing a flyer on your computer, pick fonts that are attractive and easy to read. Unless you are printing in full color, use brightly colored paper to draw attention. Scan in your own drawings or copy and paste interesting clip art or photographs. Here are a few good, royalty free, public domain clip art sites.

Classroom Clipart *www.classroomclipart.com*
More than fifty thousand free clip art, illustrations and photographs.

Clip Art ETC *etc.usf.edu/clipart*
An online service of Florida's Educational Technology Clearinghouse, with fifty thousand–plus pieces of free, quality, educational clipart.

Public Domain Clip Art *www.pdclipart.org*
A collection of more than twenty-five thousand free, public-domain clip art samples.

Wikimedia Commons *www.commons.wikimedia.org*
A huge selection (more than six million) free usable media files, including pictures and other images.

After all the work you've put into creating your poster or flyer, you will want to find the right places to hang it. If you are presenting in a school, library, church, clubhouse, or similar venue, place your posters and a stack of flyers around the building. Look beyond that conventional bulletin board; discover new places to advertise—a classroom door, the stairwell wall, the entrance door to the building. Leave flyers in the office, classrooms, teachers' mailboxes. If your school, library, or town puts out a weekly, monthly, or occasional newsletter, put in features about what's happening. You can add color photographs and spot art to make an e-mail feature stand out.

Maren Vitali, librarian at Milltown Elementary School in Bridgewater, New Jersey, writes a monthly newsletter about what's new in the library. She calls it the "Milltown Toilet Paper," and hangs a copy in the teachers' bathrooms. Her reasoning? Everyone needs something to read in the loo. She said, "I used to put it in teachers' mailboxes, but no one ever read it. Now they do." Judy used one of those bathrooms when she visited, which is how she came to read the newsletter. She admits she read the whole thing. Twice!

Public librarians can send flyers to school librarians to hand out to their students. If paper use is a concern, turn the flyer into a monthly newsletter to publicize everything that's going on in the children's room. Ask shopkeepers for window space, but carefully consider where it will attract the audience you want. The ice cream store? The toy store? The local restaurant? The garden shop?

MINI-SIGNS AND MAXI-SIGNS

People often simply ignore printed promotions. To capture these reluctant readers, try placing tiny signs, one-by-two inches or smaller, in obvious places. You can make your mini-signs on small peel-off labels that you design on your computer and print in a colorful, tiny font. Attach them to doorknobs, locker doors, milk cartons, salt shakers, or the library checkout counter. Or design business card-sized magnets to hand out. For your maxi-sign, make a huge banner and hang it over the library's front door, the entrance to the children's room, or even across the main street in your town.

SOUVENIRS AND BOOKMARKS

Giveaways make people curious enough to read the small announcement of the program you have attached. Such a souvenir need not be expensive—a cut flower, a rock, a pinecone, a seashell. Make the giveaway appropriate to the program theme. Are you having a pet show? Give away a dog biscuit with the tiny announcement connected by colorful yarn or ribbon. Make little pockets out of fabric and sew a button on the front of each. In the pocket, place a little business card printed with information on your program. Head the announcement, "Keep a Story in Your Pocket." When you hand it out, say, "You can never have too many pockets. We're giving out free stories at the library to keep in your pocket. I hope you and your children can come." Put things in colorful little gift bags. You can buy these inexpensively at your local dollar store, or you can ask people you know to donate bags they have around the house. Who doesn't love getting a goodie bag, even if there's just a tiny toy and a library flyer inside?

Bookmarks are always suitable giveaways. You can purchase spiffy commercial bookmarks from library and book promotional companies, the American Library Association (www.alastore.ala.org) and Upstart (http://upstartpromotions.com/upstart), but the ones you make yourself, labeled with program information, can be equally effective. Save used greeting cards and put them to practical use. All you need to do to turn them into bookmarks is to cut off the greeting part, then print up adhesive labels with your message and stick them on the back of the pictures. That way you recycle when you spread the word. Don't just slip a bookmark or announcement into a book—hand it directly to a child or adult with a simple oral greeting, a smile, and a reminder such as "Don't forget our story hour Wednesday. All the information is on the back!"

DOORKNOB HANGERS

When you are attempting to introduce a new program in your community, don't hesitate to borrow ideas from commercial advertisers. For example, give something away in a door-to-door canvass—perhaps a few garden seeds with a notice describing your forthcoming event. Your local garden store may have seeds they are willing to donate. Hang the surprise on the doorknobs in the neighborhood. Your subsequent story program could have a garden theme. For example, tell a "Jack and the Beanstalk" story, read or tell Margaret Read MacDonald's *Pickin' Peas* (HarperCollins, 1998), and read Kevin Henkes's *My Garden* (Greenwillow, 2010). Then have children plant seeds in little plastic flowerpots, which they can take home. Consult your local garden club or horticultural society; they may be intrigued by something that promotes their interests at the same time you are promoting yours.

BULLETIN BOARDS

The old-fashioned bulletin board is still an effective way to publicize your next story session. To use the space well, periodically change the display. If you are announcing the same event, just use a different arrangement of the information and vary your materials. Photos are a great addition. Take them during your programs, and ask a colleague or parent to take pictures of you interacting with the audience. Fabrics, tissue paper, construction paper, cut-out letters, and small objects are all suitable materials for adding color and information. If you want your bulletin board to stand out, keep the display bright, colorful, and simple, but displaying something eye catching and unexpected such as a three-dimensional object. You can set up an electronic bulletin board by projecting a PowerPoint in the room with a loop of still photos or a video of groups in the throes of an ebullient, interactive story.

CHALKBOARDS, OLD AND NEW

A chalkboard, a whiteboard, or a flannelboard hanging on a wall or resting on a table or library checkout counter can serve as a good place to post a "Daily Reminder." Because old-fashioned chalkboards are obsolete in so many schools, kids will love the way they look. Change the message daily (or at least weekly) to encourage people to look automatically for the news. To publicize a story hour to be held a week from Wednesday, for example, start your chalkboard campaign the week before with reminders, quotes, and illustrations or cover art from the stories you'll be telling. Many public libraries now use electronic chalkboards, aka digital signage systems, to post their schedules. These come wall mounted or on pedestals. Indoor models can be fairly compact. On a twenty-inch display screen you can post a slideshow of images, including your upcoming schedule, a picture of your library, and even video clips of your story hours. People will be mesmerized by the moving images and will read what you have posted.

SANDWICH BOARDS AND T-SHIRTS

The old-fashioned sandwich board still catches people's attention. Use cardboard that is not too heavy, and wear the sandwich board as you walk around a shopping center or grocery store. If the sandwich board is too over-the-top for you, have a T-shirt made. If you have an eye-catching logo and tag line on the shirt, you'll be your own best ad. You may want to make them for your participants, too. Go to Google Maps (www.maps.google.com) and type in the word T-shirts and the name of your town. Up will come a list of local places that make customized T-shirts, which can help you with a design and lettering.

BADGES, BUTTONS, BALLOONS, AND BUMPER STICKERS

Make your own button with a mininotice attractively printed on it. Simply photocopy one image, attach it to a round piece of cardboard, and affix a pin to the back. You can buy blank name tags and some stock blank buttons, or design and print your own stickers on your computer. You can buy make-your-own button kits at sites like Badge-a-Minit (www.badgeaminit.com) or design your own buttons and have them made for you at Zazzle (www.zazzle.com).Wear your badge or button everywhere.

Balloons can also serve as publicity, especially if you are trying to reach young children. Use permanent-ink markers to letter a notice or reminder on the inflated balloons. If you think you will be using this idea more than once, buy an inexpensive pump. You can also buy professionally printed balloons or bumper stickers. Look in the yellow pages under "Advertising Specialties" or online for names of merchants specializing in personalized souvenirs.

TICKETS

The best way to draw an audience is to invite people personally. It isn't always practical to address and send individual invitations, but you can invite particular groups, such as Ms. Jensen's fourth-grade class or Brownie Troop 614. Make it a practice to invite a new group to each session.

There is something about having a ticket to an event that makes the holder feel obliged and eager to attend. You may want to send out tickets on request, which provides you with a way to estimate how many children to expect. Also, you might encourage an audience by leaving tickets to be distributed in classrooms, Sunday schools, and other appropriate places. Make it easy on yourself and purchase a roll of carnival tickets at a stationery or party supply store, or create a ticket template on your computer, copy six or more images to a page, print them on colorful paper, and cut them into individual tickets. (Look up *"free invitation templates"* online for a vast array of images and formats.) You can run a batch for each story hour, if you like, updating the name of the program, the date, and the time. If you collect the tickets at the door, you can easily count attendance without taking time from the session itself.

You can also incorporate tickets into a program. Be a Story Conductor. Announce: "All aboard the Story Train. Do you have your ticket? *All aboard!*" Carry the theme through your program with train or transportation stories.

MINISPEECHES

Attending a meeting at your library or school? Ask for a few minutes to announce your project. Prepare something short and peppy to wake up your listeners and make them laugh. Then give them a printed handout on bright paper to reinforce your message. If you know in advance that you will be given some time, you might prepare a quick, snappy PowerPoint, and/or bring a poster or related artifact to hold up. Maybe even tell a story! Remember, if the principal says, "I can give you five minutes," that doesn't mean ten. Practice your pitch and time yourself before you go.

When Judy was a school librarian in Bridgewater, New Jersey, one of her favorite days at the end of the year was when the children's librarians at the Somerset County Library would visit her school to publicize their summer reading program. Each year, they created a brand-new skit based on that year's theme, and went whole hog incorporating clever props and costumes. They either went from classroom to classroom to act it out, or presented it in the cafeteria for each of the lunches. They were always wonderfully funny and inventive, and the children loved the unexpected performances. "I remember when you came last year," the kids would shout delightedly. She was only too thrilled to help them promote their fabulous summer reading club, which hundreds of her students joined each year.

TELEPHONING, E-MAILING, TEXTING, AND TWEETING

Telephoning, e-mailing, texting, and tweeting are good ways to make promotion more personal. Contact the parents in your area. You can send colorful e-mail reminders of upcoming programs or confirm that a child has signed up for one. The heading in the subject line needs to be lively enough to attract attention but clear enough that recipients don't mistake your message for spam. You can also go minimal: *R U coming to storytime? 2MORO 2 PM? CU L8R?*

NEWSPAPER PUBLICITY

Many adults are hesitant about approaching a newspaper for publicity, but announcements of upcoming events are vital community news. Write a press release—with all the names and places spelled correctly—and e-mail it to the appropriate department. You can also call a reporter at your local paper and ask if he or she (or someone else on the paper) would be interested in covering your event. Your audience will be delighted when a reporter and a photographer show up to immortalize the day, even if it's just a captioned snapshot in the "Local News" section. Getting good publicity will make budget cutters think twice before they ax library staff and cut programs like storytelling and story hours.

Don't forget to write a thank-you note to the reporter; that's a good way to cement a contact who may be able to help you in the future. If you can't get an article in the newspaper or an announcement in the paper, consider buying an ad. This may be much less expensive than you think. Try to get someone to donate the price of the ad, but if that fails, at least try for a discount.

RADIO AND TELEVISION PUBLICITY

Radio and television stations are licensed by the Federal Communications Commission, and as part of their obligation to the public, they are required to offer a certain amount of public affairs programming. This includes announcements for nonprofit organizations. They might be interested in sending out a news crew to cover your event or interview you by phone. It's worth a call. Also, try your local public-access channel. Most have "bulletin boards" that scroll information about local goings-on. Check the channel's website to find listing requirements. Be prepared to supply written copy for the announcement; the less work a station has to do, the more likely it will help you.

You may find some of these publicity ideas more useful or easier to use than others. Whatever works for you is best. The point is: Spread the word! Toot your horn! Make a splash! Let the world know what you're up to!

chapter 3

Program Basics

People are hungry for stories. It's part of our very being. Storytelling is a form of history, of immortality, too. It goes from one generation to another.

—LOUIS "STUDS" TERKEL, AUTHOR AND HISTORIAN

RECALL A BYGONE ERA—THE WIND WHISTLING AROUND A STONE house built on the heath; light from a fireplace flickering on Granny in her rocking chair, ready to tell a story; and listeners crowded close. This nostalgic scene exists mostly in our imaginations. What we are really seeing or reacting to is the ambiance evoked by the story hour, more often than not presented in the somewhat humdrum environment of a classroom or library. It is up to the storyteller to create a particular mood and convey it to our audience. Exhibits and decorations can help conjure up a desired mood.

Decorations and Exhibits

A STORYTELLING SYMBOL

Create an individual symbol that instantly proclaims "Storytime!" and use it to decorate the corner or room in which you tell stories. Consider making a standing screen ornamented with book covers or character cutouts to symbolize the story hour and serve as a backdrop. Encourage children to design a story-hour logo to sew on a banner or wall hanging. How about a large black spider on a field of red representing Anansi, the African spider that "owns all the stories"? Make a large animal or book character from plywood or papier-mâché to stand at the entrance to the story area. Hang a sign announcing an upcoming event on the figure.

Even a stuffed toy can be a symbol. The Cat in the Hat, Curious George, and Peter Rabbit are classic storybook character dolls that children will recognize. Your bookstore may have a good selection of storybook-themed dolls, stuffed toys, and puppets. If not, visit Castlemere (www.castlemerebooks.com) for a dazzling array of choices, including Olivia, Frog and Toad, Knuffle Bunny, and Paddington Bear.

Use poster board to make giant book covers. Such a "book" can serve as a permanent beginning to your story hour. Inside the covers, on individual sheets of paper, you can list the program of the day, changing the listing for each story hour.

TABLE EXHIBITS

A table placed behind the storyteller is a handy place for an exhibit. A solid-color tablecloth will add a festive air and a welcome touch of color to the room. Now you have a place to display the story-hour "wishing candle" in its special candleholder, a vase of cut flowers or a plant, and the books that the stories you will tell come from. Using an artifact, prop, or exhibit can also help children recall the story as well as arouse their curiosity. Select one object that represents each story you are telling—perhaps a small cast-iron frying pan when you present Tomie dePaola's *Fin M'Coul: The Giant of Knockmany Hill* (Holiday House, 1981) or a mango to accompany Gerald McDermott's *Monkey: A Trickster Tale from India* (Harcourt, 2011). As an after-story treat, cut open the mango and share it with everyone. Then have the children help you plant the seed. (Visit www.ehow.com/how_8726706_remove-pit-mango.html to find out how to pry open the edge of the husk with a spoon to get the seed out.)

Occasionally, you may find someone willing to lend for display a collection of objects relevant to a story you are telling. Put the objects on a table behind the children so your audience isn't tempted to look instead of listen. Tell the story, and then talk about the collection. If the objects are valuable or fragile, exhibit them in a locked glass case. Having access to such collections can help increase an awareness of the different ways that artists and artisans interpret a story.

DECORATING FOR SPECIAL PROGRAMS

It's Diwali! It's Kwanzaa! It's Father's Day! Or it's the day you plan to tell stories from China or Spain, or about dogs or the circus! Make the day special by decorating the room with student-made murals, artifacts, posters, or seasonal decorations. If you are lucky enough to have a separate room for your story hours, you can really be creative. Change it completely by stringing figured or patterned bedsheets around the walls.

If you're telling stories about the ocean, festoon the space with island props, like large inflatable palm trees, a beach umbrella and beach chairs, seashells, and lei garlands. A large inflatable shark would be a nice touch, especially if you're telling Lee Wardlaw's *Punia and the King of Sharks: A Hawaiian Folktale* (Dial, 1997) or Rafe Martin's *The Shark God* (Scholastic, 2001).

Your local party store may supply these items and more, as will the Internet, including the always-helpful Amazon.com. Even if you advise your kids beforehand to dress for the beach—including hats, flip-flops, and sunglasses—when they walk in the room, they will be dumbfounded and delighted by the decorations. For a treat afterwards, why not serve single stick popsicles?

When you need a specific prize or toy or favor, a favorite one-stop shop is Oriental Trading (www.orientaltrading.com). The company offers a dizzying supply of inexpensive little toys, favors, and doodads, including cars, finger puppets, and plastic animals. Doing that beach program? You can purchase tiny, inflatable beach balls, twenty-five to a packet, for around $10. You'll also find windup chomping teeth (perfect for Halloween), small cars, kazoos, bird whistles, a large assortment of finger puppets, and piñatas at surprisingly reasonable prices.

ARTIFACTS AND PROPS

An artifact, prop, or exhibit, when you include it as part of the story hour, may serve to focus attention, aid the listener to recall the story, or arouse curiosity. Experience will bear out that a variety of objects used in different ways makes a program visually as well as aurally interesting. Besides, looking for, selecting, or making just the right item to introduce a story can be a satisfying part of the storyteller's preparation.

At the same time, let us caution you about becoming too involved with the visual at the expense of the proper learning and telling of your story. For those who delight in "little things"—antiques and crafted objects—this can be a danger. Judy's mantra for amassing a collection of indispensable objects is: "Never throw anything out." If you do, someone will write a book about it. Then you'll say, "Oh, no! I gave away that little pair of wooden shoes!" (Her own little pair of hand-painted wooden shoes is on a shelf in her basement; she has yet to find the perfect story to go with it, but she's sure it's just a matter of time.)

Another one of Judy's mantras is from her mother, Gladys Freeman, which holds true in libraries, education, and life: "If you see it, buy it. It won't be there when you go back. You never regret the things you do buy!"

Many of the ideas suggested below may seem more appropriate for the preschool or primary program—and they are—but older children and even middle schoolers will enjoy seeing your treasured childhood stuffed animal. Bring in a football to toss when reading or telling the story *The Day Roy Riegels Ran the Wrong Way* by Dan Gutman (Bloomsbury, 2011), a true story about the Rose Bowl of 1929.

And that old cracked teapot you were about to toss is perfect to use with the alternate version of that "I'm a Little Teapot" song, which Judy learned from her sister, Sharron Freeman, when she was three. Be sure you have a sugar bowl with handles available to show afterwards.

"I'm a Little Teapot"

(Alternate Version)

I'm a little teapot, short and stout;

Here is my handle, (*Put one fist on hip.*)

Here is my . . . (*Put other fist on hip. Look at it, puzzled. Shake head; shrug shoulders. Take arms down.*)

(*Spoken*) Hmmm. Let's try that again.

I'm a little teapot, short and stout;

Here is my handle, (*Put one fist on hip.*)

Here is my . . . (*Put other fist on hip. Look baffled. Shake head; look from side to side, examining your "handles"; shrug shoulders. Take arms down.*)

(*Spoken*) Hmmm. Let's try that again. *(Smile encouragingly; nod head.)*

Repeat one more time.

Final time:

I'm a little teapot, short and stout;

Here is my handle, (*Put one fist on hip.*)

Here is my . . . (*Put other fist on hip. Look astonished. Open mouth in an "Ohhhh!"*)

(*Spoken*) Oh my goodness, oh my soul—

I'm not a teapot; I'm a SUGAR BOWL!

To help you come up with creative and inexpensive sources of crafts, displays, and props, here are some suggestions to consider.

An Alphabet of Things to Bring, Buy, Make, and Do

AUTOMOBILES, TRUCKS, TRAINS, AND OTHER TOY VEHICLES

A toy car is just the ticket when reciting the rhyming text of Phyllis Root's *Rattletrap Car* (Candlewick, 2001). When telling Jim and Kate McMullan's riotous *I Stink* (HarperCollins, 2002), narrated by a tough-talking garbage truck, or their *I'm Dirty* (HarperCollins, 2002), narrated by a hardworking backhoe loader, bring out the toy vehicles. A toy train and a toy shark will spark extra dialogue to go with the story of competing toys in Chris Barton's *Shark vs. Train* (Little, Brown, 2010).

BOXES, BAGS, AND CONTAINERS

Magic Boxes

Find a pretty container, perhaps of antique silver or carved wood. When you open it, the magic of storyland flies out. Keep the lid open until the story hour is finished. Let the children help you catch the magic and close the box for another day. Judy calls these special boxes "Magic Boxes" and has an extensive collection of them. Into one of these boxes, put an object for each story you're planning to tell, and hold up the container, saying, "I wonder what is in this box?" Children will wriggle with excitement when you pull out each item, whether it's an old-fashioned skeleton key, a pocket watch, or a strand of colorful corn kernels made into a necklace. They adore the element of mystery that a Magic Box provides. Look for hatboxes, mailboxes, jewelry boxes, pencil boxes, and, for the big splurge, music boxes. Often something is packaged in such an imaginative way that it seems as though there must be a storytelling use for it. Look for baskets; decorated bags; tea, coffee, candy, or holiday cake tins; jam jars; cookie jars; sand pails; and garden pails. For an oversize Magic Box, use a trunk, suitcase, or specially decorated cardboard box to hold the books of the day. If your trunk is pretty and small enough, it can become the permanent Surprize Box or Best Books of the Week Box in your library or classroom.

Story Bags

To make a story bag, draw the figures of animals and characters, as well as other identifiable objects from your favorite picture books on heavy-duty paper or tagboard. Cut them out and place in a large decorated bag. Let a child reach into the bag and pick out a figure. Whichever one he or she chooses represents the story or book you will tell or read. (Be sure you always have on hand the represented books, ready to read or show.) Small animals, other book-related figurines, and objects carved of wood or made of other materials also are suitable for the story bag.

COLORING BOOKS

Browse through the trade coloring books to find book-character designs or look up "coloring pages" online for a vast array you can print out. Use the pictures in an exhibit or create souvenirs of your program. Kids love to color—it satisfies their need to use their hands and fill in something with a pattern.

DOLLS AND DOLLHOUSE FURNITURE

Boys may turn up their noses at the sight of a doll, but they will still like looking at dolls you bring in, especially if the dolls are wearing interesting costumes or go with a story. At the Madame Alexander site (www.madamealexander.com) you can find replicas of Fancy Nancy, Olivia the Pig, Eloise, Ramona and Beezus, and Christopher Robin. You may also find book and fairy-tale figures at your local bookstore. You'll find beautiful ones at www.storybookfigurines.com, but these are very expensive—for your own collection at home, and not to hand to children. Don't bring anything that would lead you to grief if someone dropped it. Someone will drop it. Instead, make clothespin dolls. Buy old-fashioned wooden clothespins at your hardware store, crafts supply store (Michaels and the like), or online. Dress these with felt and fabric to represent the characters in the stories you tell.

Children are fascinated with miniature furnishings for dollhouses. Look for them at toy stores, hobby and gift shops, and, of course, garage sales and eBay. There are also shops and websites devoted exclusively to miniatures.

EXERCISE EQUIPMENT

Children sit too much these days. Whether they're watching TV, playing board or computer games, surfing the Net, reading a book, or getting through the school day at their desks, they sit, sit, sit all day. No wonder so many are out of shape. What can we do to help counter this scary trend? We can incorporate movement activities in our programs. After telling Eleanor Farjeon's *Elsie Piddock Skips in Her Sleep* (Candlewick, 2000) or *The Recess Queen* by Alexis O'Neill (Scholastic, 2002), bring out jump ropes and hold a contest. Reciting Lisa Wheeler's *Boogie Knights* (Atheneum, 2008)? Then get everyone up to do the Twist, or pull out some hula hoops. Every little movement helps kids . . . and you, too.

FINGER PUPPETS AND OTHER PUPPETS

Finger puppets are great to use with nursery rhymes and simple stories. You can make them yourself from felt, or yarn (if you knit), or buy them at craft fairs, hobby shows, or toy stores. A handmade or purchased monkey puppet for the Curious George stories or any favorite animal puppet—who becomes your constant friend and assistant—will add personality to your program. The most magnificent animal puppets out there can be found at Folkmanis Puppets (www.folkmanis.com). Beware. You will want every one of them. Designate a nook in your room as an acting area. Set up a puppet theater with a variety of puppets and stock it with a large variety of scripts for children to try out on their own in pairs or small groups. You can write these yourself, but also harvest them from books, magazines, and online. Some authors provide readers' theater scripts online for their books that you can download. Go to www.MargiePalatini.com to find scripts for many of her folktale parody picture books, including *The Cheese* (HarperCollins, 2007); *Lousy, Rotten, Stinkin' Grapes* (Simon & Schuster, 2009); and *The Web Files* (Hyperion, 2001). For older kids, go to Aaron Shepard's site, www.aaronshep.com, for his magnanimous offering of forty splendid readers' theater scripts he's written from his own books of folktale retellings.

GREETING CARDS AND POSTCARDS

Book-oriented cards make excellent exhibits. Illustrators of children's books, such as Sandra Boynton and Tomie dePaola, have created lovely cards for greeting card companies. At CafePress (www.cafepress.com) you will find cards with beautiful vintage images from classic illustrators like Kate Greenaway. Also, send your kids cards with handwritten messages every now and again. They hardly ever get any mail and will be thrilled.

HOLIDAY DECORATIONS

You may want to have special decorations for major holidays: a jack-o'-lantern, a gingerbread house, a Valentine's Day mailbox, and so on. When you go into a store festooned for the holiday, ask to see the manager. Explain you have no budget for such wonderful items, and you would be thrilled if, when the big day is past, the store would give them to you. Chances are they'll be happy to do so, and you'll be all ready for next year.

ILLUSTRATED CLOTHING

Would you like to wear an illustration from your favorite book? Or a photograph or wildly imaginative drawing made by a child in your storytelling program? One of Judy's favorite pieces of clothing is her "story shirt," a white short-sleeve shirt decorated with hand-painted characters from some of her favorite picture books. If you aren't artistic, many T-shirt shops will turn your favorite image into a T-shirt. Also check out some of the delightful tees at Wonder-Shirts (www.wonder-shirts.com) with characters including Miss Viola Swamp and Frog and Toad, and a Pigeon shirt that says "Driven to Read." There are adorable Babymouse T-shirts for sale at www.cafepress.com/Babymouse (not to mention mugs, magnets, and a wall clock), and CafePress (www.cafepress.com) has quite an array of wearable merchandise to drool over. If you can't find the tee you desire, you can design your own. And finally, look for librarian T-shirts and book-related toys at Stop Falling Productions (www.stopfalling.com).

JUNQUE

Look upon all throw-outable objects with a practiced eye. You may be a tosser, with no clutter in your house, but before you throw away those eyeglasses with no glass, the two ancient telephones in the back of the closet, or the Lawrence Welk records moldering in the basement, stop and ask yourself: "Could I use this with a story?" The eyeglasses are perfect for your dress-up box; the telephone is just what you need for having pairs of kids act out pretend conversations; and, if you're telling Daniel Pinkwater's classic automobile story, *Tooth-Gnasher Superflash* (Four Winds, 1981), the records can be car steering wheels that kids use to "drive" when you act out the story with your group.

KITES

Of course kites make splendid wall decorations, and at Picture Pretty Kites (www.pictureprettykites.com), you'll find hundreds to choose from. Have one on hand when you tell Jeff Brown's *Flat Stanley* (HarperCollins, 2006, c1964); Ying Chang Compestine's folktale-like picture book, *The Story of Kites* (Holiday House, 2003); or Florence Parry Heide's wacky *Princess Hyacinth (The Surprising Tale of a Girl Who Floated)* (Schwartz & Wade, 2009).

LIVE ANIMALS

Bring in a pet rabbit, a bird, a dog, or a cat, and then tell stories about that animal. Children will be delighted if you contact your local herpetologist, entomologist, or arachnologist to bring live animals for a show-and-tell. While you probably can't keep a cat or dog in your room—too many allergies out there—maybe you'll want to sponsor a pet gerbil, hamster, or guinea pig. No fur? A stuffed animal may do. Or, if you're up to it, how about a simple fish tank?

MAPS, MONEY, AND STAMPS

Hang on to loose change and small bills when you travel to other countries. Keep a treasure box filled with these and another filled with foreign stamps for children to peruse after a story. Or make a display with a world map and affix coins and bills on the side, with strings leading to the countries of origin. Bring out atlases and paper maps. Children who have grown up with GPS systems will be intrigued by how people found their way around in the past. On a mounted map of the world, mark with tacks or small flags the origin of the stories you will tell, and point out to the group where the story comes from.

NESTING DOLLS

Although these dolls are usually imported, they are not necessarily expensive. In Russia, they are called *matryoshka* dolls, but they also come from Scandinavia, Russia, Poland, Germany, and Japan. Tell your first story and remove the outer doll. After each successive story, remove another doll until there is only one left to say good-bye to the children. You'll find hundreds of them, some quite reasonable, at www.matryoshkastore.com. At Amazon .com, they have a nice collection—including a set of Elvis and one of the Beatles (which, OK, are really for you). Best of all, they have several types of unpainted ones, ranging from a five-piece to a fifteen-piece set. You could make your own or have older children design and paint them to go with a story. (You can use nesting boxes in the same way.)

OLD CLOTHES FOR DRESS-UP

"Hey," Judy's husband said, alarmed, "what are you doing with my old shirt?" She was taking it to school so her first graders could act out the classic Halloween story "The Little Old Lady Who Was Not Afraid of Anything" by Linda Williams (HarperCollins, 1986). She didn't think it wise to mention that she had an old pair of his pants and shoes as well. Before you toss the shirt with a little rip, the heels that are too tight, the prom dress from 1983, remember that kids would look mighty fine wearing them to act out stories. Do take these home and wash them now and then.

PUZZLES

Make use of the illustrations from book jackets. Mount them on cardboard, laminate or cover them with clear contact paper, and cut out the pieces for a puzzle. You can also make your own puzzles from scratch by drawing freehand or tracing a picture from a book. Make sure you identify the pieces by a number or symbol on the back so that you can gather them back together. You may have enough puzzles for each child or two children working as a team. When all the puzzles are put together, it's book time.

QUILLS AND OTHER WRITING IMPLEMENTS

We tell children that in the olden days, people used goose and turkey feathers as pens, dipping the tips or nibs in ink every few words. Seeing is believing. Bring in quills and other interesting writing tools, like old pens, a hornbook and stylus, parchment, or an old scroll. Make your own implements or buy them already made at www.libertybellshop.com, the Liberty Bell Shop. Children can practice writing their own names on paper with quills and ink.

RECORDINGS

Music at the beginning or the end of your session gives the program a feeling of continuity. Choose something to fit the mood of your stories from artists who specialize in music for children—like Laurie Berkner, Tom Chapin, Dan Zanes, Ralph's World, or Bill Harley—to classical pieces like "The Four Seasons" by Antonio Vivaldi or the Lieutenant Kijé Suite by Sergei Prokofiev.

STORYTELLING APRON

The storyteller's apron enables you to put objects representing each of the stories you plan to tell in the pockets. A regular cook's apron with pocket will be useful, or you can make your own. In addition to lots of other storyteller's props, Mimi's Motifs (www.mimismotifs.com) has our favorite storytelling apron ever, a wonderful multicolored, many-pocketed wonder. When children see you wearing your storytelling apron, they know good times are coming their way.

TOYS

Every year, there are new fads in toys, and some of them are just waiting for you. Case in point: Silly Bandz, rubber bands molded into shapes of various animals, objects, and even the alphabet. Judy can't imagine life without her windup chattering teeth. For stuffed animals, use an old favorite such as a worn stuffed rabbit to represent Margery Bianco's *The Velveteen Rab-*

bit (Doubleday, 2014, c1922) or a fuzzy teddy bear when you tell about Winnie-the-Pooh and Christopher Robin. You can often find toys and stuffed animals from beloved children's books, including a Cat in the Hat doll or the dolls representing Max and the monsters from *Where the Wild Things Are* by Maurice Sendak. Wait till you see the handsome array of stuffed animals, dolls, and puppets at www.merrymakersinc.com, including Bad Kitty, Dog and Bear, Miss Bindergarten, and Stillwater, the panda from Jon J Muth's Caldecott Honor–winning picture book, *Zen Shorts* (Scholastic, 2005), a marvelous one to tell.

USUAL AND UNUSUAL GAMES

Look for games you can set up in a games corner, or build a story around games or blocks. Children adore all kinds of blocks and Lego pieces; who knows how many architects and engineers got their start playing with these. Tell stories at a library, community, or school games night for children and parents.

You know Scrabble, but have you tried the word games Boggle or Bananagrams, which comes in a banana-shaped sack, and is like playing freeform Scrabble without a board? If you have space, jacks and hopscotch are classic ways to strengthen eye-hand coordination and balance. Try Jenga, where you stack the little wood blocks into a tower and then remove them, one by one, from the bottom, trying not to collapse the structure. Other games that help children develop concentration skills, build interpersonal relations, and learn patience include Mancala, Parcheesi, Chinese Checkers, and, of course, checkers and chess.

VEGETABLES AND FRUITS

Stand in the produce aisle and look at all the magnificent shapes, colors, and textures of the fruits and vegetables. If you're reading or telling a story with ties to the grocery store and its wares, bring in the real thing to admire or taste. Dried corn, gourds, and pumpkins in the fall make a spectacular display for all to admire, but so do colorful fruits like lemons, oranges, and tangerines. Artist Saxton Freymann uses actual produce to make the characters and scenery in his books: add a couple of black-eyed peas for eyes, and that zucchini becomes an alligator. Children love to identify the veggies in his *Food for Thought: The Complete Book of Concepts for Growing Minds* (Scholastic, 2005) and then create their own.

WEAVINGS AND OTHER TEXTILES

Children don't always know how things are made. If you are crafty, demonstrate knitting, crocheting, and weaving for them. They can examine their own clothing to see if it was knitted, crocheted, or woven. Bring in an old scarf and unravel a bit. Perhaps you'll want to teach your older children how to make things with yarn. A perfect tie-in book that takes you through the process, starting with shearing the sheep, is *Charlie Needs a Cloak* by Tomie dePaola (Simon & Schuster, 1973). Or go in the other direction with Simms Taback's Caldecott winner, *Joseph Had a Little Overcoat* (Viking, 1999), where Joseph turns his old and worn coat into a jacket, vest, scarf, necktie, handkerchief, and, finally, a button. It's the ultimate recycling story.

XYLOPHONES AND OTHER MUSICAL INSTRUMENTS

If you play a musical instrument, whether it's a flute, a guitar, or even a kazoo, incorporate your talent into your storytime whenever you can. Children will want to make music, too. Set up a sound corner in the library with interesting musical instruments children can try out, like hand bells, finger cymbals, maracas, a kalimba (a thumb piano from Africa), bongos drums, and egg shakers for a session that'll beat the band. (You'll find quite an

assortment of inexpensive instruments at Amazon.com if you look up children's musical instruments.) How about a six-foot piano mat that kids play by stepping on it? Look that up online—it's about $35. And don't forget a kid-size xylophone. If you tell Robert McCloskey's classic picture book *Lentil* (Viking, 1940) about a boy who plays the harmonica, bring in a harmonica and a lemon wedge. In fact, give everyone a lemon wedge so they can really get into the lip-puckering story climax.

YARD-SALE ITEMS AND OTHER ODD ARTIFACTS

It's amazing how many perfectly fine treasures are considered worthless by other people. You have to think creatively whenever and wherever you shop. One of Judy's finds is a box that looks like a big, old-fashioned book, which she found at a Victoria's Secret store in London. She fills it with an assortment of props and uses it regularly when she talks to children about the components of a great story. Other treasures she's acquired include a sporty silver Statue of Liberty crown (a wide assortment awaits you at Amazon.com); a peanut-butter-and-jelly-sandwich change purse from the Museum of Modern Art in New York City (www.coolstuffexpress.com/pbj-yummy-pocket.html); and, of course, a Brockabrella, the umbrella hat invented by Baseball Hall of Famer Lou Brock (www.umbrellahat.net). The next time you come across an interesting snow globe or a real honeycomb or a Liberty Bell pencil sharpener (Judy has one on her desk), go for it!

ZOO ANIMALS, FROM A TO Z

Start a collection of stuffed zoo animals, including the six main classes: invertebrates, amphibians, reptiles, fishes, birds, and mammals. Try to find at least one animal for each letter of the alphabet as well. Make a little enclosure for them to stay in, labeled "Our Zoo." When reading alphabet books like *Miss Bindergarten Gets Ready for Kindergarten* by Joseph Slate (Dutton, 1996), *Creature ABC* by Andrew Zuckerman (Chronicle, 2009), or *Gone Wild: An Endangered Animal Alphabet* by David McLimans (Walker, 2006), pull out your collection. Children can play with the menagerie and try to identify each animal by its first letter and by its class.

Pulling the Program Together

A good introduction or opening sets the mood for your program. You must also plan the transitions between stories, and your conclusion. Let's take a look at these components. Remember that the program begins the minute children walk through your door, so let's begin with some ways you can make your visitors feel at home.

NAME TAGS

When children arrive for your program, you may wish to distribute name tags. This is as much for you as for them. Many public librarians design new name tags for each program. It's wonderful to be able to address your charges as if you've known them forever. When you know you'll be telling stories about fruit or flowers or frogs or France, make name tags or name necklaces reflecting those themes out of construction or heavy paper. If you don't have a list of all the children's names beforehand, enlist the help of the parents or caretakers when they arrive to correctly spell the names of their charges as you (or they) write them on the tag. Running low on time? Grab blank peel-and-stick name tags; decorate them with a stamp, colored inks, or a colorful sticker; and add the child's name in big letters. You can even have the children decorate their own name tags when they arrive as a simple before-story craft.

SETTING THE MOOD

The introduction to the program often sets the mood for the entire period. A traditional opening is the lighting of a candle, which you can read about in Lucia Gonzalez's historical fiction picture book, *The Storyteller's Candle/ La velita de los cuentos* (Children's Book Press, 2008), which introduces the famed storyteller Pura Belpré, the first Puerto Rican librarian in the New York City Public Library system.

When you light the candle, the children know the time has come to settle down and listen. If you are worried about fire safety, buy a battery-operated flameless candle. After the last story is told, the storyteller or a child from the audience blows out the candle and everyone silently makes a wish.

Perhaps you want to recite a simple rhyme as you light the candle. Here's a rhyme Judy put together, based on one that librarian Alice Yucht recited:

Abracadabra, abracazoom,
Storytime magic, come into this room!
Allacadabra, allacazoom,
Light first the candle and let stories bloom.

When storytime is over, blow out the candle and say:

Allacadabra, allacazoom,
Storytime magic came into this room.
Blow out the candle; our tales are unfurled;
Gave us a journey all over the world.

If you don't want to use the candle, substitute your own trademark; ring a bell, shake a tambourine, or try some finger chimes to summon your audience. Perhaps you have a banner that you unfurl at the beginning of each program. Play a theme song on the guitar or another portable instrument. The Chinaberry catalog (www.chinaberry.com) has a star-shaped musical fairy wand that works like a tuning fork and makes a lovely *tinggggggggg*!

Setting the mood can simply mean asking a question such as "How many of you like to laugh, raise your hands?" This suggests that the story will be funny, and you have set the mood that will elicit a humorous response to whatever you tell. On the other hand, if you want to create an atmosphere of suspense, you might dim the lights and turn on a flashlight or lantern.

GETTING THE AUDIENCE'S ATTENTION

Before you begin a storytime, a class, or a big assembly, you need to capture everyone's attention. In many schools, the staff has a schoolwide signal to stop the noise, like raising your right hand with your first and index fingers upraised in a peace symbol. When children see the hands go up, they raise their own and stop talking. This is simple and effective. Ronnie Sawin, a master teacher at Van Holten School in Bridgewater, New Jersey, simply sprinkled the heads of her kindergartners with "quiet dust," which was invisible but worked every time. At Nantucket Elementary School in Nantucket, Massachusetts, teachers and their exceptional librarian, Laura Coburn, use an inexpensive but instantly effective silver bar chime called a Woodstock Percussion Zenergy Chime (easily findable online) that they strike with a little wooden mallet. This simple solo percussion instrument generates a most lovely, long-lasting ring that permeates the air. As soon as children hear it, they know to stop what they are doing, raise their right arms, and become silent.

Many teachers and librarians have an arsenal of little rhymes to get their young charges to focus. Try "One, two, three, eyes on *me*!" Children respond, "One, two, eyes on *you*!" Young children also adore silly nonsense sayings like "Criss-cross applesauce!" Follow with "Spoons in the bowl!" which means "Hands in your lap!" Or try one of these quiet-down ditties, doing the actions described in each line:

Hands #1

My hands upon my head I'll place,
Upon my shoulders, on my face;
At my waist and by my side,
Then behind me, they will hide.
Then I'll raise them way up high,
And let my fingers fly, fly, fly.
Then clap, clap, clap them,
One! Two! Three!
Now see how quiet they can be.

Hands #2

Sometimes my hands are at my side,
Then, behind my back they hide.
Sometimes I wiggle my fingers so;
I shake them fast, I shake them slow.
Sometimes my hands go clap, clap, clap;
Then I rest them in my lap.
Now they're quiet as can be,
Because it's storytime, you see.

Texas school librarian and children's book author Pat Miller incorporates some magical drama into her story hours. She says, "I start my own storytime seated next to a treasure box I made. The book I'm planning to read is hidden inside, along with a prop related to it. We recite and act out together this rhyme":

Hands #3

Sometimes my hands are by my side.
Then behind my back they hide.
Shake them fast, shake them slow,
Shake them high, shake them low.
Now they're quiet as can be, (cross hands on lap)
Mrs. Miller will read to me.

"Then the child of the day opens the box, shows the prop (the book is still hidden, covered with a gold cloth), and accepts from the group their three guesses for the name of the book, based on the prop. As the child reaches for a corner of the gold cloth, we all chant, 'Hocus-pocus, show the book!' The child dramatically lifts off the gold cloth and then shows the book, which we proceed to read together."

Sometimes Judy simply says, "*Show* me you're ready!" That's the signal for children to sit up straight and pay attention. When they do, she smiles and says, "Thank you for being such excellent listeners."

If some children continue to talk or fidget, praise the children who are ready. Try going overboard, clutching palm to chest and exclaiming, "Oh, be still my heart! I love the way Julia is sitting and listening so beautifully. What could be better than telling stories to children who show me they can't wait to hear them? Thank you, Julia! You just made my day! No, my week! No, my *whole year*!"

Julia will beam and laugh. With a heartfelt little speech like that, watch the rest of the group try to exceed your expectations. Positive feedback is usually far more effective than negative: "I adore the way Row Two is sitting right now. You are perfectly perfect, Row Two." Row Two beams. Rows One and Three sit up straighter, hoping for a compliment. Give them one. "And Row One and Three, look how fabulous you are, too. You are all the most marvelous children in the whole world. Maybe even the universe."

And yet, sometimes it's just plain hard to get young kids quiet. This rhyme is a good one for participation.

Wiggles

I wiggle my fingers, (hands in air, wiggle your fingers)
I wiggle my toes, (look down and wiggle your toes)
I wiggle my shoulders, (move your shoulders)
I wiggle my nose. (wiggle your nose)
Now, no more wiggles (wiggle your pointer finger "no" from side to side)
Are left in me, (use your thumbs to point to yourself)
So I will be still (clap loudly)
As still can be. (whisper this line and fold your hands in your lap)

Still wiggly? Try the active approach, acknowledging it. "OK, it's time to shake the sillies out, waggle the wiggles, and turn on the ears. Can you copycat me? Let's go!" Pat your head and rub your stomach, and then pat your stomach and rub your head. Start with simple motions in a sequence. Clap slowly twice, then three times fast. Your children will be delighted to try to repeat your pattern. Keep things simple, or do sillier or more complicated motions to see if they can keep up. End with a big clap, and say, "And now, a *story*!"

Introducing a Story

If you have planned your program around a theme, you may want to make a general introduction to each story. Suit the introduction to the group and to yourself, but keep it brief, taking care not to overwhelm the story itself.

One way to introduce the individual story is with a personal comment. Tell your audience where you learned it, why you like it, or how it relates to a personal incident. Another style of introduction is more academic. Look up some background information beforehand. Briefly discuss the author, the type of story you have chosen, or its country of origin, but don't make your introduction sound like a lecture; sound enthusiastic when you present the information. You can often find useful material in the preface, on flap copy, or on the copyright page. The best collections of folk and fairy tales will include information about the lands and the peoples from whom the stories were collected. Don't overlook the encyclopedia and Wikipedia.com—which will surprise you with their information about specific stories—as sources for a lively, informative introduction.

If you are telling tales from a variety of countries, put together a wee PowerPoint of images that personify those countries: Big Ben, the Coliseum, and the Eiffel Tower may be familiar to you, but they may not be known to your audience. At www.google.com/images, you can find pictures of a huge array of national monuments, buildings, and natural wonders to provide your kids with a travelogue that will make them want to visit some of those places one day.

The book itself can provide yet another introductory approach. Display it and tell your listeners that in it is the story they are about to hear. You might also exhibit or give one-sentence booktalks for several books containing similar stories, either variants of the one you are about to tell, or ones with related themes. You will reinforce the idea that stories that are told often come from books.

If you want to try a theatrical flourish to introduce your story, borrow a useful device from vaudeville and silent movies: an easel holding large cards. On each card print the title of the story you will tell and the title of the book it comes from, if they differ. Display the appropriate title card immediately before you tell the story. To see an array of these old cards, which were often black with white letters, go back to www.google.com/images and type in the keywords "*silent movie title cards*." A bit of further online searching will turn up templates with fancy borders for making the cards.

Transitions

The atmosphere or mood you wish to maintain should dictate your handling of the time between stories in your program. If you look for common threads in each story, it's not difficult to come up with a graceful transition sentence. Let's say the two stories you will be telling are the English folktale "The Old Woman and Her Pig" (on page 100) and the African folktale *Mabela the Clever* by Margaret Read MacDonald (Albert Whitman, 2001). At the end of the first story, ask, "Wasn't that piggy stubborn and uncooperative? Why do you think he refused to do what he was told?" Pause for their responses. Then say, "Now we're going to meet a mouse who learns it's not always a good thing to do just what bigger creatures tell you to do," and dive into *Mabela.* Thinking out the connections between stories makes your program flow effortlessly.

If time permits you might give a brief booktalk to introduce a new addition to the library or to promote an old favorite, or use poetry, magic, music and participation activities (games, responsive songs, riddles, or creative dramatics) as transitions from one story to another.

Closing the Program

Some storytellers sing a song or recite the same rhyme to begin and end the story hour. Do what you find works for you. A simple "Thank you for listening" might be sufficient. If the story hour opens with a ritual, perhaps you will want to close it with a similar ritual, such as blowing out the candle.

To end her storytimes, elementary school librarian, Catalina Charles, from Lansing, New York, says, simply:

Snip, snap, snout,
This tale is told out.

She snuffs out the candle on "out." Very effective. You'll recall that that's the ending to the Norwegian folktale, "The Three Billy Goats Gruff."

In Nepal, at the end of a story, the teller often recites this verse:

Garland of gold to the listener.
Garland of flowers to the teller.
May this tale go to heaven
and come down to be told again.

Is there something you would like your listeners to do at the close of your program? If you are in the library, invite children to look at, touch, or play with exhibit material or encourage them to browse the shelves and check out an armload of books. Don't forget to remind the group about the next program.

SOUVENIRS

The book you featured in your story hour might just lend itself to inexpensive or virtually free souvenirs for that special occasion, so keep your imagination open. Favors for the audience can transform a storytelling program into a joyous event. It's probably not feasible to provide a memento at each presentation; but when you find something appropriate and timely, hand it out after the program.

Bookmarks make useful souvenirs. They can be decorative or informational—announcing a future story session, for example. Even ordinary objects take on significance when associated with a story. After telling the Japanese fairy tale "Momotaro," about the little boy who comes out of a peach pit, Caroline gave everyone a peach pit saved from summer and spray-painted gold. Telling a variant of "Stone Soup" suggests that each child in the audience go home with a pretty stone. A simple kidney bean glued to a colorful little circle of poster board will make that "Jack and the Beanstalk" retelling even more memorable, especially when you tell the children that you are pretty sure it's a magic bean.

Telling Native American stories today? A small, colorful bead strung on a cord may end up a cherished gift. Give children a little birthday candle to celebrate Hans Christian Andersen's birthday. Origami, the age-old Japanese art of paper folding, can be used in conjunction with storytelling to create a variety of lovely favors. Children can make a paper-folded dog to take home after they listen to a favorite dog story. If you don't know how to make one, go to YouTube, type *origami* and *dog* into the search bar, and treat yourself to an online tutorial. Any small present, especially if unexpected, is endowed with a certain magic.

Why wait for a traditional holiday? Originate a special event of your own to celebrate. Teach the children step-by-step how to make a paper frog after you tell them the Grimm Brothers' fairy tale "The Frog Prince," to observe Kindness Day, a holiday you invented to remind everyone how important it is to treat others as you would wish to be treated, including frogs. Find the text of the story on page 109.

Sometimes something to eat is the magic ingredient needed to round out a program, but be forewarned. Many schools no longer permit you to give food to children because of food allergies and other dietary restrictions.

Always check with the school nurse before you make any preparations. If you're in a public library, confer with parents about any possible problems and keep a list. Fruit is usually a good option.

If food allergies aren't a problem, animal crackers make fine souvenirs after a zoo-themed program. How about cinnamon-flavored rice cakes after telling Ying Chang Compestine's Chinese New Year story, *The Runaway Rice Cake* (Simon & Schuster, 2001). Send everyone home with a lollipop when you read Rukhsana Khan's *Big Red Lollipop* (Viking, 2010), a story of two sisters who go to a birthday party. Did you know October is National Pizza Month? Have a pizza party for a small group after telling *The Little Red Hen (Makes a Pizza)* by Philemon Sturges (Dutton, 1999). Children can also make and take home pretend pizzas out of clay, or color the rim of a paper plate brown, add a red construction paper circle for sauce, a yellow circle for cheese, and cut out paper shapes for mushrooms, pepperoni, and whatever else you might like.

SOMETHING TO TAKE HOME

Here are a few more easy and inexpensive souvenirs to give out after a story.

Alphabet letters. (Look for refrigerator magnet letters, die cut letters on heavystock paper, or Silly Bandz, rubber bands shaped like alphabet letters.) To remember any alphabet books, including Nick Bruel's *Bad Kitty* (Roaring Brook, 2005), Lisa Campbell Ernst's *The Letters Are Lost* (Viking, 1996), Laura Vaccaro Seeger's *The Hidden Alphabet* (Roaring Brook, 2003), and Judy Sierra's *The Sleepy Little Alphabet: A Bedtime Story from Alphabet Town.*

Apple seeds. (It won't take long to save enough to hand out.) To remember Eden Ross Lipson's *Applesauce Season* (Roaring Brook, 2009), in which a boy and his grandmother make applesauce; and Alice Schertle's *Down the Road* (Harcourt, 1995), where young Hetty breaks all the eggs in her basket when she stops to pick apples on her way home from the general store. And don't forget Marjorie Priceman's *How to Make an Apple Pie and See the World* (Knopf, 1994). Show how apples grow with *How Do Apples Grow* by Betsy Maestro (HarperCollins, 1992).

Balloons. (Do not have to be blown up!) To remember "In Which Eeyore Has a Birthday and Gets Two Presents" in A. A. Milne's *Winnie-the-*

Pooh (Dutton, 1926). Also perfect for Florence Parry Heide's picture book, *Princess Hyacinth (The Surprising Tale of a Girl Who Floated)* (Schwartz & Wade, 2009), in which a young princess needs to be weighted down lest she float away.

Beads. (Available at craft or hobby shops.) To remember the maiden's lost blue bead that the fox must find in Nonny Hogrogian's Caldecott winner, *One Fine Day* (Macmillan, 1971).

Beans. To remember "Jack and the Beanstalk" and compare it with Mary Pope Osborne's *Kate and the Beanstalk* (Atheneum, 2000). Also a natural with *Mice and Beans* by Pam Muñoz Ryan (Scholastic, 2001).

Buttons. To remember Arnold Lobel's "A Lost Button" from *Frog and Toad Are Friends* (HarperCollins, 1970); Judy Sierra's *Tasty Baby Belly Buttons: A Japanese Folktale* (Knopf, 1999); and, of course, Simms Taback's *Joseph Had a Little Overcoat* (Viking, 1999).

Carrots. (From a bag of miniature ones.) To remember Candace Fleming's *Muncha! Muncha! Muncha!* (Simon & Schuster, 2002), *Tops & Bottoms* by Janet Stevens (Harcourt, 1995), Ruth Krauss's *The Carrot Seed* (HarperCollins, 1945), Jackie French's *Diary of a Wombat* (Clarion, 2003), and especially *Creepy Carrots!* by Aaron Reynolds and Peter Brown (Simon & Schuster, 2012).

Chalk. To remember *Chalk* by Bill Thomson (Marshall Cavendish, 2010), a dramatic wordless picture book about three kids who draw a scary dinosaur on the pavement and it comes to life.

Cherries or cherry pits. To remember Marjorie Priceman's *How to Make a Cherry Pie and See the U.S.A.* (Knopf, 2008) and Vera B. Williams's *Cherries and Cherry Pits* (Greenwillow, 1986).

Cheerios or doughnut holes. To remember the chapter "The Doughnuts," about a doughnut machine run amok, in Robert McCloskey's classic *Homer Price* (Viking, 1943).

Chocolate chip cookies (or just a chocolate chip). To remember James Marshall's *George and Martha* (Houghton Mifflin, 1972), Laura Joffe Numeroff's *If You Give a Mouse a Cookie* (HarperCollins, 1985), and Amy Krouse Rosenthal's *Cookies: Bite-Size Life Lessons* (HarperCollins, 2006).

Chopsticks. To remember Ying Chang Compestine's *The Story of Chopsticks* (Holiday House, 2001) and Ina R. Friedman's *How My Parents Learned to Eat* (Houghton Mifflin, 1984).

Flowers. To remember Kevin Henkes's *My Garden* (Greenwillow, 2010).

Fortune cookies. To remember Grace Lin's *Fortune Cookie Fortunes* (Knopf, 2004).

Gold coins. (Fake ones, of course.) To remember Melinda Long's *How I Became a Pirate* (Harcourt, 2003).

Grapes. To remember Margie Palatini's *Lousy Rotten Stinkin' Grapes* (Simon & Schuster, 2009).

Leaves. (Colorful autumn ones are best, if you can wait till October.) To remember Lois Ehlert's *Leaf Man* (Harcourt, 2005).

Orange pits. To remember Patricia Polacco's *An Orange for Frankie* (Philomel, 2004).

Paper-folded boats and airplanes. To remember H. A. Rey's *Curious George Rides a Bike* (Houghton Mifflin, 1952), or Randall de Sève's *Toy Boat* (Philomel, 2007), or *My Teacher is a Monster! (No, I Am Not.)* by Peter Brown (Little, Brown, 2014).

Pasta. (Uncooked large ziti would work well, maybe strung on yarn as an after-story craft.) To remember Tomie dePaola's *Strega Nona* (Prentice-Hall, 1975).

Peach pits. (Paint them gold.) To remember David Elliott's *Finn Throws a Fit* (Candlewick, 2009), where toddler Finn decides he doesn't like peaches today.

Peas. To remember "The Princess and the Pea" by Hans Christian Andersen, Deborah Blumenthal's *Don't Let the Peas Touch!: And Other Stories* (Scholastic, 2004), Amy Krouse Rosenthal's *Little Pea* (Chronicle, 2005), and George McClements's *Night of the Veggie Monster* (Bloomsbury, 2008).

Play money. To remember Rosemary Wells's *Bunny Money* (Dial, 1997), from which you can photocopy the bunny money on the endpapers onto green paper, or David M. Schwartz's *If You Made a Million* (Lothrop, 1989).

Potatoes. (Buy fingerlings or other small varieties.) To remember John Coy's *Two Old Potatoes and Me* (Knopf, 2003), Cynthia DeFelice's *One Potato, Two Potato* (Farrar, 2006), or Tomie dePaola's *Jamie O'Rourke and the Big Potato: An Irish Folktale* (Putnam, 1992).

Pumpkin seeds. (Save them from the jack-o'-lantern.) To remember Stephen Savage's splendidly spooky *Ten Orange Pumpkins* (Dial, 2013), Cathryn Falwell's *Mystery Vine: A Pumpkin Surprise* (Greenwillow, 2009), Margaret McNamara's *How Many Seeds in a Pumpkin?* (Schwartz & Wade, 2007), Marisa Montes's *Los Gatos Black on Halloween* (Henry Holt, 2006), and don't forget Linda Williams's *The Little Old Lady Who Was Not Afraid of Anything* (HarperCollins, 1986). Find out more about how pumpkins grow with Wendy Pfeffer's *From Seed to Pumpkin* (HarperCollins, 2004).

Raisins. To remember Russell Hoban's *A Baby Sister for Frances* (HarperCollins, 1964).

Rope or twine. (Cut 8-inch lengths and knot the ends.) To remember Jerry Pinkney's *The Lion & the Mouse* (Little, Brown, 2009).

Seashells. To remember Suzy Lee's wordless picture book, *Wave* (Chronicle, 2008), David Soman's *Three Bears in a Boat* (Dial, 2014), and the tongue twister "She sells seashells by the seashore."

Spoons. (Plastic ones.) To remember Amy Krouse Rosenthal's *Spoon* (Disney/Hyperion, 2009).

States. (From a jigsaw puzzle of the fifty states, especially when there's already a piece or two missing.) To remember Laurie Keller's *The Scrambled States of America* (Henry Holt, 2008).

Sticks. To remember *Anansi and the Magic Stick* by Eric A. Kimmel (Orchard, 2001) and Antoinette Portis's *Not a Stick* (HarperCollins, 2008).

Stones, pebbles or rocks. (Available free on the beach or on the ground, or as polished little rocks purchased inexpensively at the aquarium or garden shop.) To remember Eric A. Kimmel's *Anansi and the Moss-Covered Rock* (Orchard, 1991), Leslie McGuirk's *If Rocks Could Sing: A Discovered Alphabet* (Tricycle, 2011), and William Steig's *Sylvester and the Magic Pebble* (Simon & Schuster, 2005, c1969).

Umbrellas. (Look for the colorful little paper ones they put in fancy drinks.) To remember Jan Brett's *The Umbrella* (Putnam, 2004) and Jon J Muth's *Zen Shorts* (Scholastic, 2005).

Vegetable seeds. (Buy at less than half price at the end of the growing season from nurseries.) To remember Ruth Krauss's *The Carrot Seed* (HarperCollins, 1945) and Dianna Aston's beautiful nonfiction picture book, *A Seed Is Sleepy* (Chronicle, 2007).

Discipline, or Holding Your Own

It's easy to pretend that there is no such thing as a discipline problem during story hour. After all, how could anyone not want to hear a story? But we all know discipline problems happen. Although each person must react to situations as he or she thinks best, we have a few general thoughts on establishing a respectful and positive atmosphere.

First off, teaching is a cult of personality; it is performance art. All teachers are storytellers. For an infusion of inspiration and affirmation, and to see how teachers are made, not born, meet a self-effacing man who questioned his own competence in his field, and in desperation, told his students searing stories about his impoverished childhood in Limerick, Ireland. "My life saved my life," wrote the late Frank McCourt in *Teacher Man: A Memoir* (Scribner, 2005), his account of thirty years teaching high school English in the New York City public schools. His students would say to him, "Hey, Mr. McCourt, you should write a book." Those stories he told became the basis of his bestselling memoir and Pulitzer Prize winning *Angela's Ashes: A Memoir* (Scribner, 1996), published when he was 66.

In an interview with the *Toronto Sun* in 2000, McCourt said, "We were all storytellers growing up. That's all we had. There was no TV or radio. We'd sit around the fire and make up stories. My dad was a great storyteller. We'd mention a neighbor, and he'd make up a story. But I also had to be a great storyteller to survive teaching. I spent 30 years in the classroom. When you stand before 170 teenagers each day, you have to get and keep their attention. Their attention span is about seven minutes, which is the time between commercials. So you have to stay on your toes."[1]

So how do we stay on our toes? Basically the trick to it is this: if you are fair with kids and truly like them, if you share a bit of yourself and your unique personality, and if you tell them stories, most children—not all, and not all the time—will respond positively. Each adult, whether you're a teacher, librarian, parent, scout leader, or a grandparent, needs to work out discipline techniques to use with children. We collect them like little nuggets over the years and add them to our bag o' tricks. One important thing you've probably learned from experience is that positive feedback works better than negative, and that, at least for preteens, sarcasm is unfair, unkind, and unproductive. Children know you're saying something mean, but don't know why or how to respond to it, and it ends up being demeaning for them. (With high school kids, they get your humor and may respond well to it.)

Getting angry doesn't work either; children learn quickly how to tune out a yeller. Speaking very softly when children are being loud can make them stop and listen to hear what you are saying. This can be very effective in telling stories and in getting your audience to pay attention.

LEARNING NAMES

Usually, the better you know your group, the better they will behave. Learning their names or having them wear name tags until you do makes your discipline technique so much more effective than saying, "Little girl with the red shirt and blue sneakers, I need you to stop pulling out the threads of our story rug."

All the children will stop and examine their own clothing to see if they match your description, and you've just lost everyone's attention. Whoops. Not effective. Meanwhile the little girl with the viselike fingers continues to dismantle your carpet. Saying, "Jane, please stop pulling on the rug," is instantly specific and usually effective.

If you're bad with names, make yourself a seating chart for each group, and you'll always know who is who. More and more schools have photos of the children linked to their attendance records—see if you can get a copy.

If you're a school librarian who sees a zillion classes each week, it's not easy to keep all the names straight. You get to know the really good ones and the really bad ones right away. For the rest, you listen for name clues, or call kids "sweetie" or "kiddo." Judy says, "I learned early on not to refer to my students as 'Hey, guys' and 'You guys' when one fourth-grade girl corrected me sternly, saying, 'We're not all guys here, you know.' Point taken. Instead, call everyone 'folks' or 'students' or 'kids.' Children don't necessarily like to be reminded that they are 'children,' so I don't use that term much."

Sixth-grade teacher Peter Kennedy, at the Hilltown Cooperative Public Charter School in Williamsburg, Massachusetts, tells his new class on the first day of school each year, "There is only one of me, but twenty of you.

You already know my name, but it will take me some time before I know all of yours. Therefore, until I can remember your names, I will call you all Bob, even the girls. However, if I do have to call you Bob, first, you must not take offense, because I am old, and then you must tell me your real name again. You will then have my permission to call me any silly name you like, and we both can laugh about it and then get on with our lives. Soon I will know all of your names."

Teachers like that get their kids loving them on the first day of school with their honesty, sense of humor, and obvious affection for their students. Working with children is never easy, but it is incredibly rewarding, Bob.

HANDLING DISRUPTIONS, INTERRUPTIONS, AND MISBEHAVIORS

Not every disruption is a destructive one. You should not necessarily consider it a problem if children articulate their reactions: "Look at that elephant!" "Oh, no, she better watch out!" Such verbal reactions reflect interest and attention. You want your listeners to become emotionally and physically invested in the stories you tell. Encourage them to join in on refrains, to fill in words, and, sometimes, to predict what they think will happen next.

What looks like out-of-control to some may be just you and your group having a fine old time together. Telling stories is just plain fun to do, and for children, listening to them is pure joy. When they are rolling on the floor laughing at the antics of Anansi the Spider, there is no better feeling, with all those happy endorphins bouncing around the room.

When you're telling or reading a story to younger children—and perhaps you are describing the shoes the elves made for the shoemaker—sometimes a hand will go up, waving frantically so you can't ignore it. "Yes, Zoey, what is it?" Nine times out of ten, Zoey's comment will have absolutely nothing to do with the story or even the urgent need to run to the loo. It's more often some hilariously and tenuously connected piece of essential (at least to that child) information like, "My mother, she took me to the mall, and we were looking for shoes and there was this dog . . ." You gently stop Zoey's monologue, and say, "That is very interesting, Zoey. Let's talk about it after we finish our story."

Storyteller Laura Simms uses a compelling way to get children to listen attentively. Say to your group, "Unless it is really important, you must never interrupt a storyteller. If you do, the story could just fly out of my head, and you and I will never know how the story will turn out. That would be a terrible thing." Then pause and say, dramatically, "Oh, dear. Where was I? I think the story just flew out of my head. Can you help me get it back?" The children will retell the story thus far, and then you say, "Oh, good, I've got it back now. Thank you for helping me remember."

Judy notes that Alice Yucht, a marvelous storyteller and former middle school librarian, used to say to her kids, "Never interrupt a storyteller unless you are bleeding or dying." That no-nonsense statement works wonders in getting older listeners to pay attention.

Then there's the little boy at the back of the room who is rolling on the floor and looks like he's paying no attention to your story at all. He seems to be in his own little world. There could be a variety of reasons he's stirring up a fuss back there: for extra attention, or because he's bored or having a bad day, or maybe he's feeling angry and wants to start a commotion to have his anger acknowledged. Sometimes the most disruptive child is testing you, but deep inside, he'd love to feel like you understand and like him. A hyperactive child may have trouble sitting still, but it doesn't necessarily mean he is not listening to your story. Make a connection by catching his eye frequently and involving him in the story. When you make good eye contact with your audience, that boy in the back feels like you are telling the story to him.

When you come up against misbehavers, it may be that children don't remember or don't understand the rules of your room. If you don't have rules, you might want to make some simple ones and share them clearly. In the face of disruption, stay firm, fair, and consistent.

Your rules can be as simple as:

1. Respect yourself.
2. Respect others.
3. Respect your library/classroom.
4. "When given the choice between being right or being kind, choose kind."

This last quote is by the author and motivational speaker Dr. Wayne W. Dyer. It is an essential component of a most inspirational, memorable, and quiet bombshell of a fiction book for middle grade readers, *Wonder* by R. J. Palacio (Random House, 2012), about a boy named Augie Pullman who, because of severe facial deformities requiring twenty-seven surgeries, has been homeschooled his whole life—until this year. Read this book aloud to an obstreperous class and they will be transformed.

For the child who is starting to disrupt your group, there's "the look," an expression every grown-up who works with kids needs to master. It clearly says, "I don't like what you're doing and you need to stop it now." Give her a chance to correct her own behavior. Usually, she'll get the idea and straighten up. If she stops there, smile and say, "Excellent, Molly. Nice job." You may still need to get up and walk over to that child, though, making eye contact as you continue to talk with the group. Your physical presence is often enough to stop itchy kids in their tracks. Or say softly, for her ears only, "Is that appropriate behavior for our room?"

If misbehavior continues or accelerates, Judy recommends upgrading "the look" to "the hairy eyeball"—a steady glare, or narrowing or widening of the eyes, accompanied by a finger point and a shake of the head. For a quick tutorial, she suggests looking the portrait of Miss Viola Swamp on the back cover of Harry Allard's *Miss Nelson Is Missing* (Houghton Mifflin, 1977). If the child is still unaware of your displeasure, however, say her name in a warning tone. Still no reaction? At this point, stop being subtle and say, "Molly, I need you to stop doing that."

One reason children cut up is they're sitting next to others who are doing the same thing. Don't be afraid to rearrange seating, splitting up the troublemakers. When someone breaks a rule or acts disrespectfully, you may want to give a time-out. Say, "If you're not ready to be with our group, I'll need to ask you to take a break until you're ready to join us again." If the child continues to disrupt, say, sorrowfully, "I'm so sorry, Brendon. You do need a bit of a break. There's a chair over there (point to a chair on the outskirts) with your name on it. Go take a seat there now. When you're ready to join us again, you may come back." One librarian calls this "taking a vacation, since on a vacation the idea is to clear your mind."

If you are telling a story or leading the children in a creative dramatics activity, Brendon would much prefer not to be sent to Chair Siberia. He'll say, "I'll be good. I promise." At this point, you need to decide whether he can keep that promise, and usually he can. Just the warning is enough for many kids. If he does land in the time-out chair, don't forget he's there. After a few minutes, says, "Brendon, you're behaving so beautifully. I'd love to have you come back and join us now."

You may be able to minimize problems of discipline if the story hour is an elective activity. If someone wants to come to the story hour, which is a special treat, he or she must behave or not be allowed to come the next time. In a school setting, however, this is not usually an option—you are expected to deal with your students' behavior problems. (However, if you are trying to handle the outburst of an emotionally disturbed student who has become uncontrollable, by all means call the office or a coworker for help.)

Then again, perhaps it's something you're doing and don't even realize it. How's your pacing when you interact with children? Maybe you're going too slowly or quickly and they're either bored or confused. If you're giving your listeners time to get bored, misbehavior will happen. How's your attitude towards your group? If you're talking down to them or acting scornful, annoyed, or uncaring, they'll pick up on it. They want you to appreciate them, and if you show you do, your chances of discipline problems will lessen.

It is well to remember that not everyone is interested in books and stories. You may notice children—especially young adults—rolling their eyes and making it clear that you are the most boring, uncool speaker the world has ever known. This reaction may actually have nothing to do with you.

In one junior high Judy visited, the librarian told her how excited the kids were about her visit. Yet, during her program, the students sighed disdainfully and looked bored. Judy says, "I had the audacity to ask them to sing a song with me. Most just stared, aghast. I told stories. They looked like they weren't listening. I gave some riveting booktalks. They looked unmoved. When I finished, they applauded politely. They weren't the toughest crowd I had seen, for they weren't rowdy, just infused with teen ennui."

When she finished, she waited patiently for what she hoped would come next. She was not disappointed. As the class stood up to leave, a gaggle of students meandered to the front of the room and started picking up the books she had showcased and asking all kinds of questions. They wanted to talk with a grown-up who had obviously read and loved the same books they did. Their bored looks didn't mean they weren't tuned in and enjoying the program. They were just being adolescents. Whew. What a relief.

If you are presenting programs to older kids, fifth grade and up, their behavior can veer from subdued to contemptuous to obnoxious. You will need to work hard to earn their respect and attention. If your stories skew too young, audiences will be offended (unless they are at a family story hour with younger siblings, in which case they grant themselves special dispensation to enjoy your stories). Remember, you seem really, really old to them, and they will need to decide if you are worthy of their attention. You don't need to use their slang and pretend you're a teenager to gain their respect. Start with short grabbers—stories that will surprise and startle them—and then show and tell them about books to make them desperate to read.

Even when you are well prepared, sometimes there are circumstances beyond your control. Judy recalls doing an evening storytelling program for several hundred children and parents at an all-school pajama party. After children had a shared read-aloud time with their families, completed a crafts activity, and had a snack, it was time for them to watch her, the storyteller.

Unfortunately, by that time, the kids were tired and cranky, the littlest ones were howling or racing up and down the gym and onto the stage, and the parents had retreated into groups to have a chatfest at full volume. The principal had disappeared, the teachers figured it was the parents' job to make the kids quiet down and listen, and there Judy was, trying to tell stories and sing songs. She says, "I earned my pay that night, that's all I can say. I couldn't really discipline the troops, ask for help, or make everyone pay attention. What can you do in a situation like that? Laugh and make the best of it."

When Judy was asked to do another such program in a different school, she was understandably apprehensive. It was the night before Halloween. As she pulled into the parking lot, she could see, standing by the front door, people dressed as vampires and witches in black capes and long black dresses, their faces transformed with white, green, and blood. Those were the principal and several teachers, waiting to greet her. As she wheeled her book- and prop-filled suitcases up the walkway, she passed tombstones set into the grass. "I take it this isn't one of those schools where they're not allowed to celebrate Halloween," she said to the teachers. "No way," they said cheerfully. "We look forward to this all fall."

Inside, the hallways were festooned with cobwebs, with bats hanging from the ceilings, and children dressed in costumes were milling excitedly in the corridors. She figured she was in for another disaster. "This can't end well," she said to herself. And yet, it was a polar opposite experience. The children and parents got involved in her scary-but-not-too-scary stories, and all were perfectly behaved. She had a blast, and so did they. You just never know.

And, finally, you can gain control of an obstreperous group with a great story, though it may take some time to get them on your side. One fifth-grade class Judy faced as a school librarian was loud, mouthy, disrespectful, and scornful that she could tell them anything they cared to know. She brought out the big guns. She told them "Mr. Fox," the English folktale, collected by Joseph Jacobs. (You may know the German variant, told by the Brothers Grimm, called "The Robber Bridegroom." The Grimm version is every bit as gory as Jacobs's, and they'll love it, too.)

Mr. Fox

An English Folktale Retold by Joseph Jacobs

Lady Mary was young, and Lady Mary was fair. She had two brothers, and more suitors than she could count. But of them all, the bravest and most gallant was a Mr. Fox, whom she met when she was down at her father's country house. No one knew who Mr. Fox was; but he was certainly brave, and surely rich, and of all her admirers, Lady Mary cared for him alone. At last, it was agreed upon between them that they should be married. Lady Mary asked Mr. Fox where they should live, and he described to her his castle, and where it was; but, strange to say, did not ask her, or her brothers to come and see it.

So one day, near the wedding day, when her brothers were out, and Mr. Fox was away for a day or two on business, as he said, Lady Mary set out for Mr. Fox's castle. And after many searchings, she came at last to it, and a fine, strong house it was, with high walls and a deep moat. And when she came up to the gateway she saw written on it:

Be Bold, Be Bold.

But as the gate was open, she went through it, and found no one there. So she went up to the doorway, and over it she found written:

Be Bold, Be Bold, But Not Too Bold.

Still she went on, till she came into the hall, and went up the broad stairs till she came to a door in the gallery, over which was written:

Be Bold, Be Bold, But Not Too Bold, Lest That Your Heart's Blood Should Run Cold.

But Lady Mary was a brave one, she was, and she opened the door, and what do you think she saw? Why, bodies and skeletons of beautiful young ladies all stained with blood. So Lady Mary thought it was high time to get out of that horrid place, and she closed the door, went through the gallery, and was just going down the stairs, and out of the hall, when who should she see through the window, but Mr. Fox dragging a beautiful young lady along from the gateway to the door.

Lady Mary rushed downstairs, and hid herself behind a cask, just in time, as Mr. Fox came in with the poor young lady who seemed to have fainted. Just as he got near Lady Mary, Mr. Fox saw a diamond ring glittering on the finger of the young lady he was dragging, and he tried to pull it off. But it was tightly fixed, and would not come off, so Mr. Fox cursed and swore, and drew his sword, raised it, and brought it down upon the hand of the poor lady.

The sword cut off the hand, which jumped up into the air, and fell—of all places in the world—into Lady Mary's lap. Mr. Fox looked about a bit, but did not think of looking behind the cask, so at last he went on dragging the young lady up the stairs into the bloody chamber.

As soon as she heard him pass through the gallery, Lady Mary crept out of the door, down through the gateway, and ran home as fast as she could.

Now it happened that the very next day the marriage contract of Lady Mary and Mr. Fox was to be signed, and there was a splendid breakfast before that. And when Mr. Fox was seated at table opposite Lady Mary, he looked at her. "How pale you are this morning, my dear."

"Yes," said she, "I had a bad night's rest last night. I had horrible dreams."

"Dreams go by contraries," said Mr. Fox, "but tell us your dream, and your sweet voice will make the time pass till the happy hour comes."

"I dreamed," said Lady Mary, "that I went yestermorn to your castle, and I found it in the woods, with high walls, and a deep moat, and over the gateway was written:

Be Bold, Be Bold.

"But it is not so, and it was not so," said Mr. Fox.

"And when I came to the doorway over it was written:

Be Bold, Be Bold, But Not Too Bold.

"It is not so, and it was not so," said Mr. Fox.

"And then I went upstairs, and came to a gallery, at the end of which was a door, on which was written:

Be Bold, Be Bold, But Not Too Bold, Lest That Your Heart's Blood Should Run Cold.

"It is not so, and it was not so," said Mr. Fox.

"And then—and then I opened the door, and the room was filled with bodies and skeletons of poor dead women, all stained with their blood."

"It is not so, and it was not so. And God forbid it should be so," said Mr. Fox.

"I then dreamed that I rushed down the gallery, and just as I was going down the stairs, I saw you, Mr. Fox, coming up to the hall door, dragging after you a poor young lady, rich and beautiful."

"It is not so, and it was not so. And God forbid it should be so," said Mr. Fox.

"I rushed downstairs, just in time to hide myself behind a cask, when you, Mr. Fox, came in dragging the young lady by the arm. And, as you passed me, Mr. Fox, I thought I saw you try and get off her diamond ring, and when you could not, Mr. Fox, it seemed to me in my dream, that you out with your sword and hacked off the poor lady's hand to get the ring."

"It is not so, and it was not so. And God forbid it should be so," said Mr. Fox, and was going to say something else as he rose from his seat, when Lady Mary cried out:

"But it is so, and it was so. Here's hand and ring I have to show," and pulled out the lady's hand from her dress, and pointed it straight at Mr. Fox.

At once her brothers and her friends drew their swords and cut Mr. Fox into a thousand pieces.

To make the story even more dramatic, beforehand, Judy stuffed a thin white plastic surgical glove with cotton balls (both courtesy of the school nurse), taped the open end, and added red, press-on nails and an imitation diamond ring. Then she tucked it into her pocket. When she reached the heartstopping climax of the story, she drew out the hand, just as Lady Mary did, pointing it at the group. They shrank back and screamed. (The hand looked amazingly real from a few feet away.) Their final reaction: it was best story they ever heard. And she never had a bit of trouble with that class ever again. True story.

Almost everyone enjoys a story, whether it is told or read, but not every story will appeal equally to everyone who hears it. In fact, you may never know what has impressed a child. It could be your voice, the language of the story you've just told, its characters, its plot, your gestures or lack of them, the flowers on the table, the doll that represents the story's central character, or the special story-related activity or treat you provided afterwards.

Your enthusiasm for the stories you share, your evident enjoyment of the books from which you select those stories, and the rapport you establish with your audience and each of its members may stimulate some of the nonreaders among them to read a book or two themselves. And this could be habit forming, which makes all the planning you do and all the effort you expend on your program worth every minute. Happy telling!

NOTE

1. Dennis McClellan, "Frank McCourt Dies at 78; Late-Blooming Author of 'Angela's Ashes'," *LA Times*, July 20, 2009, www.latimes.com/local/obituaries/la-me-frank-mccourt20-2009jul20-story.html #page=1.

chapter 4

Selecting, Preparing, and Telling the Story

If you're going to have a story, have a big story, or none at all.

—JOSEPH CAMPBELL, AUTHOR AND MYTHOLOGIST

FOR THE PURIST, THE ULTIMATE IN STORYTELLING IS TO TELL A story without props or pictures—just you and the story. However, whether you tell a story simply standing or sitting in front of an audience, or go whole hog on a stage full of production items, your storytelling techniques will be the same. The more you practice and tell your stories, the better you will be as a storyteller. As for being a world-class storyteller, a leader in the field, that is a different matter, for storytelling is like other arts: in order to be truly great, you probably have to be born with inner talent and spend your life honing it. Never mind. You don't need to be the Pavarotti or the Streisand of the storytelling world. Your job is to pick stories that suit you, learn them well, and share them with others. Let's start at the beginning to see how the process works.

Selecting the Story

The key to a successful program lies in the story or stories that you use. Planning, production, and promotion are vital, but the story remains the single most important element. Above all, choose a story that you like and one that fits your personality.

If you think of yourself as vivacious and sparkling, you might enjoy telling a funny or silly folktale; if you are naturally quiet or shy, it might work best to choose a romantic or magical tale. You don't have to actually sit down and analyze your psyche, but the stories you choose will reflect your inner self. What you are looking for are stories that speak to you—that sing to you, even. Sometimes they will grab you by the throat and demand, "Tell me to someone!" Keep your eyes peeled for stories that stop you in your tracks.

You'll need to read through many stories until you find ones that appeal to you. As you rummage through story collections, myths, epics, short stories, picture books, and other materials suitable for storytelling, you will find something that appeals and is usually suitable for your storytelling repertoire. Everything you read—a family story, a folktale, an anecdote, a newspaper article, or something you came across online—is fair game. Everything is a story.

Although you may begin by using stories familiar to you, you will soon want to search for new material. When you exhaust your local collections, use interlibrary loan to get your hands on stories you would like to see. At work, at conferences, and online, ask librarians, teachers, and friends who tell stories to name their favorites. On vacations, visit the local library and ask if the librarians keep records of the stories they tell. Listen to the stories that other storytellers have posted online, and, if you're on a listserv like LM_Net (for school librarians), PUBYAC (for public children's and YA librarians), or STORYTELL (for storytellers), check their archives or post a query asking people to tell you their favorite tales to tell. You will gather endless suggestions of already tried and successful stories.

Chapters 5 through 8 contain extensive, hand-selected annotated booklists, filled with hundreds of books and stories Caroline and Judy think are marvelous to tell. Go through our stellar picks of picture books and folktales—both single stories and collections—and mark off the ones that surprise, startle, and satisfy you. Many marvelous old stories can be found online, and we've added the URLs for scores of these. Your job is to figure out which stories you can't live without.

There are other storytellers out there who have done some of the heavy lifting for you, publishing collections of tales that are easy to tell, and giving you step-by-step directions on how to tell them well. Margaret Read

MacDonald, Anne Pellowski, Dianne de las Casas, Pleasant DeSpain, and storytelling spouses Martha Hamilton and Mitch Weiss have all written multiple books filled with deliciously fast and funny stories you can read today and tell tomorrow. You'll see them represented in the booklists in this chapter. These folks are master storytellers, so why not try out some of their tried-and-trues? Many professional storytellers have produced their own storytelling tapes. These are useful because they give you an opportunity to hear different styles of telling. Imitation can be a sincere form of flattery, of course, but such recordings are also a ready-made source of well-told stories. Many are available for free online. For instance, the Center for Children's Books at the Graduate School of Library and Information Science at the University of Illinois at Urbana-Champaign has been holding an annual storytelling festival since 2003. They have posted audio recordings of dozens of tellings by well-known storytellers such as Janice Del Negro, Betsy Hearne, and Dan Keding. You'll find the audios at http://ccb.lis.illinois.edu/storytellingaudio.html. If you visit Amazon.com, look up storytelling under "Music" or "MP3 Downloads." You'll be able to locate and download recordings by veteran tellers, including Willy Claflin, Donald Davis, Carmen Agra Deedy, Bill Harley, David Holt, Mary Jo Huff, Jay O'Callahan, Laura Simms, and the late, great Jackie Torrence.

Taking a storytelling class is a grand way to nudge you into telling stories and building a good collection. As you listen to someone else tell a story, the possibilities are laid out for you. You think, "Hmmm. I could tell that. I think I'd want to use a different pace, though." The first time you tell it, you have that other person's voice in your head, guiding you through the sequence. By the tenth time, the story will have your voiceprints all over it. Judy took a memorable summer course in storytelling at Rutgers University—taught by the elegant and eloquent Laura Simms—many years back and still remembers the stories Laura told back then and the stories her classmates told.

Borrow like crazy. If you hear your friend or a professional storyteller tell a story you love, make it yours. Add your own spin, plus the bells and whistles that make the telling work for you. Of course, if you tell a story you heard from someone else, be sure to give credit. Remember that while it's fine to embrace a story here and there from other tellers, don't go overboard. You need to amass and develop your own singular repertoire from a wide variety of sources.

STORY FOLDERS

When you find something that captivates you, don't say, "Oh, I'm sure I'll remember where I found this." You won't. Honest. Stop and add it to your "Stories to Learn" folder right then and there.

You'll want to keep two story folders—one of photocopied stories you have already learned, and another of stories you would like to learn. If you find texts of some of your stories online, bookmark or save them on your computer, but also print out hard copies, making sure the URL is on the first page in case you need to find it again. With books, be sure to write the source of the story—including the title of the story and the book's title, author, publisher, and copyright date—on the first page of your photocopy, so you can track it down easily if you need to. You will be grateful for that hard copy, which you can either tuck away in your folder for later or carry around with you everywhere while you are learning the story.

Once you start to amass a collection of stories, look through them to see if you can identify patterns. You don't want to tell too many stories of the same type. Mix it up. As you get comfortable with the learning process, add new genres to your folder—a Russian fairy tale, a Greek myth, a story by Oscar Wilde, a narrative poem. One story may dovetail into a particular holiday program; another may be from a country that interests you. You'll find some tales that tie in perfectly to your school's science or social studies curriculum and others that you liked as a child. A good program requires balance.

You won't learn all the stories you collect, but it's better to have more than you need so you have a good choice. It's a good idea to learn as many tales as you can early on. You won't regret the effort. But even if you learn just one new story a year, you will soon have a tidy collection to tell. It feels very satisfying, too, when you can take a new story from the "Stories to Learn" folder and move it to the "Stories Already Learned" folder.

I'VE GOT A LITTLE LIST

Keep a simple but ongoing list of all the stories in your repertoire. If you are asked unexpectedly to tell a story, you can simply whip out your little list from your purse, pocket, or smartphone and decide which one to do. The list is especially useful as an indicator that you need to broaden your horizons. One glance will tell you that it's time to look for a suitable tall tale because you already know so many stories about witches or tricksters.

If you work at an institution, a school, library, or religious institution where you tell stories on a regular basis; if you run a birthday-party storytelling business; or if you plan to become a professional storyteller, you will want to keep records of your storytelling activities. If you are a seriously organized kind of person, you could set up an Excel spreadsheet. After a program, you might want to jot down comments on the proceedings and on the success or failure of your selections. Keep these pages in a file so when you're planning a similar program, you can refer back to them.

Judy keeps a loose-leaf binder with a page for every program she has presented tucked into a plastic sleeve. When she visits a school or library, she writes up a set list of all the stories, songs, chants, riddles, poems, and booktalks she intends to use in each performance. She labels each page with the date, place, and age levels of her audiences. As soon as the program is over, she marks the material she used with a dot of magic marker. If she is asked back to that school the next year, she can easily look at her set list and make sure she doesn't duplicate the same material. Let's say she's been asked to give three one-hour assemblies at an elementary school in October. She can page through her notebook and look up the Halloween-related programs she did in years past and put together a set list based on her programs of tried-and-trues, plus any new material she's learned in the past year. Every time you learn a new story, poem, song, or riddle, it adds pizzazz to your presentations.

Preparing the Story

For your very first story, you'll want to choose something easy to tell that suits your storyteller's voice and personality. You will probably want to begin with a simple folktale. An authored story, one that relies heavily on the flavor of the language—like Rudyard Kipling's "The Elephant's Child"—really has to be learned almost word for word. This is a more difficult project and can be tackled later. Don't get fancy or crazy; a three-minute story will be just fine. This is what you will soon recognize as a filler story, one you can tell anytime when there are a few minutes to fill. Not every story can or should be an epic. A fast, fun story will make you feel successful right away, and you'll have it forever. It will go into long-term memory and be there whenever you need it. Judy still tells and loves the first stories she ever learned.

After you have chosen a story that you feel is worth your time, the actual learning begins.

LEARNING THE STORY

No one can tell you the "correct way" to master a story. We all have our own methods of learning new material. Your first attempt may take a great deal of time, but after you learn how *you* learn, the process will become much easier. When some tellers select a story, they retype the whole thing, especially if it's in picture-book format. They feel that retyping the story helps them get the essence of the tale into their heads. Some prefer to recopy the story by hand, as a sort of kinesthetic learning experience—the story travels up their arm as they write it and nestles in their brain so they can better remember it. If that works for you, great.

Here's another technique, one we swear by. When you select a new story to tell, begin by reading it all the way through at least three times. Then start telling it to yourself. If you forget a section, stop for that session. The next time, reread the story again and then start telling it to yourself from the beginning again, getting as far as you can before you get stuck. Pretty soon, you'll find that you've just retold the whole thing. Like writing a first draft of a novel, a new story will be full of rough spots that need fixing. It will sound choppy. You'll forget parts. It will be inelegant. Read it again and then tell it again. It will improve a bit every time, so keep at it, repeating it over and over.

You'll be amazed at the number of spare moments you can find in your day: standing in line to get into a movie, in the waiting room at the dentist, waiting for a bus, soaking in the tub, microwaving leftovers. How wonderful to put all that waiting time to real use! People may look at you funny, seeing you mumble a story to yourself, but pay them no mind. The story is king.

Judy is more of an auditory learner. She likes to record herself telling a new story and play it in the car, telling it aloud as she tries to keep up with the pace of her recorded version. It helps her work on phrasing, fluency, expression, and in seeing the story unfold in her mind's eye like a movie. Nowadays, you can record your stories on your iPhone, using the Voice Memos app. (Judy's best advice? Keep your eyes on the road.)

Once you get through one unimpeded telling, it's time to try your story on someone else. Everyone is a potential guinea pig, starting with your family. Children are critical and appreciative, roommates are amused, spouses are sometimes bored, pets are noncommittal. Friends are willing, at least the first time. But strangers, caught unaware, can be the best listeners of all. Try this: You're out for a day of skiing and find yourself on a ski lift with a man you don't know in the opposite chair, a fifteen-minute ride with no escape. Simply ask, "Want to hear a story?" He has to say yes, so tell your story. Imagine how he'll describe this experience when he returns from his ski trip.

Or this: You are on a train. The mom across from you is trying, without success, to quiet down her obstreperous child. Lean over and say, "Can I tell you a story?" Do it. It's good practice. The more you actually tell the story the better a storyteller you will be. Once you've told it a dozen times, it will be yours forever.

Just as aspiring authors join the Society of Children's Book Writers and Illustrators to find a forum for sharing their writing, you may find a group for storytellers in your state. Participating in such groups is a wonderful incentive to learn new material, and you will benefit from the helpful suggestions and gentle critiques of fellow tellers, not to mention the opportunity to appropriate new stories. See if your public librarian has any information about groups in your area, or start your own.

TO MEMORIZE OR NOT TO MEMORIZE

Your next question will probably be, "Should I memorize the story?" The answer is, that depends. Some storytellers feel that, except in special cases, memorization should be kept at a minimum or not be a part of learning a story at all. We don't agree. In nearly every instance, the stories you tell will have been selected from books. The source you are using was adapted by someone. If you choose your material carefully, your author will be competent as a collector and as a writer. Unless you feel that your phrasing is better, why not lean on the printed word?

This does not mean that you must sit down and learn your story word for word. It simply means that you should start by memorizing the beginning and ending of a work, key phrases or repeated refrains, and maybe a particularly enchanting passage or two. Later, when you feel you know the whole story, you can begin working on what the words mean and how to express those meanings. Beginners often make the mistake of thinking they are ready for a group of children once they have learned the words of the story. You need to feel so comfortable with the language that you will not panic if you forget where you are in the story. You must also be able to make an emotional connection—to feel the events of the story.

One suggestion that may help is to list in sequence the major events of a story in your mind or on paper. After all, you can't kill the dragon until the hero has met that fearsome beast. Think logically, and you will learn logically. After you start telling the story to audiences, you will find yourself making subtle changes; you are making it your own.

When Caroline began taping a children's television storytelling series, her director asked her for a script. She gave him a copy of a folktale taken from a book. Halfway through rehearsal, she saw the director jumping around and tearing at his hair. He stopped the show and started ranting through the loudspeaker, "What king? There's no king here!" Indeed, she had added a character without even realizing it and thought that she was telling the story exactly as printed. Eventually they decided not to use scripts at all, since she changed the stories with each telling!

At times, you will find a story that is too long to learn, or one that has a good plot but is written in stilted or unsuitable language. It's tempting to try to cut or rewrite the story to suit your own purposes. If you are a beginner, you might look for another story to learn, because adapting a story can be tricky. This is not to say that you should never do it; it just means that you must be very careful not to edit the essence out of it. You may be able to find another version of the story that better fits your needs.

Telling the Story

Now that you have selected and learned and practiced your story, you are ready to tell it to a real audience, whether it's a preschool story hour or an assembly program for middle school kids. The most important advice we can give you is this: Do not "act out" the story. You are not an actor. Don't leap from side to side to show your audience who is speaking in a dialogue. Don't use your voice to convey characterization, unless you have had voice training. Portraying Father Bear with a big, powerful voice and a squeaky voice for Baby Bear turns out to be a disaster for some people when they inadvertently switch voices midstory. Characterization emerges through descriptive language: "a little wisp of a girl . . ." or "he was so thin he could only eat noodles." Let the language tell the story.

On the other hand, a regional story is very much improved with an authentic dialect. A good Irish brogue improves an Irish story 100 percent. However, be aware that some dialects can be offensive to their respective ethnic groups if they are used incorrectly. If you come from an ethnic or national background and have the chops for rendering a particular accent with reasonable authenticity, you might want to try a story with it.

WEIRD WORDS

Difficult words can be a problem. If you don't know what a word means, look it up. Don't guess. It is embarrassing as well as unprofessional to say a word sweetly and find out the word is an insult that should have been said with a certain amount of venom your voice. And you don't want to be caught without a correct answer when someone asks you to define a calabash, a cudgel, or a dreidel.

You can define a strange word in a story if you can do it without breaking the flow, but it isn't always essential. Often, unfamiliar words can be understood by the context in which they are used. Nor should you simply remove a word and substitute something easier; doing so can ruin the spirit of the story. Children love long, meaty words and can learn them faster than adults do. Don't be afraid to use them.

Sometimes if a word or phrase is central to the understanding of the story, you can explain it before the telling. One of Caroline's favorite stories is Isaac Bashevis Singer's "The First Shlemiel." She told the story many times in New York, where it was received with delight. The first time she told it in Oregon, however, it didn't get the same reaction. It turned out that many in that audience didn't know the meaning of the Yiddish word *shlemiel.* After that experience, she regularly prefaced the story thusly: "The difference between a shlemiel and a shlimazel is that a shlemiel is the kind of a guy who is always spilling his soup and a shlimazel is the guy he spills it on."

Sometimes a good word can lead to an interesting discussion. In Joseph Jacobs's English folktale "The Travels of a Fox," the Fox says to each woman whose house he visits, "May I leave my bag here while I go to Squintums?" He never tells you what or where Squintums might be. After you finish telling the story, ask your listeners, "So, what or where is this 'Squintums' the fox keeps talking about?" Guaranteed, they'll have a variety of different and interesting speculations, depending on where their imaginations have taken them. When Judy told this story to a class of first graders, the children speculated that Squintums was the fox's house, a town, and even a restaurant. One child said, "I think that fox was really just hiding in the woods until he made sure the woman of the house looked in his bag, so he could come back and take something from her." Perceptive kid.

What to Wear

You've decorated the room, prepared a story table, checked your equipment, and put together a riveting program. What have you forgotten? You, the presenter. What are you going to wear? You have probably seen storytellers before. Often they wear funny hats, flowing skirts, diaphanous scarves, and interesting vests. If that makes you cringe, you can wear anything you think your audience will find interesting. You can look for outfits that complement your stories: a frog hat, a fresh flower pinned to your shirt, or even an alligator purse. It's all part of the fun. Children love to look at what you're wearing. Don't wear anything that might be particularly distracting. Beware of the locket that you unconsciously twist, the loose change in your pocket that you can't stop rattling, or the lock of hair you keep flipping out of your eyes. Ladies, if you're working with young children, keep the makeup to a minimum and the cleavage covered.

Some people choose to wear the same distinctive article of clothing for each story hour; this may be a storytelling apron or they may copy the African custom of wearing a story hat. Judy has a favorite pair of boots that she wears whenever she tells stories to children. They were designed by a twelve-year-old New York City schoolgirl who won a shoe store's contest for her design. The red and white boots, with two raised eyes and a nose on the toe box, have become part of Judy's official storytelling outfit and lead to much speculation by children. They call out, "Are those alligators?" "They look like dogs." "No, I think they're dragons!" The best part is that the kids are now ready and eager to listen to anything said by the lady who would wear such crazy shoes. Thanks to her happy feet, Judy is able to establish a rapport with her audience before she has even said a word.

Standing or Sitting?

Here are two good reasons for standing while telling a story: First, it can be easier express oneself with body movements. Second, one can maintain a more formal atmosphere; standing distinguishes the storyteller from the audience and creates the ambiance of theater.

A case for sitting can be made for exactly the opposite reasons. Sitting in a chair or on a stool confines movement so the telling is what makes the impact. If you and your audience are sitting, the atmosphere is more intimate. Choose the way that works best for you, the situation, and the story you are telling.

Equipment Checklist

If you plan to do any multimedia storytelling, you will surely use equipment of some kind. After you decide on your program, be sure to arrange for the equipment you will need. An easel or flip chart, a felt board, and a table or two were pretty much all you needed in the olden days, and maybe all you need now.

On the other hand, maybe your PowerPoint program requires an LCD or DLP projector and cordless remote clicker, plus a screen. Many teachers and librarians use interactive whiteboards like the SMART Board and the Promethean board. If you are playing recorded music, will it be on an MP3 player or iPod, or just an old-fashioned CD player? Or will you play it from your computer or tablet, connected to speakers? (Realize that all this technology can become obsolete at any moment, as new and more powerful machines hit the stores with dizzying speed.)

PROJECTION SCREEN

Start with a projection screen. If you've still got one from your overhead or slide projector days, great—they're still good! You can get a traditional, classroom-size pull-down screen for around $50, but oversize models, as well as those that electrically retract, can cost into the thousands. You want to buy the screen first because it will help determine the size of the projection you need from your data projector. Later, you might experiment with rear projecting; that is, placing the projector *behind* a translucent material like a sheet. This method allows you to move more freely throughout the room, as you won't be walking between the beam and the screen. Be sure to test it with your model of data projector.

PROJECTOR

Data projectors cost upwards of $300, but don't assume that you need the most expensive model. DLP projectors (digital light processing, using tiny mirrors and a color wheel) are the latest technology, superseding the LCD (liquid crystal display). For classroom-size spaces, an economy model will probably do just fine. You'll want to check with your local tech support folks and share the specifications you have for it. Some models have brighter lumens (meaning they emit more light), which is better for large rooms and those with abundant light. Some models can be ceiling mounted; others are lightweight and best suited for portable use. Most come with remote control and the ability to lock them to a cart or table to prevent theft. They usually have varying methods of focusing and "squaring" or keystoning the image so it doesn't look crooked on the screen. Most models can connect to a computer, tablet or handheld device, DVD player, or a document camera.

DOCUMENT CAMERA

If you would like to be able to share images from a picture book on a large screen or do a draw-and-tell story for a large group, you may want to acquire a document camera. Easily transportable, a document camera, which supersedes the clunkier (but still useful) overhead projectors of yore, is a video camera mounted on a short tripod. Anything placed on the table under the camera—from a picture book to a puppet to a prop—will be transmitted through the document camera and through to the data projector onto a screen. Some document cameras—such as the inexpensive and lightweight Point 2 View from iPevo—connect through your computer.

Many presenters use their own laptop, netbook computer, or iPad-like device and store slides and images on it. Ask your computer vendor what special adapters—nicknamed "dongles"—your computer might need to connect to the data projector. Other presenters create their presentations at home and transfer them to the host organization's setup via e-mail, online storage, or a flash drive. If you will be using a host's equipment to display text, use standard fonts in lieu of unusual ones so that they render correctly. Fonts like Helvetica, Arial, Verdana, Trebuchet, Georgia, and Times New Roman are safe bets.

PRESENTATION REMOTE

A presentation remote costs under $100 and allows you to control a computer's slideshow without having to be near the projector. This is especially helpful if you are a kinesthetic storyteller who enjoys moving about the room. If you have music that accompanies your presentation, you'll want a set of speakers with a cord that specifically fits the 1/8-inch jack on your computer. Microphones are generally set up using a separate sound system. All of this is expensive, but many schools and libraries already have some or all the equipment you'll need.

THE LAPEL MICROPHONE, YOUR LIFESAVER

If you are speaking to a large group or talking over an extended period of time, the most important piece of equipment you will want is a microphone.

Teachers and librarians routinely destroy their voices with all the jawing they do each day. Did you know that vocal cord nodules—small, inflammatory, or fibrous growths on the vocal cords of people who constantly strain their voices—are also called screamer's nodule, singer's nodule, and teacher's nodule? Teachers are thirty-two times more likely to have vocal problems, thanks to needing to speak louder and longer than most professionals.[1] That's one reason some school districts have invested in cordless lapel mics for their staffs. It especially helps those children with even minimal hearing loss who have trouble following the teacher when there's classroom noise. It helps children focus better and gives the teacher far better group control, and those behavior problems become easier to resolve. All these advantages will help you when you are telling stories to kids, too.

Easiest to use is the cordless, clip-on lapel mic, with a battery-powered body-pack transmitter, the size of a deck of cards, which clips onto your belt or back pocket. This leaves your hands free to hold up props, puppets, or books; to write on a board or a flip chart; to tell a paperfolding story; or to play an instrument. You have the freedom of being able to move around on stage or into the audience, and the assurance of being heard perfectly by everyone in the room.

A handheld cordless mic is fine if you are a comedian doing standup—and many storytellers use them masterfully—but if you need to use your hands for props or puppets, it can be bulky and awkward. If you use a mic attached to a floor stand, you will be tethered to one spot, standing straight, which is hard on the knees, though rock singers do well with them. An over-the-head mic can look weird and be uncomfortable, or can be almost imperceptible, and some storytellers prefer them. The cordless, clip-on lavaliere mic—pretty much invisible to your audience and easy to switch off if you need to—is a godsend. (Be sure to press the mute button when speaking privately to someone, or everyone will listen in. And, most important, take off the danged thing before you visit the restroom!)

Well before a presentation, even if you send the person in charge an e-mail listing all your equipment needs, know that foul-ups do still happen. In one school where Judy was to be giving one-hour assemblies all day, the principal handed her an over-the-head mic, saying, "We don't have the lapel mic you requested. This is all we've got." Unfortunately, the headpiece was child-size, and the attached mic only came to her cheek, instead of near her mouth. Better still, every two minutes, the whole apparatus would pop off her head. This made for general merriment amongst the children in the audience. She still shudders when she thinks of that day, but at least she had a mic.

This stands in stark contrast to what happened to a well-known children's book author on one of her school visits. When she arrived, they told her blithely, "About that mic you wanted? We don't have one. Sorry." Not wanting to appear uncooperative or prima donna–ish, she instead ratcheted up her vocal volume to be heard by each of her large groups. By the end of the day, her voice was gone. She had stripped her vocal cords and had to cancel her next two weeks of speaking engagements.

"No, I don't need a microphone. I have a very loud voice," you say? Do reconsider. It's better for your listeners if you don't have to bellow. The point of using a mic is to unobtrusively but effectively enable your audience to hear every word, even when you speak softly, and give you total vocal control without straining your vocal cords. Even when you are barely murmuring, your voice becomes almost magically omnipresent, and you can talk over your group when you're telling a noisy participation story without appearing to yell. One baffled little boy, hearing Judy's voice float above the crowd in a school gym during one of her storytelling presentations, looked around wildly, and then said, "How did you do that?!" Judy pointed to the little black bud clipped to her shirt and said, "It's the magic of technology."

Throat hurts from talking too much? Congested with a drippy throat? When giving a presentation, drink water or weak warm tea to stay hydrated. You'll swear by Throat Coat tea, made by Traditional Medicinals, found in the herbal-tea section of your supermarket, and Entertainer's Secret Throat Relief spray. You can find both on Amazon. Whatever you do, take care of those pipes. You can't tell stories when your throat is on the fritz.

Setting It All Up

Set up chairs, exhibits, and equipment well before your audience arrives. If your program is being sponsored by an outside organization and/or someone else is coordinating your visit, be sure to let the person in charge know all your needs and requirements well in advance of the program so there are no unwelcome surprises when you arrive. The rule of thumb is, the more technology, the more things go wrong. The PowerPoint won't open, the DLP projector blows a mega-expensive bulb, or you can't find the playlist you thought you had on your iPhone. You might have performance nerves before you begin a program, but when the technology fails, you'll want to pull out your hair and throw your computer across the room. Resist the urge. Breathe. Look for someone under twenty-five to fix it for you. There. Much better!

Pack a long heavy-duty extension cord or two (the orange kind), a multi-outlet surge-protector strip, and a three- to two-prong adapter. In many presentation venues, the number of electrical outlets may be limited or not located near your presentation spot, and it's much easier to bring your own than ask your host to track one down, especially during evening hours, when the maintenance crew may have gone home for the day. Tape down any cords to prevent you or your audience from tripping and/or knocking over your equipment. Cloth gaffer tape is best, as it doesn't leave a sticky residue; duct tape will do in a pinch. Some places have low-pile floor mats to place over the cords.

Test out your equipment before the program. Check the projector focus; if you're giving a PowerPoint presentation, run through your slides. (Always have a backup of your PowerPoint on a thumb drive in case the original crashes or the computer dies. It happens.) Have a backup plan (duplicate equipment or a low-tech storytelling option) in case of total mechanical failure.

Unless you are looking for an unusual dramatic effect, be sure that your acting space is separate from that of the projector beam, or the image will project onto you, creating a large shadow on the screen. Scope out the light switches in the room. In many cases, it will be easier for your audience to see images crisply if the lights right above the screen are dimmed or turned off. If they can't be adjusted, you could turn the lights off, but then you run the risk that there might be snoring. This is why it is wonderful to have a DLP projector that can stand up to a well-lighted room. It's not so much fun to tell stories in the dark unless you're in the woods somewhere.

Pay attention to all the connecting cables and connectors for all your equipment, which can be a dizzying array, including the XLR audio cable (from the mixer to the sound system in the wall), the VGA cable (from the projector to the computer), and the power cords for the mixer, receiver, projector, and computer. If they belong to you, label them with your name so you can't overlook them and leave them behind. Do be sure to label every single piece of your personal equipment with fluorescent tape, tags, or laminated business cards so it can be returned to you if misplaced. Bring extra cords, batteries, bulbs, and maybe some chocolate for stress.

Judy says, "I was in Orlando, Florida, late on a Sunday afternoon, setting up for my all-day presentation the next day, when I realized that I had brought along the power cord to my husband's Mac, which, of course, was not compatible with mine. Gasp! Choke! Scream! The tech guy at the hotel said, 'No problem. There's an Apple store in the mall, not that far away, and I can give you a ride.' Away we raced. When we got there, they had just closed the store for a meeting. Desperate, I hammered on the big glass doors, and caught the eye of an employee. Explaining my predicament through the door—'Out of town! From New Jersey! Big presentation tomorrow! Wrong power cord! Help! Save me!'—I was elated when he opened the door and fetched me a brand-new cord. It was a very expensive error—$80 for the cord and a big tip for the hotel tech guy who saved my bacon."

Lessons learned: pay better attention when packing, bring extra cords when possible, and be grateful for the kindness of strangers—especially tech folk, often the nicest, most helpful people anywhere.

Performance Pitfalls

You may be completely unaware of distracting movements you make when you speak in public. Maybe you bite your lip, sway from side to side, or close your eyes when you talk. Ask your friends to give you an honest critique, or film yourself telling a story to analyze your tics and traits. You may be horrified to see the wacky little things you do, but it's better to know about them early on. Maybe one of these performance pitfalls has your name on it.

- *Do you speak too fast?* In an effort to "get it over with," we sometimes race through material. As a first-year storyteller at the New York Public Library, Caroline was observed by a storytelling supervisor who came to observe her story hour. She told Harold Courlander's "The Goat Well" from *The Fire on the Mountain and Other Ethiopian Stories* (Henry Holt, 1950). Afterwards the supervisor told her, "Miss Feller, you have good expression. Someday you might be a good storyteller, but that story usually takes fifteen minutes to tell and you told it in four minutes and thirty-eight seconds." Whoops.

  If you don't have enough time to do justice to a story, pick another one. In one of Judy's graduate storytelling classes, she gave the assignment to choose and learn a simple story, no longer than five minutes. One student picked an elaborate fairy tale she loved, stripped it of all "nonessential" action and description, and told it at breakneck pace to make the five-minute time limit. What's wrong with this? First off, your listeners use their mind's eye to visualize the story. If it zips by too fast, there's not enough time to become emotionally invested. Second, the story lost its heart and resonance when all the supporting details were chopped out. If you're taking the time to learn a story, give it the space it deserves. If you have five minutes left in a program, save that great twenty-minute story for next time.

Remember that your audience is hearing your story for, perhaps, the first time. They are trying to understand your words and make sense of the plot, all at the same time. Watch them carefully to make sure they are comprehending you.

- *Do you speak too slowly?* Sometimes the whole pace of a story drops. Some people tend to talk too deliberately, almost caressing each word. This can also happen if you tell the story too often. You might actually be bored by it. Snap out of it!

- *Do you speak too softly?* Remember that everyone has to hear you. Speak up and out. Don't be afraid to be heard. Use a microphone if your group is large, but remember that using one takes some experience, especially a standing or a handheld one. The most common pitfall is to stand too close, thereby distorting the sound and also obstructing the audience's view of the speaker. The opposite problem is standing too far away; no one will hear you despite the aid. A wireless clip-on lapel one is far less obtrusive and easy to use.

- *Is your voice too high?* Many women's voices are naturally high. If yours is very high, practice dropping your voice a bit when you speak publicly. Record yourself to hear how you sound when telling a story and adjust your voice accordingly.

- *Do you speak in a monotone?* In the rush to get your story out there, you may not be thinking about your delivery. Your voice is your Stradivarius. If it stays on one note, the song will be boring. Authentic enthusiasm, where your voice goes up and down, gets loud and soft, makes a story more compelling. Don't go overboard, but make sure you're speaking and reading aloud with expression.

- *Do you act passively?* When you give a program, you are in charge of the room. Own it. Stand up straight and project confidence. Your audience needs to make a personal and emotional connection. Even if you are shy in real life, you can be bold and brave as a storyteller. Project your own life force in what we call "storyteller's charisma."
- *Do you avoid eye contact?* When you are talking to a group, make its members feel as though you are talking to them individually. This is the great advantage of traditional storytelling. Freed from props and books, you are able to establish direct eye contact with every single member of your audience. Glance at a select few in a random pattern. You will find yourself grateful for that someone who smiles and nods her head with approval. Try not to lose hope if someone falls asleep; you may have done it yourself when you were very tired. Just remember that most of the audience is listening.
- *Do you use distracting gestures?* To gesture or not to gesture? The answer is: it's up to you. One of Caroline's graduate students used to tell stories as if he were tied to a post and told not to move a muscle, not even to blink; yet his voice was mesmerizing and listeners fell completely under his spell. Other tellers move around quite a bit and use hand gestures. If the question of what to do with your hands is at first a problem for you, lightly clasp them behind you. When you feel that you must demonstrate the smallest or the tallest, show the size with your hands and again put them behind your back. If the gesturing gets in the way of the story, remember less can be more.
- *Are you using language correctly?* We need to model good grammar and speech patterns for our listeners. It's very easy to revert to sloppy form. *Like* and *you know* are two of the worst offenders, and they are the bane of a storyteller's vocabulary. Banish them. It's jarring, dreadful, and just plain wrong. Many of the stories you will tell are antiques, so treat them reverently. Modern phrasing and incorrect usage don't belong in the land of Once upon a Time. When you insert them into stories you're telling, it breaks the mood and compromises your storyteller's voice.

  Each time Judy teaches her graduate storytelling class at Pratt Institute in NYC, one of the first things she does is ban the use of "uh" and "like" and "you know" and "so I'm like" by all of her students. There's nothing worse than a story that begins, "Once upon a time, there were three little pigs. One day their mother was like, 'It's time for you to leave and find homes of your own.' So they head off into the forest where they have to, like, you know, build their own houses."

It's eye-opening for the students to not be allowed to say those words, even in casual conversation, for, like, 10 whole minutes, y'know? Actually, though, it makes them very conscious of the way they use words from then on. It is true that it makes you sound a bit dim when you resort to those ubiquitous phrases. "Like" and "you know" are often used as fillers or as emphasis or to give us time to think of the next thing we want to say. Judy teaches her students to pause or take a breath, instead.

Another thing that's hard for beginning storytellers to master is the past tense. Did you notice the shifting tenses in "The Three Little Pigs" story above? That's no darn good. Jokes are usually told in the present tense, but stories from once-upon-a-time really need to be set in the past, unless you have a good reason for doing otherwise. At first, new tellers will shift their tenses from past to present willy nilly, back and forth within a story they're telling. Some students, probably the ones who have never studied grammar in school, don't even know the difference between the two tenses. until they become more aware of how a story should sound.

As teachers and librarians, we need to model language effectively with our students, whether they're five or fifteen or fifty. It's so easy to revert to sloppy form, and "like" and "you know" are two of the worst offenders. If we put a quarter in a jar for each time we use those words, we'll either stop using them pretty fast or collect enough cold cash to take a nice little weekend trip. Either way, it's a win-win situation.

- *Do you speak down to your audience?* Just as it's off-putting to hear well-meaning adults babble in baby talk to a toddler, sometimes storytellers can speak condescendingly to an audience, whether it's made up of preschoolers or adolescents. With young children, we sometimes can lapse into a singsong cadence, using a syrupy, icky-sweet voice that just sounds insincere. Enthusiasm and expression are all good, but be aware that children don't like being talked down to any more than you do. You also want to project warmth and sincerity as a person and storyteller, looking upon the audience as your peers, not your subjects. While your listeners may well adore you, if your persona is too forbidding or if you see yourself as "the great one," they could find you egotistical instead of down-to-earth.

LOSING TRACK OF OR FORGETTING THE STORY

It happens to the inexperienced and the experienced: you suddenly go blank. What should you do? Stop, and think. That is the only way out. Sometimes you have to just quietly stand there until the story comes back to you. The possibility of forgetting is a good reason to bring along a copy of the story or exhibit the book the story comes from. You can always glance at the text. Your listeners won't mind a bit, or even notice if you do. Sometimes merely looking at a book's cover will help you regain your place. Just don't panic.

Occasionally you'll need to recover piece of the story you forgot to tell. It happens when you're not paying enough attention to your story and/or your audience. All of a sudden, your brain runs cold and you think, "Did I forget that part?" or "Am I repeating something I already said?" or, worst of all, "Where am I?" Chances are good that you've let your mind wander, thinking about, oh, chocolate or something. Now you must snap to it and figure out how to rescue your story.

Let's say you're telling the Indian folktale "The Cat and the Parrot" (page 127), and you realize you left out one of the many characters the cat scarfs down in his swallowing spree. That's when you say, simply, "And did I mention that the greedy cat also ate, slip slop gobble, an entire elephant? Let me go back a bit and tell you about it." That "and did I mention" phrase will stand you in good stead. Add it to your bag of tricks. Fix your mistake, and move on.

STAGE FRIGHT

More serious than forgetting is getting waylaid by stage fright, which manifests in symptoms ranging from nausea and hot flashes to a quavering voice and frequent trips to the restroom. Some of us never have it; some of us always have it. Stage fright symptoms are part of your body's primary threat response, also known as "fight or flight syndrome." What happens to you in stage-fright mode? Your muscles contract and start to tremble; your vocal cords stretch, making your voice tighten; and your hands and feet feel cold and clammy. You start to breathe rapidly. Because your blood pressure rises, you start to sweat so your body doesn't overheat, and your heart starts pumping quicker, thumping in your chest.

Should you give up and go home now? Don't be hasty. This is mighty unpleasant and unwelcome, but it's something you can and will master with practice. Here's the first rule to dispel stage fright: the audience is rooting for you; they want you to succeed.

Performance Exercises

If you get overly nervous before a performance, here are a few tips. On the morning of a performance, do an aerobic workout to give you energy. Yoga can help you focus. Even a brisk walk beforehand or doing a few stretches is an excellent strategy.

If you feel your heart pounding or your throat going dry, change your behavior. Trick your body into doing something different. March quickly, shake your arms and legs vigorously, roll your head, and even jump up and down. Clench and relax your fists, kick your legs, and, if you can do this inconspicuously, howl. If not, sing a silly song or recite a nonsense poem. Laugh out loud. It will help you relax. Stage fright makes you feel stressed, but weirdly excited, too. You should be excited. You're going to have so much fun on stage, you'll get a sugar high without the calories.

Speaking of sugar, avoid it before you perform; your blood-sugar level will drop after the high wears off. Also steer clear of milk, which creates phlegm, and caffeine, which stimulates the adrenal glands and makes you jittery, not to mention all those trips to the loo. Drink water, no ice.

HOW TO BREATHE

Did you know that most people breathe shallowly, using only the tops of their lungs? If you are a speaker or singer, you need to breathe from the diaphragm. Deep, slow breathing helps you relax, take in more oxygen, and expel more carbon dioxide. Your heart will stop racing, and you'll have better vocal control when you speak in public.

How do you breathe from your diaphragm? Put your hands on your belly to see if you do it naturally. Breathe in slowly, from your nose. If you feel your abdomen expanding, pushing out when you breathe in, and going in when you breathe out, you are engaging your diaphragm. Teach your kids how to do this, too.

Now try this blood pressure–reducing trick: Rest your tongue behind your front teeth. Inhale through your nose to the count of four. Hold your breath while you count to seven. Exhale in a long whoosh, to the count of eight, pushing out the air from your mouth, held slightly ajar, your tongue still resting on the roof. Do this four or five times. Do it at night when you go to bed, and you'll probably relax and fall asleep faster.

Here's another good exercise: breathe in and out of your nose quickly, like an angry bull, for up to thirty seconds. (Some kids do this when they get really mad.) It'll give you energy and clear your head.

HOW TO WARM UP

Judy's wonderful niece, Caitlin Freeman, who teaches voice, contributed the following practical suggestions for speakers and singers warming up for performance:

Start out standing with your feet a hip's width apart, arms at your sides, face forward. Imagine your chin and the back of your head resting on a level platter. Make sure your eyes are looking straight forward in front of you. Your tongue rests at the tip of your bottom teeth.

Every in breath starts with an out breath. When you start an exercise, breathe out first, and then breathe back in to get a greater volume of fresh air in your lungs. Breathe from the diaphragm. As you go through the exercises, sing across the room or out the window to an imagined person, someone who is a bit restless and needs you to get their attention. (Sing a song you know or just sing the word "hello" for starters.)

If you feel phlegm in your throat, do not worry about it. Worrying about it will make it worse. Keep seeing out in front of you, give yourself lots of space in your mouth, remember to keep your tongue at the tip of your bottom teeth, and sing "over" the phlegm—that is, don't press through the phlegm, but keep your tone buoyant over it.

Singing Exercises

Here are three of Caitlin's simple, excellent vocal exercises you can do anywhere. In lieu of a piano, a pitchpipe, which you can buy for under $20, will be helpful, as will a harmonica or virtual piano keyboard online.

TONING Start on middle C. Breathe out first, then breathe in. On an "Ah," sing as long as your breath lasts, without pushing. Breathe back in. On an "Ah," tone a D. Repeat up the scale and back down.

SIRENS IN FIFTHS Start on middle C. Breathe out first, then breathe in. On an "Ah," swoop slowly from middle C down to the F below middle C and back up to middle C.

Repeat sirens in fifths from:

C# to F# to C#
D to G to D
D# to G# to D#
E to A to E

And so on.

1-3-5 (TRIAD) CHORDS Start on the chord middle C-E-G. Breathe out first, then breathe in. On a "Ma-mo-may-mee-moo," sing up the chord and back down, C-E-G-E-C. Repeat up and down the keyboard:

C-E-G-E-C
C#-F-G#-F-C#
D-F#-A-F#-D

And so on.

Sing the three notes of the chords as you work your way up the keyboard, and feel free to vary the vowel/consonant combinations:

Ma-mo-may-mee-moo
Ba-bo-bay-bee-boo
La-lo-lay-lee-loo
Fa-fo-fay-fee-foo
Ha-ho-hay-hee-hoo
Sha-sho-shay-shee-shoo

And so on.

HOW TO SPEAK

Here is more essential advice from Caitlin Freeman.

- Imagine that your voice is a beach ball buoyed aloft by a powerful fan. Your goal is to speak in the middle of your speaking range, not so low that the beach ball falls onto the fan in "vocal fry," and not so high that it blows off into the stratosphere. Vocal fry (also called creak, glottal fry, glottal rattle, or glottal scrape) is the tone at the very bottom of your register where your voice produces a popping or rattling tone. (Tune in to those teenage girls talking in their flat, bored, low monotones, and you'll hear it.) It's not great for your voice.

- If you feel phlegm in your throat, keep speaking "over" it in the middle of your range. Vocal fry will increase the amount of phlegm on the vocal folds (it is the throat's way of lubricating the vocal folds from the friction of the vocal fry), so make sure to keep your voice elevated.
- Sing your words and phrases. Every word you speak is intoned on a pitch, usually within a relatively small range of your voice (about five notes or so). Imagine that those pitches are part of a song that you are singing. Make your speech musical by "singing" your words in the middle of your speaking range.
- Imagine that your chin and the back of your head are supported on a level platter. Notice when your chin tucks down into your neck, juts forward, or raises up toward the ceiling, and remind yourself to keep your chin level.
- Keep your eyes straight ahead. Picture a line drawn around the room that is exactly level with your gaze. Follow this track when you speak. Find landmarks that correspond with this imaginary line, and speak to them. Wherever you turn your head, find your line.
- Imagine that you are speaking to someone who is a little distracted. Use the above techniques to make this person realize that what you are saying is important.

Speaking Exercise

Here's what some actors memorize and recite, slowly at first and then faster, when they're warming up their voices, tongue, mouth, and facial muscles before a performance. The first one is a chorus from *The Mikado* by Gilbert and Sullivan, in which various characters decline to trade places with a man awaiting execution.

To Sit in Solemn Silence

> *To sit in solemn silence on a dull, dark dock,*
> *In a pestilential prison with a life-long lock,*
> *Awaiting the sensation of a short, sharp shock,*
> *From a cheap and chippy chopper on a big black block!*

This second selection is from *Merrie England*, a comic opera written by Basil Hood and Edward German in 1902. In a play-within-the-play, Queen Elizabeth I watches as players put on a Masque of "St. George and the Dragon." The first verse below is recited by a princess who is going to be sacrificed to the Dragon; the second verse is by her father, the King of Egypt.

Oh, Here's a To-Do to Die To-Day

Oh, here's a to-do, to die to-day
At a minute or two to two,
A thing distinctly hard to say,
But a harder thing to do.
For they'll beat a tattoo at two to two,
A rat-a-tattoo at two. Boohoo!
And the Dragon will come
When he hears the drum
At a minute or two to two to-day,
At a minute or two to two!

Why hullabaloo? You die to-day
At a minute or two to two,
A thing distinctly hard to say
But an easy thing to do!
For they'll beat a tattoo at two to two,
A rat-a-tat-tat tattoo for you!
And the Dragon will come
When he hears the drum;
There's nothing for you to do but stay,
And the Dragon will do for you!

You can teach these delicious verses to your children as well. First, do each line as a call-and-response. Then put it all together and recite it with them several times, increasing your speed each time. It really gives your facial muscles a nice workout when you enunciate each word carefully, and your nerves will be soothed.

An oft-repeated story regarding stage fright is one attributed to Winston Churchill, who supposedly said (or didn't) something like, "I never feel stage fright anymore; I just imagine that the whole audience is naked, but I, the speaker, am fully clothed." OK, that's just plain creepy. Let your audience members keep their knickers on, and you concentrate on slow, deep breathing, visualizing your story, and making eye contact with your eager listeners. And remember—this will be fun, both for your listeners and for you. Your performance jitters will vanish once you get started. Honest.

Four Stories to Learn

No point in putting things off. Let's jump right in with several stories and analyses of how you might approach each one. For your first and easiest story to tell, we've picked an old English cumulative tale, "The Old Woman and Her Pig," one of Judy's favorite standbys to tell to ages two to six.

The Old Woman and Her Pig

An Old English Folktale Retold by Joseph Jacobs

An old woman was sweeping the floor of her house, and she found a little crooked sixpence in the nest of a mouse. "What," said she, "shall I do with this little sixpence? I know! I will go to market, and buy myself a sweet little pig."

So she went to the market and she bought herself a pig. As she was coming home, she came to a stile, but the pig would not go over it. She said, "Pig, Pig, jump over the stile, or we shan't get home tonight."

But the stubborn pig said, "I won't!"

She went a little further, and she met a dog. She said to the dog, "Dog, Dog, bite Pig; Pig won't jump over the stile, and we shan't get home tonight." But the dog said, "I won't!"

She went a little further, and she met a stick. So she said: "Stick, Stick, beat Dog! Dog won't bite Pig; Piggy won't get over the stile, and we shan't get home tonight." But the stick said, "I won't!"

She went a little further, and she met a fire. So she said: "Fire, Fire, burn Stick; Stick won't beat Dog; Dog won't bite Pig; Piggy won't get over the stile, and we shan't get home tonight." But the fire said, "I won't!"

She went a little further, and she met some water. So she said: "Water, Water, quench Fire; Fire won't burn Stick; Stick won't beat Dog; Dog won't bite Pig; Piggy won't get over the stile, and we shan't get home tonight." But the water said, "I won't!"

She went a little further, and she met an ox. So she said: "Ox, Ox, drink Water; Water won't quench Fire; Fire won't burn Stick; Stick won't beat Dog;

Dog won't bite Pig; Piggy won't get over the stile, and we shan't get home tonight." But the ox said, "I won't!"

She went a little further, and she met a butcher. So she said: "Butcher, Butcher, kill Ox; Ox won't drink Water; Water won't quench Fire; Fire won't burn Stick; Stick won't beat Dog; Dog won't bite Pig; Piggy won't get over the stile, and we shan't get home tonight." But the butcher said, "I won't!"

She went a little further, and she met a rope. So she said: "Rope, Rope, hang Butcher; Butcher won't kill Ox; Ox won't drink Water; Water won't quench Fire; Fire won't burn Stick; Stick won't beat Dog; Dog won't bite Pig; Piggy won't get over the stile, and we shan't get home tonight." But the rope said, "I won't!"

She went a little further, and she met a rat. So she said: "Rat, Rat, gnaw Rope; Rope won't hang Butcher; Butcher won't kill Ox; Ox won't drink Water; Water won't quench Fire; Fire won't burn Stick; Stick won't beat Dog; Dog won't bite Pig; Piggy won't get over the stile, and we shan't get home tonight." But the rat said, "I won't!"

She went a little further, and she met a cat. So she said: "Cat, Cat, kill Rat; Rat won't gnaw Rope; Rope won't hang Butcher; Butcher won't kill Ox; Ox won't drink Water; Water won't quench Fire; Fire won't burn Stick; Stick won't beat Dog; Dog won't bite Pig; Piggy won't get over the stile, and we shan't get home tonight."

But the cat said to her, "If you will go to yonder cow, and fetch me a saucer of milk, I will kill the rat."

So away went the old woman to the cow. But the cow said to her: "If you will go to yonder haystack, and fetch me a handful of hay, I'll give you the milk."

So away went the old woman to the haystack; and she brought the hay to the cow. As soon as the cow had eaten the hay, she gave the old woman the milk, and away she went with it in a saucer to the cat.

As soon as the cat had lapped up the milk . . . the cat began to kill the rat, the rat began to gnaw the rope, the rope began to hang the butcher, the butcher began to kill the ox, the ox began to drink the water, the water began to quench the fire, the fire began to burn the stick, the stick began to beat the dog, the dog began to bite the pig, the little pig in a fright jumped over the stile, and so the old woman got home that night.

PARSING "THE OLD WOMAN AND HER PIG"

Cumulative tales are usually told to younger children, who enjoy the repeated refrains and the predictability of the story. Such stories are pretty simple to learn; you just need to visualize and recall the cause-and-effect sequence; in this case, the roster of each nay-saying creature the old woman encounters. Concentrate and you'll see the cat lapping up the milk. Maybe you'll want to stop and act out that part in pantomime (encouraging your listeners to join in), and then pretend to lick your paws before setting down to the work of catching the rat. Then visualize the cat catching the rat, the rat gnawing the rope, and so on.

Judy has made a few small changes in this version to make the telling more fluid and inclusive. Each time the old woman says " . . . Pig won't jump over the stile; and I shan't get home tonight," Judy thought it was more inclusive to say, "Pig won't jump over the stile; and *we* shan't get home tonight." If you like it better in its original form, change it back.

The second change switches a passive response into an active one. The original text reads, "But the dog would not." After trying out this story with children, it quickly became apparent to use interactive dialogue here, so Judy changed it to, "But the dog said, 'I won't!'" Now children can join in on the refrain, which they do with great expression, a shake of the head, and sometimes even a stamp of the foot.

The third change is one you can make if you or your audience are squeamish. Although it's part of the absurdist fun, the characters use some drastic strong-arm tactics to goad creatures into action in the tale. The poor old woman is at the end of her rope with all these obstructionists. Can you blame her for using bit of intimidation to make each slacker hop to it? However, if the old woman's directive to "hang Butcher" is too medieval for you or your audience, change it to "tie Butcher." Also, the cat could start to catch (instead of kill) the rat. True, no actual characters are harmed in the course of the story—the cat *begins* to kill the rat, but never actually does it. It won't harm the story to make such adjustments.

Vocabulary alert: The word *stile* may stop you in your tracks; assume it will do the same to your listeners. Find pictures of stiles online to show the children so they understand why the piggy is reluctant to jump over it.

This story begs for audience participation. You will find that even young children can recall the entire sequence, which consists of ten actions, and recite the ever-lengthening refrain with you. They also love to predict what the next character will be. Say, "What do you think the old woman can find to quench the fire?" and they'll all yell, "Water!" (They'll quickly intuit the meaning of the word *quench* from the context of the story and happily add it to their own vocabularies from now on.)

After you tell the story, have the children form a long line and act out the whole thing. To ensure that each child gets a part, you can cast more than one child to play each part—two sticks or three cats, for instance.

Hand out long strips of paper and see if your kids can draw each character in sequence, assembled in that great long line. Chances are good that they will remember the whole thing. (You may want to try this exercise yourself while you are learning the story so you have a visual record of its sequence. Drawing the steps to a story like this will help you visualize each action as you tell it.)

It's fun to tell one version and read the others so children can compare them. After you tell the story, share Margaret Read MacDonald's picture-book version, *The Old Woman and Her Pig* (HarperCollins, 2007), which is rich in chantable refrains. Then pull out a New England variant, Jim Aylesworth's charmer, *Aunt Pitty Patty's Piggy* (Scholastic, 1999), in which Aunt Pitty Patty's niece tries to get everyone and everything she meets to help her make the stubborn piggy enter the gate. The refrain in this book is "It's gettin' late, and piggy's by the gate sayin', 'No, no, no, I will not go!'" There's even a Polish version, "The Pear Tree," in which a pear tree won't let go of its pears. You will find it in *Polish Folktales and Folklore* by Michael Malinowski and Anne Pellowski (Libraries Unlimited, 2009).

Here's an interesting note, as we look at the folk process. "Chad Gadya," which in Aramaic means "one goat," is a cumulative Jewish folk song that is sung at the end of the Passover seder. The song can be traced back to fifteenth century Germany. The last verse will certainly seem familiar now:

Chad Gaya

Then came the Holy One, Blessed be He
And killed the angel of death
That killed the slaughterer
That killed the ox
That drank the water
That quenched the fire

That burned the stick
That beat the dog
That bit the cat
That ate the kid
That my father bought for two coins
One kid, one kid!

That wasn't so hard to learn, was it? Our second story, "Tyll Paints the Duke's Portrait," features that merry German prankster, Tyll Ulenspiegel (pronounced Till OIL-en-spee-gull). The language is more sophisticated in this one, though it's actually a tale you can tell to any age.

Tyll Paints the Duke's Portrait

Retold by Caroline Feller Bauer

Clip, clop. Clip, clop. Here comes Tyll Ulenspiegel riding his old gray donkey into town. And here comes the Duke riding on his sleek black horse.

"Good morning, your Honor," hails Tyll.

"Good morning to you," says the Duke. "What brings you to town?"

"I'm a portrait artist looking for work."

"Is that so?" says the Duke. "I just happen to be looking for someone to paint my family and the people of the court on the wall of my throne room. Let me see your work."

Tyll opens one of the saddlebags and takes out a painting of two older people and a dog.

"My parents and Ignatz, their dog," he introduces his relatives with a flourish.

"Nice work," says the Duke. "You're hired."

"Not so fast," says Tyll. "I have a few requests for my working conditions."

"Anything you want," says the Duke.

And that is how Tyll Ulenspiegel spent four months at court. His donkey had a private stall and its own groom. The donkey was brushed twice a day and ate heartily of the freshest green grass.

As for Tyll, he had requested three meals a day and a snack before bedtime. He was pampered by a servant who ran his bath and washed his painting smock.

Each day Tyll went to the chamber where the wall portrait was to be painted. He always carefully locked the door so that no one would enter while he was at work. "No one is to see the mural until I am ready to show it."

Every afternoon, Tyll entertained the Duke's family and their friends at tea, the tea provided by the Duke, of course. The guests were all curious to see their portraits and were constantly admonishing Tyll.

The Grand Duchess was so old that even she had forgotten how many years she had saluted the daily rising of the sun. She always wore her best for tea with Tyll. "I know I am no longer beautiful," she would croak, "but in my day I was famous for the curl in my hair and the twinkle in my eye. I hope that you will paint me as I was in my twenties. Remember that my skin was as smooth and as rosy as the first apples of fall."

Tyll always smiled. "You are beautiful today, my lady."

The Duke's eldest daughter visited Tyll at teatime, too. "Please, pretty please, may I see the portrait of me? I hope you didn't paint my bangs. I don't want to be remembered forever with this haircut. It was a mistake. Nurse cut it this way."

Tyll always smiled. "No, my lady, you can not see the portrait until it is done, but of course I painted you with the hairstyle of your dreams."

Even the Duke himself, who surely had other things to do, came by for tea one day. He was accompanied by his steward and his advisor. They all made requests for the mural.

"I hope you will represent me with a fuller beard."

"I can no longer fit into my purple pantaloons, but I'm sure you won't paint my stomach. It's here only temporarily."

"I had more hair when I was younger. I certainly hope the mural will depict me with a full head of hair."

Tyll always smiled. "I am listening to your requests."

Every day Tyll would disappear into the throne room, where the mural was to be painted. He took his paints and his brushes and a good book to read. Hours later he emerged yawning with fatigue.

Court members and friends waited at the door until Tyll emerged. "Is it finished yet?" But Tyll was having too much fun. "No, the mural isn't finished, but it would help to have venison for dinner, please, and a bit of chocolate cake."

At teatime the Duke's cook came by. "I hear that the entire household is being represented in your wall mural. I certainly hope that you will paint me holding my new puppy. She is a member of the family, too."

The Duke's groom had a request, too. "The mare is expecting her foal next month. I hope you will include it. Make it a stallion, please."

Tyll always smiled at the requests. "I'm sure you will all be pleased."

The Duke's five-year-old son was Tyll's most devoted admirer. He never requested how he should be painted. He only wanted Tyll to read to him and share his tea. Together they ate cream puffs and marzipan. They shared picture books. Little Peter learned to smile just like his friend Tyll.

But what was Tyll doing in the throne room? Why wasn't the painting done? The Duke was impatient. "My father-in-law will be visiting next week. I would like to show him the portraits. I insist that you finish the painting."

Tyll agreed. He demanded a bag of gold for more paint, and a horse and buggy to fetch it from the market. He needed money to buy red velvet curtains, and he would also like the Duke to provide him with a cottage. "Just a humble house, Your Lordship."

The Duke was anxious to see the finished painting. "Yes, yes, whatever you want," he wearily agreed.

The Duke's father-in-law arrived. There was a feast and dancing. "Now we shall see the painting," announced the Duke. The entire household gathered outside the throne room.

"Ladies and Gentlemen," intoned Tyll. "You are about to see my masterpiece. As you know, it has taken four months to paint it. I have had suggestions from each and every one of you and I have listened and satisfied your wishes. I think that you will be pleased with my interpretation of this lovely assemblage."

The Grand Duchess, the Duke, his children, the people of the court, and the household all filed into the throne room. The wall was completely covered with a red velvet curtain with gold tassels. The court musicians played a fanfare, and Tyll pulled the curtain aside.

The people gasped. The wall was blank, completely white. There was nothing to see. No one said anything. They were all waiting for the Duke's reaction. The Duke and his father-in-law were too astonished to speak.

"Each of you asked me to paint you as you, yourself, saw yourself. Now you can gaze at your portraits and see exactly what you would like to see."

"But," sputtered the Duke, "there is nothing to see."

"Father," said young Peter. "You are wrong. I see what I want to see. There I am right in the middle of the picture eating cream puffs with Tyll."

The Duke laughed. "Yes, you are right. I see my whole family dressed for a party, perpetually young. Let us all have some cream puffs."

Clip, clop. Clip, clop. There is Tyll's donkey. He is being led by a groom who is switching flies off his back as they stroll through town. And there is Tyll with the Duke's son, young Peter, taking tea in front of Tyll's new house. He no longer paints portraits.

PARSING "TYLL PAINTS THE DUKE'S PORTRAIT"

Now let's get to work. First, read the story the first time to see if it appeals to you. It does? Good! Now read it again—this time paying special attention to the plot. Sound familiar? It's a variant of Hans Christian Andersen's "The Emperor's New Clothes." Recognizing that you already know the point of the story will make it easier to learn.

Now list on paper, or in your head, the ten major story events in sequence. Here's our list:

1. Tyll comes to town and represents himself as a portrait painter to the Duke.
2. He is hired to paint a portrait of the Duke's family and staff on the throne room wall and set up in comfortable quarters.
3. Over four months, various members of the Duke's family give Tyll suggestions for the portrait, including the Grand Duchess, the Duke's daughter, the Duke, the cook, the groom, and Peter, the Duke's five-year-old son.
4. Tyll claims to be painting but doesn't show his work; he reads, eats well, and asks for more money.
5. The Duke and his entourage assemble in the throne room by the velvet-covered wall.
6. Tyll pulls the curtain aside and everyone gasps to see only a blank white wall.
7. Tyll says, "Each of you asked me to paint you as you, yourself, saw yourself. Now you can gaze at your portraits and see exactly what you would like to see."
8. The Duke's son, Peter, says: "I see what I want to see."
9. The Duke recognizes that he has been duped, but takes it in good humor.
10. Tyll enjoys his new leisure with the Duke's young son.

You see, ten sentences can tell the whole story. The action of writing it down helps you to recall the sequence and imprint it in your brain. Read the story again to see if you missed anything important. When you do this, you are setting the story more firmly in your mind (and in your mind's eye). Now do it again.

Next, add the touches that make it a story worth telling (and hearing). Caroline's version is told in the clicking cadence of the opening "clip, clop" of the donkey's hooves. Note that Caroline told the first scene where Tyll meets the Duke in present tense, and then moved into the past tense for the rest of the story. (Oh, you didn't notice? You should. As we have already said, most folktales are told in the past tense, fitting for "Once upon a time" tales, while jokes are usually told in the present tense. Caroline liked the way the present tense worked here, though.)

If you don't care for the way Caroline told it, incorporate your own style; her version is certainly not set in stone. She chose several members of the court—the Grand Duchess, the Duke's daughter, the Duke, his steward, his advisor, and even the cook to make certain requests. Use these characters or make up your own. Add your mother-in-law or your best friend.

We're suggesting that you may tweak a story by adding or subtracting details. As we mentioned earlier, however, another way to learn a story is essentially to memorize the words as they are written. If you are a memorizer, that's fine. If you are not, the details of the story will change slightly each time you tell it, and that's fine, too. Stories evolve.

Look for key lines you want to memorize, such as Tyll's statement in #7 above. If you cannot improve on a line, it is worth memorizing it. Usually, you will want to commit to memory the first and last paragraphs so you have a smooth start and finish.

Read the story over several more times to form a mental picture of each scene. Can you see the room where Tyll is "painting?" What's he doing in there all day? (And what do you think he is reading?) And little Peter? What does he look like? How about the Cook's cream puffs? What do they taste like? It helps to visualize the setting and the characters and to hear the dialogue in your head.

What kind of person is Tyll, and why didn't the Duke get angry with him upon realizing he'd been fooled? Do you know anyone like Tyll? Is there a bit of Tyll in you, maybe? Think deeply about the characters in a story and their motivations.

Want some background into the character, based on an actual person of that name who died in 1350? Go to www.story-lovers.com/liststilulen spiegelstories.html for some fascinating connections. Notice his name is spelled many different ways, including Tyl, Til and Till, plus Eulenspiegel and Uilenspiegel. Composer Richard Strauss even wrote a musical piece about him—"Till Ulenspiegel's Merry Pranks"—in 1895, which Vaslav Nijinsky then choreographed as a ballet in 1916.

Now that you are comfortable with the order of the story, play with the voice, the intonation, and the gestures that may help your listeners see the characters you are representing. You may want to touch your "bald head" or show the girth of your stomach with your arms. Be subtle, though. This is not a pantomime, though it is fun to mime Tyll's opening of that red velvet curtain with a flourish.

Now it's time to tell your story out loud to a spouse, a relative, a good friend, or even your cat. Don't worry that it is still a rough effort and that you stammer and forget bits. After you know the words better, you will perfect your telling. Actually, the story will feel more natural each time you run through it. Once you have told it aloud ten times, it will be familiar, like an old friend. However, telling to ten or twenty people is very different from an audience of one. The story is not yours until you see how a larger group reacts to it. You will then know where to tighten your telling to make it flow more naturally and bring out the humor.

Next let's examine "The Frog-King" or, as it's also called, "The Frog Prince" by the Brothers Grimm. It's an interesting tale for several reasons. First of all, unlike so many of the stark and, well, grim, fairy tales the brothers collected and retold back in the early nineteenth century, this one has marvelously visual scenes infused with humor. It's the first story Judy remembers learning in the storytelling class she took at Rutgers University, taught by that transcendent New York City storyteller, Laura Simms, and it has stayed in her head lo these many decades.

The Frog-King; Or, Iron Henry

Retold by Jacob and Wilhelm Grimm

from Grimm's Household Tales, *translated by Margaret Hunt, 1884*

In olden times when wishing still helped one, there lived a king whose daughters were all beautiful, but the youngest was so beautiful that the sun itself, which has seen so much, was astonished whenever it shone on her face.

Close by the king's castle lay a great dark forest, and under an old linden tree in the forest was a well. When the day was very warm, the princess went out into the forest and sat down by the side of the cool fountain. When she was bored, she took a golden ball, and threw it up on high and caught it. This ball was her favorite plaything.

Now, it so happened that on one occasion the princess's golden ball did not fall into her outstretched hands, but onto the ground beyond, and rolled straight into the water. The king's daughter followed it with her eyes, but it vanished, and the well was deep—so deep that the bottom could not be seen.

At this she began to cry, and cried louder and louder, and could not be comforted. And as she thus lamented, someone said to her, "What ails you, king's daughter? You weep so that even a stone would show pity."

She looked round to the side whence the voice came, and saw a frog stretching forth its big, ugly head from the water. "Ah, old water splasher, is it you?" she said, "I am weeping for my golden ball, which has fallen into the well."

"Be quiet, and do not cry," answered the frog, "I can help you, but what will you give me if I bring your plaything up again?"

"Whatever you will have, dear frog," said she, "My clothes, my pearls and jewels, and even the golden crown which I am wearing."

The frog answered, "I do not care for your clothes, your pearls and jewels, nor for your golden crown, but if you will love me and let me be your companion and playfellow, and sit by you at your little table, and eat off your little golden plate, and drink out of your little cup, and sleep in your little bed—if you will promise me this, I will go down below, and bring you your golden ball up again."

"Oh yes," said she, "I promise you all you wish, if you will but bring me my ball back again." But she thought, "How the silly frog does talk. All he does is to sit in the water with the other frogs, and croak. He can be no companion to any human being."

But the frog, when he had received this promise, put his head into the water and sank down, and in a short while came swimming up again with the ball in his mouth, and threw it on the grass. The king's daughter was delighted to see her pretty plaything once more, and picked it up, and ran away with it.

"Wait, wait," said the frog. "Princess, take me with you. I can't run as you can." But what did it avail him to scream his *croak, croak, croak* after her, as loudly as he could. She did not listen to it, but ran home and soon forgot the poor frog, who was forced to go back into his well again.

The next day when the princess had seated herself at table with the king and all the courtiers, and was eating from her little golden plate, something came creeping—*splish splash, splish splash*—up the marble staircase. When it had got to the top, it knocked at the door and cried, "Princess, youngest princess, open the door for me."

She ran to see who was outside, but when she opened the door, there sat the frog in front of it. Then she slammed the door in great haste, sat down to dinner again, and was quite frightened.

The king saw plainly that her heart was beating violently, and said, "My child, what are you so afraid of? Is there perchance a giant outside who wants to carry you away?"

"Ah, no," replied she. "It is no giant, but a disgusting frog."

"What does a frog want with you?"

"Ah, dear Father, yesterday as I was in the forest sitting by the well, playing, my golden ball fell into the water. And because I cried so, the frog brought it out again for me, and because he so insisted, I promised him he should be my companion, but I never thought he would be able to come out of his water. And now he is outside there, and wants to come in to me."

In the meantime, the frog knocked a second time, and cried,

"Princess, youngest Princess, open the door for me;

"Do you not know what you said to me yesterday by the cool waters of the well?

"Princess, youngest Princess, open the door for me."

Then said the king, "That which you have promised must you perform. Go and let him in."

Reluctantly, she went and opened the door. The frog hopped in and followed her, step by step, to her chair. There he sat and cried, "Lift me up beside you."

She delayed, until at last the king commanded her to do it. Once the frog was on the chair, he wanted to be on the table, and when he was on the table, he said, "Now, push your little golden plate nearer to me that we may eat together."

She did this, but it was easy to see that she did not do it willingly. The frog enjoyed what he ate, but almost every mouthful she took choked her.

At length he said, "I have eaten and am satisfied, but now I am tired. Carry me into your little room and make your little silken bed ready, and we will both lie down and go to sleep."

The king's daughter began to cry, for she was afraid of the cold frog, which she did not like to touch, and which was now to sleep in her pretty, clean little bed. But the king grew angry and said, "He who helped you when you were in trouble ought not afterwards to be despised by you."

So she took hold of the frog with two fingers, carried him upstairs to her bedroom, and put him in a corner. When she was in bed, he crept to her and said, "I am tired. I want to sleep as well as you. Lift me up or I will tell your father."

At this, she was terribly angry, and took him up and threw him with all her might against the wall. "Now, will you be quiet, odious frog," said she.

But when he fell down, he was no frog but a king's son with kind and beautiful eyes. Then he told her how he had been bewitched by a wicked witch, and how no one could have delivered him from the well but herself, and that tomorrow they would go together into his kingdom.

Then they went to sleep, and next morning when the sun awoke them, a carriage came driving up with eight white horses, which had white ostrich feathers on their heads, and were harnessed with golden chains. Behind them stood the young king's servant, Faithful Henry. Faithful Henry had been so unhappy when his master was changed into a frog, that he had caused three iron bands to be laid round his heart, lest it should burst with grief and sadness.

The carriage was to conduct the young king into his kingdom. Faithful Henry helped them both in, and was full of joy because of this deliverance. And when they had driven a part of the way, the king's son heard a cracking behind him as if something had broken. So he turned round and cried, "Henry, the carriage is breaking."

"No, master, it is not the carriage. It is a band round my heart, which was put there in my great pain when you were a frog and imprisoned in the well."

Again and once again while they were on their way, something cracked, and each time the king's son thought the carriage was breaking. But, no, it was only the bands that were springing from the heart of Faithful Henry because his master was set free and was happy at last.

PARSING "THE FROG-KING"

"In olden times when wishing still helped one . . ." Doesn't that marvelous first line make you wish that you lived in olden times?

Sometimes, scenes of a story and lines of dialogue run through your head like an old movie. You envision the princess at the well, weeping piteously after her golden ball rolls into the water. The frog surfaces: "Ah, old water splasher, is it you?" the princess says. "Wait, wait," cries the frog as the princess runs off, leaving him behind. "Princess, take me with you. I can't run as you can." Can't you just see that in your mind's eye? Then there's the unhappy princess picking up the frog with two fingers and carrying him up the stairs to her bedroom, where she sets him in a corner.

One of Judy's favorite parts of the story is when the frog comes over to the princess's bed and says, "I am tired, and I want to sleep as well as you do. Pick me up or I'll tell your father." The princess, quite at the end of her tether, dashes him against the wall, only to watch in amazement as a handsome prince "with kind and beautiful eyes" appears in the frog's stead.

The two then go to sleep in her bed, a detail you will doubtless leave out when telling the story to children. Instead, some tellers end the story with a tagline about the two falling in love and getting married. Note there is no kissing of the frog in this story. People always assume this is the tale where the princess kisses the frog to make him revert to his prince persona, but that's not the case here. Just so you know. Actually there is that serious and poignant ending with the prince's faithful servant, Faithful Henry, or, as the title calls him, Iron Henry (sometimes known instead as Iron Hans). You'll need to decide whether you want to include that last scene, but it's a stirring one.

In her classic collection *Tales from Grimm*, Wanda Gág used this refrain in her version of the story:

Youngest daughter of the king, open the door for me;
Mind your words at the old well spring; open the door for me.

It has a better cadence, don't you think? Really, each translation of Grimm will be slightly different; the Grimm Brothers themselves rewrote and padded their 1812 version in 1857. See the side-by-side comparison done by D. L. Ashliman at www.pitt.edu/~dash/frogking.html.

In making the story your own, think about your facial expressions as you say the dialogue from the three main characters. What voice and intonation will you use for each of them? If you have come up with a way of speaking for each of the characters, do the voices fit the tone of the story, and can you sustain those voices throughout the story? Will your mood be lighthearted or more solemn?

Once again—and we can't say this too many times—you need to be living the story in your head as you tell it. Visualize the well and the golden ball sinking out of sight. Listeners will first feel sorry for the princess having lost her favorite plaything. They've been there themselves. Then their allegiance will change and they'll root for the maligned frog. They may find their sympathies shifting several more times, depending on your delivery. For even the simplest story you choose to tell, you will find layers of meaning, emotion, symbolism, and wisdom that emerge every time you perform it. And each time, your knowledge and appreciation of the story will grow. If you select well, you will never grow tired of that tale. It will continue to speak to you over the years.

Do some research on the stories you choose. "The Frog-King" is discussed at length at www.surlalunefairytales.com/frogking and at www.pitt.edu/~dash/frog.html#grimm1; both sites feature the full text and variants of the story from other countries. As well, there are four sensational children's books we recommend as modern-day tie-ins. Jon Scieszka's *The Frog Prince Continued* (Viking, 1991) imagines life for the former frog and his princess after "happily ever after"; *The Prince of the Pond: Otherwise Known as De Fawg Pin* by Donna Jo Napoli, (Dutton, 1992), a middle grade chapter book, introduces the prince during the frog part of his life; and in Stephanie Calmenson's parody *The Frog Principal* (Scholastic, 2001), an elementary school principal is turned into a, well, you know. Finally, the heartless princess is particularly nasty to the poor frog in Adam Gidwitz's fairy tale–inspired novel, *In a Glass Grimmly* (Dutton, 2012).

Relearning a Story

Obviously, you are not going to all the trouble of learning a story to tell it only once—or at least, we hope you're not. However, there are some stories you'll only use once a year for special days, such as Christmas or the first day of spring. Or you may be actively engaged in storytelling activities one year, but not the next. What do you do when you want to reuse a story that has been dormant in your mind?

That's where keeping a hard copy of each story on hand comes in. If you have a copy in your "Stories Already Learned" folder, you can read it through a time or two, shine it up a bit, and you're ready to go. Revisiting a story is usually easier, especially if you learned it well initially, but you'll still need to retrieve it from where it's idling in your long-term memory. Sometimes you will be astonished to discover that when you tell the story the next time you do it even better than you did before. Somewhere, somehow, the story has jelled and truly become your own. Nevertheless, don't take a chance on your memory when dredging up an old story. Always review the tale before telling it.

Making a Story Your Own

Go back to the text of a story you learned many years before and you will probably find that you have omitted some parts and added others, tweaking your telling to fit your style and personality. You may say something in an interesting way and like your wording so much that you repeat it the next time, until it is a natural part of the story. Or you may forget something and realize it wasn't that important, so you leave it out the next time, too. This is all part of the natural evolution of your storytelling. You hone the story to make each word work, although your telling may still be slightly different every time you share it.

In Arnold Lobel's little easy-reader classic, *Mouse Tales* (HarperCollins, 1972), Papa Mouse tells one bedtime story to each of his seven children. One of them, "The Journey," is a mini-story about a young mouse who sets off in a car to visit his mother. Over the course of the story, he roller-skates, tramps, walks, and runs until he finally makes it to his mother's house. In the last line, she says, "Hello, my son. You are looking fine—and what nice new feet you have!" Delicate spot art highlights his progression, but the story works perfectly well without the pictures.

Some years ago, when Judy was teaching her storytelling course at Pratt Institute, John Peters stopped by to tell some stories. John—who retired in 2010 as the supervising librarian of the New York Public Library's Children's Center at 42nd Street after more than thirty years at various branch libraries—is a witty guy who has a way with a story. He announced that he was going to tell "The Journey," and she settled in happily to hear the familiar tale.

The story he told was so wildly different from the original that it knocked her back on her heels. Unlike Lobel's story, it was full of zooms, crashes, and wonderful noises as the mouse ventured forth. Over the years of telling it, the story had evolved, and while its genesis was there, John had made it his own. "This is the tale," he says, "that got me thinking that stories are a lot like viruses—not exactly independent living entities but capable through mysterious processes of growing, changing, spreading, and eliciting a vast range of responses from their hosts. I've been telling 'The Journey' since the early 1980s, and it still comes out a little different each time." He suggests that tellers "start slowly to give the audience time to catch the rhythm, and gradually speed up. Use zooms, screeches and other sound effects as appropriate, plus a broadly expressive hand clap or knee slap at each crash. The plotline can be extended—rocket ship, jet plane, car, motorcycle, speedboat, bicycle, skateboard, roller skates, boots, sneakers—or abridged as inclination and audience interest dictate."

The Journey

Loosely based on "The Journey" from Arnold Lobel's Mouse Tales
Retold and Reimagined by John Peters

Once there was a mouse who went to visit his mother. He started, as you would start, by closing and locking his door (*turn key*), climbing into his car (*climb in*), and driving down the road (*steer*). Being a mouse, you know, he did not drive slowly—oh, no no! He drove fast. How fast? Pretty fast! In fact, he went zooooommming down the street sooo fast that when he went around a corner—CRASH! He wrecked his car!

But Mouse was having a lucky day, and right there on the corner (*point*) was a man selling . . . motorcycles. So Mouse bought himself a motorcycle and zooooomed off. Do you think he went slowly? That's right, he went fast. Sooo fast that when he went around a corner—SMASH! He totaled that motorcycle.

BUT, Mouse was having a really lucky day, and right there on the corner was a woman selling . . . bicycles. Mouse bought himself a bicycle and zooooomed off. How fast do you think he went? How fast? That's right, he went sooo fast that when he went around a corner—CRASH! There went the bicycle.

BUT, what kind of day was Mouse having? That's right, and there on that corner was a man selling . . . skateboards. So Mouse bought himself a skateboard and went skaaaaating down the street. How fast? Oh yes—that fast, ahundredmilesanhour, until he went around a corner—and, CRASH! He destroyed that skateboard.

BUT, what kind of day was Mouse having? (*By this time, your audience is pretty much telling the story. You don't have to shout over them, just nod, keep eye contact, and supply the next line.*) Right, a lucky day, and right there on the corner was a woman selling . . . boots. So Mouse bought himself new boots and went marching down the road. Did he march slowly? You know he didn't! He marched sooo fast, that when he went around a corner—POW! His boots fell off!

It was a lucky day for Mouse, though, right? And, at that very corner, was a man selling sneakers! (*or* "Reeboks!" *or insert a favorite brand*) Mouse bought himself new sneakers, and went running down the road. Slowly? No, no! He went fast. Sooo fast that when he went skidding around a corner . . . his sneakers melted off!

Now, Mouse was having what kind of day? That's right, but there are two kinds of luck . . . and this time he had some of the bad kind, because there was nobody at that corner. So, Mouse walked on in his bare feet. Did he walk slowly? Of course not. He went fast, sooo fast that when he went screeching around a corner . . . HIS FEET FELL OFF!

Now, what kind of day was Mouse having? Riiight, and this time the good luck came back, because right on that corner was a woman selling . . . FEET! Mouse bought himself new feet, and trotted all the way to his mother's house.

When he knocked on the door, his mother came out and gave him a big hug, and a big kiss, and said, "My son! How nice to see you! And, saaaayyyy, I like your new feet!"

Use John's tale as role model in how to rethink a story when you start to tell it. Children become active participants in the narrative from the beginning, and rejoice in all of the clamor. From John's text it's easy to see how listeners can join in and fill in the many repeated phrases. Just like Mouse, you will be having a lucky day when you tell it, too, adding your own style and making the story your own.

NOTE

1. "Voice Strain in Teachers, Especially Females," *Medical News Today,* October 27, 2009; www.medicalnewstoday.com/articles/168872.php.

SOURCES FOR STORYTELLING

The Lost Donkey

Retold by Caroline Feller Bauer

A friend came to the Goha and said, "I am sorry, Goha. The donkey you lent me has run away. He is lost."

The Goha was very sad. The donkey was the only thing he owned. The next moment he was happy. He sang for joy.

The friend said, "Goha, why are you happy? Your donkey is lost."

The Goha said, "I am happy because if I had been on the donkey, I would be lost too."

Where will you find material for telling? You can lose yourself at the library, of course. There you will find both narrative and nonnarrative selections aplenty: folklore, poetry, picture books, informational books, short stories, fiction—enough for a lifetime of storytelling. The Internet is also a rich source of materials, with hundreds of classic tales in public domain.

The following sections explore some of the different types of material you may want to use, and identify some of our favorite tellable selections.

chapter 5

Folklore

If you want your children to be intelligent, read them fairy tales. If you want them to be more intelligent, read them more fairy tales.

—ALBERT EINSTEIN

WE SUGGEST STARTING YOUR STORYTELLING JOURNEY with folktales, stories loved by children through the generations. In the first half of this chapter, we will lay out and define some of the basic genres of folk literature; in the second half, we will conduct an around-the-world tour of stories, broken down by continent and/or geographic region.

What Is a Folktale?

The late Stith Thompson, a famed authority on the folktale, defined the traditional prose tale as a story "which has been handed down from generation to generation either in writing or by word of mouth." As few of us have access to oral story sources these days, we usually take our material from print. Scholars might argue that published folktales do not belong to the true tradition because they can no longer develop and change, but as storytellers, we keep the tradition alive by conveying not only the plot of the story, but also the story's spirit and style in our telling. If you want to learn more about folktales, begin with some of the scholarly studies listed at the end of this chapter. In many story collections, folklorists provide extensive documentation regarding the source of the story, the circumstances under which it was collected, what parts were deleted, or what additions were made. Some of the material may be useful when you introduce a story to your audience.

Familiar stories such as "Goldilocks and the Three Bears," "Little Red Riding Hood," and "Cinderella" are all examples of the folktale. The versions of these stories with which we are most familiar originate in three different countries: "The Three Bears" from England, "Little Red Riding Hood" from Germany, and "Cinderella" from France. All three stories exist in many versions. In fact, there are many hundreds of variants of the Cinderella story from around the world.

The formula for virtually all folktales is the same: characters are faced with a problem or obstacle that they cleverly or heroically resolve, often (though not always) leading to a happy ending. Usually folktales are devoid of long descriptive passages and concentrate almost entirely on plot. Characters are not developed to any great extent; they tend to be stereotypes of good or evil, cleverness or stupidity. The shorter folktales rely on a single theme: the triumph of good over evil or of a poor man over a rich man (which, in folktale parlance, is often the same thing). Dive into the 398.2 section of the library, especially those old dusty, musty collections, which may contain untold treasures. Here's a quick little reference guide. Snap your fingers as you recite this chant, and have your kids join in on the refrain. They'll never forget where the folk and fairy tale section of the library is.

Look for 398.2

By Judy Freeman

If you want a good story, let me tell you what to do—

LOOK FOR 398.2, LOOK FOR 398.2!

Prince or princess in hot water, trouble with a witch's brew—

LOOK FOR 398.2, LOOK FOR 398.2!

Fierce and fire-breathing dragons, shiny scales of green and blue—

LOOK FOR 398.2, LOOK FOR 398.2!

Ogres, leprechauns, and goblins all are waiting just for you—

LOOK FOR 398.2, LOOK FOR 398.2!

Find a tale from every country, from Australia to Peru—

LOOK FOR 398.2, LOOK FOR 398.2!

That's all you've got to do!

It is useful to be aware of the major types of folktales. Identification of common themes can help you create thematic programs and broaden your repertoire to include particular categories of tales or motifs that appeal to you or your audiences. There are many subsets of folk and fairy tales, and one story can often fit into several categories.

What follows is a breakdown of popular story types, each type accompanied by an annotated booklist of treasured titles, plus a careful selection of Internet resources. Because many stories can be told to a wide range of ages, we decided to give you some loose audience guidelines for the books we suggest. In the end, of course, it's up to you to pick the stories you love and match them with the listeners who will best appreciate them.

P: Primary (preschool through grade 3; toddlers to age 8)
I: Intermediate (grade 3 through 6; ages 8 to 11)
A: Advanced (grade 6 and up; ages 11 to 111)

Beast Tales

Many folktales deal with animals that are really humans in disguise, exhibiting recognizable human faults. These are often called "beast tales." They differ from animal fables in that fables exist to impart a moral, a lesson that we less-than-perfect humans can take to heart. Beast tales feature animals as the main characters; they can act alone or with humans. The stories are often comical, but there are exceptions, as in the case of "Little Red Riding Hood," which ends badly for the wolf. (The story has evolved since Charles Perrault's version, first printed in 1697, where the wolf eats the girl, and that's it for her. That version was told as a warning to young women not to fool around with Wolves, a euphemism for young men, but that version is certainly not one you need to tell to young children. . . .) The simpler tales, such as "The Three Little Pigs" and "The Three Billy Goats Gruff," are easily learned and appropriate for small children, but don't assume your audience is familiar with even these most basic stories. Do you know the parts in "The Three Little Pigs" about the apple tree and the butter churn? If not, then you don't know the complete version either. You'll find Paul Galdone's picture-book rendition (Houghton Mifflin Harcourt, c1974 p2011) satisfying and symmetrical, unlike the far more inauthentic Disney movie version (though who doesn't love the song "Who's Afraid of the Big Bad Wolf?"). Of course, in the original version the first two pigs get eaten, but really, it's partly their own fault for building such flimsy dwellings.

Beast or animal stories often employ the repetition of refrains and/or events, in what we call repetitive or cumulative tales. When an animal gets both ravenously hungry and greedy and gobbles up everyone or thing in sight, we call the ensuing tale a swallowing story. Another type of beast tale is the trickster tale, which often features animals. There are many subsets of folk and fairy tales, and one story can often fit into several categories.

Look at the many Anansi the Spider stories from Africa and the Caribbean, for one example. Sometimes he is a spider, which would make those stories beast tales, but he can also be a human man. He can be wise and profound, as in Gail E. Haley's *A Story, a Story* (Aladdin, 1970), where he performs three impossible tasks for the Sky God and spreads the world's first stories. He can also be foolish, a noodlehead, outwitted by others, as in *Anansi Goes Fishing* (Holiday House, 1992) by Eric A. Kimmel. Sometimes his greedy machinations lead to the creation of something new, as in the Harold Courlander pourquoi (how-and-why) tale you'll find on page 193, "Two Feasts for Anansi," where we discover why spiders have such skinny waists. However, because he is most often wily, conniving, and cunning, we decided to list the stories about him under "Trickster Tales" on page 132. Find a few more stories to tell in chapter 8 under "Anansi" on page 280.

REPETITIVE AND CUMULATIVE TALES

These formula tales, sometimes called "chain tales" or "circular stories," are the easiest to learn because they have a minimal plot that unfolds in a set sequence and often have a repetitive, rhythmic refrain. They are particularly popular with young children, who love saying the same thing over and over. You will be amazed at how well listeners recall the order in which the actions occur, and how quickly they catch on to the refrain. When your language arts curriculum calls for a lesson on cause and effect, tell one of these tales to exemplify the concept.

Typical of the repetitive story is the foolish Henny Penny who meets Cocky Locky, Ducky Daddles, Goosey Loosey, Turkey Lurkey, and Foxy Woxy on the way to tell the king that the sky is falling. In "The Gingerbread Boy," the proud, newly baked gingerbread hero rushes away from his gathering pursuers and taunts, "Run! Run! As fast as you can! You can't catch me, I'm the Gingerbread Man!"

Joseph Jacobs's English folktale "The Cat and the Mouse" delights youngsters with its rhythmic refrain. Tell this charming English cumulative/circular tale along with "The Old Woman and Her Pig" (page 100) for a storytime about nice cats and not-so-nice cats. This little yarn is easy to learn and fun to act out, thanks to all the repetitions. It will also remind you of Nonny Hogrogian's Caldecott winner, *One Fine Day*, an Armenian folktale about a fox whose tail is cut off by an old woman who refuses to sew it back until he replaces the milk he has taken from her.

Let's have a look.

The Cat and the Mouse

From Popular Rhymes and Nursery *Tales:* A Sequel to the Nursery Rhymes of England *by James Orchard Halliwell-Phillipps (London: John Russell Smith, 1849)*

The cat and the mouse
Played in the malt-house.
The cat bit the mouse's tail off.
"Pray, puss, give me my tail," begged the mouse.

"No," said the cat, "I'll not give you your tail, till you go to the cow, and fetch me some milk."

First she leapt, and then she ran,
Till she came to the cow, and thus began:

"Pray, Cow, give me milk, that I may give Cat milk, that Cat may give me my own tail again."

"No," said the cow, "I will give you no milk, till you go to the farmer and get me some hay."

First she leapt, and then she ran,
Till she came to the farmer, and thus began:

"Pray, Farmer, give me hay, that I may give Cow hay, that Cow may give me milk, that I may give Cat milk, that Cat may give me my own tail again."

"No," says the farmer, "I'll give you no hay, till you go to the butcher and fetch me some meat."

First she leapt, and then she ran,
Till she came to the butcher, and thus began:

"Pray, Butcher, give me meat, that I may give Farmer meat, that Farmer may give me hay, that I may give Cow hay, that Cow may give me milk, that I may give Cat milk, that cat may give me my own tail again."

"No," says the butcher, "I'll give you no meat, till you go the baker and fetch me some bread."

First she leapt, and then she ran,

Till she came to the baker, and thus began:

"Pray, Baker, give me bread, that I may give Butcher bread, that Butcher may give me meat, that I may give Farmer meat, that Farmer may give me hay, that I may give Cow hay, that Cow may give me milk, that I may give Cat milk, that Cat may give me my own tail again."

"Yes," says the baker, I'll give you some bread,

"But if you eat my meal, I'll cut off your head."

Then the baker gave Mouse bread, and Mouse gave Butcher bread, and Butcher gave Mouse meat, and Mouse gave Farmer meat, and Farmer gave Mouse hay, and Mouse gave Cow hay, and Cow gave Mouse milk, and Mouse gave Cat milk, and Cat gave Mouse her own tail again!

And so she leapt, and so she ran,

For the mouse had her own tail again.

SWALLOWING STORIES

Another type of tale that children find endlessly delicious is the swallowing story, a subset of repetitive and cumulative tales, in which a greedy person or animal eats everything and/or everyone in sight. Mirra Ginsburg's picture book *Clay Boy*; "Sody Saleratus" from Richard Chase's *Grandfather Tales* (Houghton Mifflin, 1948); and "Hoimie the Woim," from Judy Freeman's *Once Upon a Time* (Libraries Unlimited, 2007) are good examples, as is Simms Taback's riotous picture book *There Was an Old Lady Who Swallowed a Fly,* based on the old song. If you can locate a copy, Jack Kent's picture book of a Danish folktale, *The Fat Cat,* features an ever-expanding yellow cat that devours with relish a number of objects, animals, and people until a crafty woodcutter puts an end to the greedy thing. Margaret Read MacDonald retold her own version in *The Fat Cat: A Danish Folktale.*

Here's a variant from India that will make children crave five hundred little cakes. This cumulative tale would work well with puppets for each of the creatures the cat eats, and with audience participation for the menacingly gleeful refrain of "slip! slop! gobble!" If you want to share a picture-book version of the story, read Meilo So's dapper and spirited *Gobble, Gobble, Slip, Slop: A Tale of a Very Greedy Cat.*

The Cat and the Parrot

Retold by Sara Cone Bryant in Best Stories to Tell to Children *(Houghton Mifflin, 1912)*

Once there was a cat, and a parrot. And they had agreed to ask each other to dinner, turn and turn about: first the cat should ask the parrot, then the parrot should invite the cat, and so on. It was the cat's turn first.

Now the cat was very mean. He provided nothing at all for dinner except a pint of milk, a little slice of fish, and a biscuit. The parrot was too polite to complain, but he did not have a very good time.

When it was his turn to invite the cat, he cooked a fine dinner. He had a roast of meat, a pot of tea, a basket of fruit, and, best of all, he baked a whole clothes-basketful of little cakes!—little, brown, crispy, spicy cakes! Oh, I should say as many as five hundred. And he put four hundred and ninety-eight of the cakes before the cat, keeping only two for himself. Well, the cat ate the roast, and drank the tea, and sucked the fruit, and then he began on the pile of cakes. He ate all the four hundred and ninety-eight cakes, and then he looked round and said:

"I'm hungry; haven't you anything to eat?"

"Why," said the parrot, "here are my two cakes, if you want them."

The cat ate up the two cakes, and then he licked his chops and said, "I am beginning to get an appetite; have you anything to eat?"

"Well, really," said the parrot, who was now rather angry, "I don't see anything more, unless you wish to eat me!" He thought the cat would be ashamed when he heard that. But the cat just looked at him, licked his chops again, and—slip! slop! gobble!—down his throat went the parrot!

Then the cat started down the street. An old woman was standing nearby, and she had seen the whole thing. She was shocked that the cat should eat his friend. "Why, Cat!" she said. "How dreadful of you to eat your friend the parrot!"

"Parrot, indeed!" said the cat. "What's a parrot to me? I've a great mind to eat you, too." And, before you could say "Jack Robinson"—slip! slop! gobble!—down went the old woman!

Then the cat started down the road again, walking like this, because he felt so fine. Pretty soon he met a man driving a donkey. The man was beating the donkey, to hurry him up, and when he saw the cat he said, "Get out of my way, Cat; I'm in a hurry and my donkey might tread on you."

"Donkey, indeed!" said the cat. "Much I care for a donkey! I have eaten five hundred cakes, I've eaten my friend the parrot, I've eaten an old woman. What's to hinder my eating a miserable man and a donkey?"

And—slip! slop! gobble!—down went the old man and the donkey.

Then the cat walked on down the road, jauntily, like this. After a little while, he met a procession, coming that way. The king was at the head, walking proudly with his newly married bride, and behind him were his soldiers, marching, and behind them were ever and ever so many elephants, walking two by two. The king felt very kind to everybody, because he had just been married, and he said to the cat, "Get out of my way, Pussycat, get out of my way. My elephants might hurt you."

"Hurt me!" said the cat, shaking his fat sides. "Ho, ho! I've eaten five hundred cakes, I've eaten my friend the parrot, I've eaten an old woman, I've eaten a man and a donkey; what's to hinder my eating a beggarly king?"

And slip! slop! gobble! down went the king; down went the queen; down went the soldiers—and down went all the elephants!

Then the cat went on, more slowly; he had really had enough to eat, now. But a little farther on he met two land crabs, scuttling along in the dust. "Get out of our way, Pussycat," they squeaked.

"Ho, ho, ho!" cried the cat in a terrible voice. "I've eaten five hundred cakes, I've eaten my friend the parrot, I've eaten an old woman, a man with a donkey, a king, a queen, his men-at-arms, and all his elephants; and now I'll eat you too."

And slip! slop! gobble!—down went the two land crabs.

When the land crabs got down inside, they began to look around. It was very dark, but they could see the poor king sitting in a corner with his bride on his arm; she had fainted. Near them were the men-at-arms, treading on one another's toes, and the elephants still trying to form in twos, but they couldn't because there was not room. In the opposite corner sat the old woman, and near her stood the man and his donkey. But in the other corner was a great pile of cakes, and by them perched the parrot, his feathers all drooping.

"Let's get to work!" said the land crabs. And *snip, snap,* they began to make a little hole in the side, with their sharp claws. *Snip, snap, snip, snap,* till it was big enough to get through. Then out they scuttled.

Then out walked the king, carrying his bride; out marched the men-at-arms; out tramped the elephants, two by two; out came the old man, beating his donkey; out walked the old woman, scolding the cat; and last of all, out hopped the parrot, holding a cake in each claw. (You remember, two cakes were all he wanted?)

But the poor cat had to spend the whole day sewing up the hole in his coat!

BOOKLIST: BEAST TALES, INCLUDING CUMULATIVE AND REPETITIVE TALES AND SWALLOWING STORIES

Aardema, Verna. *Bringing the Rain to Kapiti Plain.* *Illus. by Beatriz Vidal. Dial, 1981.* This African cumulative tale, in rhyming "This Is the House That Jack Built" style, explains how Ki-Pat shot an arrow into the clouds to end the drought. (P)

Aardema, Verna. *Traveling to Tondo: A Tale of the Nkundo of Zaire.* *Illus. by Will Hillenbrand. Knopf, 1991.* Bowane the civet cat invites his friends—the pigeon, snake, and tortoise—to travel with him to meet his bride-to-be. (P)

Ada, Alma Flor. *The Rooster Who Went to His Uncle's Wedding: A Latin American Folktale.* *Illus. by Kathleen Kuchera. Putnam, 1993.* "What to do? Peck or not peck?" the hungry rooster ponders as he contemplates a perfect kernel of corn lying in a mud puddle. Also see Lucia M. Gonzalez's version below, *The Bossy Gallito.* (P)

Asbjørnsen, P. C., and J. E. Moe. *The Three Billy Goats Gruff.* *Illus. by Marcia Brown. Harcourt, 1957.* The troll is pretty scary in this authentic version of the Norwegian folktale. (P)

Aylesworth, Jim. *Aunt Pitty Patty's Piggy.* *Illus. by Barbara McClintock. Scholastic, 1999.* Aunt Pitty Patty's niece tries to enlist everyone and everything she meets to make stubborn Piggy enter the gate in this version of "The Old Woman and Her Pig." (P)

Aylesworth, Jim. *The Gingerbread Man.* *Illus. by Barbara McClintock. Scholastic, 1998.* Quaint, old-fashioned pen-and-ink-and-watercolor illustrations are just right for this charming chase tale. (P)

Aylesworth, Jim. *The Mitten.* *Illus. by Barbara McClintock. Scholastic, 2009.* A little boy loses his hand-knitted red mitten in the snow, but one by one, the animals find it and crawl inside, to stay warm. (P)

Aylesworth, Jim. *The Tale of Tricky Fox: A New England Trickster Tale.* *Illus. by Barbara McClintock. Scholastic, 2001.* Tricky Fox boasts that he can fool a human into putting a fat pig into his sack. (P)

Brett, Jan. *Goldilocks and the Three Bears.* *Illus. by the author. Putnam, 1987.* This classic tale is richly detailed, with bear-filled borders and ornaments. (P)

Brett, Jan. *The Mitten: A Ukrainian Folktale.* *Illus. by the author. Putnam, 1989.* Compare this ornate version of the overstuffed mitten tale with Jim Aylesworth's version, above, and Alvin Tresselt's *The Mitten: An Old Ukrainian Folktale* (illus. by Yaroslava; Lothrop, 1964). (P)

Buehner, Caralyn, and Mark Buehner. *Goldilocks and the Three Bears.* *Illus. by Mark Buehner. Dial, 2007.* This Goldilocks totes a jump rope and wears cowboy boots. (P)

Dee, Ruby. *Two Ways to Count to Ten: A Liberian Folktale.* *Illus. by Susan Meddaugh. Holt, 1988.* "I will be king. I can do this thing!" each animal says—but only one can win. (P, I)

Divakaruni, Chitra Banerjee. *Grandma and the Great Gourd: A Bengali Folktale.* *Roaring Brook, 2013.* On her way to visit her daughter, Grandma encounters a hungry fox, a black bear, and a tiger, all of whom want to eat her. Compare this version with Jessica Souhami's *No Dinner! The Story of the Old Woman and the Pumpkin*, below.

Egielski, Richard. *The Gingerbread Boy.* *Illus. by the author. HarperCollins, 1997.* This version is set in New York City's Central Park. (P)

Emberley, Rebecca, and Ed Emberley. *Chicken Little.* *Illus. by Rebecca Emberley and Ed Emberley. Roaring Brook, 2009.* Not the "brightest chicken in the coop," Chicken Little is hit on the noggin with an acorn and rushes off, crying, "The sky is falling! We must run for our lives!" (P)

Emberley, Rebecca, and Ed Emberley. *The Red Hen.* *Illus. by Rebecca Emberley and Ed Emberley. Roaring Brook, 2010.* No one will help Red Hen prepare her new recipe for a "Simply Splendid Cake." (P)

Galdone, Paul. *The Gingerbread Boy.* *Illus. by the author. Clarion, 1975.* A classic version of a familiar tale. (P)

Galdone, Paul. *Henny Penny.* *Illus. by the author. Clarion, 1968.* "The sky is falling!" cries the simple hen. (P)

Galdone, Paul. *The Little Red Hen.* *Illus. by the author. Clarion, 1973.* No one wants to help Hen with the bread making until it's time to eat it. (P)

Galdone, Paul. *The Three Bears.* *Illus. by the author. Clarion, 1972.* Classic version of the classic beast tale, plus Goldilocks. (P)

Galdone, Paul. *The Three Billy Goats Gruff.* *Illus. by the author. Clarion, 1973.* Three goats encounter a mean troll and survive. (P)

Galdone, Paul. *The Three Little Pigs.* *Illus. by the author. Clarion, 1979.* A classic version. (P)

Ginsburg, Mirra. *Clay Boy: Adapted from a Russian Folk Tale.* *Illus. by Jos. A. Smith. Greenwillow, 1997.* The insatiable clay boy swallows everyone in the village. (P)

Gonzalez, Lucia M. *The Bossy Gallito: A Traditional Cuban Folktale.* *Illus. by Lulu Delacre. Scholastic, 1994.* On his way to his uncle's wedding, a bossy little rooster tries to make the grass, a goat, a stick, fire, water, and the sun clean his dirty beak. Also see Alma Flor Ada's similar *The Rooster Who Went to His Uncle's Wedding,* above.

Hogrogian, Nonny. *One Fine Day.* *Illus. by the author. Macmillan, 1971.* A fox begs an old woman to sew his tail back, but before she will do it, he needs to find her some milk. (P)

Kimmel, Eric A. *The Gingerbread Man.* *Illus. by Megan Lloyd. Holiday House, 1993.* "I'll run and run as fast as I can. You can't catch me. I'm the gingerbread man!" (P)

MacDonald, Margaret Read. *The Fat Cat: A Danish Folktale.* *Illus. by Julie Paschkis. August House Little Folk, 2001.* A hungry cat swallows his friend, the mouse, and everyone else who dares to call him fat. Compare with Meilo So's *Gobble, Gobble, Slip, Slop,* below.

MacDonald, Margaret Read. *The Old Woman and Her Pig.* *Illus. by John Kanzler. HarperCollins, 2007.* An old woman can't get her new pig to cross the bridge to get home. For the original text of this English cumulative tale, see page 100 in this book. Compare it with Jim Aylesworth's New England–based version, *Aunt Pitty Patty's Piggy,* above.

Marshall, James. *Goldilocks and the Three Bears.* *Illus. by the author. Dial, 1988.* "They must have kitties," Goldilocks exclaims, upon finding fur in the bears' house. (P)

Marshall, James. *The Three Little Pigs.* *Illus. by the author. Dial, 1989.* Not fractured, exactly, but a very funny version. (P)

McGovern, Ann. *Too Much Noise.* *Illus. by Simms Taback. Houghton Mifflin, 1967.* A man can't sleep until he brings all his animals into the house. (P)

Moser, Barry. *The Three Little Pigs.* *Illus. by the author. Little, Brown, 2001.* This is the whole story, complete with apple-tree and butter-churn scenes. (P)

So, Meilo. *Gobble, Gobble, Slip, Slop: A Tale of a Very Greedy Cat.* *Illus. by the author. Knopf, 2004.* In a folktale from India, a ravenous cat swallows his friend, the parrot—and a whole host of other folks, too. Compare with Margaret Read MacDonald's *The Fat Cat,* above. (P)

Souhami, Jessica. *No Dinner! The Story of the Old Woman and the Pumpkin.* *Illus. by the author. Frances Lincoln, 2012, c2000.* In a folktale from India, an old woman, on her way through the forest to visit her granddaughter, tricks a wolf, a tiger, and a bear into not eating her. Compare this with *Grandma and the Great Gourd* by Chitra Banerjee Divakaruni (Roaring Book Press, 2013). (P)

Spirin, Gennady. *Goldilocks and the Three Bears.* *Illus. by the author. Marshall Cavendish, 2009.* Sumptuous watercolor and colored-pencil illustrations show the bears and that little blond scamp all clad in flowing Renaissance clothing. (P)

Taback, Simms. *There Was an Old Lady Who Swallowed a Fly.* *Illus. by the author. Viking, 1997.* A riotous picture-book version of a ubiquitous swallowing song. (P)

Vamos, Samantha R. *The Cazuela That the Farm Maiden Stirred.* *Illus. by Rafael López. Charlesbridge, 2011.* In this Hispanic cumulative story, written in the style of "This Is the House That Jack Built," a young woman makes *arroz con leche* (rice pudding), with ingredients gathered by the *cabra* (goat), the *vaca* (cow), and the *gallina* (chicken). (P)

Zemach, Margot. *The Three Little Pigs: An Old Story.* *Illus. by the author. Farrar, 1988.* Wonderful Zemach illustrations elevate this classic tale. (P)

WEBSITE

Folklore and Mythology Electronic Texts. *www.pitt.edu/~dash/folktexts.html* This site features a wealth of folk- and fairy-tale texts, ed. and/or trans. by D. L. Ashliman of the University of Pittsburgh, listed alphabetically by subject, including "The Gingerbread Boy" and other "Runaway Pancake" stories at www.pitt.edu/~dash/type2025.html and nine variants of "The Three Little Pigs" at www.pitt.edu/~dash/type0124.html.

Trickster Tales

In your reading you will find many tales that revolve around an animal or human character who seems to be wise and foolish at the same time, and who tries to use his cleverness to trick his adversaries. These bad actors are often unrepentant and fail to learn their lessons.

We love these tricksters in spite of (and maybe because of) their irresponsible acts. They are so high spirited or conniving they make us laugh. They are almost always male, though some notable exceptions can be found in Robert D. San Souci's *Sister Tricksters.* Tricksters frequently represent the underdogs in society, and we root for them to succeed against the fat cats, the bigwigs, and the powerful.

Tricksters can be found around the globe. We've already met the German folk character Tyll Ulenspiegel in the story "Tyll Paints the Duke's Portrait," on page 104. Baron Munchausen, another German tall-tale character, inevitably emerges triumphant from the conflicts in his humorous adventures, as does Hershel of Ostropol, from the Jewish literature tradition. The popular Turkish folk character, Nasreddin Hodja (also spelled Hoca, and called

Goha in Egypt), is a combination fool, prophet, wise man, and trickster, who avenges himself with ingenious trickery. There's Pedro Urdemales in South American folklore, and in Haitian folklore, Uncle Bouqui or Bouki, who is often bested by his friend Ti Malice.

In Ghana and other parts of West Africa, you will find Kwaku Anansi, also called Anansi the Spider—sometimes human, sometimes a spider—who never learns his lessons. Stories about him migrated from Africa with slaves brought to Jamaica and the Caribbean, where Anansi is known as Ananse, Anancy, and even Aunt Nancy, and to the Americas, as did the Brer Rabbit stories. Interestingly, the Native American trickster, Iktomi, of the Lakota tribes, can also appear as a man or a spider.

In African American folklore, the trickster may be small, weak, oppressed, and belittled. Thanks to his quick wit and clever tongue, however, he always gets the better of foolish and greedy authority figures. High John, the smartest slave on the plantation, ever outsmarts Old Master. Steve Sanfield, a popular professional storyteller, collected and retold sixteen of these stories in *The Adventures of High John the Conqueror*. Then there's Brer Rabbit who outsmarts Brers Bear, Fox, and Wolf in the Uncle Remus stories, retold by Joel Chandler Harris (1845–1908). Most of us have heard a version of Brer Rabbit and the tar-baby story. Virginia Hamilton retold a delightful variant of this tale from the Sea Islands of South Carolina in her humorous picture book *Bruh Rabbit and the Tar Baby Girl.*

As a trickster, Hare or Rabbit hails from many countries, including Gerald McDermott's *Zomo the Rabbit: A Trickster Tale from West Africa.* You'll see rabbits stirring up trouble in Native American folklore, as depicted in Gretchen Will Mayo's *Big Trouble for Tricky Rabbit!* Compère Lapin is a trickster rabbit from Cajun and Creole traditions, as you'll find in the collection *Why Lapin's Ears Are Long, and Other Tales from the Louisiana Bayou* by Sharon Arms Doucet. Those trickster rabbits evolved into the cartoon persona of the great Bugs Bunny.

Sometimes, you'll read one tale and say, "Hey, I know I read another story just like that!" You can compare and contrast these variants with your audience. In *The Tale of Rabbit and Coyote* from Mexico, retold by Tony Johnston, Rabbit talks Coyote into holding back a rock to keep it from crushing the world. In *Love and Roast Chicken: A Trickster Tale from the Andes Mountains* by Barbara Knutson, Cuy the guinea pig does the same thing to Tió Antonio, the hungry but gullible fox. Through picture books, you can meet other trickster animals from all over the world, including Monkey in Gerald McDermott's *Monkey: A Trickster Tale from India,* who tricks Crocodile three times.

In many Native American legends, Coyote and Raven may be tricksters, but they are also credited with creating the world. Other mythological gods as tricksters include the Greek god Hermes, known as Mercury in Roman myths; Loki in Norse mythology; and Maui from Hawaii and New Zealand, who first brought fire to the humans. Look up *trickster* on Wikipedia and you'll see links to more than a hundred diverse characters and cultures, from Azeban of the Abenaki Indians to Reynard the Fox from France. Everyone loves a trickster.

Speaking of foxes, try this Finnish folktale where Bear is no match for Fox, who knows just how to get him talking.

The Bear Says North

A Story from Finland, Retold by Caroline Feller Bauer

Bear was quite pleased with himself. He had caught a pheasant all by himself. He was anxious to show it off to admiring fans. He stood in the middle of the forest path, gently holding the pheasant between his teeth.

The first animal to happen by was Fox. Fox saw that Bear was holding a nice plump pheasant. He wondered how he could trick Bear.

Bear paced back and forth on the forest path, hoping that Fox would say something admiring. Instead, Fox quietly said, "Hello, Bear. How are you today?"

Of course Bear couldn't talk with a pheasant in his mouth, so he just mumbled through his teeth: "Mmmmm."

"I couldn't understand you, Bear. How is the hunting today?"

Bear couldn't talk and felt mighty frustrated that Fox didn't mention the pheasant in his mouth that was beginning to feel uncomfortable. "Mmmmm," mumbled Bear.

Fox continued to ignore Bear's prize and asked, "Please tell me, which way is the wind blowing?" Bear couldn't answer without opening his mouth and mumbled and grunted once again: "Mmmmmm."

"I really would like to know, Bear, which way is the wind blowing?" Fox insisted. "It's blowing from the south? Are you sure? It doesn't feel like a southern breeze. Perhaps I misunderstood you. Which way did you say the wind was blowing?"

Bear was furious. Why didn't fox say anything about his pheasant? And why did he want to know which way the wind was blowing? Without thinking, Bear opened his mouth and said, "North."

The pheasant flew away. "Oh," wailed Bear. "I've lost the bird. You made me open my mouth!" Bear raged at Fox.

"I didn't do anything," said Fox. "I just asked you which way the wind was blowing."

"You can't say 'north' without opening your mouth." Bear cried.

"If it had been me, I wouldn't have said 'north.'"

"What would you have said?" asked the disappointed Bear.

Fox opened his mouth just enough to be able to say, "East."

BOOKLIST: TRICKSTER TALES

Aardema, Verna. *Borreguita and the Coyote.* *Illus. by Petra Mathers. Knopf, 1991.* A little lamb gets the best of Coyote. (P, I)

Arkhurst, Joyce Cooper. *The Adventures of Spider: West African Folktales.* *Illus. by Jerry Pinkney. Little, Brown, 1964.* Six delightful trickster tales from Liberia and Ghana; Caldecott illustrator Jerry Pinkney's first children's book! (P, I, A)

Courlander, Harold. *The Piece of Fire and Other Haitian Tales.* *Illus. by Beth Krush and Joe Krush.* Harcourt, 1964. Includes plenty of jocular tales about the Haitian trickster Bouki. (I, A)

DeSpain, Pleasant. *Tales of Tricksters.* *Illus. by Don Bell. August House, 2001.* Compact volume of nine brief, easy-to-learn, funny folktales from around the world. (P, I, A)

Doucet, Sharon Arms. *Why Lapin's Ears Are Long and Other Tales from the Louisiana Bayou.* *Illus. by David Catrow. Orchard, 1997.* These three Creole and Cajun trickster tales about Compère Lapin (Brother Rabbit) will keep kids laughing. The companion book is *Lapin Plays Possum: Trickster Tales from the Louisiana Bayou* (Farrar, 2002). (P, I)

Goble, Paul. *Iktomi and the Boulder: A Plains Indian Story.* *Illus. by the author. Orchard, 1988.* A humorous Native American trickster/pourquoi tale explains why bats have flat noses. (P, I)

Hamilton, Virginia. *Bruh Rabbit and the Tar Baby Girl.* *Illus. by James E. Ransome. Blue Sky/Scholastic, 2003.* "Don't throw me in the briar bush," Bruh Rabbit begs in this variant of the classic African American trickster tale. Another version is "Lapin Tangles with Tee Tar Bébé" in *Lapin Plays Possum: Trickster Tales from the Louisiana Bayou,* adapted by Sharon Doucet (Farrar, 2002). (P, I)

Janish, Heinz. *The Fantastic Adventures of Baron Munchausen: Traditional and Newly Discovered Tales of Karl Friedrich Hieronymus von Munchausen.* *Tr. by Belinda*

Cooper. Illus. by Aljoscha Blau. Enchanted Lion, 2010. Eleven tall tales about the German adventurer. (I, A)

Jaquith, Priscilla. *Bo Rabbit Smart for True: Folktales from the Gullah.* *Illus. by Ed Young. Philomel, 1981.* Four African-based animal trickster tales from the Sea Islands of Georgia and South Carolina. (P, I)

Kimmel, Eric A. *The Adventures of Hershel of Ostropol.* *Illus. by Trina Schart Hyman. Holiday House, 1995.* In a collection of ten hilarious tales, meet Hershel, a legendary Jewish trickster and folk hero who actually lived in Ukraine in the early nineteenth century. (I, A)

Kimmel, Eric A. *Anansi and the Moss-Covered Rock.* *Illus. by Janet Stevens. Holiday House, 1988.* The trickster spider makes off with everyone's food. Follow up with other titles in this comical series of picture books, including *Anansi and the Magic Stick* (2001), *Anansi and the Talking Melon* (1994), and *Anansi Goes Fishing* (1992). (P, I)

Knutson, Barbara. *Love and Roast Chicken: A Trickster Tale from the Andes Mountains.* *Illus. by the author. Carolrhoda, 2004.* Cuy the guinea pig tricks Tió Antonio, the hungry but gullible fox. (P)

Lester, Julius. *Uncle Remus: The Complete Tales.* *Illus. by Jerry Pinkney. Dial, 1999.* A compilation of all four of Lester's folksy retellings of Joel Chandler Harris's Brer Rabbit tales, traditional African American trickster tales from the American South. (I, A)

Matthews, John, and Caitlin Matthews. *Trick of the Tale: A Collection of Trickster Tales.* *Illus. by Tomislav Tomic. Candlewick, 2008.* Twenty animal-trickster tales span the globe from Asia to Africa, the Americas, and Europe. (P, I, A)

Mayo, Gretchen Will. *Big Trouble for Tricky Rabbit!* *Illus. by the author. Walker, 1994.* Five easy-to-read, cheerful stories in the Native American Trickster Tales series that includes *Here Comes Tricky Rabbit!* (1994), *Meet Tricky Coyote!* (1993), and *That Tricky Coyote!* (1993). (P, I)

McDermott, Gerald. *Coyote: A Trickster Tale from the American Southwest.* *Illus. by the author. Harcourt, 1994.* In a comical Zuni legend, trickster Coyote attempts to fly with the crows. (P, I)

McDermott, Gerald. *Monkey: A Trickster Tale from India.* *Illus. by the author. Houghton Mifflin Harcourt, 2011.* Monkey climbs aboard Crocodile's back to get to the mangoes on an island in the river. (P)

McDermott, Gerald. *Zomo the Rabbit: A Trickster Tale from West Africa.* *Illus. by the author. Harcourt, 1992.* In order to gain wisdom, Zomo must complete three impossible and dangerous tasks. (P, I)

Sanfield, Steve. *The Adventures of High John the Conqueror.* *Illus. by John Ward. Orchard, 1989.* Sixteen trickster tales based on the legendary antics of an African American folk hero from the days of slavery. (A)

San Souci, Robert D. *Sister Tricksters: Rollicking Tales of Clever Females.* *Illus. by Daniel San Souci. August House, 2006.* Meet Molly Hare, Miz Duck, Miz Grasshopper, and Miz Goose in eight tales from down South. (P, I, A)

Sherlock, Philip M. *Anansi, the Spider Man: Jamaican Folk Tales.* *Illus. by Marcia Brown. Crowell, 1954.* There are fifteen Anansi stories in this classic and appealing collection. (A, I)

Sherman, Josepha. *Trickster Tales: Forty Folk Stories from Around the World.* *Illus. by David Boston. August House, 1996.* Wide-ranging collection including Anansi, Tyl Eulenspiegel, Raven, and Coyote—but refreshingly, most of the tricksters featured are far less ubiquitous. (I, A)

Stevens, Janet. *Tops & Bottoms.* *Illus. by the author. Harcourt, 1995.* Hare offers to plant and harvest crops for Bear and split the veggies, which *seems* like a good idea . . . . (P, I)

Walker, Barbara K. *A Treasury of Turkish Folktales for Children.* *Linnet Books, 1988.* Quirky humor runs through these thirty-four fairy tales and tales of the foolish wise man, Nasreddin Hoca. (I, A)

WEBSITES: TRICKSTER TALES

American Folklore: A-Z Story Index *www.americanfolklore.net*
This helpful site from S. E. Schlosser has a link to retellings of more than a dozen American trickster tales (http://americanfolklore.net/folklore/tricksters). There's also a section on obtaining permissions to use them.

EDSITEment! The Best of the Humanities on the Web *http://edsitement.neh.gov*
An educational site run by the National Endowment for the Humanities, the Verizon Foundation, and the National Trust for the Humanities features an extensive lesson plan, "Aesop and Ananse: Animal Fables and Trickster Tales."

Folklore and Mythology Electronic Texts *www.pitt.edu/~dash/folktexts.html*
The site features a wealth of folk- and fairy-tale texts edited and/or translated by D. L. Ashliman, listed alphabetically by subject, including twenty-five Hodja stories at www.pitt.edu/~dash/hodja.html, with information about the trickster/fool/wise man, and a host of spellings of his name. It also includes "Playing Dead," six tales of tricky foxes from a variety of countries, at www.pitt.edu/~dash/type0001.html.

Drolls and Humorous Stories (Sillies, Fools, and Noodleheads)

Stories that make your audience laugh are fun to tell. If your audience laughs, you know right away the story has been well received. Drolls rely on ridiculous situations or clueless characters to create their humor. Some fools are tricksters who are not as smart as they think they are and who are outfoxed on a regular basis. Some fools are smarter than they look and end up triumphant. Still others are irredeemably foolish but often triumph anyway. In many stories, the youngest of three brothers, considered by his family to be hopelessly dim, is the one who defeats the ogre, wins the princess, or ends up wealthy. Other characters are so silly that we can't help but laugh at their witless ways. These witless characters are sometimes called "noodleheads," "numbskulls," or "simpletons."

In Puerto Rico, you'll find stories about Juan Bobo; in South America, there's Pedro Urdemales; in England, there's Foolish Jack; in India, Mogul Emperor Akbar; and in Turkey, Nasreddin Hodja, a learned man who can be a fool or a wise man in disguise. In Jewish folklore the mythical town of Chelm is populated entirely by fools. (Pronounce the *Ch* of *Chelm* gutterly, at the back of your throat.)

Nobel Prize–winning author Isaac Bashevis Singer often wrote about Jewish life in Poland where he grew up, and his two story collections for children—*When Shlemiel Went to Warsaw & Other Stories* and the Newbery Honor winner *Zlateh the Goat and Other Stories*—are filled with Chelm tales and other treasures for the storyteller. Judy's favorite, from *Zlateh the Goat*, has always been "The Snow in Chelm," where the silvery snow that falls on Hanukkah night shimmers like pearls and diamonds on the ground. To preserve the treasure that has fallen from the sky, the seven Elders, the village's oldest and greatest fools, come up with a brilliant plan. First they worry that a messenger, if sent to each house to warn people not to go outside until the treasure has been gathered, will himself trample the snow. With an unerring sense of unreason, they arrange for Gimpel the errand boy to stand on a table, carried by four others, so his feet will not trample the snow.

Many years ago, while examining a map of Poland to locate the city of Lodz, near the village where her husband's family lived before World War II, Judy found a city called Chelm. She asked her father-in-law, Yankiv Feldman, if the fools of Chelm stories were based on that place. He laughed and said, "Chelm is a fictional town of fools. But when I lived in Poland, this is what would happen when you met someone from the real town of Chelm.

You would say, innocently, 'So where are you from?' and the person would reply, defensively, 'Well, you're not so smart, either!' And then you'd realize that person was from Chelm. They were very touchy about it." Not that you could blame them for being sensitive about being mistaken for fools.

According to Judy's cousin, Mira Stillman, the Yiddish expression for Chelm-like thinking is "kop moyech," which means, literally, "head brain," referring to the lack thereof. A typical story of the citizens of Chelm goes like this:

The Logs in Chelm

Retold by Caroline Feller Bauer

Once the people of Chelm thought they could make money by selling lumber from the mountain that overlooked their town. For weeks the strongest men of Chelm chopped down the largest trees and hacked off the branches until they had a fine pile of large logs. Then it took another month for a team of men to carry the great tree trunks down the mountain. At last the colossal job was almost done.

Two strangers arrived in town on that final day. They watched in amazement and amusement as the men dragged the last massive log down the endless slope. "Why didn't you just roll the logs down the hill instead of carrying them?" asked one of the strangers.

"What an excellent idea!" exclaimed the men of Chelm. "Why didn't we think of that? Let's do it."

And with that the team hoisted up a log and began the long trek back up the mountain, so when they reached the top they could roll it back down again.

"Those strangers were right!" the men of Chelm exclaimed. "It's much easier when you roll the logs."

BOOKLIST: DROLLS AND HUMOROUS STORIES (SILLIES, FOOLS, AND NOODLEHEADS)

Demi. *The Hungry Coat: A Tale from Turkey.* *Illus. by the author. McElderry, 2004.* Ostracized for wearing an old, smelly coat to a rich friend's banquet, Nasrettin Hoca changes into a fine silk coat and feeds his dinner to it. (P, I, A)

Hamilton, Martha, and Mitch Weiss. *Noodlehead Stories: World Tales Kids Can Read & Tell.* *Illus. by Ariane Elsammak. August House, 2000.* Twenty-three easy-to-tell tales about foolish folk from many lands. (P, I)

Johnson-Davies, Denys. *Goha the Wise Fool.* *Illus. by Hany El Saed Ahmed, from drawings by Hag Hamdy Mohamed Fattouh. Philomel, 2005.* Fifteen short, droll tales about Goha, the well-meaning fool, trickster, and sage from Egyptian folklore. (P, I, A)

Montes, Marisa. *Juan Bobo Goes to Work: A Puerto Rican Folktale.* *Illus. by Joe Cepeda. HarperCollins, 2000.* Juan Bobo goes to work on Don Pepe's farm, but the foolish boy does everything wrong. (P, I)

Salley, Coleen. *Epossumondas.* *Illus. by Janet Stevens. Harcourt, 2002.* Each time a little possum tries to carry home gifts from his auntie, his exasperated mama says, "Epossumondas, you don't have the sense you were born with." Follow with *Why Epossumondas Has No Hair on His Tail* (2004) and *Epossumondas Plays Possum* (2009). (P)

Sanfield, Steve. *The Feather Merchants, and Other Tales of the Fools of Chelm.* *Illus. by Mikhail Magaril. Orchard, 1991.* Thirteen lively Jewish tales of the silly folk of Chelm. (I, A)

Schwartz, Alvin. *There Is a Carrot in My Ear, and Other Noodle Tales.* *Illus. by Karen Ann Weinhaus. HarperCollins, 1982.* Six easy-to-read stories, based on folklore, about a family of sillies. (P)

Simon, Solomon. *The Wise Men of Helm and Their Merry Tales.* *Trans. by Ben Bengal and David Simon. Illus. by Lillian Fischel. Behrman House, 1995, c1945.* Twenty-two Yiddish stories about the Polish town of fools. (I, A)

Singer, Isaac Bashevis. *Zlateh the Goat and Other Stories.* *Trans. by the author and Elizabeth Shub. Illus. by Maurice Sendak. HarperCollins, 1966.* Seven irresistible Jewish tales set in the shtetls of Poland, including some about Chelm, famed town of fools. For a complete collection of Singer's short stories, including those in *When Shlemiel Went to Warsaw & Other Stories* (Farrar, 1969), scare up a copy of *The Fools of Chelm and Their History* (Farrar, 1973). (I, A)

Singh, Rina. *The Foolish Men of Agra, and Other Tales of Mogul India.* *Illus. by Farida Zaman. Key Porter, 1998.* Ten wry, funny tales of Mogul Emperor Akbar and his wise advisor, Birbal. (I, A)

Taback, Simms. *Kibitzers and Fools: Tales My Zayda (Grandfather) Told Me.* *Illus. by the author. Viking, 2005.* Thirteen short, comical Jewish tales about a variety of fools, from nebbishes to schnooks. (P, I, A)

WEBSITES: DROLLS AND HUMOROUS STORIES (SILLIES, FOOLS, AND NOODLEHEADS)

Beauty and the Beast Storytellers
beautyandthebeaststorytellers.com/pdf/noodleheadUnit.pdf
See "Writing Noodlehead Stories: A Unit for Second through Sixth Graders," an extensive lesson plan developed by Martha Hamilton and Mitch Weiss, aka Beauty and the Beast Storytellers, as an addendum to their book, *Children Tell Stories: Teaching and Using Storytelling in the Classroom* (Richard C. Owen, 2005).

Folklore and Mythology Electronic Texts *www.pitt.edu/~dash/folktexts.html*
A wealth of folk- and fairy-tale texts, edited and/or translated by D. L. Ashliman, are listed alphabetically by subject, including "Count Themselves" (six tales about groups of men who can't seem to count themselves) at www.pitt.edu/~dash/type1287.html; "The Moon in the Well" (four tales of fools who think the moon has fallen into the well); and "Nasreddin Hodja: Tales of the Turkish Trickster" (with the texts of 25 Hodja stories) at www.pitt.edu/~dash/hodja.html.

Hatter's Classics: Noodleheads: The Wisdom of Fools
www.eldrbarry.net/roos/books/hatrsbks.htm
Information, links, and stories about the Wise Men of Gotham, the fools of Chelm, Till Eulenspiegel, and others.

Nasreddin Hodja *u.cs.biu.ac.il/~schiff/Net/front.html*
More than one hundred Hodja stories, compiled by Alpay Kabacali and illustrated by Fatih M. Durmus.

Pourquoi Tales ("How-and-Why" Stories)

How-and-why stories—often referred to as pourquoi (pronounced poor-KWAH) tales, from the French word for "why"—explain how and why a physical or cultural phenomenon began. Some of these stories are closely related to myths. Remember the Greek myth about inquisitive Pandora unleashing bad karma into the world? Creation stories constitute the first pourquoi tales. Virginia Hamilton's *In the Beginning: Creation Stories from Around the World* is a handsomely illustrated collection, comprised of twenty-five creation myths from many different cultures. The African folktale *Why the Sun and the Moon Live in the Sky*, retold by Elphinstone Dayrell, explains their celestial origin. In Eric Maddern's *The Fire Children: A West African Folk Tale*, two lonely spirit people shape little clay children, which they bake in the fire for different amounts of time, which explains why we are all different colors today.

Some pourquoi tales explain how an animal acquired its singular characteristics. These tend to be more lighthearted, such as the Native American tale *How Chipmunk Got His Stripes* by Joseph Bruchac. In the Caldecott-winning African folktale *Why Mosquitoes Buzz in People's Ears* by Verna Aardema, Mosquito's lie to Iguana sets off a disastrous chain of events. After exploring a variety of how-and-why stories, children may wish to choose an animal with a singular characteristic or a scientific phenomenon—why cats hiss, why snow is white, why people sneeze—and write their own folklore-ish explanation. It's also fun to introduce a related pourquoi tale when you are teaching science or geography as an alternative explanation of how something originated. Here's an example, an oldie-but-goodie from Norway.

Why the Bear Is Stumpy-Tailed

Adapted by Judy Freeman from Popular Tales from the Norse *by Peter Christen Asbjøornsen and Jøorgen Moe, Translated by George Webbe Dasent (1904)*

One day Bear met Fox, who came slinking along with a string of fish he had stolen.

"Where did you get those fish?" asked Bear.

"Oh, dear Bruin, I've been out fishing and caught them," said the sly Fox.

Seeing that tempting string of fish, Bear had a mind to learn to fish, too. He begged Fox to tell him how to do it.

"Oh, it will be an easy task for you," answered Fox, "and you'll learn it with no trouble at all. You've only got to go to the river, which is now frozen over. Walk out upon the ice, cut a little hole in it, and stick your big, bushy tail down into the water. You must go on holding it there as long as you can. You're not to mind if your tail smarts a little, for that just means the fish are biting. The longer you can hold it there, the more fish you'll get. When you decide your tail is full enough with fish, you must yank your tail out of the hole—all at once, with a cross pull sideways, and with a strong pull too."

"That sounds easy enough," Bear thought to himself, and down to the river he went. There he did as Fox had said. He cut a hole in the ice, and lowered his long, bushy tail into the freezing water. He held his tail a long, long time down in the hole, till it was fast frozen in. It began to smart—not just a little, but a lot. "I must have many fish holding onto my tail," the greedy Bear said. Then, remembering Fox's instructions, he yanked out his tail out of the hole—all at once, with a cross pull sideways, and with a strong pull too, and it snapped short off. And that's why Bruin goes about with a short, stumpy tail this very day.

BOOKLIST: POURQUOI TALES ("HOW-AND-WHY" STORIES)

Aardema, Verna. ***Why Mosquitoes Buzz in People's Ears.*** *Illus. by Leo and Diane Dillon. Dial, 1975.* This classic Caldecott Medal book is a cumulative pourquoi tale that ends with a good slap. (P)

Bruchac, Joseph. ***The First Strawberries: A Cherokee Story.*** *Illus. by Anna Vojtech. Dial, 1993.* When the first man on earth hurts his wife's feelings and she leaves him, the sun creates the first strawberries as the man's apology. (I, A)

Bruchac, Joseph, and James Bruchac. ***How Chipmunk Got His Stripes: A Tale of Bragging and Teasing.*** *Illus. by Jose Aruego and Ariane Dewey. Dial, 2001.* In a Native American tale from the East Coast, Brown Squirrel asks bragging Bear to stop the sun from rising. (P)

Dayrell, Elphinstone. ***Why the Sun and the Moon Live in the Sky: An African Folktale.*** *Illus. by Blair Lent. Houghton Mifflin, 1968.* An African tale explaining the heavens. (P, I)

Gerson, Mary-Joan. ***Why the Sky Is Far Away: A Nigerian Folktale.*** *Illus. by Carla Golembe. Little, Brown, 1992.* The people are punished after Adese eats too much of the delicious sky. (P, I, A)

Goble, Paul. ***Iktomi and the Boulder: A Plains Indian Story.*** *Illus. by the author. Orchard, 1988.* A humorous Native American trickster and pourquoi tale explaining why bats have flat noses. (P, I)

Haley, Gail E. ***A Story, a Story.*** *Illus. by the author. Atheneum, 1970.* In an African pourquoi tale, which was awarded a Caldecott Medal, Anansi the Spider spreads the world's first stories. (P, I)

Hamilton, Martha, and Mitch Weiss. ***How & Why Stories: World Tales Kids Can Read & Tell.*** *Illus. by Carol Lyon. August House, 1999.* Twenty-five brief, easy-to-learn and-tell pourquoi tales from North and South America, Asia, Europe, and Africa. (P, I)

Hausman, Gerald. ***How Chipmunk Got Tiny Feet.*** *Illus. by Ashley Wolff. HarperCollins, 1995.* Seven enjoyable Native American animal pourquoi tales. (P, I)

Hong, Lily Toy. ***How the Ox Star Fell from Heaven.*** *Illus. by the author. Albert Whitman, 1991.* This Chinese tale explains why we eat three times a day, and why oxen are now beasts of burden. (P, I)

Kimmel, Eric A. ***Ten Suns: A Chinese Legend.*** *Illus. by YongSheng Xuan. Holiday House, 1998.* How the emperor's ten sons disobeyed him and why there is only one sun in the sky as a result. (I)

Maddern, Eric. ***The Fire Children: A West African Folk Tale.*** *Illus. by Frané Lessac. Frances Lincoln, 2006, c1993.* Discover how people came to be all different colors. (P, I)

Young, Ed. *Cat and Rat: The Legend of the Chinese Zodiac.* *Illus. by the author. Henry Holt, 1995.* Cat and Rat hope to win the Jade Emperor's race and have a year in the Chinese calendar named after them. (P, I)

WEBSITES: POURQUOI TALES ("HOW-AND-WHY" STORIES)

First People—The Legends *www.firstpeople.us/FP-Html-Legends*
"Dedicated to all First People of the Americas and Canada, better known as Turtle Island." This truly remarkable, child-friendly site features texts of more than 1,300 Native American legends, listed alphabetically by tribe; many of them are pourquoi tales.

Pourquoi Tales Lesson Plan Blog *whystories.wordpress.com*
Lesson materials, resources, and links. Click on "Pourquoi Examples" to watch a wonderful Cherokee storyteller share "How Rabbit Lost Its Tail."

Jump Tales, Scary Stories, and Urban Legends

Those stories you told at summer camp or on overnights that ended in a scream are called jump tales. Other scary stories might be about ghosts, goblins, creatures, monsters, and other things that go bump in the night. Urban legends are the tales that you swear are true, that you claim you heard from your friend's cousin, like the one about the vanishing hitchhiker, a girl who leaves her sweater behind in the car, except you find out that she died ten years ago. What is it about these stories that scare the daylights out of some people and make others shriek with delight?

Be cognizant of your audience, especially children, when you tell the scarier examples from this genre. The children may seem to be laughing, but some will be truly terrified if they are too young or too faint of heart. Then again, second graders may clutch each other in mock fear when you tell a simple jump story like "Tillie." ("Tillie, I'm on the first step . . . Tillie, I'm on the second step . . ."), but they realize that you, their storyteller, will guide them safely to the end ("Tillie, I GOTCHA!") when they can give a little shriek and then laugh. That works fine.

Who doesn't know this one, the original jump tale, the first one that many children hear? They love to chime in.

The Teeny-Tiny Woman

An English Jump Tale Collected by Folklorist Joseph Jacobs

Once upon a time there was a teeny-tiny woman who lived in a teeny-tiny house in a teeny-tiny village. Now, one day this teeny-tiny woman put on her teeny-tiny bonnet, and went out of her teeny-tiny house to take a teeny-tiny walk. And when this teeny-tiny woman had gone a teeny-tiny way, she came to a teeny-tiny gate; so the teeny-tiny woman opened the teeny-tiny gate, and went into a teeny-tiny churchyard. And when this teeny-tiny woman had got into the teeny-tiny churchyard, she saw a teeny-tiny bone on a teeny-tiny grave, and the teeny-tiny woman said to her teeny-tiny self, "This teeny-tiny bone will make me some teeny-tiny soup for my teeny-tiny supper." So the teeny-tiny woman put the teeny-tiny bone into her teeny-tiny pocket, and went home to her teeny-tiny house.

Now, when the teeny-tiny woman got home to her teeny-tiny house, she was a teeny-tiny bit tired; so she went up her teeny-tiny stairs to her teeny-tiny bed, and put the teeny-tiny bone into a teeny-tiny cupboard. And when this teeny-tiny woman had been to sleep a teeny-tiny time, she was awakened by a teeny-tiny voice from the teeny-tiny cupboard, which said: "*Give me my bone!*"

And this teeny-tiny woman was a teeny-tiny frightened, so she hid her teeny-tiny head under her teeny-tiny covers and went to sleep again. And when she had been to sleep again a teeny-tiny time, the teeny-tiny voice again cried out from the teeny-tiny cupboard a teeny-tiny louder, "*Give me my bone!*"

This made the teeny-tiny woman a teeny-tiny more frightened, so she hid her teeny-tiny head a teeny-tiny bit further under the teeny-tiny covers. And when the teeny-tiny woman had been to sleep again a teeny-tiny time, the teeny-tiny voice from the teeny-tiny cupboard said again a teeny-tiny louder, "*Give me my bone!*"

And this teeny-tiny woman was a teeny-tiny bit more frightened, but she put her teeny-tiny head out of the teeny tiny covers, and said in her loudest teeny-tiny voice, "*TAKE IT!*"

BOOKLIST: JUMP TALES, SCARY STORIES, AND URBAN LEGENDS

De Las Casas, Dianne. *Scared Silly: 25 Tales to Tickle and Thrill.* *Libraries Unlimited, 2009.* Silly, scary, jump tales, most of them peppy rewrites of ones you know, just begging for a campfire or a darkened room. (Professional)

Galdone, Johanna. *The Tailypo: A Ghost Story.* *Illus. by Paul Galdone. Clarion, 1977.* After an old man chops off, cooks, and eats the tail of a cat-like varmint, the critter returns, wanting its "tailypo" back. (I)

Galdone, Paul. *The Teeny-Tiny Woman: A Ghost Story.* *Illus. by the author. Clarion, 1984.* "Give me my bone!" says the teeny-tiny voice. (P)

Half-Minute Horrors. *Ed. by Susan Rich. Harper, 2009.* Seventy little two-page jump stories you can read in thirty seconds, by major children's book authors, including Lane Smith, Neil Gaiman, Jack Gantos, James Patterson, and R. L. Stine. (I)

Hamilton, Martha, and Mitch Weiss. *Scared Witless: Thirteen Eerie Tales to Tell.* *Illus. by Kevin Pope. August House, 2006.* Mostly funny jump tales, with tips for telling. (Professional)

Hoberman, Mary Ann. *You Read to Me, I'll Read to You: Very Scary Stories to Read Together.* *Little, Brown, 2007.* Little funny/scary rhyming stories for two voices. (P)

Holt, David, and Bill Mooney, retels. *Spiders in the Hairdo: Modern Urban Legends.* *August House, 1999.* Fifty of the most common urban legends, including, of course, "The Vanishing Hitchhiker." (A)

MacDonald, Margaret Read. *When the Lights Go Out: Twenty Scary Tales to Tell.* *Illus. by Roxane Murphy. H. W. Wilson, 1988.* Twenty fun jump stories children will scream over, with suggestions on how to tell them. (Professional)

Olson, Arielle N., and Howard Schwartz. *More Bones: Scary Stories from Around the World.* *Illus. by E. M. Gist. Viking, 2008.* Short and not terribly frightening, these twenty-two folktales are good for telling, as are the stories in the companion book, *Ask the Bones: Scary Stories from Around the World* (1999). (I, A)

Parkhurst, Liz Smith. *The August House Book of Scary Stories: Spooky Tales for Telling Out Loud.* *August House, 2009.* Twenty chillers with a book cover that will give you pause. (I, A)

San Souci, Robert D. *Short & Shivery: Thirty Chilling Tales.* *Illus. by Katherine Coville. Doubleday, 1987.* Ghastly little tales from all over the globe featuring a nifty assortment of ghosts, skeletons, witches, wizards, and more. Follow up with *More Short & Shivery: Thirty Chilling Tales* (1994) and *Even More Short & Shivery: Thirty Chilling Tales* (1997); then try San Souci's *Haunted Houses* (Henry Holt, 2010). (I, A)

Schwartz, Alvin. *Ghosts! Ghostly Tales from Folklore.* *Illus. by Victoria Chess. HarperCollins, 1991.* Seven humorous, easy-to-read-and-tell, not-too-chilling ghost stories for youngest readers when they cry, "Don't you have any scary books?" Also hand them Schwartz's similarly formatted *In a Dark, Dark Room and Other Scary Stories* (1984). (P)

Schwartz, Alvin. *Scary Stories to Tell in the Dark.* *Illus. by Brett Helquist. HarperCollins, 1981.* These short, chilling jump tales work beautifully as transitions between longer selections, and you can't survive without the wickedly fun companion books: *More Scary Stories to Tell in the Dark* (1984) and *Scary Stories 3: More Tales to Chill Your Bones* (1991). These titles get banned a lot. (I, A)

Stine, R. L., comp. *Beware! R. L. Stine Picks His Favorite Scary Stories.* *HarperCollins, 2002.* Twenty-three deliberately icky stories and poems from leading adult and children's book authors, including Ray Bradbury, Edward Gorey, William Sleator, and Alvin Schwartz.

Young, Richard, and Judy Dockrey Young. *Favorite Scary Stories of American Children.* *Illus. by Don Bell. August House, 1999.* The twenty-three scary stories in this eclectic, entertaining, and sometimes hair-raising collection are rated for ages five to six, seven to eight, and nine to ten. (P, I)

WEBSITES: JUMP TALES, SCARY STORIES, AND URBAN LEGENDS

American Folklore: Urban Legends
http://americanfolklore.net/folklore/urban-legends
Retellings of almost two dozen American urban legends, written by website master and author Sandy Schlosser.

Jackie Torrence *http://jackietorrence.com*
No one told a story better than Jackie, whose recordings are available to purchase and/or download. "Tales for Scary Times" contains four tales, including "The Golden Arm."

Snopes.com *http://snopes.com*
An "internet reference source for urban legends, folklore, myths, rumors, and misinformation." At www.snopes.com/horrors you can look up any urban legend people claim is true and find the story behind it. The Vanishing Hitchhiker legend, for instance, has been around for centuries, going back to the days when people rode horses instead of cars.

Story Lovers World: Halloween Stories
www.story-lovers.com/barebonesstories.html#monsterinmyhouse
You'll find an alphabetical list of 105 Halloween stories with full texts and notes, including a rich collection of jump tales, contributed by tellers. Don't read these before bed.

Fairy Tales

Fairy tales are a subset of folktales, which are a subset of folklore. So all fairy tales are folktales, but not all folktales are fairy tales. What exactly constitutes a fairy tale? The rule of thumb is this: if the story is an old folktale set in a once-upon-a-time land of castles and enchanted forests, contains a matter-of-fact melding of magic, enchantments, impossible quests, and wishes; is peopled by a combination of royalty or commoners, talking animals that converse with humans, dragons, or other magical not-exactly-human creatures; and/or features fantastical elements (objects with astonishing powers, like cloaks of invisibility, seven-league boots, or magic mirrors), we call it a fairy tale.

Fairy tales have people, usually young ones, as their protagonists and include aspects of adventure and romance. Foolish lads, youngest brothers or sisters, and clever royals in search of a mate or a fortune are led on bracing adventures that take them deep inside a hill, under the sea, or up a glass mountain. Their journeys wrap up with a happily-ever-after ending—sometimes even a wedding (though this is not a requirement). Usually the characterizations are scanty: heroes and heroines, whether they are princes and princesses or simple peasants, are kind and good, while their enemies are often portrayed as greedy, grasping, and venal. Guess who almost always wins? Real life should be as satisfying as fairy tales, where trolls, giants, ogres, goblins, witches, or even nasty siblings are punished for their wicked ways. Wizards and enchanters can be nice guys or fearsome opponents, and although stepmothers are often in competition with their downtrodden stepchildren, fairy godmothers prove valuable allies.

Fairy tales often involve animals that converse and interact matter-of-factly with human beings. In the German "The Fisherman and His Wife," a fish grants wishes to the fisherman's ungrateful spouse, who craves larger and more opulent houses and positions of authority. In the French fairy tale "Puss in Boots," a cat takes care of his master and defeats an ogre, while in the Finnish variant, "Mighty Mikko," a gentle, clever fox guides his master into marrying a princess.

Enchanted humans are often found to take on an animal form. In the well-known German story, "The Frog Prince," a prince lives his life as a frog until he is freed by a princess. (See the story on page 109.)

Supernatural characters abound in fairy tales. Scandinavian trolls and ogres; Irish fairies and leprechauns; Slavic domovoi; and Japanese *oni*, *kappa*, and *tengu* are just a few. Some of these creatures are downright evil; others may be a blessing for those who come in contact with them. If you become interested in one of these folk characters, gather a number of stories together and create an entire program around it. To see an extensive alphabetical list of more than a thousand of such creatures from all over the world, each with its own link to a definition and description, visit Wikipedia at http://en.wikipedia.org/wiki/List_of_legendary_creatures. You will be amazed.

Why are they called "fairy tales" if they don't necessarily have fairies in them? The answer to that is . . . because. The French called them "*contes de fées*," which translates as "tales of fairies." "Rapunzel," "Sleeping Beauty," "Hansel and Gretel," "Snow White and the Seven Dwarfs," "The Twelve Dancing Princesses," "Jack and the Beanstalk," "Beauty and the Beast," "East of the Sun, West of the Moon," "Aladdin and the Wonderful Lamp," "Ali Baba and the Forty Thieves," and "Momotaro the Peach Boy" are some of the tales we know best.

The collections that turned many people on to fairy tales are the dozen "color" compendiums, which Andrew Lang wrote in the late-nineteenth century, starting with *The Blue Fairy Book* in 1889. Dover has kept all of these books in print: Blue, Brown, Crimson, Green, Grey, Lilac, Olive, Orange, Pink, Red, Violet, and Yellow. It's well worth collecting them. They are treasure troves of tales from all over the world.

Back in the 1970s, the great Virginia Haviland (1911–1988)—the children's librarian of the Library of Congress, whose credo was "The right book for the right child at the right time"—compiled a series of stories for children: sixteen small, enticing volumes, starting with *Favorite Fairy Tales Told in Ireland,* in 1961. Each book contains six to eight representative tales from a single country. The illustrated retellings are full of flair for storytellers. The books are long out of print, but your library may have copies, or you may find them online. It's unfortunate that they are not more readily available, as they are unsurpassed for encouraging children to read a collection instead of a single story. The countries represented are Czechoslovakia, Denmark, England, France, Germany, Greece, India, Ireland, Italy, Japan, Norway, Poland, Russia, Scotland, Spain, and Sweden. For more suggestions of fairy-tale literature, see also the booklists in chapter 6.

On the Virtual 6th Grade Book Club wiki at boundtoplease.wikispaces.com, where sixth-grade students have published their book reviews, Sofia writes, "My book is called *Favorite Folktales from Around the World*, by Jane Yolen. This is a book of folktales (as you can probably tell from the title). My favorite story in this book is 'Li Chi Slays the Serpent,' because it actually has a girl for a heroine, unlike other stories where all the women do is stay home and cry." Good point. It is true that women play passive roles in most (but not all) fairy tales, but that is a reflection of the times in which they were told. Sofia and other girls need to know that women made up the majority of storytellers who told their folktales to the men like Perrault, Grimm, and Jacobs who wrote them down. Times have changed, thankfully, and it's gratifying to find strong, independent female protagonists in new stories.

And then there's "Cinderella," the most famous of all the romantic stories. She may not be an action hero (and unfortunately she's influenced generations of young women to hope Prince Charming will sweep them off their tiny, glass-slippered feet), but we nevertheless revere her and cheer when she shows up those ghastly stepsisters. The version most of us know (with the glass slipper and the pumpkin coach) was written down in France by Charles Perrault at the end of the seventeenth century, but there are so many variants that a storyteller could specialize in telling Cinderella stories. The ancient Egyptians told the story of a Greek slave girl, Rhodopis, who married a pharaoh. She's called Aschenputtel in Germany, Settareh in Iran, Yeh-Shen in China, and Cenerentola in Italy. Native Americans tell the story of "Little Burn Face" or "Sootface" or "The Rough-Face Girl." We have listed some of the best-known, still-in-print picture-book versions of Cinderella below. You'll find more listed, along with ways to use them, in Judy's book *Once Upon a Time.* There are twenty-three printed versions of the story, from Europe, Asia, and North America, available online at www.pitt.edu/~dash/grimm0510a.html.

BOOKLIST: CINDERELLA STORIES

Climo, Shirley. ***The Egyptian Cinderella.*** *Illus. by Ruth Heller. Crowell, 1989.* One of the world's oldest Cinderella stories, first recorded in the first century B.C. (P, I)

Climo, Shirley. ***The Korean Cinderella.*** *Illus. by the author. HarperCollins, 1993.* Pear Blossom's stepsisters call her Little Pig, a tokgabi or goblin comes to her aid, and she loses her straw sandal. (P, I)

Climo, Shirley. ***The Persian Cinderella.*** *Illus. by Robert Florczak. HarperCollins, 1999.* Settareh will have to stay home from the New Year festival of No Ruz. (P, I)

Coburn, Jewell Reinhart, adapt. with Tzexa Cherta Lee. ***Jouanah: A Hmong Cinderella.*** *Illus. by Anne Sibley O'Brien. Shen's Books, 1996.* A tender Cinderella story from the Hmong people of Laos, in which Jouanah's mother transforms herself into a cow. (P, I)

Fleischman, Paul. ***Glass Slipper, Gold Sandal: A Worldwide Cinderella.*** *Illus. by Julie Paschkis. Henry Holt, 2007.* A graceful composite of Cinderella variants from seventeen countries. (P, I)

Han, Oki S., and Stephanie Haboush Plunkett. ***Kongi and Potgi: A Cinderella Story from Korea.*** *Illus. by Oki S. Han. Dial, 1996.* Potgi is made to do all the work, until an ox becomes her helpmate. (P, I)

Jaffe, Nina. ***The Way Meat Loves Salt: A Cinderella Tale from the Jewish Tradition.*** *Illus. by Louise August. Henry Holt, 1998.* When the rabbi's daughter, Mireleh, tells him she loves him "the way meat loves salt," he misunderstands and casts her out of the house. Also see a US version, *Moss Gown* by William Hooks (Clarion, 1987). (P, I)

Karlin, Barbara. ***Cinderella.*** *Illus. by James Marshall. Little, Brown, 1989.* A traditional French version, but with marvelously goofy illustrations. (P, I)

Louie, Ai-Ling. ***Yeh-Shen: A Cinderella Story from China.*** *Illus. by Ed Young. Philomel, 1982.* A magic fish is the girl's confidant in this tale that dates back more than a thousand years. (P, I)

Manna, Anthony L., and Soula Mitakidou. ***The Orphan: A Cinderella Story from Greece.*** *Illus. by Giselle Potter. Schwartz & Wade, 2011.* With the help of Mother Nature and her children, an orphan girl in delicate blue shoes meets her prince at church. (P, I)

Martin, Rafe. ***The Rough-Face Girl.*** *Illus. by David Shannon. Putnam, 1992.* In a solemn Algonquin Indian Cinderella variant, a young girl, scarred and burned from tending the fire, is the only one who can see the Invisible Being. See also *Sootface: An Ojibwa Cinderella Story* by Robert D. San Souci, below. (P, I)

McClintock, Barbara. *Cinderella.* *Illus. by the author. Scholastic, 2005.* Cinderella forgives her stepsisters in this version, based on Charles Perrault's original telling from seventeenth-century France. (P, I)

Perrault, Charles. *Cinderella; Or, The Little Glass Slipper.* *Trans. and illus. by Marcia Brown. Scribner, 1954.* Caldecott winner, illustrated with French baroque–style watercolors. (P, I)

Pollock, Penny. *The Turkey Girl: A Zuni Cinderella Story.* *Illus. by Ed Young. Little, Brown, 1996.* Wanting to attend the Dance of the Sacred Bird, the Turkey Girl is granted her wish by the turkeys she attends so faithfully. (P, I)

San Souci, Robert D. *Cendrillon: A Caribbean Cinderella.* *Illus. by Brian Pinkney. Simon & Schuster, 1998.* On the island of Martinique, a *nannin'* (or godmother) explains how she helped poor Cendrillon attend a birthday ball. (P, I)

San Souci, Robert D. *Sootface: An Ojibwa Cinderella Story.* *Illus. by Daniel San Souci. Doubleday, 1994.* Only Sootface passes the test of the invisible warrior. See also *The Rough-Face Girl* by Rafe Martin, above. (P, I)

Schroeder, Alan. *Smoky Mountain Rose: An Appalachian Cinderella.* *Illus. by Brad Sneed. Dial, 1997.* A talking hog helps poor Rose get to rich feller Seb's shindig, where she and Jeb square-dance till midnight. (P, I)

WEBSITES: CINDERELLA STORIES

The Cinderella Project

www.usm.edu/media/english/fairytales/cinderella/cinderella.html

Part of the de Grummond Research Collection at the University of Southern Mississippi and edited by Michael N. Salada, this text and image archive includes a dozen English-language versions of "Cinderella" published between 1729 and 1912.

Mi'Kmaq Indian Cinderella and the Invisible One

www.kstrom.net/isk/stories/cinder3.html

Text and commentary, prepared by Paula Giese, introduces a Native American variant collected in Nova Scotia by a Baptist missionary in the mid-nineteenth century.

Fables

Fables are short, didactic tales that attempt to teach a useful truth or lesson or convey a moral. The main characters are often animals that behave as foolishly as humans sometimes do. Some fables are so well-known that expressions from them—such as "sour grapes," "the boy who cried wolf," "don't count your chickens before they hatch," and "slow and steady wins the race"—have become part of our everyday language. Children may understand the message underlying the fable, but they'll enjoy the tale most for its story line. Some fables present philosophical concepts that are too abstract for young children to comprehend; these are best left for more mature listeners.

Because so many fables feature animals, which are favorite topics among children, there have been many editions of fables published especially for kids. Tell a fable at the beginning of a storytelling session. They are easy to learn and may stimulate some serious thought in young listeners. Only one or two fables at a time, please—unless you are introducing the topic and having children act out some of the fables you tell.

AESOP'S FABLES

The best-known fables are those known as Aesop's fables. It is believed that Aesop was a Greek slave who lived about 600 BC, but since he left no written records, we have no way of ascertaining hard facts about his life or works. Indeed, there's no real evidence that he actually existed, although Aristotle, Herodotus, and Plutarch all wrote about him.

The earliest-known written versions of these stories were recorded in Latin by Phaedrus in the first century AD. In the third century, Babrius wrote a collection of three hundred of the fables in Greek verse. Subsequent compilations were made by Aviares in the fourth century, and by Romulus in the tenth century. Later, these fables reached Northern Europe and were printed by William Caxton, England's first printer, in 1484. They have survived until the present in various versions. There is no one accepted written standard.

Many artists have illustrated Aesop's fables. Traditionalists will particularly enjoy looking at the black-and-white silhouettes and full-color paintings Arthur Rackham did for V. S. Vernon Jones's 1912 translation, *Aesop's Fables.* More recently, the 2010 Caldecott Medal went to Jerry Pinkney, whose magnificent watercolors elucidate the almost wordless *The Lion & the Mouse,* one of Aesop's best-known fables. Read aloud a prose version, and then have your group retell the story along with Pinkney's illustrations. Then read aloud the same story, told in rhyme for two voices, from Mary Ann Hoberman's *You Read to Me, I'll Read to You: Very Short Fables to Read Together,* where the fable is told from both characters' points of view.

Speaking of lions, still a favorite modern adaptation of an Aesop's fable is James Daugherty's picture book *Andy and the Lion,* published in 1938, in which a boy pulls a thorn out of a lion's paw, the same basic theme as in "Androcles and the Lion." Then there's Margie Palatini's bossy fox in her updated telling of *Lousy Rotten Stinkin' Grapes*, which you can compare with the simple fable, "The Fox and the Grapes." Here's the original story as printed by William Caxton in 1484, which you may want to have your students read and translate into more modern English. If you'd like to see what the original looked like in print, you can see the facsimile of the book at mythfolklore.net/aesopica/caxton/41.htm.

Of the Foxe and of the Raysyns

He is not wyse / that desyreth to haue a thynge whiche he may not haue / As reciteth this fable Of a foxe / whiche loked and beheld the raysyns that grewe vpon an hyghe vyne / the whiche raysyns he moche desyred for to ete them / And whanne he sawe that none he myght gete / he torned his sorowe in to Ioye / and sayd these raysyns ben sowre / and yf I had some I wold not ete them / *And therfore this fable sheweth that he is wyse / whiche fayneth not to desyre that thynge the whiche he may not haue /*

FABLES OF LA FONTAINE

Jean de La Fontaine (1621–1695) used various sources, including Aesop, for his verse fables, which first appeared in 1688. French schoolchildren know the fables almost as well as American children know their Mother Goose. They hear them when they are young and study them in school, memorizing them for recitation contests. Although La Fontaine suffers somewhat in translation into English, his poems are still delightful versions of the traditional fables. There are several collections available, but not many particularly for children. One good one is *Fables* (part of the Everyman's Library Children's Classics), a facsimile of a 1931 edition translated into English verse by Sir Edward Marsh.

FABLES OF INDIA

The Panchatantra, which contains the earliest recorded fables of India, originated somewhere around the third century BC. In these Hindu fables, written in Sanskrit, the Vishnu Sarma attempts to teach the three sons of the king some principles of conduct that they are expected to follow. There are some two hundred delightful versions of *The Panchatantra*, recorded in more than fifty languages. These fables, which are much more complex than those of Aesop or La Fontaine, contain stories within stories.

The Hitopadesa, or *Book of Good Counsels*, is a rearrangement of *The Panchatantra* with a few additional stories that date from the tenth century. Marcia Brown's excellent picture book, *Once a Mouse*—which won the Caldecott Medal in 1962—popularized one story from this collection. In this story, a hermit befriends a mouse and turns him into various animal forms. When the mouse, now a proud tiger, expresses his ungratefulness to the hermit, he is turned once more into a humble little mouse.

The Jatakas are a series of animal stories describing the lessons of life that Gautama Buddha preached in northeast India between 563 BC and 483 BC. The stories, numbering some five hundred, remained in the oral tradition until several hundred years after Buddha's death, when they were written down in the Pali language. Although they were first translated into English in the nineteenth century, these fables have been told and enjoyed for over two thousand years in various parts of the world. One recent collection appropriate for children is Demi's *Buddha Stories*.

Jataka Tales and *More Jataka Tales*, Ellen C. Babbitt's collections, written for children and published in 1912, have been brought back into print. In one fable from *Jataka Tales*, "The Turtle Who Couldn't Stop Talking," a turtle meets some geese that are flying back to their home. The turtle would like to join them and the geese suggest that he hold a stick between his teeth while they each take an end and fly into the air. When the village children see the odd sight they jeer and laugh at the turtle. Because he is unable to keep quiet, the foolish turtle lets go of the stick to answer the children and falls to his death. There are many version of this story told in different cultures as a pourquoi tale. Comparatively lucky for the turtle, they usually end with just his shell becoming cracked.

The following story taken from *The Panchatantra* is also told in many other cultures. You'll find several versions at www.pitt.edu/~dash/type2031c.html and a Zuni Indian version at www.firstpeople.us/FP-Html-Legends/WhoIsTheStrongest-Zuni.html. A Japanese version is Gerald McDermott's dramatic picture book, *The Stonecutter: A Japanese Folk Tale*.

The Mouse Maiden

A Folktale from India, from The Panchatantra
Retold by Judy Freeman

A wise and holy man had just finished bathing in the Ganges, the sacred Indian river, when a falcon flew by with a mouse in its beak. The falcon opened its mouth for a moment, and the mouse fell down, down, down, into the holy man's outstretched hand. He looked at the mouse in surprise, and then transformed it into a little girl. He and his wife had always yearned for a child, so he took the girl home. They were overjoyed to have a daughter and brought her up with great love and care.

When the time came for the girl to be married, the holy man said, "I will summon the exalted and powerful sun god and present you to him as his wife."

He prayed, and soon the blazing sun itself appeared. "Holy man, why have you summoned me?" the sun demanded.

The wise man was unafraid. "Behold!" he said. "Here is my dear young daughter. If she will have you, won't you take her as your wife?" He then turned to his daughter and said, "My daughter, does this exalted being please you, this sun god who lights the three worlds?"

The daughter shook her head disdainfully and said, "Father, he is too hot. I do not want him. Summon a better one!"

The holy man said to the sun, "Exalted one, is there a being more powerful than you?"

The sun replied, "Yes, there is one more powerful than I. Look up in the sky and see the cloud, who covers me, making me invisible."

The father summoned the cloud and said to his daughter, "My daughter, would you prefer this cloud as a husband?"

She said, "No, he is too dark and cold. I do not want him. Summon a better one!"

The father asked the cloud, "Is there anyone more powerful than you?"

The cloud answered, "The wind is more powerful than I. Put your hand into the air and feel the wind. When the wind blows, I am scattered here, there, and everywhere."

Now the wise man summoned the wind and said, "My daughter, would you prefer this wind as a husband?"

She said, "No, he is too breezy for me. I do not want him. Summon a better one!"

The holy man asked, "Wind, is there anyone more powerful than you?"

The wind said, "The mountain is more powerful than I, for however hard I bluster, I cannot blow him down."

Then the father summoned the mountain and said to the girl, "My daughter, would you prefer this mountain as a husband?"

She answered, "No, he is too tall and rugged for me. I do not want him. Summon a better one!"

The wise man was feeling desperate. He asked the mountain, "Listen, most powerful of all mountains, is there anyone more powerful than you?"

The mountain answered, "There is only one creature more powerful than I. The mouse is the most powerful. Only mice can tunnel though my rocky surface and gnaw holes in my body."

Now the wise man summoned a tiny mouse and held it in his hand. He showed her the mouse and said, "My daughter, would you prefer this mouse king as a husband?"

Seeing the mouse, she was delighted. "He is of my own kind!" she said. "Dearest Father, make me into a mouse and I will marry him!"

Once again, through his power of holiness, he transformed her, this time back into a little mouse. And so the two strong mice were married and they were content.

BOOKLIST: FABLES

Babbitt, Ellen C. *Jataka Tales.* *Illus. by Ellsworth Young. Yesterday's Classics, 2006, c1912.* Eighteen Jataka fables, first published a century ago, including "The Monkey and the Crocodile," which Paul Galdone published as a picture book, below. Also see *More Jataka Tales* (2008, c1922). (P, I)

Brown, Marcia. *Once a Mouse . . . : A Fable Cut in Wood.* *Illus. by the author. Atheneum, 1961.* A mouse is given a chance to be a bigger, more powerful animal. (P)

Carle, Eric. *The Rabbit and the Turtle: Aesop's Fables.* *Illus. by the author. Orchard, 2008.* Eleven fables, one per double page, each face a luminous full-page illustration. (P, I)

Chaucer, Geoffrey. *Chanticleer and the Fox.* *Adapted and illus. by Barbara Cooney. Crowell, 1958.* This Caldecott Medal–picture book is an adaptation of Chaucer's "The Nun's Priest's Tale" from *The Canterbury Tales* (which is itself a story adapted from Aesop's "The Cock and the Fox"), where a proud rooster succumbs to the flattery of a fox. (P, I)

Daugherty, James. *Andy and the Lion: A Tale of Kindness Remembered; Or, The Power of Gratitude.* *Illus. by the author. Viking, 1938.* In this modern-day parallel to the fable "Androcles and the Lion," Andy helps a lion with a thorn in its paw. (P)

Demi. *Buddha Stories.* *Illus. by the author. Henry Holt, 1997.* Eleven brief Jataka tales—parables about people and animals, attributed to Buddha 2,500 years ago—are printed on dark indigo paper with illustrations and text done in fine lines of gold. (I, A)

Demi. *A Chinese Zoo: Fables and Proverbs.* Illus. by the author. Harcourt, 1987. Each of thirteen fables is printed beside a sumptuous fan-shaped illustration. (P, I)

Galdone, Paul. *The Monkey and the Crocodile: A Jataka Tale from India.* *Illus. by the author. Clarion, 1969.* Fable of a hungry croc and the cunning monkey he plans to eat. (P)

Hoberman, Mary Ann. *You Read to Me, I'll Read to You: Very Short Fables to Read Together.* *Illus. by Michael Emberley. Little, Brown, 2010.* Thirteen fables are retold in rhyme from the contrasting points of view of animal duos. (P, I)

Jones, V. S. Vernon. *Aesop's Fables.* *Illus. by Arthur Rackham. Dover, 2009, c1912.* Classic collection of close to three hundred fables. (I, A)

La Fontaine, Jean de. *The Complete Fables of La Fontaine: A New Translation in Verse.* *Trans. by Craig Hill. Illus. by Edward Sorel. Arcade, 2011.* More than two hundred fables, retold in rhyme in the spirit of the original French. Fine for older readers and adults as an introduction to La Fontaine's satirical poems, first published in 1688. (A)

La Fontaine, Jean de. *Fables.* *Illus. by R. de la Nézière. Trans. by Sir Edward Marsh. Knopf, 2001.* A volume in the Everyman's Library Children's Classics series, this facsimile of a 1931 edition, translated into English verse, contains five dozen of La Fontaine's fables, including "The Grasshopper and the Ant" and "The Town Mouse and the Country Mouse." (I, A)

Lobel, Arnold. *Fables.* *Illus. by the author. HarperCollins, 1980.* Twenty original and drolly illustrated animal tales for which Lobel won a Caldecott Medal. (P, I, A)

Lowry, Amy. *Fox Tails: Four Fables from Aesop.* *Illus. by the author. Holiday House, 2012.* In four fables linked together, Fox can't reach the grapes he craves, goads a crow into dropping a piece of cheese, tricks a goat into helping him out of a well, and gets his comeuppance from a stork who invites him for dinner. (P, I)

McClintock, Barbara. *Animal Fables from Aesop.* *Adapted and illus. by the author. Godine, 1991.* Nine animal fables, illustrated in nineteenth century–style pen and ink and watercolors, focus on foxes and wolves. (P, I)

Morpurgo, Michael. *The McElderry Book of Aesop's Fables.* *Illus. by Emma Chichester Clark. McElderry, 2005.* Twenty-one fables introduce the usual assortment of misbehaving and misguided rats, dogs, foxes, and crows. (P, I, A)

Palatini, Margie. *Lousy Rotten Stinkin' Grapes.* *Illus. by Barry Moser. Simon & Schuster, 2009.* Unable to reach a tantalizing bunch of grapes, Fox—who considers himself sly, clever, and smart—makes a plan to get them with the help of other animals. (P, I)

Pinkney, Jerry. *Aesop's Fables.* *Retold and illus. by Jerry Pinkney. SeaStar, 2000.* Pinkney's signature lush watercolors invigorate sixty well-told Aesop's fables. (P, I, A)

Pinkney, Jerry. *The Lion & the Mouse.* *Illus. by the author. Little, Brown, 2009.* Pinkney won the 2010 Caldecott Medal for this majestic, wordless "retelling" of the Aesop fable about the lion that spares a mouse and is, in turn, saved by the mouse. (P, I, A)

Pinkney, Jerry. *The Tortoise and the Hare: An Aesop Fable.* *Illus. by the author. Little, Brown, 2013.* Told mostly through captivating watercolors, showing the tortoise in a blue cap trudging slow and steady through a Sonoran desert landscape—and triumphing over the hare, of course. (P)

Scieszka, Jon. *Squids Will Be Squids: Fresh Morals, Beastly Fables.* *Illus. by Lane Smith. Viking, 1998.* Eighteen modern, hip fables feature crazy combos of characters like Straw and Matches. (I, A)

Stevens, Janet. *The Tortoise and the Hare: An Aesop Fable.* *Illus. by the author. Holiday House, 1984.* The classic story, jazzed up a bit with the two competitors in running shorts and sneakers. (P)

WEBSITES: FABLES

Aesopica: Aesop's Fables in English, Latin, and Greek
http://mythfolklore.net/aesopica

This site features a massive index by subject, linked to the stories in English, as retold by Laura Gibbs in her book *Aesop's Fables* (Oxford Univ. Press, 2008). Gibbs also provides links to early printed books of Aesop and many stories told in Latin and Greek.

Aesop's Fables *www.umass.edu/aesop*

For many years, students in Professor Copper Giloth's Introduction to Computing in the Fine Arts class at University of Massachusetts–Amherst have illustrated and retold Aesop's fables as a class assignment. Peruse several dozen fables here, from simple HTML pages to Macromedia Flash-based animated ones with sound and interactivity.

Aesop's Fables Online Collection *www.aesopfables.com*

The site features all 655 of Aesop's fables, indexed in table format, with morals, illustrations, lesson plan links, and Real Audio narrations.

Bartleby *www.bartleby.com/17/1*
Part of Bartleby—"Great Books Online"—from the Harvard Classics, Vol. XVII, Part 1, published in 1909, these eighty-two fables are charmingly retold by English folklorist, Joseph Jacobs.

Carlson Fable Collection *http://creighton.edu/aesop*
Father Greg Carlson has collected fables and fable-related artifacts for more than thirty years. His site includes scholarly commentary on the fables, and more than 3,500 images of fable-themed objects he has also assembled.

Folklore and Mythology Electronic Texts *www.pitt.edu/~dash/folktexts.html*
Texts and commentary on thousands of stories, arranged by themes, motifs, and story titles, edited and or translated by D. L. Ashliman, and including full texts and links to hundreds of fables.

Myths, Legends, and Epics

The words *myth*, *legend*, and *epic* are sometimes used interchangeably. Traditionally, myths have been regarded as stories that represent the attempts of early people to explain human existence and the nature of the world around them. Whether these tales were actually part of the religion of ancient cultures is not always clear, but we generally define a myth as having something to do with religion. Our most familiar myths feature the gods and goddesses of Greek, Roman, and Norse cultures, while Native American mythology is also well represented in many single tales and collections.

A *legend* usually refers to a story relating to the history of a culture. Legends revolve around an incident that supposedly took place or a person who may have lived. In most instances, however, the story has been told so often and embellished to such an extent that it would be very difficult to discover a factual basis. Did Robin Hood and King Arthur actually live? Was the Swiss hero William Tell a real person? Did he actually shoot an apple from his son's head? These and other legends like them provide a wealth of material for the storyteller.

Whereas myths focus on the gods, epics are ongoing legends that center on earthly heroes. Originally the epics were collections of songs or poems about a particular hero and his adventures, but modern authors have translated and/or retold these stories in prose form, which makes them particularly useful to the storyteller. Usually the epic hero is one whose character and moral code express not only universal but also national ideals, and the tales, therefore, impart a nationalistic flavor. While one adventure is sometimes extracted from an epic and presented as a single tale (it would then be categorized as a legend), the appeal of the epic lies in following the complete adventures of the hero, often from birth to death. Most adults will recognize some of their old childhood favorites in the epic literature—*The Odyssey*, *The Iliad*, and Robin Hood being the most ubiquitous and enjoyable for older children and teens.

While a folktale can usually be enjoyed without any knowledge of the culture of its origin, myths and legends cannot so easily be removed from their cultural context. The relationships of the gods and the patterns of the culture are expressed in continuous relationships rather than in individual tales. Like most folklore, the stories were originally told orally. If they seem too long or complicated for telling, some condensing may be desirable; but care must be taken not to shorten or simplify them so drastically that the majesty and power of the ancient tales are lost. Some writers have attempted to adapt myths and legends for very young children, but that often necessitates stripping away the beautiful language and philosophical musings, leaving only the bare threads of the plot.

Historically myths and legends have been most understood and appreciated by young adults, but with the success of Rick Riordan's myth-based novels, including *The Lightning Thief* (Greek mythology) and *The Red Pyramid* (Egyptian mythology), middle graders have joined in the fun.

It is also important to note that the myths we read are not necessarily translations of the original story. The literary styles of writers who do the retellings vary widely. While some versions are well suited for oral storytelling, others are best for individual readers. Storytellers who wish to introduce mythology to children should take the time to sample several collections.

GREEK AND ROMAN MYTHS AND LEGENDS

The stories of the gods and heroes of ancient Greece and Rome are among many storytellers' favorite myths. With their fantastic events, abundant action, and complex characters and relationships, these myths comment on human and divine foibles, explain natural phenomena, and describe the beginning of the world. While the capricious cruelty of the gods often causes painful tragedy for humans, the myths nevertheless exude a sunny optimism that celebrates the beauty and excitement in life.

There are many new retellings of and informational books about Greek and Roman mythology, but three books remain standard reading for storytellers. As an introduction to Greek mythology, Robert Graves's *Greek Gods and Heroes* is an entertaining look at the classics. Noted classicist Edith Hamilton's scholarly *Mythology* includes valuable background that you may wish to include in your introduction to a storytelling program. To share with younger children, Ingri and Edgar D'Aulaire's *Book of Greek Myths* has a humorous and earthy folktale quality that is reflected in both the text and illustrations. Whether you enjoy stark or poetic prose, collections of stories, or a single favorite tale, these books offer a rich array of stories to share with your listeners.

GREEK EPICS

The Iliad and *The Odyssey* of Homer are probably the most famous Greek epics. *The Iliad,* which relates the events of the Trojan War, is extremely complex and confusing (not to mention violent). The central figure is Achilles, but many other legendary heroes also take part, among them Agamemnon, Patrocles, Hector, and Priam. *The Odyssey,* which is much easier to understand, relates the strange and wonderful adventures that befall Odysseus on his return voyage to Ithaca after the capture of Troy. Adult versions of these Homeric epics are usually too difficult and racy for children, but there are several adaptations or retellings designed for younger readers that provide storytellers with some appropriate material. You'll find some included in the booklist below on page 164.

NORSE MYTHS

The Norse myths of Iceland are contained in two collections, the Elder or Poetic Edda and Younger or Prose Edda. The Poetic Edda tells of the creation of the world and the evolution of the gods. It also contains the Norse epic story of Sigurd the Volsung. The Prose Edda is a collection of important Norse myths, gathered in the thirteenth century, about Odin, Thor, Loki, Freya, and Baldur. Incidentally, the word *edda* originally meant "great-grandmother," which gives a rather folksy air to these sometimes difficult stories.

Norse myths seem considerably more somber than those of the Greeks and Romans, though the exploits of the trickster god Loki provide some humor. Unlike the immortal deities of classical Greek and Roman mythology, the Norse gods are mortal and are preparing to perish in a tragic battle at the end of the world. There are several excellent versions. Padraic Colum relates both the myths and the hero or epic tales in his classic 1912 collection, *The Children's Homer: Adventures of Odysseus and the Tale of Troy*, which has been reissued multiple times. The amply illustrated *D'Aulaires' Book of Norse Myths* emphasizes points of beauty and humor in the sometimes dark tales of the North. Its retelling will entice a somewhat younger age group, as will the excellent collections from handsomely illustrated volumes by Lise Lunge-Larsen, Mary Pope Osborne, and Neil Philip.

Pair your Norse tales with stories or readings from middle grade fiction books like Livi Michael's *City of Dogs* (Putnam, 2007), a fantasy that merges contemporary London with the possible ending of the Nine Worlds, and ties it in with the death of Balder. Nancy Farmer's *The Sea of Trolls* (Atheneum, 2004), in which siblings Jack and Lucy are kidnapped by the Viking berserker, Olaf One-Brow, is a wild, dangerous, but often droll adventure on the North Sea in the late eighth century that pulls in Norse and Celtic mythology, Vikings, dragons, trolls, and some wonderful language and storytelling.

OTHER EPICS

What is the world's oldest recorded story? So far, it's "The Epic of Gilgamesh" from ancient Mesopotamia. Thousands of clay tablets with cuneiform writing were excavated from what is now Iraq, starting in the 1840s. Dating back to 2700 BC, the writings tell the story of the legendary Gilgamesh, king of the Sumerian city of Uruk. Although Gilgamesh was probably an actual person, in the stories he's described as two-thirds god and one-third man. There have been several children's books about Gilgamesh, the most accessible and compelling being Geraldine McCaughrean's *Gilgamesh the Hero*. You can find the complete first translation of Gilgamesh online at www.sacred-texts.com/ane/eog/index.htm.

From India, *The Ramayana* is a collection of ancient Sanskrit stories, dating from the fifth to fourth centuries BC. Frequently told through dance, the stories describe the earthly life of the god Vishnu in his human form as Prince Rama. The tales relate Prince Rama's marriage to Sita and the adventures they share before her death. A classic telling in English is R. K. Narayan's *The Ramayana: A Shortened Modern Prose Version of the Indian Epic*.

The oldest epic written in English is *Beowulf*, an Anglo-Saxon saga believed to have been composed in the eighth century. It celebrates the courage, strength, wit, and cunning by which Beowulf destroys the man-eating monster Grendel, Grendel's cruel mother, and a fiendish dragon. Both Robert Nye and Seamus Heaney have written strongly dramatic prose versions, which render the action with all its gory details. Eric A. Kimmel, Michael Morpurgo, Gareth Hinds, and James Rumford have written versions that you may find more suitable for using with young people.

The exploits of Robin Hood, one of the most popular children's heroes, appear in several forms of literature and film, including prose stories and numerous old English ballads. These stories of Robin, Little John, Will Scarlet, Friar Tuck, and Maid Marian are filled with wit, courage, and fellowship. Although Robin Hood is an outlaw, he embodies many exemplary traits. His robbing of the rich to give to the poor may be a questionable ethic, but many of his followers see it as a brave attempt at justice. Howard Pyle's version, *The Merry Adventures of Robin Hood,* is a superb classic, good for reading aloud or for extracting incidents for an oral presentation.

King Arthur is the hero of a long series of medieval romances. Arthurian stories in the oral tradition were first written down in French, the language of the English court in Norman times. Sir Thomas Malory's fifteenth-century version, *Le Morte d'Arthur*—with tales of this romantic figure and his chivalrous knights—has been the source for later versions, of which Lord Tennyson's narrative poem "Idylls of the King" is typical. The concept of chivalry exemplified by Arthur and his knights reflects a more sophisticated ethic than that of the Robin Hood epic, but whether or not children understand chivalry as such, they find knights and their ladies particularly fascinating. More than a century ago, Howard Pyle, who so aptly portrayed Robin Hood, wrote an excellent version of this epic, *The Story of King Arthur and His Knights,* which remains popular in newer editions. Children will appreciate Margaret Hodges's *The Kitchen Knight: A Tale of King Arthur* and *Merlin and the Making of the King,* both illustrated with Trina Schart Hyman's dignified artwork.

You may also want to investigate tales of other national epic heroes: Ireland's Cuchulain and Finn McCool, Spain's El Cid, France's Roland, and Germany's Siegfried.

BOOKLIST: MYTHS, LEGENDS, AND EPICS

Burleigh, Robert. *Pandora.* *Illus. by Raúl Colón. Harcourt, 2002.* Pandora is warned not to open the mysterious jar that Zeus gave to her husband. Does she listen? (I, A)

Clayton, Sally Pomme. *Persephone.* *Illus. by Virginia Lee. Eerdmans, 2009.* "You will be Queen and light up my kingdom," Hades, King of the Underworld, tells her. (I, A)

Colum, Padraic. *The Children's Homer: Adventures of Odysseus and the Tale of Troy.* *Illus. by Willy Pogány. Aladdin, 2004, c1918.* Challenging language, but a masterful retelling of *The Odyssey* and *The Iliad* by an Irish poet. (A)

Coolidge, Olivia E. *Greek Myths.* *Illus. by Edouard Sandoz. Houghton Mifflin, 2001, c1949.* Reissue of a basic intro to the gods. (A)

Craft, M. Charlotte. *Cupid and Psyche.* *Illus. by K. Y. Craft. Morrow, 1996.* Cupid accidentally nicks himself with his own arrow and falls in love with Psyche. (I, A)

Crossley-Holland, Kevin. *The Norse Myths.* *Pantheon, 1981.* Thirty-two well-told tales start with the creation of the world and end with final story of Ragnarok. (A)

D'Aulaire, Ingri, and Edgar Parin D'Aulaire. *D'Aulaires' Book of Norse Myths.* *Illus. by the authors. New York Review of Books, 2005, c1967.* Gorgeously illustrated classic volume about Odin, Thor, Loki, and all the other gods, goddesses, giants, and Norse creatures. (I)

D'Aulaire, Ingri, and Edgar Parin D'Aulaire. *Ingri and Edgar Parin D'Aulaire's Book of Greek Myths.* *Illus. by the authors. Doubleday, 1962.* An oversize, classic compilation with forty-six stories of misbehaving gods and goddesses. (I)

Demi. *King Midas: The Golden Touch.* *Illus. by the author. McElderry, 2002.* In two tales, King Midas judges a music contest between Apollo and Pan and wishes for too much gold. (P, I)

Evslin, Bernard. *The Adventures of Ulysses.* *Illus. by William Hunter. Scholastic, 1969.* Tales of Ulysses's arduous journey home after the Trojan War. (A)

Graves, Robert. *Greek Gods and Heroes.* *Illus. by Dimitri Davis. Doubleday, 1960.* Lively two- to three-page retellings of twenty-seven myths. (A)

Hamilton, Edith. *Mythology.* *Illus. by Steele Savage. Little, Brown, 1942.* Classic collection of Greek, Roman, and Norse myths and legends. (A)

Hamilton, Virginia. *In the Beginning: Creation Stories from Around the World.* *Illus. by Barry Moser. Harcourt, 1988.* Twenty-five fascinating creation myths. (I, A)

Hodges, Margaret. *The Kitchen Knight: A Tale of King Arthur.* *Illus. by Trina Schart Hyman. Holiday, 1990.* Hiding his noble lineage and serving as a kitchen boy in King Arthur's court, Gareth proves his worthiness. Magnificent medieval-style illustrations. (I, A)

Hodges, Margaret. *Merlin and the Making of the King.* *Illus. by Trina Schart Hyman. Holiday House, 2004.* Three of the best-known English legends of King Arthur—"The Sword in the Stone," "Excalibur," and "The Lady of the Lake"—describe his crowning, marriage, and death. (I, A)

Hodges, Margaret. *Saint George and the Dragon: A Golden Legend.* *Adapted by Margaret Hodges from Edmund Spenser's "Faerie Queen." Illus. by Trina Schart Hyman. Little, Brown, 1984.* Una recruits the Red Cross Knight to slay a mighty dragon that plagues her father's kingdom. Based on Spenser's sixteenth-century epic poem from England. (I, A)

Kimmel, Eric A. ***The Hero Beowulf.*** *Illus. by Leonard Everett Fisher. Farrar, 2005.* Gloriously creepy picture-book version of the oldest surviving epic poem in English literature. (I, A)

Kimmel, Eric A. ***The McElderry Book of Greek Myths.*** *Illus. by Pep Montserrat. McElderry, 2008.* A dozen of the best-known ones. (I)

Lanier, Sidney, ed. ***The Boy's King Arthur.*** *Illus. by N. C. Wyeth. Dover, 2006, c1917.* Unabridged republication, with Wyeth's exciting color paintings. (I, A)

Low, Alice. ***The Macmillan Book of Greek Gods and Heroes.*** *Illus. by Arvis Stewart. Macmillan, 1985.* More than thirty myths in an attractive volume give a good overview of Greek mythology and legends. (I, A)

Lunge-Larsen, Lise. ***The Adventures of Thor the Thunder God.*** *Illus. by Jim Madsen. Houghton Mifflin, 2007.* Eight Norse legends featuring Thor and his mighty hammer. (I, A)

Lunge-Larsen, Lise. ***Gifts from the Gods: Ancient Words & Wisdom from Greek and Roman Mythology.*** *Illus. by Gareth Hinds. Houghton Mifflin, 2011.* Derivations and myths behind each of seventeen words commonly used in English, including *Achilles' heel, fate, fury,* and *genius.* Read one chapter a day and your kids will ace the SATs someday. (I, A)

Lupton, Hugh, and Daniel Morden. ***The Adventures of Odysseus.*** *Illus. by Christina Balit. Barefoot, 2006.* Odysseus narrates the stories of his own nine-year voyage home from the Trojan War. (I, A)

McCaughrean, Geraldine. ***The Bronze Cauldron: Myths and Legends of the World.*** *Illus. by Bee Willey. McElderry, 1998.* A remarkable collection of twenty-seven myths and legends from five continents. Equally splendid are the tales in McCaughrean's companion collections, *The Crystal Pool* (1999), *The Golden Hoard* (1996), and *The Silver Treasure* (1997). (I, A)

McCaughrean, Geraldine. ***Gilgamesh the Hero: The Epic of Gilgamesh.*** *Illus. by David Parkins. Eerdmans, 2003.* This elegant collection of twelve epic adventures of mighty King Gilgamesh and the Wild Man, Enkidu—based on seventh-century-BC Assyrian clay tablets—is the first of all buddy stories. (I, A)

McCaughrean, Geraldine. ***Roman Myths.*** *Illus. by Emma Chichester Clark. McElderry, 2001.* Noble and surprising collection of fifteen classic tales from ancient Rome. (I, A)

Morpurgo, Michael. ***Sir Gawain & the Green Knight.*** *Illus. by Michael Foreman. Candlewick, 2004.* A giant and fearsome knight challenges Sir Gawain to chop off his head in this King Arthur tale from England. (I, A)

Narayan, R. K. ***The Ramayana: A Shortened Modern Prose Version of the Indian Epic.*** *Viking, 1972.* Based on an eleventh-century account of the adventures of Hindu deity, Rama, an incarnation of the god Vishnu. (A)

Nye, Robert. ***Beowulf: A New Telling.*** *Illus. by Alan E. Cober. Hill and Wang, 1968.* A prose version of the epic poem of how the great warrior Beowulf defeated the fearsome monster Grendel. (A)

Osborne, Mary Pope. ***Favorite Greek Myths.*** *Illus. by Troy Howell. Scholastic, 1989.* An elegant retelling of twelve myths, most of which are based upon the Roman poet Ovid's "Metamorphoses." (I, A)

Osborne, Mary Pope. ***Favorite Norse Myths.*** *Illus. by Troy Howell. Scholastic, 1996.* Battles, squabbles, and adventures of Norse gods and goddesses. (I, A)

Philip, Neil. ***Odin's Family: Myths of the Vikings.*** *Illus. by Maryclare Foa. Orchard, 1996.* From the creation of the earth to the twilight of the gods.

Pyle, Howard. ***The Merry Adventures of Robin Hood.*** *Illus. by the author. Dover, 1965, c1903.* Not an easy read, with all the *thee*s and *thou*s, but an unabridged replication of Pyle's classic recounting of the epic tales, with his handsome black-and-white illustrations. (I, A)

Pyle, Howard. ***The Story of King Arthur and His Knights.*** *Illus. by the author. Sterling, 2004, c1903.* A facsimile edition of the classic retelling of the Camelot legends. (I, A)

Reinhart, Matthew, and Robert Sabuda. ***Gods & Heroes.*** *Candlewick, 2010.* Visually thrilling, this pop-up paper-engineered book gives an overview of major deities from Egyptian, Greek, Norse, Asian, and New World mythologies. The Encyclopedia Mythologica series also includes *Fairies and Magical Creatures* (2008) and *Dragons & Monsters* (2011). (I, A)

Riordan, Rick. ***Percy Jackson's Greek Gods.*** *Illus. by John Rocco. Disney/Hyperion, 2014. (I, A)* Percy Jackson, the ADHD demigod you've met in the Percy Jacksons and the Olympians series, starting with *The Lightning Thief*, narrates the inside scoop on the creation and history of Ancient Greece's major gods and goddesses. Hilarity, violence, and mayhem erupts on every gorgeous oversized page, with chapter titles like "Persephone Marries Her Stalker" and "Zeus Kills Everyone." (I, A)

Rumford, James. ***Beowulf: A Hero's Tale Retold.*** *Illus. by the author. Houghton Mifflin, 2007.* A visual feast and skillful retelling/distillation of the ninth-century hero poem about the stalwart young knight Beowulf, the ogre Grendel and his evil mother, and a flying fire-snake. (I, A)

San Souci, Robert D. ***Robin Hood and the Golden Arrow.*** *Illus. by E. B. Lewis. Orchard, 2010.* Disguised as a beggar, Robin enters the Sheriff of Nottingham's archery contest. (P, I)

Souhami, Jessica. ***Rama and the Demon King: An Ancient Tale from India.*** *Illus. by the author. Frances Lincoln, 1997.* In a Hindu tale from The Ramayana, Prince Rama is aided by a monkey army to rescue his wife, Sita, when she is kidnapped by Ravana, the ten-headed demon king. (P, I)

Sutcliff, Rosemary. ***Black Ships Before Troy! The Story of "The Iliad."*** *Illus. by Alan Lee. Delacorte, 1993.* A prose retelling of Homer's epic poem "The Iliad" with magnificent sweeping paintings across each page. (I, A)

Sutcliff, Rosemary. ***The Wanderings of Odysseus: The Story of "The Odyssey."*** *Illus. by Alan Lee. Frances Lincoln, 2005, c1995.* Odysseus and his men leave Troy and sail off for home. (I, A)

Vinge, Joan D. ***The Random House Book of Greek Myths.*** *Illus. by Oren Sherman. Random House, 1999.* Fourteen well-told myths of major and minor gods, with handsome paintings. (I, A)

WEBSITES: MYTHS, LEGENDS, AND EPICS

Best of Legends *http://bestoflegends.org*
Links to texts of King Arthur, Robin Hood, the Brothers Grimm, and Andrew Lang's Fairy Books series, edited by Paula Katherine Marmor.

Encyclopedia Mythica *www.pantheon.org*
Extensive encyclopedia of mythology, folklore, and religion, including myths, heroes, Arthurian legends, creatures and characters from folklore, an image gallery, and an invaluable pronunciation guide for English speakers.

Folklore and Mythology Electronic Texts *www.pitt.edu/~dash/mythlinks.html*
Includes links and stories of "Germanic (Especially Old Norse) Mythology and Culture" edited and/or translated by D. L. Ashliman.

Greek Mythology Link *www.maicar.com/GML*
"Primarily concerned with the creative, artistic, literary and inspiring aspects of the Greek myths," this site offers a collection of Greek myths, retold by author Carlos Parada.

Internet Sacred Text Archive *www.sacred-texts.com*
This archive is the "largest freely available archive of online books about religion, mythology, folklore and the esoteric on the Internet." Look up any country, continent, culture, or religion and read complete texts of books of myths in public no longer protected by copyright, including the complete *Bullfinch's Mythology*, written by Thomas Bullfinch in 1855.

Mr. Donn's Social Studies Site *www.mrdonn.org*

Comprehensive site for teachers and children with free lesson plans for teachers, games, activities, and PowerPoints on a huge range of topics, including ancient civilizations, world history, and American history.

Myth Index *www.mythindex.com*

Dictionary of more than 3,700 names in Greek mythology and another 500-plus in Roman mythology.

Mythmania *www.mythman.com*

Click on the "Homework Help" link to find thorough descriptions and images of each god, goddess, heroes, and other mortal characters and creatures in Greek mythology.

Myths and Legends *http://myths.e2bn.org*

Five dozen myths and legends, mostly from the British Isles, which children can read and/or hear. The site includes an interesting "Add a Story" feature that allows children to enter their own stories, either retold from folklore or made up.

Myths Writing Workshop with Jane Yolen
teacher.scholastic.com/writewit/mff/mythswshop_index.htm

A guide for children by author Jane Yolen on writing myths about natural phenomena and how they came to be.

Theoi Greek Mythology *www.theoi.com*

A spectacularly illustrated, free reference guide to gods (*theoi*) and other characters in Greek mythology and religion.

Religious Stories

Oral presentation has traditionally played an important part in the teaching of religion. The teacher or leader stands or sits in front of a group and tells a story based on the religious principles of the order. Today storytelling is still used as a way to teach religious concepts as well as relate stories that entertain.

Oscar Wilde, the talented nineteenth-century playwright, contributed to children's literature with his book of original fairy tales. The most impressive of these is "The Selfish Giant." Because the giant lets no one visit his lovely garden, winter lingers within its walls while it is springtime outside. When the neighborhood children sneak into the garden and the trees burst into blossom, the giant befriends a little boy. Years later the boy, a Christ figure, accompanies the giant to the garden of Paradise. Children may not understand the religious symbolism, but they will still appreciate the beautifully written tale, which is a good example of the religious influence on written and oral sources.

For those seeking religious stories, a wealth of material is available. But do remember that just because a story doesn't specifically mention religion doesn't mean that it might not serve your purpose.

Books based on Judeo-Christian heritage are various and easy for storytellers to find. You can choose from many interpretations of the Bible. In *Tomie dePaola's Book of Bible Stories: New International Version,* full-color art accompanies the retellings of stories from both the Old and New Testaments. Mary Pope Osborne and Natalie Pope Boyce's *The Random House Book of Bible Stories* is another attractive collection, just right for an audience of children.

Retellings of single Bible stories are popular. Isaac Bashevis Singer's picture book, *Why Noah Chose the Dove,* illustrated with Eric Carle's tissue paper collages, shows animals arguing about which of them is most worthy. It is the dove who says, "Each one of us has something the other doesn't have, given us by God who created us all." At that point Noah invites all the animals into the ark.

The husband-and-wife team Leo and Diane Dillon took on "The Book of Ecclesiastes" in the Bible with their magnificently illustrated interpretation of *To Everything There Is a Season.* You can then sing the Pete Seeger version of the verses, "Turn, Turn, Turn," set to music. Speaking of music, Ashley Bryan's joyful picture book, *Let It Shine: Three Favorite Spirituals,* will get everyone singing. Those interested in using their storytelling skills in their church or synagogue activities can find an endless supply of source materials for visual presentation, storytelling, and reading aloud.

Through stories, children can learn of other cultures and religions and note the similarities and differences between them. One Jewish legend, gloriously illustrated as a picture book but suitable for a wide age range, is David Wisniewski's Caldecott Medal–winning story, *The Golem,* in which a lump of clay fashioned into a man becomes a monster with a power all its own.

Below are some great single titles and story collections that deal with religious themes.

BOOKLIST: RELIGIOUS STORIES

Adler, David A. ***The Story of Hanukkah.*** *Illus. by Jill Weber. Holiday House, 2011.* Simply told picture-book account of the destruction of Jerusalem by King Antiochus IV more than two thousand years ago and how the Maccabees fought back. (P, I)

Bernier-Grand, Carmen T. ***Our Lady of Guadalupe.*** *Illus. by Tonya Engel. Marshall Cavendish, 2012.* A picture-book retelling of the story of Juan Diego, who at age fifty-seven in 1531, reported four apparitions of the Virgin Mary near what is now Mexico City. (P, I)

Bryan, Ashley. ***Let It Shine: Three Favorite Spirituals.*** *Illus. by the author. Atheneum, 2007.* Wildly colorful illustrations accompany the lyrics to "This Little Light of Mine," "Oh, When the Saints Go Marching In," and "He's Got the Whole World in His Hands." (P, I)

Davis, Aubrey. ***Bagels from Benny.*** *Illus. by Dusan Petricic. Kids Can, 2003.* Young Benny leaves a bag of bagels in the synagogue for God every week in a heartwarming story based on an old Jewish folktale. (P)

Demi. ***Buddha.*** *Illus. by the author. Henry Holt, 1996.* In a glowingly illustrated picture book biography, follow the prince, Siddhartha, on his journey to enlightenment and to becoming Buddha. Demi has done several stunning picture book biographies of religious figures, including *Gandhi* (McElderry, 2001), *Jesus* (McElderry, 2005), *Joan of Arc* (Marshall Cavendish, 2011), *The Legend of Lao Tzu and the Tao Te Ching* (McElderry, 2007), *The Legend* *of Saint Nicholas* (McElderry, 2003), *Muhammad* (McElderry, 2003), *Rumi: Whirling Dervish* (Marshall Cavendish, 2009), and *Saint Francis of Assisi* (Wisdom Tales, 2012). (I)

Demi. *Buddha Stories.* *Illus. by the author. Henry Holt, 1997.* Eleven brief Jataka tales—parables about people and animals—attributed to Buddha some 2,500 years ago, are printed on indigo paper with text and illustrations in gold. (I, A)

DePaola, Tomie. *Christopher: The Holy Giant.* *Illus. by the author. Holiday House, 1994.* The legend of the giant, Reprobus, who wished to serve "the mightiest of all," and whom Jesus renames Christopher, or Bearer-of-Christ. (P, I)

DePaola, Tomie. *The Clown of God: An Old Story.* *Illus. by the author. Harcourt, 1978.* Giovanni, a street urchin, becomes a juggler, but finds fulfillment only when he performs for a statue of the Holy Child on Christmas. (P, I)

DePaola, Tomie. *The Legend of Old Befana: An Italian Christmas Story.* *Illus. by the author. Harcourt, 1980.* An old woman sets out to find the Child King and visits sleeping children, leaving them gifts from her basket. (P, I)

DePaola, Tomie. *The Legend of the Poinsettia.* *Illus. by the author. Putnam, 1994.* With no other gift to offer Baby Jesus in her church in Mexico on Christmas, young Lucida brings an armful of weeds that transform into the first poinsettias. (P, I)

DePaola, Tomie. *Patrick: Patron Saint of Ireland.* *Illus. by the author. Holiday House, 1992.* Picture book biography of Ireland's patron saint, plus five legends about his life. (P, I)

DePaola, Tomie. *Tomie dePaola's Book of Bible Stories: New International Version.* *Putnam, 1990.* Thirty-seven stories from the Old and New Testament, from the creation to the resurrection. (P, I)

Dillon, Leo, and Diane Dillon. *To Everything There Is a Season.* *Illus. by the authors. Scholastic, 1998.* Breathtaking illustrations accompany the well-known verses from the Book of Ecclesiastes in the Bible. (P, I, A)

Ganeri, Anita. *Sikh Stories.* *Illus. by Rachael Phillips. Picture Window Books, 2006.* A collection of eight well-told and illustrated Sikh tales, part of the Traditional Religious Tales series, all by Ganeri, including *Buddhist Stories, Christian Stories, Islamic Stories,* and *Jewish Stories,* all published in 2006. (I, A)

Gavin, Jamila. *Tales from India: Stories of Creation and the Cosmos.* *Illus. by Amanda Hall. Candlewick/Templar, 2011.* Ten ornately illustrated Hindu myths about how the world began and the birth of the gods. (I, A)

Goldin, Barbara Diamond. *Cakes and Miracles: A Purim Tale.* *Illus. by Jaime Zollars. Marshall Cavendish, 2010, c1991.* A blind boy, Hershel, finds a way to celebrate Purim with the baking of the traditional cookie, the hamantaschen. (P)

Hodges, Margaret. *Moses.* *Illus. by Barry Moser. Harcourt, 2007.* Handsome watercolors portray the life of Moses, from the basket in the bulrushes to the Ten Commandments. (P, I)

Kimmel, Eric A. *The Story of Esther: A Purim Tale.* *Illus. by Jill Weber. Holiday House, 2011.* Old Testament story of Queen Esther, the Jewish wife of the Persian king Ahasuerus, who thwarted the murderous plans of Haman, the king's disloyal minister. (P, I)

Krishnaswami, Uma. *The Broken Tusk: Stories of the Hindu God Ganesha.* *Illus. by Maniam Selven. August House, 1996.* A collection of seventeen short stories about Ganesha, the elephant-headed Hindu god. (I, A)

McFarlane, Marilyn. *Sacred Stories: Wisdom from World Religions.* *Aladdin, 2011.* Creation stories and other myths from six major religions: Buddhism, Christianity, Hinduism, Islam, Judaism, and Native American. (I, A)

Moore, Emma V. *Manu's Ark: India's Tale of the Great Flood.* *Illus. by the author. Mandala, 2012.* In this picture book rendition, King Manu, the father of Man, prays to Vishnu to keep the world safe, and in return finds a tiny talking and ever-growing fish, an incarnation of Vishnu known as Matsya. (I, A)

Nelson, Kadir. *He's Got the Whole World in His Hands.* *Illus. by the author. Dial, 2005.* Glorious picture book illustrating the lyrics to the spiritual, featuring an African American boy and his multiethnic family. (P, I)

Osborne, Mary Pope, and Natalie Pope Boyce. *The Random House Book of Bible Stories.* *Illus. by Michael Welply. Random House, 2009.* Fifty-six well-told and well-known stories from the Old and New Testaments. (P, I)

Paterson, Katherine. *Brother Sun, Sister Moon: Saint Francis of Assisi's Canticle of the Creatures.* *Illus. by Pamela Dalton. Handprint, 2011.* Gorgeous folk art–style cut-paper illustrations grace this adaptation of Saint Francis of Assisi's song of praise, which he wrote in 1224. (P, I, A)

Pilling, Ann. *The Kingfisher Book of Bible Stories.* *Illus. by Kady MacDonald Denton. Kingfisher, 2003.* Ninety-three well-known stories from the Old and New Testaments, with notation of chapter and verse. (P, I, A)

Pinkney, Jerry. *Noah's Ark.* *Illus. by the author. SeaStar Books, 2002.* Beautifully illustrated Caldecott Honor picture book retelling of the flood story. (P, I)

Sabuda, Robert. *Saint Valentine.* *Atheneum, 1992.* The legend of Valentine, a Roman priest and physician, illustrated with intricate mosaics made of tiny paper squares. (P, I)

Schwartz, Howard. *Elijah's Violin and Other Jewish Fairy Tales.* *Illus. by Linda Heller. Oxford University Press, 1994, c1983.* An impressive assortment of thirty-six fairy tales and legends, many from the Talmud, hailing from Eastern Europe, the Middle East, and other far-flung places. (I, A)

Singer, Isaac Bashevis. ***Why Noah Chose the Dove.*** *Trans. by Elizabeth Shub. Illus. by Eric Carle. Farrar, 1973.* Lovely picture-book account of how the dove became Noah's messenger. (P, I)

Souhami, Jessica. ***Rama and the Demon King: An Ancient Tale from India.*** *Illus. by the author. Frances Lincoln, 1997.* See page 168.

Spier, Peter. ***Noah's Ark.*** *Illus. by the author. Doubleday, 1977.* This Caldecott winner is a mostly wordless picture book told in minutely detailed pen and ink and watercolors. (P)

Stampler, Ann Redisch. ***The Wooden Sword: A Jewish Folktale from Afghanistan.*** *Illus. by Carol Liddiment. Albert Whitman, 2012.* When the shah, disguised as a poor traveler, meets a poor shoemaker and his wife, he decides to test the man's claim that if one path is blocked, God will lead him to another. (P, I, A)

Wilde, Oscar. ***The Happy Prince and Other Stories.*** *Illus. by Lars Bo. Penguin, 1996, 1962.* Nine of Wilde's more spiritual short stories originally published in 1888, including "The Selfish Giant" and "The Star Child." You can find all of Wilde's short stories on Project Gutenberg at www.gutenberg.org/ebooks/902 or the Literature Network at www.online-literature.com/poe/177. (I, A)

Wisniewski, David. ***The Golem.*** *Illus. by the author. Clarion, 1996.* The chief rabbi in sixteenth-century Prague makes a clay giant in the image of a man to protect the Jews from their enemies. A Caldecott Medal winner. (I, A)

chapter 6

Around the World with Folk and Fairy Tales

The universe is made of stories, not of atoms.

—MURIEL RUKEYSER, AMERICAN POET

ONE OBVIOUS THEMATIC CHOICE WHEN TELLING OR SHARING stories is to present an assemblage of tales from a particular region, country, and/or culture. Well-written collections and picture books of single tales from every part of the world are widely available. We now take you and your audience on a virtual tour of six of the seven continents (the penguins in Antarctica don't tell stories) and demonstrate that people on the other side of the world are not so different after all.

TALES FROM EUROPE

Many of the stories in the first books of fairy tales ever published in Europe are still read and relished by children in Western Europe and America. Let's dig into some of them.

Tales from France (and Italy)

One of the earliest books, *Histoires ou contes du temps passé avec des moralités* (*Histories or tales of long ago with morals*) and subtitled *Contes de ma mere l'oye* (*Tales of Mother Goose*), was published in 1697. Charles Perrault (1628–1703), usually credited with authorship, collected the folktales. He rewrote them for the amusement of the adults at the French court, but they became popular with children as well. The eight tales in his collection (whose subtitle, incidentally, seems to be the first mention of "Mother Goose") were "The Sleeping Beauty," "Little Red Riding Hood," "Blue Beard," "Puss in Boots," "Diamonds and Toads," "Cinderella," "Riquet with the Tuft," and "Tom Thumb." Perrault added morals to the stories for the amusement of adults; they are usually omitted for children.

Other French tales, some of which were written in the same period as Perrault's, are also enjoyed today. If you think these were all twee tales written by male aristocrats, read Terri Windling's essay "Les Contes des Fées: The Literary Fairy Tales of France" (www.endicott-studio.com/rdrm/forconte.html). Women actually wrote a number of the tales. Comtesse D'Aulnoy, for example, wrote "The White Cat," and Madame LePrince de Beaumont wrote "Beauty and the Beast," both of which appear in many story collections.

Many credit Perrault with inventing the written fairy-tale genre, but the first recorded book of fairy tales was composed a century earlier, though not released until 1634. The book, *Il Pentamerone,* written by Italian poet Giambattista Basile and published after his death, greatly influenced the fairy-tale movement in France sixty years later. The Brothers Grimm considered it to be the first national collection of fairy tales. The book contains the earliest known written versions of such classics as "Sleeping Beauty" ("The Sun and the Moon and Talia"), "Cinderella" ("Cenerentola"), "Puss in Boots" ("Gagliuso"), "Rapunzel" ("Petrosinella"), and many others. You can easily find and read all the stories online.

In fact, there was one even earlier book of tales: *The Facetious Nights of Straparola,* by Giovanni Francesco Straparola (which is probably a pseudonym, since it means "babbler" in Italian), an Italian writer and fairy-tale collector. Published in the sixteenth century during the course of several years (1550–1553), it contains a collection of seventy-five stories, some the first written versions of familiar fairy tales, though most are far too bawdy for children. In one story, "Constantino Fortunato," a magical cat helps a poor young man gain riches and the hand of a princess, and even become the king of Bohemia. This is the earliest-known version of "Puss in Boots."

It seems as if each succeeding generation ripped off the stories of its predecessors, adding new wrinkles and plot points. We're not complaining. It's fascinating to compare the Italian stories with the later French, German, and English versions and to realize we are still telling, reading, and loving these stories hundreds of years later.

BOOKLIST: TALES FROM FRANCE

Galdone, Paul. *Puss in Boots.* *Illus. by the author. Clarion, 1976.* A smart cat helps a poor young man defeat an ogre and win a princess. (P, I)

Huck, Charlotte. *Toads and Diamonds.* *Illus. by Anita Lobel. Greenwillow, 1996.* An old woman rewards helpful Renée with diamonds that fall from her lips; her rude stepsister, Francine, is punished with toads and snakes. (P, I)

McClintock, Barbara. *Cinderella.* *Illus. by the author. Scholastic, 2005.* Cinderella forgives her stepsisters in this comely version, which is based on Charles Perrault's original telling from the seventeenth century. (P, I)

Perrault, Charles. *Cinderella; Or, The Little Glass Slipper.* *Trans. and illus. by Marcia Brown. Scribner, 1954.* See page 152.

Perrault, Charles. *The Complete Fairy Tales of Charles Perrault.* *Trans. by Neil Philip and Nicoletta Simborowski. Illus. by Sally Holmes. Clarion, 1993.* An attractive volume of all eleven tales attributed to the French folklorist, including a "Little Red Riding Hood" with no rescue at the end, "Sleeping Beauty," and "Bluebeard." (P, I, A)

Perrault, Charles. *Puss in Boots.* *Illus. by Fred Marcellino. Farrar, 1990.* The Caldecott Honor art for this version of the poor-boy-makes-good-thanks-to-his-cat story is a must to share. (P, I)

Tales from Germany

In Germany, Jacob Grimm (1785–1863) and Wilhelm Grimm (1786–1859) collected folktales as part of their study of philology in order to examine the roots of the German language. Their first volume of *Kinder und Hausmarchen* (Children's and Household Tales) was published in 1812, and subsequent volumes followed in later years. The stories were transcribed mostly as the brothers heard them from storytellers, and though they allowed people to believe the stories came from country peasants or villagers, many were from middle-class or aristocratic acquaintances.

The brothers made many modifications to the stories, editing their original retellings in subsequent editions, including changing the characters of the mothers in "Hansel and Gretel" and "Snow White and the Seven Dwarfs" into stepmothers. (Perhaps this is why stepmothers have gotten such a bad rap all these years.) Many of the 212 tales in the complete collection are inappropriate for children (and a few are disturbingly anti-Semitic), but some have been popular for generations—among them, "Rapunzel," "Rumpelstiltskin," and "The Bremen Town Musicians."

The tales reach us today in many different translations and versions. A large library can easily have a whole shelf of different books devoted to Grimm's fairy tales. Which version should you use to learn and tell these tales? If you took the time to study each version of Grimm, each version of the Arabian Nights, and each version of Perrault, you could become an expert folklorist, but you might never have time to learn a story! As a beginner, trust the judgment of experienced storytellers. Also check your local library; it may have a printed or online storytelling bibliography based on its collection. The diverse annotated bibliographies in this and the following chapters will help you. There is, of course, no one perfect version of a collection of a tale. For instance, even though many new beautifully and colorfully illustrated translations of the tales are now available, you may end up preferring the retellings in books like Wanda Gág's *Tales from Grimm* and *More Tales from Grimm*.

There's no question that one should introduce tales by the Brothers Grimm to children, but keep in mind that, for a variety of reasons, many of the stories are unsuitable for younger audiences. You will discover that much of what is portrayed is symbolic of the struggle between good and evil; the triumph of good often comes from some sort of sacrifice. Violence is a concern in many of the tales, but rarely is the sacrifice portrayed with the blood and gore that many children are exposed to by today's media. For example, in "The Seven Ravens" a young woman searching for her seven bewitched brothers cuts off her finger to use as a key to open the door of a glass mountain. Her act symbolizes a sacrifice in exchange for love and forgiveness, but the act is actually overshadowed by the brothers' return to their human form and their reunion with their sister. If a young child seems frightened by a story from Grimm, then set aside the stories until the child is more mature and able to deal with the tale's frightening aspects.

BOOKLIST: TALES FROM GERMANY

Altmann, Anna E. ***The Seven Swabians, and Other German Folktales.*** *Libraries Unlimited, 2006.* Part of the World Folklore series, this features more than eighty folktales, historical background, recipes, and color photos. (Professional)

Babbitt, Natalie. ***Ouch! A Tale from Grimm.*** *Illus. by Fred Marcellino. HarperCollins, 1998.* The king sends Marco off on an errand to hell, where the Devil's own grandmother helps him collect three golden hairs from the Devil's head. (I, A)

Coombs, Kate. ***Hans My Hedgehog: A Tale from the Brothers Grimm.*** *Illus. by John Nickle. Atheneum, 2012.* Born half boy and half hedgehog, a young man retreats to the forest, rescues two kings, and finds a princess who lifts the spell that has ruled his life. (P, I, A)

Gág, Wanda. ***Tales from Grimm.*** *Tr. and illus. by Wanda Gág. University of Minnesota Press, 2006, c1936.* Along with *More Tales from Grimm* (2006, c1947), this classic collection of sixteen Grimm's fairy tales is marvelously accessible for kids. (P, I)

Galdone, Paul. ***Rumpelstiltskin.*** *Illus. by the author. Clarion, 1985.* A splendid rendering of the Grimm brothers' tale. (P, I)

Grimm, Jacob, and Wilhelm Grimm. ***The Complete Fairy Tales of the Brothers Grimm.*** *Third expanded ed. Tr. by Jack Zipes. Random House, 1996.* Weighing in at eight hundred pages, this complete collection includes 242 tales, including several dozen previously untranslated and fragmentary ones. Many are wildly inappropriate for children, so be forewarned. (Professional)

Grimm, Jacob, and Wilhelm Grimm. ***Grimm's Fairy Tales.*** *Illus. by Arthur Rackham. Calla Editions, 1992.* A handsome edition of thirty-seven stories with numerous color plates and black-and-white illustrations by the great Arthur Rackham, circa 1907. (I, A)

Grimm, Jacob, and Wilhelm Grimm. ***The Juniper Tree and Other Tales from Grimm.*** *Tr. by Lore Segal and Randall Jarrell. Illus. by Maurice Sendak. Farrar, 1973.* This two-volume set is filled with grim and melancholy tales, but oh, those exquisite pencil illustrations! (I, A)

Hyman, Trina Schart. ***Little Red Riding Hood.*** *Illus. by the author. Holiday House, 1983.* This version's delicate pen and inks illustrations won Hyman a Caldecott Honor. (P, I)

Kimmel, Eric A. ***Iron John.*** *Illus. by Trina Schart Hyman. Holiday House, 1994.* Young Prince Walter frees wild man Iron John from the king's cage. See also *Iron Hans: A Grimm's Fairy Tale* by Stephen Mitchell, below. (I, A)

Lesser, Rika. ***Hansel and Gretel.*** *Illus. by Paul O. Zelinsky. Dodd, Mead, 1984.* The classic Grimm tale, for which Zelinsky won his first Caldecott Honor. (P, I)

Marshall, James. *Hansel and Gretel.* *Illus. by the author. Dial, 1990.* Marshall's wicked witch is sublime, with her bulging bosom and ribbons in her blonde hair. (P, I)

Marshall, James. *Red Riding Hood.* *Illus. by the author. Dial, 1987.* Rescued from the wolf's belly, Red's granny says, "It was so dark in there I couldn't read a word!" (P)

Mitchell, Stephen. *Iron Hans: A Grimms' Fairy Tale.* *Illus. by Matt Tavares. Candlewick, 2007.* A young prince lets the caged wild man free and goes with him to the forest. Have children compare this one with Eric A. Kimmel's version, above. (P, I)

Pinkney, Jerry. *Little Red Riding Hood.* *Illus. by the author. Little, Brown, 2007.* On a snowy day, Mama sends her sweet little girl with a basket of chicken soup and raisin muffins to grandmother's house, where the wolf awaits. (P, I)

Pirotta, Saviour. *The McElderry Book of Grimms' Fairy Tales.* *Illus. by Emma Chichester Clark. McElderry, 2002.* Attractive compilation of ten familiar tales. (P, I, A)

Pullman, Philip. *Fairy Tales from the Brothers Grimm.* *Viking, 2012.* Fifty tales in a splendid new English retelling by the author of the His Dark Materials trilogy. (I, A)

Schlitz, Laura Amy. *The Bearskinner: A Tale of the Brothers Grimm.* *Candlewick, 2007.* In exchange for riches, a hungry soldier makes a deal with the Devil to wear a bear skin and not bathe for seven years. (I, A)

Tatar, Maria, ed. *The Annotated Brothers Grimm.* *Bicentennial ed. Illus. with paintings and reprods. W. W. Norton, 2012.* New translations of thirty-seven household tales, many known to children, and an additional seven stories in a "Tales for Adults" chapter. Each story is accompanied by margin notes and numerous period illustrations. (Professional)

Zelinsky, Paul O. *Rapunzel.* *Illus. by the author. Dutton, 1997.* The sumptuous Italianate paintings accompanying this somber fairy tale about the girl with all that hair won Zelinsky a Caldecott Medal. (I, A)

Zelinsky, Paul O. *Rumpelstiltskin.* *Illus. by the author. Dutton, 1986.* Zelinsky's medieval-style paintings for the story of the man who spun straw into gold earned him a Caldecott Honor. (P, I)

Tales from the British Isles

The name that stands out above all others as collector of English tales is Joseph Jacobs (1854–1916), whose *English Fairy Tales* was published in 1890, followed by *More English Fairy Tales* (1894), *Celtic Fairy Tales* (1892), *More Celtic Fairy Tales* (1894), *Indian Fairy Tales* (1912) and *European Folk and Fairy Tales* (1916). He was inspired by Perrault and the Brothers Grimm, but his purpose in collecting was somewhat different: he was deliberately trying to find stories for children. Although his retellings leave out incidents that he felt would be inappropriate for young listeners, he recorded his omissions in notes at the end of his collections. If heavy dialects made reading difficult, he changed the language slightly, but his tales, nevertheless, still retain their original folk flavor.

The stories that Jacobs collected ranged from simple nursery favorites, such as "Jack and the Beanstalk," "The Story of the Three Bears," "The Story of the Three Little Pigs," and "Teeny-Tiny," to the more sophisticated "Cap o' Rushes," a variant of Cinderella. Unlike German folktales, which are often rather somber, Jacobs's stories and other English tales contain more than a measure of humor. Giants and giant killers abound in these tales, including the stalwart, sturdy Molly Whuppie, the title heroine who outwits a giant. No simpering ninny awaiting rescue from a prince is she! Jacobs's tales may not be considered authentic folklore, since he added literary attributes (as did Perrault, the Brothers Grimm, and so many authors, come to think of it), but his versions have a distinctive flair. Consider the many bowdlerized versions of "The Three Little Pigs." Now enjoy Jacobs's original introduction to the popular story, published in *English Fairy Tales* (1890):

> Once upon a time when pigs spoke rhyme
> And monkeys chewed tobacco,
> And hens took snuff to make them tough,
> And ducks went quack, quack, quack-o!
>
> There was an old sow with three little pigs, and as she had not enough to keep them, she sent them out to seek their fortune.

These days you might be castigated for mentioning chewing tobacco, and children won't know what snuff is; this is still a charming way to begin a story.

The other sources of English folktales readily available to children came from well-known Scottish folklorist Andrew Lang (1844–1912), who was also a well-known poet, novelist, and historian. Lang included English tales with other stories he collected from all over the world in his famous "color" fairy books, beginning with *The Blue Fairy Book* (1889).

The popularity of English stories has inspired some fine picture-book versions, but in our opinion, reserve them mostly for individual reading after the story has been told. An oral presentation of "Master of All Masters" has got to be funnier without pictures, no matter how skillful the art is. See if you don't agree.

Master of All Masters

Retold by Joseph Jacobs

This English folktale, collected by Joseph Jacobs, is a thesaurus lover's delight. You'll need to memorize the servant girl's final speech, delivered in a fine panic. Compare the story with Cynthia DeFelice's picture-book reworking of it, Nelly May Has Her Say, *illustrated by Henry Cole.*

A girl once went to the fair to hire herself for servant. At last a funny-looking old gentleman engaged her, and took her home to his house. When she got there, he told her that he had something to teach her, for in his house he had his own names for things.

He said to her, "What will you call me?"

"Master or mister, or whatever you please sir," says she.

He said: "You must call me 'master of all masters.' And what would you call this?" he said, pointing to his bed.

"Bed or couch, or whatever you please, sir."

"No, that's my 'barnacle.' And what do you call these?" said he pointing to his pantaloons.

"Breeches or trousers, or whatever you please, sir."

"You must call them 'squibs and crackers.' And what would you call her?" he said, pointing to the cat.

"Cat or kit, or whatever you please, sir."

"You must call her 'white-faced simminy.' And this now," says he, showing the fire, "what would you call this?"

"Fire or flame, or whatever you please, sir."

"You must call it 'hot cockalorum.' And what's this?" he went on, pointing to the water.

"Water or wet, or whatever you please, sir."

"No, 'pondalorum' is its name. And what do you call all this?" asked he, as he pointed to the house.

"House or cottage, or whatever you please, sir."

"You must call it 'high-topper mountain.'"

That very night the servant woke her master up in a fright and said: "Master of all masters, get out of your barnacle and put on your squibs and crackers. For white-faced simminy has got a spark of hot cockalorum on its tail, and unless you get some pondalorum, high-topper mountain will be all on hot cockalorum."

. . . That's all.

BOOKLIST: TALES FROM THE BRITISH ISLES

For English legends and epics about Beowulf, King Arthur, and Robin Hood, see the booklist on page 164.

Beneduce, Ann Keay. *Jack and the Beanstalk.* *Illus. by Gennady Spirin. Philomel, 1999.* Based on an 1881 version of the Old English fairy tale, in which Jack climbs the beanstalk and avenges his father. (P, I)

Brown, Marcia. *Dick Whittington and His Cat.* *Illus. by the author. Scribner, 1950.* A legend about a poor boy who, with the help of his cat, came up in the world and became the mayor of London in the early-fifteenth century. (I, A)

Byrd, Robert. *Finn MacCoul and His Fearless Wife: A Giant of a Tale from Ireland.* *Illus. by the author.* Dutton, 1999. Finn's wife Oonagh tries to shield her giant husband, Finn, from that big bully, Cucullin. Compare with *Fin M'Coul, the Giant of Knockmany Hill* by Tomie dePaola and *Mrs. McCool and the Giant Cuhullin* by Jessica Souhami, both below. (I, A)

DeFelice, Cynthia. *Nelly May Has Her Say.* *Illus. by Henry Cole. Farrar/Margaret Ferguson, 2013.* Accepting a job as housekeeper and cook at the castle, Nelly May is instructed by Lord Pinkwinkle to use his special names for things. A comical rewrite of Joseph Jacobs's story "Master of All Masters," above. (P, I)

DePaola, Tomie. *Fin M'Coul, the Giant of Knockmany Hill.* *Illus. by the author. Holiday House, 1981.* Irish giant and his clever wife, Oonah, outsmart the giant bully, Cucullin. Compare with Robert Byrd's *Finn MacCoul and His Fearless Wife* and Jessica Souhami's *Mrs. McCool and the Giant Cuhullin.* (P, I, A)

DePaola, Tomie. *Jamie O'Rourke and the Big Potato: An Irish Folktale.* *Illus. by the author. Putnam, 1992.* With his wife in bed with a bad back, lazy Jamie is worried he'll starve, until he meets a leprechaun who grants his wish to grow the world's biggest *pratie* (potato). (P, I)

Galdone, Paul. *Jack and the Beanstalk.* *Illus. by the author. Clarion, 1974.* A classic version of the English fairy tale. (P, I)

Glassie, Henry. *Irish Folktales.* *Pantheon, 1997.* This volume in the Pantheon Fairy Tale and Folklore Library series is comprised of 125 tales divided into sections: The Old Story, Faith, Wit, Mystery, History, and Fireside Tales. (Professional)

Huck, Charlotte. *The Black Bull of Norroway: A Scottish Tale.* *Illus. by Anita Lobel. Greenwillow, 2001.* Peggy Ann, youngest and merriest of three sisters, says she would even be content to marry the Black Bull of Norroway—and that's just what comes to take her away. (I, A)

Huck, Charlotte. *Princess Furball.* *Illus. by Anita Lobel. Greenwillow, 1989.* About to be betrothed to an ogre, an English princess insists she must first have three fancy gowns and a coat made of a thousand different kinds of fur. (P, I)

Jacobs, Joseph. *English Fairy Tales.* *Illus. by John Batten. Knopf, 1993.* Part of the Everyman's Library Children's Classics series, this volume contains almost ninety tales collected by folklorist Joseph Jacobs in 1890. Continue the folk fest with *More English Folk and Fairy Tales* (Flying Chipmunk, 2009) and *Celtic Fairy Tales* (Dover, 1968), which has a fine collection of Irish, Scottish, and Welsh tales. (P, I)

Keding, Dan, and Amy Douglas. *English Folktales.* *Libraries Unlimited, 2005.* In the World Folklore series, this collection features fifty folktales to read aloud and/or tell, with background notes on each. (Professional)

Kellogg, Steven. *Jack and the Beanstalk.* *Illus. by the author. Morrow, 1991.* Kellogg's glowing watercolors portray the English giant as a sharp-toothed ogre. (P, I)

Krull, Kathleen. *A Pot o' Gold: A Treasury of Irish Stories, Poetry, Folklore, and (of Course) Blarney.* *Illus. by David McPhail. Disney/Hyperion, 2004.* More than two dozen stories, plus poems, songs, and recipes. (P, I)

McNeil, Heather. *The Celtic Breeze: Stories of the Otherworld from Scotland, Ireland, and Wales.* *Libraries Unlimited, 2001.* In this entry in the World Folklore series, McNeil brings together seventeen ballads and fifteen lesser-known tales from the Hebrides about fairies, mermaids, changelings, and ghosts, adding historical background and color photos. (Professional)

Osborne, Mary Pope. *Favorite Medieval Tales.* *Illus. by Troy Howell. Scholastic, 1998.* Nine classic English tales, including "Beowulf," "The Sword in the Stone," "Robin Hood and His Merry Men," and "Chanticleer and the Fox." (I, A)

Reeves, James. *Stories from England.* *Illus. by Joan Kiddell-Monroe. Oxford, 2009, c1954.* Nineteen tales, including "The Story of Tom Thumb," "Tom

Tit Tot," and "Dick Whittington"; originally published as *English Fables and Fairy Stories.* (I, A)

San Souci, Robert D. *The Well at the End of the World.* *Illus. by Rebecca Walsh. Chronicle, 2004.* An English fairy tale about plain but practical Princess Rosamond and her father, the king of Colchester, who weds the beautiful but dangerous Lady Zantippa. (P, I)

Souhami, Jessica. *Mrs. McCool and the Giant Cuhullin: An Irish Tale.* *Illus. by the author. Henry Holt, 2002.* The Irish giant Cuhullin plans to pound giant Finn McCool, but Finn's wife has a plan to defeat the bully. See also *Finn MacCoul and His Fearless Wife* by Robert Byrd and *Fin M'Coul, the Giant of Knockmany Hill* by Tomie dePaola, above. (P, I)

Zemach, Harve. *Duffy and the Devil: A Cornish Tale.* *Illus. by Margot Zemach. Farrar, 1973.* In an uproarious variant of "Rumpelstiltskin" from Cornwall, England, Squire Lovel's new wife, Duffy, makes a deal with the squinty-eyed devil to do all her knitting and spinning. (P, I, A)

Tales from Scandinavia

When storytellers think of Norwegian and Scandinavian folktales, they inevitably come up with three names. The first is Denmark's Hans Christian Andersen. Andersen was primarily a writer, not a collector of folklore. While he retold and used elements of Danish folklore, many of his stories are completely original—what we call "literary" folk and fairy tales. For this reason, you'll find more about him in his own segment in chapter 7, under "Literary Tales and Short Stories" on page 254.

Unlike Andersen, Peter Christian Asbjørnsen (1812–1855) and Jorgen E. Moe (1813–1882) collected tales they heard from peasant storytellers in Norway and published them in a famous collection, *East o' the Sun and West o' the Moon.* Much of the popularity and success of this collection in English-speaking countries can be attributed to the excellent translation done by the English scholar, George Webbe Dasent (1817–1896). You'll find simple stories for the very young, such as the rhythmic "The Three Billy Goats Gruff" and the comical, "Why the Bear Is Stumpy-Tailed," (for which you'll find the text on page 142).

When you think of Norway, you also envision those wonderfully visual stories of terrifying trolls usually outwitted by clever simple folk. You will find some wonderful troll tales in Ingri and Edgar Parin D'Aulaire's *D'Aulaires' Book of Trolls.* Equally shivery and satisfying is Lise Lunge-Larsen's *The Troll with No Heart in His Body, and Other Tales of Trolls from Norway.*

While you're on a troll roll, read aloud or booktalk Katherine Langrish's middle grade novel, *Troll Fell* (HarperCollins, 2004), that ties in Norse mythology and characters like trolls, orphans, dogs, and Granny Greenteeth. Newly orphaned Peer Ulfsson, who is worked half to death by his cruel twin uncles in their mill, makes friends with the Nis, a house spirit, and a spunky girl named Hilde, who help him thwart his uncles' plan to sell him off to the trolls.

Not every Norwegian tale has a troll in it, of course. A nonchalant humor prevails in tales like "Gudbrand-on-the-Hillside," in which everything that Gudbrand does, no matter how foolish, is supported with good humor by his loving wife. Then there's "The Husband Who Was to Mind the House," about a man whose housekeeping efforts end in humorous disaster. And don't forget the story of the pompous squire who is used to having everything he wants, even his choice of brides.

The Squire's Bride

Retold by Gudrun Thorne-Thomsen in East o' the Sun and West o' the Moon
(Chicago: Row, Peterson and Company, 1912)

There was once a very rich squire who owned a large farm, had plenty of silver at the bottom of his chest, and money in the bank besides; but there was something he had not, and that was a wife.

One day a neighbor's daughter was working for him in the hayfield. The squire liked her very much and, as she was a poor man's daughter, he thought that if he only mentioned marriage she would be more than glad to take him at once. So he said to her, "I've been thinking I want to marry."

"Well, one may think of many things," said the lassie, as she stood there and smiled slyly. She really thought the old fellow ought to be thinking of something that behooved him better than getting married at his time of life.

"Now, you see," he said, "I was thinking that you should be my wife!"

"No, thank you," said she, "and much obliged for the honor."

The squire was not used to being gainsaid, and the more she refused him, the more he wanted her. But the lassie would not listen to him at all. So the old man sent for her father and told him that, if he could talk his daughter over and arrange the whole matter for him, he would forgive him the money he had lent him, and would give him the piece of land which lay close to his meadow into the bargain.

"Yes, yes, be sure I'll bring the lass to her senses," said the father. "She is only a child and does not know what is best for her."

But all his coaxing, all his threats, and all his talking went for naught. She would not have the old miser if he sat buried in gold up to his ears, she said.

The squire waited and waited, but at last he got angry and told the father that he had to settle the matter at once if he expected him to stand by his bargain, for now he would wait no longer.

The squire's neighbor knew no other way out of it, but to let the squire get everything ready for the wedding; then, when the parson and the wedding guests had arrived, the squire would send for the lassie as if she were wanted for some work on the farm. When she got there, they would marry her right away, in such a hurry that she would have no time to think it over.

When the guests had arrived, the squire called one of his farm lads, told him to run down to his neighbor and ask him to send up immediately what he had promised.

"But if you are not back with her in a twinkling," he said, shaking his fist at him, "I'll—"

He did not finish, for the lad ran off as if he had been shot at.

"My master has sent me to ask for that which you promised him," said the lad, when he got to the neighbor, "but, pray, lose no time, for master is terribly busy today."

"Yes, yes! Run down in the meadow and take her with you—there she goes," answered the neighbor.

The lad ran off and when he came to the meadow, he found the daughter there raking the hay.

"I am to fetch what your father has promised my master," said the lad.

"Ah, ha!" thought she, "is that what they are up to?" And with a wicked twinkle of the eye, she said, "Oh, yes, it's that little bay mare of ours, I suppose. You had better go and take her. She stands tethered on the other side of the pea field."

The boy jumped on the back of the bay mare and rode home at full gallop.

"Have you got her with you?" asked the squire.

"She is down at the door," said the lad.

"Take her up to the room my mother had," said the squire.

"But, master, how can I?" said the lad.

"Do as I tell you," said the squire. "And if you can't manage her alone, get the men to help you," for he thought the lassie might be stubborn.

When the lad saw his master's face, he knew it would be no use to argue. So he went and got all the farmhands together to help him. Some pulled at the head and the forelegs of the mare and others pushed from behind, and at last they got her upstairs and into the room. There lay all the wedding finery ready.

"Well, that's done, master!" said the lad, while he wiped his wet brow, "but it was the worst job I have ever had here on the farm."

"Never mind, never mind, you shall not have done it for nothing," said his master, and he pulled a bright silver coin out of his pocket and gave it to the lad. "Now send the women up to dress her."

"But, I say, master!"

"None of your talk!" cried the squire. "Tell them to hold her while they dress her, and mind not to forget either wreath or crown."

The lad ran into the kitchen. "Listen, here, lasses," he called out, "you are to go upstairs and dress up the bay mare as a bride. I suppose master wants to play a joke on his guests."

The women laughed and laughed, but ran upstairs and dressed the bay mare in everything that was there. And then the lad went and told his master that now she was all ready, with wreath and crown and all.

"Very well, bring her down. I will receive her at the door myself," said the squire.

There was a clatter and a thumping on the stairs, for that bride, you know, had no silken slippers on. When

the door was opened and the squire's bride entered the room, you can imagine there was laughing and tittering and grinning enough.

And as for the squire, they say he never went courting again.

BOOKLIST: TALES FROM SCANDINAVIA

Asbjørnsen, Peter C., and Jorgen E. Moe. *Norwegian Folk Tales.* *Trans. by Pat Shaw Iversen and Carl Norman. Illus. by Erik Werenskiold and Theodor Kittelsen. Pantheon, 1982.* A collection of three dozen tales, in the Pantheon Fairy Tale and Folklore Library series. (P, I, A)

Dasent, George Webbe. *East o' the Sun and West o' the Moon.* *Tr. by George Webbe Dasent. Illus. by Erik Werenskiold. Dover, 1970.* Includes classic folktales collected by Peter Christen Asbjørnsen, and Jorgen E. Moe, including "Gudbrand-on-the Hillside," "The Husband Who Was to Mind the House," "The Three Billy Goats Gruff," "Why the Bear Is Stumpy-Tailed," and "Why the Sea Is Salt." (P, I, A)

Dasent, George Webbe. *East of the Sun and West of the Moon.* *Illus. by P. J. Lynch. Candlewick, 1992.* In this Norwegian fairy tale, a man gives his youngest daughter to a white bear, which transforms into a man each night. (I, A)

D'Aulaire, Ingri, and Edgar Parin D'Aulaire. *D'Aulaire's Book of Trolls.* *Illus. by the authors. Doubleday, 1972.* All you need to know about Norway's forest trolls, mountain trolls, and bridge trolls. (P, I, A)

Lunge-Larsen, Lise. *The Troll with No Heart in His Body, and Other Tales of Trolls from Norway.* *Illus. by Betsy Bowen. Houghton Mifflin, 1999.* Nine great troll stories, illustrated with large, troll-filled woodcuts. (P, I)

BOOKLIST: OTHER TALES FROM EUROPE

Afanasev, Aleksandr. *Russian Fairy Tales.* *Pantheon, 1976.* Pantheon Fairy Tale and Folklore Library series; a selection of almost two hundred tales from the original three-volume 1945 edition. You will be most familiar with stories about Ivan (comparable to the English Jack) and the witch Baba Yaga, and the tale about the giant turnip that was so difficult to pull out of the ground. (Professional)

Alley, Zoe B. *There's a Wolf at the Door.* *Illus. by R. W. Alley. Roaring Brook, 2008.* In each of five well-known tales, presented in oversize comic-book format, the wolf ends up still hungry. The companion book is *There's a Princess in the Palace* (2010). (P)

Cousins, Lucy. ***Yummy: Eight Favorite Fairy Tales.*** *Illus. by the author. Candlewick, 2009.* The eight standard folktales in this yummy oversize volume for young kids are bold, cheery, and a bit gory. (P)

Demi. ***The Firebird.*** *Illus. by the author. Henry Holt, 1994.* In this classic Russian fairy tale, Tsar Ivan insists that Dimitry bring him the Firebird, or lose his head. (P, I)

DePaola, Tomie. ***The Mysterious Giant of Barletta: An Italian Folktale.*** *Illus. by the author. Harcourt, 1984.* A town's giant statue comes to life to dissuade an army invasion. (P, I)

DePaola, Tomie. ***Tomie dePaola's Favorite Nursery Tales.*** *Illus. by the author. Putnam, 1986.* Twenty-five favorites, including "The Three Bears," "The Three Little Pigs," and other traditional fables and poems, illustrated in dePaola's distinctive style. (P)

De Regniers, Beatrice Schenk. ***Little Sister and the Month Brothers.*** *Illus. by Margot Tomes. Marshall Cavendish, 2009, c1976.* A Czechoslovakian story about a girl sent by her heartless stepmother to find flowers and strawberries during a winter blizzard. (P, I)

Gág, Wanda. ***Gone Is Gone; Or, The Story of a Man Who Wanted to Do Housework.*** *Illus. by the author. University of Minnesota Press, 2003, c1935.* In a tale from Bohemia, now the Czech Republic, Farmer Fritzl thinks he works harder than his wife, Liesi, so the two trade jobs for the day. (P, I)

Geras, Adele. ***My Grandmother's Stories: A Collection of Jewish Folk Tales.*** *Illus. by Jael Jordan. Knopf, 1990.* The narrator relates ten stories from the Jewish tradition that she heard as a child from her grandmother, ranging from a story about the fools in Chelm to one about wise King Solomon. (P, I)

Keding, Dan. ***Stories of Hope and Spirit: Folktales from Eastern Europe.*** *August House, 2004.* Twelve tales the author collected, many from his own Croatian maternal grandmother, who told him stories from the old country. (I, A)

Kimmel, Eric A. ***Bearhead: A Russian Folktale.*** Illus. by Charles Mikolaycak. Holiday House, 1991. A man with a bear's head takes directions literally when he becomes a servant to a witch. (P, I, A)

Kimmel Eric A. ***Medio Pollito: A Spanish Tale.*** *Illus. by Valeria Docampo. Marshall Cavendish, 2010.* A little half chick—with one leg, one eye, one wing, half a comb, and half a beak—sets out for the city. (P)

Livo, Norma J., and George O. Livo. ***The Enchanted Wood and Other Tales from Finland.*** *Libraries Unlimited, 1999.* World Folklore series; includes twenty folktales, proverbs, recipes, historical background, and color photos. (Professional)

Lunge-Larson, Lise. ***The Hidden Folk: Stories of Fairies, Dwarves, Selkies, and Other Secret Beings.*** *Illus. by Beth Krommes. Houghton Mifflin, 2004.* Eight stories from Norway and Northern Europe about small magical creatures. (P, I)

MacDonald, Margaret Read. ***Fat Cat: A Danish Folktale.*** *Illus. by Julie Paschkis. August House Little Folk, 2001.* With a "SLIP SLOP SLUUURP!" this cat eats everyone. (P)

MacDonald, Margaret Read. ***Little Rooster's Diamond Button.*** *Illus. by Will Terry. Albert Whitman, 2007.* In this Hungarian folktale, Little Rooster wants the king to return his diamond button. (P, I)

Maddern, Eric. ***Nail Soup.*** *Illus. by Paul Hess. Frances Lincoln, 2009.* In this Swedish variant of "Stone Soup," a traveler makes soup for a stingy old woman, using only a rusty old nail (and a few other choice ingredients she grudgingly provides). Compare with Harve and Marot Zemach's *Nail Soup: A Swedish Folk Tale* (Follett, 1964), and Marcia Brown's French version, *Stone Soup: An Old Tale* (Scribner, 1947). (P, I)

Malinowski, Michael, and Anne Pellowski. ***Polish Folktales and Folklore.*** *Libraries Unlimited, 2009.* Fifty-five folktales, historical background, recipes, games, riddles, and color photos in a volume from the World Folklore series. (Professional)

Marshall, Bonnie. ***The Flower of Paradise and Other Armenian Tales.*** *Libraries Unlimited, 2007.* World Folklore series; includes sixty folktales, with historical background, activities, recipes, and color photos. (Professional)

Marshall, Bonnie. ***The Snow Maiden and Other Russian Tales.*** *Libraries Unlimited, 2004.* World Folklore series; includes thirty folktales, with historical background, activities, recipes, and color photos. Also see her *Tales from the Heart of the Balkans* (2001). (Professional)

McDonald, Megan. ***The Hinky Pink: An Old Tale Retold.*** *Illus. by Brian Floca. Atheneum, 2008.* Seamstress Anabel has only one week to make the finest dress in all of Florence, but there's a mysterious little creature in her room that won't let her sleep. (P, I)

Meder, Theo. ***The Flying Dutchman, and Other Folktales from the Netherlands.*** *Libraries Unlimited, 2008.* Another volume in the World Folklore series, with more than eighty folktales, plus historical background and color photos. (Professional)

Mitakidou, Soula, and Anthony L. Manna, with Melpomeni Kanatsouli. ***Folktales from Greece: A Treasury of Delights.*** *Libraries Unlimited, 2002.* Twenty folktales, with historical background and color photos; an entry in the World Folklore series. (Professional)

Ransome, Arthur. ***The Fool of the World and the Flying Ship.*** *Illus. by Uri Shulevitz. Farrar, 1968.* A Russian fool wins the czar's daughter. (P, I)

Shepard, Aaron. ***The Princess Mouse: A Tale of Finland.*** *Illus. by Leonid Gore. Atheneum, 2003.* Mikko takes a mouse for his sweetheart. (P, I)

Shepard, Aaron. ***The Sea King's Daughter: A Russian Legend.*** *Illus. by Gennady Spirin. Atheneum, 1997.* Sadko plays his music for the King of the Sea. (P, I)

Singer, Isaac Bashevis. ***Zlateh the Goat, and Other Stories.*** *Illus. by Maurice Sendak. HarperCollins, 1966.* Seven irresistible Jewish tales set in the shtetls of Poland, including some from Chelm, famed town of fools. Also look for the companion book, *When Shlemiel Went to Warsaw, and Other Stories* (Farrar, 1968), or a copy of Singer's compilation of both books and more, *The Fools of Chelm and Their History* (Farrar, 1973), both out of print. (I, A)

Suwyn, Barbara J. ***The Magic Egg, and Other Tales from Ukraine.*** *Libraries Unlimited, 1997.* This World Folklore series volume includes thirty-three folktales, historical background, and color photos. (Professional)

Tatar, Maria, ed. ***The Annotated Classic Fairy Tales.*** *Illus. with paintings and reprods. W. W. Norton, 2002.* Translations of twenty-six well-known fairy tales from Germany, France, England, and Russia, along with five Hans Christian Andersen tales, with margin notes and period illustrations for each story. Tatar has also done *The Annotated Brothers Grimm* (2012) and *The Annotated Hans Christian Andersen* (2007). (Professional)

TALES FROM AFRICA

There are an estimated three thousand groups and tribes in Africa, and between two and three thousand languages are spoken in the more than fifty countries. Christianity dominates in the southern half of the continent and Islam the northern half, although there are also a number of African-based traditional folk religions. With this sort of diversity, it's folly to try and categorize the folklore of the continent. You'll find creation myths and pourquoi tales, animal fables, and trickster tales. You'll meet hunters, farmers, herders, fishermen, villagers, kings, chiefs, sons and daughters, and supernatural beings, but the most ubiquitous characters in African folklore for children are the animals: birds, chameleons, tortoises, rabbits, monkeys, crocodiles, wolves, leopards, lions, zebras, giraffes, rhinos, and elephants. Often the small animals endeavor to trick the larger more powerful ones. Of course, you'll meet the original Anansi the Spider, from the Ashanti in West Africa, but there are other wily tricksters, too, including rabbits, hares, tortoises, and even hyenas. Hare from East Africa became Brer (Brother) Rabbit in the American south. Brer Rabbit's troubles with the tar baby (characterized as "stick fast" tales in folklore) originated in Africa.

One of the most dogged collectors and eloquent retellers of folklore was Harold Courlander (1908–1996), who studied the cultures and collected folklore—music and stories—from Africa, Haiti, Indonesia, Asia, and the United States, particularly the Hopi Indians and African Americans. His memorable collections of stories for children include *The Fire on the Mountain and Other Ethiopian Stories* (Henry Holt, 1950), *The Hat-Shaking Dance, and Other Ashanti Tales from Ghana* (Harcourt, 1957), and *The Piece of Fire and Other Haitian Tales* (Harcourt, 1964). *The Cow-Tail Switch, and Other West African Stories* was selected as a Newbery Honor Book in 1948; it is the only Courlander collection for children still in print.

Every wonder why spiders are so skinny? Here's the real reason.

Two Feasts for Anansi

From The Hat-Shaking Dance, and Other Ashanti Tales from Ghana,
Retold by Harold Courlander

Kwaku Anansi's thin belly came from greed. It is said that one year there was a wedding feast in the town of Kibbes, and another wedding feast in the town of Diabee, and they were both on the same day. Anansi asked himself: "Which feast will I go to?" He thought, and then he said: "I am very hungry. I will go to both. I will eat first at the place where the food is served first, and afterwards I will go to the other place and eat again."

But Anansi couldn't find out which of the feasts would come first. He went to Diabee and asked: "When will the food be served?" But they couldn't tell him. So he went then to the town of Kibbes and asked: "What time will the food be given out?" But they didn't know. He went back and forth between the two towns, first the one and then the other, until he was weary. But still he knew nothing about when the food would be given out.

So Kwaku Anansi bought two long ropes, and he sent for his sons Intikuma and Kweku Tsin. He tied both ropes around his middle. He gave the end of one rope to Intikuma, saying: "Take this end of the rope with you and go to Diabee. When they start giving out the food, pull hard on the rope and I will come." He gave the end of the other rope to Kweku Tsin, saying: "Take this with you to Kibbes. When the feast begins, pull hard and I will come. This way I will know where the food is given out first."

So Intikuma went to Diabee, taking the end of one rope with him, and Kweku Tsin went to Kibbes, taking the end of the other rope with him. Each of them stood in the town and waited to give the signal.

But when the feasts began in Diabee and Kibbes, they began at the very same moment. Intikuma pulled and Kweku Tisn pulled. As they both pulled very hard, Anansi couldn't go one way or another. He was halfway between, and he couldn't move. His sons pulled harder and harder, and they didn't stop until the feasts were ended and the food was gone. Then they went to see what had detained their father.

They found him where they had left him, but he didn't look the same. Where the ropes had squeezed him around the middle he had become very small. And this way he has always remained. The spider carries with him forever the mark of greed.

BOOKLIST: TALES FROM AFRICA

Aardema, Verna. ***Misoso: Once upon a Time Tales from Africa.*** *Illus. by Reynold Ruffins. Knopf, 1994.* Top-notch collection of twelve animal folktales. (P, I)

Aardema, Verna. ***Who's in Rabbit's House?*** *Illus. by Leo and Diane Dillon. Dial, 1977.* Rabbit and his friends are afraid of The Long One, who has ensconced himself inside Rabbit's house. (P, I)

Abrahams, Roger. ***African Folktales:*** *Traditional Stories of the Black World.* Pantheon, 1999. From the Pantheon Fairy Tale and Folklore Library series, here are ninety-five stories from south of the Sahara, collected and/or retold by Abrahams. (Professional)

Bryan, Ashley. ***Ashley Bryan's African Tales, Uh-Huh.*** *Illus. by the author. Atheneum, 1998.* A splendid collection of myths, legends, trickster tales, and other folktales, containing the full text of three collections: *The Ox of the Wonderful Horns* (1971), *Beat the Story-Drum, Pum-Pum* (1980), and *Lion and the Ostrich Chicks* (1986). (P, I)

Courlander, Harold, and George Herzog. ***The Cow-Tail Switch, and Other West African Stories.*** *Illus. by Madye Lee Chastain. Henry Holt, 1947.* These seventeen tales, collected and retold by Courlander, are superb for sharing. (I, A)

Dayrell, Elphinstone. *Why the Sun and the Moon Live in the Sky: An African Folktale.* *Illus. by Blair Lent. Houghton, 1968.* African pourquoi tale explaining the heavens. (P, I)

Diakité, Baba Wagué. *The Hatseller and the Monkeys: A West African Folktale.* *Illus. by the author. Scholastic, 1999.* Hatseller BaMusa is horrified when he wakes from his nap and finds all his hats are gone, stolen by monkeys up in the mango tree. Compare this with *Caps for Sale* by Esphyr Slobodkina (HarperCollins, 1985, c1947). (P, I)

Diakité, Baba Wagué. *The Hunterman and the Crocodile: A West African Folktale.* *Illus. by the author. Scholastic, 1997.* Donso the Hunterman helps Bamba the crocodile across the river and then looks for a way out when the croc plans to eat him. (P, I)

Diakité, Baba Wagué. *The Magic Gourd.* *Illus. by the author. Scholastic, 2003.* In a West African story, Dogo Zan (Brother Rabbit) is given a gourd that fills itself with food and water, and greedy Mansa Jugu, the king, wants it. (P, I)

Grifalconi, Ann. *The Village of Round and Square Houses.* *Illus. by the author. Little, Brown, 1986.* After a volcanic eruption near a small village in Central Africa, the men move to square houses and the women to round ones. (P, I)

Knutson, Barbara. *How the Guinea Fowl Got Her Spots: A Swahili Tale of Friendship.* *Illus. by the author. Carolrhoda, 1990.* After Guinea Fowl frightens Lion away, Cow rewards her by camouflaging her feathers. (P, I)

Kurtz, Jane. *Fire on the Mountain.* *Illus. by E. B. Lewis. Simon & Schuster, 1994.* In Eritrea, young Alemayu, watcher of cows, spends the night outside, keeping warm by focusing the glow from a shepherd's fire across the mountain. (P, I)

Kurtz, Jane. *Trouble.* *Illus. by Durga Bernhard. Harcourt, 1997.* In a comical Eritrean folktale from the east coast of Africa, young Tekleh heads to the hills to graze his goats. (P, I)

Lewis, I. Murphy. *Why Ostriches Don't Fly, and Other Tales from the African Bush.* *Libraries Unlimited, 1997.* Part of the World Folklore series, this features fifteen folktales, plus historical background and color photos. (Professional)

MacDonald, Margaret Read. *Mabela the Clever.* *Illus. by Tim Coffey. Albert Whitman, 2001.* In this sweet story from Sierra Leone, Mabela is the only mouse who pays attention when a big orange cat entreats the mice to follow it into the forest. (P, I)

McDermott, Gerald. *Anansi the Spider: A Tale from the Ashanti.* *Illus. by the author. Henry Holt, 1972.* Anansi story from Ghana about how the moon came to be. (P, I)

McNeil, Heather. *Hyena and the Moon: Stories to Tell from Kenya.* *Libraries Unlimited, 1994.* Ten folktales collected by the author from seven of Kenya's forty ethnic groups, with historical background and photos. A World Folklore series volume. (Professional)

Mollel, Tololwa M. *The Orphan Boy: A Maasai Story.* *Illus. by Paul Morin. Clarion, 1991.* Why the planet Venus is known to the Maasai as Kileken, the orphan boy. (P, I)

Mollel, Tololwa M. *Subira, Subira.* *Illus. by Linda Saport. Clarion, 2000.* In Tanzania, after Mother dies and Tatu cannot get her little brother to obey her, she seeks help from a spirit woman who tells her to pluck three whiskers from a lion. Another affecting version of the same story, this one from Ethiopia, is *Pulling the Lion's Tail* by Jane Kurtz (Simon & Schuster, 1995). (P, I)

Musgrove, Margaret. *The Spider Weaver: A Legend of Kente Cloth.* *Illus. by Julia Cairns. Scholastic, 2001.* Watching a spider weave her web, master weavers Koragu and Ameyaw are inspired to develop a new kind of colorful woven cloth in this story from Ghana. (P, I)

Onyefulu, Obi. *Chinye: A West African Folk Tale.* *Illus. by Evie Safarewicz. Frances Lincoln, 2007, c1994.* In a good sister/bad sister story, Chinye is sent by her stepmother to fetch water from the stream late at night, and is taken home by a kind old woman who tests her obedience. The African American version of this tale is the Caldecott Honor Book *The Talking Eggs* by Robert D. San Souci, illustrated by Jerry Pinkney (Dial, 1989). (P, I)

Shepard, Aaron. *Master Man: A Tall Tale of Nigeria.* *Illus. by David Wisniewski. HarperCollins, 2001.* Shadusa decides to call himself Master Man, but soon finds out there are others far stronger than he is. (P, I)

Steptoe, John. *Mufaro's Beautiful Daughters: An African Tale.* *Illus. by the author. Lothrop, 1987.* One good daughter and one bad; each hopes the king will choose her to be his queen. (P, I)

Washington, Donna L. *A Pride of African Tales.* *Illus. by James Ransome. HarperCollins, 2004.* Six rich and thoughtful stories from West Africa. (I, A)

TALES FROM THE MIDDLE EAST

Although the Middle East simmers and sizzles and erupts in constant conflicts and wars, we can all identify with the folktales of the region, whether they recount the silly wisdom of Egypt's Goha or take us to the ornate backdrop of the Arabian Nights.

What we often call "The Arabian Nights" is actually "The 1,001 Nights," collected fairy tales, written in Arabic, gathered from the Middle East, Central Asia, and North Africa. The roots of the stories go back to the folklore of

Persia, India, Egypt, and Mesopotamia. The first English-language edition of the tales was published in 1706, but some of the earliest Arabic tales were recorded in the eighth century, with stories from other cultures added over the ensuing centuries. These tales are not for children, as evidenced by Sir Richard Burton's translation *The Book of the Thousand Nights and a Night* (www.sacred-texts.com/neu/burt1k1) that he published as a ten-volume set in 1885. Indeed, the problem storytellers face is finding tales that can be stripped of the abundant sex, violence, and ornate language for younger audiences.

The tales begin this way: After discovering that his brother's wife and his own have been unfaithful, the Persian king Shahryar decides that all women are no good, so he marries a new virgin each night, and has her beheaded in the morning. (You can see why this is tricky to explain to children. . . .) Scheherazade, the vizier's daughter and a consummate student of stories, marries the king and tells him an engrossing story, stopping at the most exciting part. Naturally, Shahryar can't behead her until he hears the rest of the tale, but the next night she finishes one story and tells half of another. After 1,001 nights of tales about flying horses, wish-granting *jinns*, dreams that come true, and lovers torn apart and reunited, Shahryar realizes that Scheherazade, who now has three young sons, is the perfect woman, thus ending his murderous rampage. Whew.

The stories we know best from the collection are "Aladdin and the Wonderful Lamp," "Ali Baba and the Forty Thieves," and "The Ebony Horse." Visit http://en.wikipedia.org/wiki/One_Thousand_and_One_Nights for a complete list of tales and background information.

BOOKLIST: TALES FROM THE MIDDLE EAST

Demi. *The Hungry Coat: A Tale from Turkey.* *Illus. by the author. McElderry, 2004.* Ostracized for wearing an old, smelly coat to a rich friend's banquet, Nasrettin Hoca returns wearing a fine silk coat and feeds his dinner to it. (P, I, A)

Edgecomb, Diane. *A Fire in My Heart: Kurdish Tales.* *Libraries Unlimited, 2008.* A World Folklore series volume, this includes thirty-three folktales, historical background, recipes, games, and color photos. (Professional)

Henderson, Kathy. *Lugalbanda: The Boy Who Got Caught Up in a War.* *Illus. by Jane Ray. Candlewick, 2006.* One of the oldest stories in the world—told aloud five thousand years ago in ancient Sumer (now Iraq)—this tale relates how young Prince Lugalbanda helps bring peace to his city of Uruk. (I, A)

Hickox, Rebecca. ***The Golden Sandal: A Middle Eastern Cinderella Story.*** *Illus. by Will Hillenbrand. Holiday House, 1998.* In Iraq, Maha begs her fisherman father to marry the kind widow who lives nearby, and you know how those things always turn out. (P, I)

Hussain, Shahrukh, and Mucha Archer. ***The Wise Fool: Fables from the Islamic World.*** *Barefoot, 2011.* Twenty-two lavishly illustrated tales of the Mulla Nasruddin, sometimes judge, sometimes jester. (I, A)

Johnson-Davies, Denys. ***Goha the Wise Fool.*** *Illus. by Hany El Saed Ahmed from drawings by Hag Hamdy Mohamed Fattouh. Philomel, 2005.* Fifteen short, droll tales about Goha, the well-meaning fool, trickster, and sage from Egyptian folklore. (P, I, A)

Kimmel, Eric A. ***Joha Makes a Wish: A Middle Eastern Tale.*** *Illus. by Omar Rayyam Marshall Cavendish, 2010.* On his way to Baghdad, Joha finds a wishing stick that grants the opposite of what he wishes for. (P, I, A)

MacDonald, Margaret Read. ***Tunjur! Tunjur! Tunjur! A Palestinian Folktale.*** *Illus. by Alik Arzoumanian. Marshall Cavendish, 2006.* Wishing for a child to love, "even if it is nothing more than a cooking pot," a woman's wish comes true in the guise of a naughty little pot. (P)

Philip, Neil. ***The Arabian Nights.*** *Illus. by Sheila Moxley. Orchard, 1994.* Introducing fifteen tales—some familiar, all exotic and compelling—narrated by Scheherazade herself. (I, A)

Singh, Rina. ***Nearly Nonsense: Hoja Tales from Turkey.*** *Illus. by Farida Zaman. Tundra, 2011.* Ten comical tales about the mullah Nasrudin Hoja, wise fool and trickster. (I, A)

Soifer, Margaret, and Irwin Shapiro. ***Tenggren's Golden Tales from the Arabian Nights.*** *Illus. by Gustaf Tenggren. Golden Books, 2003, c1957.* Ten of the 1,001 stories Scheherazade told to her husband, the woman-hating king, which saved her life. (I, A)

Tarnowska, Wafa'. ***The Arabian Nights.*** *Illus. by Carole Hénaff. Barefoot, 2010.* Eight of the 1,001 tales, beginning with "Shahriyar Meets Shahrazade," the explanation of why the king beheads a new bride each morning until one woman stops him with a nightly dose of stories. (A)

Walker, Barbara K. ***A Treasury of Turkish Folktales for Children.*** *Linnet Books, 1988.* Quirky humor runs through these thirty-four fairy tales and tales of the foolish wise man Nasreddin Hoca. (I, A)

WEBSITES: TALES FROM THE MIDDLE EAST

Nasreddin Hodja *http://u.cs.biu.ac.il/~schiff/Net/front.html*
More than one hundred Hodja stories compiled by Alpay Kabacali, plus a biography of the learned man and a bibliography.

"One Thousand and One Nights"
http://en.wikipedia.org/wiki/One_Thousand_and_One_Nights
An extensive Wikipedia article with many links, including a list of stories, a list of characters, and access to several online translated versions of the stories.

TALES FROM ASIA

Variants of tales told in China may be found in Japan, Korea, or Vietnam, and animal fables from Malaysia may have roots in India. Stories travel just as we do, and cultures can be similar. In this section we have brought together stories about transforming teakettles, songless sparrows, and flying dragons. Antagonists include fierce tigers, terrifying ghosts, demons, and man-eating snakes. Protagonists—peach boys, monkey kings, royal children, and the poor and powerless—are compassionate and generous to others but frugal with themselves. They are trustworthy, loyal, and responsible when asked to complete a task, and clever in times of danger.

We have separate booklists for China and Japan as there are so many good titles from these countries. Our third list is an assortment of other splendid stories from India, Pakistan, Korea, Thailand, and other Asian countries.

Tales from China

The myths, legends, and folktales of China rely heavily on gods and goddesses, emperors and empresses, giants, ghosts, and wise elders. Recurring animal characters include serpents, monkeys, tigers, birds, and, of course, the king of all mythical creatures, the dragon. Unlike European dragons, which medieval knights were always trying to knock off, Chinese dragons are symbols of good luck. They are one of the twelve creatures of the zodiac, the other eleven being real animals.

Is there such a thing as an unselfish person? Let's go back to the Ming Dynasty (1368–1644), whence this story comes, and see what things were like in those days.

The Pointing Finger

From Sweet and Sour: Tales from China,
Retold by Carol Kendall and Yao-wen Li (Illus. by Shirley Felts; Seabury, 1978)

Even P'eng-lai has its tedious days, and when time hung heavy over that fairy mountain isle in the Eastern Sea, the Eight Immortals that dwelt there remembered and talked of their previous existence as mortals on earth. Upon occasion they took disguise and transported themselves from P'eng-lai to their old world to nose about in human affairs in hope of discovering improvements in human nature. On the whole, however, they found the mortals of today to have the same shortcomings and the same longcomings as those of yesterday.

It came about that one of the Immortals, on such a nosing-about expedition, was seeking an unselfish man. He vowed that when he found a man without the taint of greed in his heart, he would make of him an Immortal on the spot and transport him to P'eng-lai Mountain. Forthwith.

His test for avarice was simple. Upon meeting a foot traveler in a lane or road, he would turn a pebble into gold by pointing his finger at it. He would then offer the golden pebble to the traveler.

The first person he met accepted the pebble eagerly, but then, turning it over and over between his fingers, his eyes beginning to gleam and glint, he said, "Can you do the same thing again? To those?" and he pointed to a small heap of stones at their feet.

The Immortal shook his head sadly and went on.

The second person looked at the proffered golden pebble long and thoughtfully. "Ah," he finally said, his eyes narrowed in calculation, "but this is a fine thing you would give me. It will feed my family for a year, and feed them well, but what then? Back to rice water and elm bark? That would be a cruelty. How could I face their tears and laments? Kind sir, as it is such an effortless task for you, perhaps you could turn your finger towards something larger, like, for example"—and he pointed at a boulder as big as himself beside the road—"that bit of stone?"

All along the way the story was the same, until the Immortal despaired of finding a human being whose cupidity did not outweigh his gratitude. After many a weary mile's walking, he came upon a man of middle years stumping along the lane, and greeting him, said, "I should like to make you a present." He pointed his finger at a stone and it turned into gold before their eyes.

The man studied the gleaming chunk of stone, his head canted to one side. "What sort of trick is that?" he asked with a frown.

"No trick," said the Immortal. "Pick it up. Or would you prefer a larger stone?" He pointed his finger at a small rock and it instantly blossomed gold. "Take it, brother. It is yours. I give it to you."

The man thought a while, then slowly shook his head. "No-o-o. Not that it's not a very clever trick, and a pretty sight to see."

With growing excitement the Immortal pointed at a larger rock and a larger, until their eyes were dazzled by the glint of gold all around them, but each time the man shook his head, and each time the shake became more decisive. Had he found his unselfish man at last? Should he transform him this instant into an Immortal and carry him back to P'eng-lai?

"But every human being desires *something*," the Immortal said, all but convinced that this was untrue. "Tell me what it is you want!"

"Your finger," said the man.

BOOKLIST: TALES FROM CHINA

Carpenter, Frances. ***Tales of a Chinese Grandmother: 30 Traditional Tales from China.*** *Illus. by Malthe Hasselriis. Tuttle, 2001, c1937.* A grandmother tells stories to her two grandchildren. (P, I, A)

Davison, Gary Marvin. ***Tales from the Taiwanese.*** *Libraries Unlimited, 2004.* From the World Folklore series, this volume includes twenty-eight folktales, with background notes and one recipe per story. (Professional)

Helft, Claude. ***Chinese Mythology: Stories of Creation and Invention.*** *Trans. from the French by Michael Hariton and Claudia Bedrick. Illus. by Chen Jiang Hong. Enchanted Lion, 2007.* A slim, attractive volume with an introduction to creation tales of gods and goddesses, emperors, and mere mortals. (I, A)

Kendall, Carol, and Li, Yao-wen. ***Sweet and Sour: Tales from China.*** *Illus. by Shirley Felts. Seabury, 1978.* A lovely selection of twenty-four folktales that take us from ancient to modern China. (I, A)

Kimmel, Eric A. ***Ten Suns: A Chinese Legend.*** *Illus. by YongSheng Xuan. Holiday House, 1998.* This pourquoi tale explains why there is only one sun in the sky. (P, I)

Roberts, Moss. ***Chinese Fairy Tales and Fantasies.*** *Pantheon, 1980.* Ninety-two mostly brief folktales that "blend the everyday life of mortals, the fabulous kingdom of birds and beasts, and the supernatural world of gods and ghosts." (Professional)

Simonds, Nina, and Leslie Swartz. *Moonbeams, Dumplings & Dragon Boats: A Treasury of Chinese Holiday Tales, Activities & Recipes.* *Illus. by Meilo So. Harcourt, 2002.* A festive collection of stories, riddles, crafts, and food, celebrating five major Chinese festivals. (I)

Yep, Laurence. *The Dragon Prince: A Chinese Beauty and the Beast Tale.* *Illus. by Kam Mak. HarperCollins, 1997.* A farmer's youngest daughter, Seven, agrees to marry a terrifying dragon so it will spare her father's life. (P, I)

Young, Ed. *Lon Po Po: A Red-Riding Hood Story from China.* *Illus. by the author. Philomel, 1989.* Ed Young won a Caldecott Medal for his ethereal, wolf-infused illustrations. (P, I)

Young, Ed. *Mouse Match: A Chinese Folktale.* *Illus. by the author. Harcourt, 1997.* Papa and Mama Mouse look for the most powerful one in the world to marry their wonderful daughter. The story, formatted as an accordion book, or codex, opens out into a spectacular eighteen-foot-long mural in English on one side and in Chinese characters on the other. (P, I)

Young, Ed. *The Sons of the Dragon King: A Chinese Legend.* *Illus. by the author. Atheneum, 2004.* Pondering the singular talents of his nine sons, the Dragon King finds a new job or role for which each is best suited. (P, I)

Yuan, Haiwang. *The Magic Lotus Lantern and Other Tales from the Han Chinese.* *Libraries Unlimited, 2006.* In the World Folklore series, this entry includes fifty folktales, plus historical background, recipes, proverbs, and color photos. Also see the author's *Princess Peacock: Tales from the Other Peoples of China* (2008). (Professional)

Tales from Japan

Japanese stories are filled with odd creatures and monsters, including three-eyed horned ogres called *oni, kappa* or water monkeys, and beaked, bird-like spirits called *tengu.* Review the annotated list with links of more than two hundred legendary creatures from Japan at http://en.wikipedia.org/wiki. The tales are rife with enchantments and with animal transformations; for example, where tanuki (often translated into English as "badgers" or "raccoons," though they're really a different species, also called raccoon dogs) turn themselves into teakettles, and *kitsune* (mischievous foxes) or cranes transform themselves into beautiful young women. There's also a strong moral overtone in Japanese stories, with retribution for the cruel and greedy, and lifelong rewards for the simple, humble folk who are kind and gentle at heart.

Brave boys are born in unusual ways and lead unusual lives. Momotaro the Peach Boy, for example, was sent by heaven in a large peach to be the child of an elderly couple. Tiny Issun-Boshi (Little One Inch, similar to the English Tom Thumb and Hans Christian Andersen's Thumbelina), born to elderly parents, sets off to see the world and rescue a princess with his sword (a sewing needle), boat (a soup bowl), and oars (chopsticks). After Urashima Taro, a fisherman, rescues a turtle, he is invited to the palace of the Dragon God, where he stays for three days. When he returns, he discovers that—much like the unfortunate Rip van Winkle—he's really been away for three hundred years.

BOOKLIST: TALES FROM JAPAN

Bodkin, Odds. ***The Crane Wife.*** *Illus. by Gennady Spirin. Harcourt, 1998.* After nursing an injured crane back to health, Osamu, a Japanese sail maker, marries Yukiko, a mysterious woman who weaves a magical sail. Compare with *Dawn* by Molly Bang (SeaStar, 1992, c1983). (P, I)

Fujita, Hiroko. ***Folktales from the Japanese Countryside.*** *Edited by Fran Stallings with Harold Wright and Miki Sakurai. Libraries Unlimited, 2008.* World Folklore series; includes more than forty folktales, plus historical background, recipes, games, crafts, and color photos. (Professional)

Hodges, Margaret. ***The Boy Who Drew Cats.*** *Illus. by Aki Sogabe. Holiday House, 2002.* Brought to a temple to be educated, a young Japanese boy cannot stop drawing cats all over the temple walls. (P, I)

Kajikawa, Kimiko. ***Tsunami!*** *Illus. by Ed Young. Philomel, 2009.* A wise and wealthy old rice farmer called Ojiisan ("Grandfather") sets his own rice fields ablaze to warn villagers of an impending tsunami. (P, I)

Kimmel, Eric A. ***Three Samurai Cats: A Story from Japan.*** *Illus. by Mordicai Gerstein. Holiday House, 2003.* Unable to rid his castle of a savage, rampaging rat, the daimyo, a powerful Japanese lord, seeks a tough samurai cat to help. (P, I)

McDermott, Gerald. ***The Stonecutter: A Japanese Folk Tale.*** *Illus. by the author. Viking, 1975.* A lowly stonecutter envies everything more powerful than he. (P, I)

Mosel, Arlene. ***The Funny Little Woman.*** *Illus. by Blair Lent. Dutton, 1972.* Japanese ogres called *oni* kidnap the funny little woman to cook their rice. (P)

Paterson, Katherine. ***The Tale of the Mandarin Ducks.*** *Illus. by Leo and Diane Dillon. Lodestar, 1990.* In a Japanese tale, Yasuko, a kitchen maid, and Shozu, a one-eyed former samurai, are condemned to death for freeing a captive drake. (P, I, A)

Say, Allen. ***Under the Cherry Blossom Tree: An Old Japanese Tale.*** *Illus. by the author. HarperCollins, 1974.* When he swallows a cherry pit, a mean old man grows a cherry tree atop his head. (P, I)

Sierra, Judy. ***Tasty Baby Belly Buttons: A Japanese Folktale.*** *Illus. by Meilo So. Knopf, 1999.* When wicked *oni* kidnap all the babies of a village, a brave baby, Uriko-hime (the melon princess), sets out to rescue them. (P, I)

Snyder, Dianne. ***The Boy of the Three-Year Nap.*** *Illus. by Allen Say. Houghton Mifflin, 1988.* Taro, a lazy Japanese boy who has never had a real job, tricks a rich merchant into arranging a marriage with his daughter. (P, I)

Stamm, Claus. ***Three Strong Women: A Tall Tale from Japan.*** *Illus. by Jean Tseng and Mou-sien Tseng. Viking, 1990.* On his way to a wrestling match, a mighty wrestler meets a young woman, her mother, and her grandmother, all of whom are far stronger than he. (P, I, A)

Tyler, Royall, ed. ***Japanese Tales.*** *Pantheon, 1987.* Just one good example of the Pantheon Fairy Tale and Folklore Library series—an excellent adult reference, each of which contains scores of stories. (Professional)

A SAMPLING OF OTHER TALES FROM ASIA

Blia Xiong. ***Nine-in-One, Grr! Grr! A Folktale from the Hmong People of Laos.*** *Adapted by Cathy Spagnoli. Illus. by Nancy Hom. Children's Book Press, 1989.* After the god Shao promises Tiger nine cubs each year, Bird fears for the safety of the other weaker animals and intervenes. (P, I)

Curry, Lindy Soon. ***A Tiger by the Tail and Other Stories from the Heart of Korea.*** *Libraries Unlimited, 1999.* Twenty-five folktales, with background notes on each in the standard format of the World Folklore series. (Professional)

Dashdondog, Zhambyn, and Borolzoi Dashdondog. ***Mongolian Folktales.*** *Libraries Unlimited, 2009.* Sixty-one folktales, historical background, recipes, riddles, games, crafts, and color photos are included in this volume of the World Folklore series. (Professional)

De Las Casas, Dianne. ***Kamishibai Story Theater: The Art of Picture Telling.*** *Illus. by Philip Chow. Teacher Ideas Press, 2006.* Twenty-five Asian folktales for grades 2 through 6, adapted for story-card presentations, a type of Japanese storytelling.

Divakaruni, Chitra Banerjee. ***Grandma and the Great Gourd: A Bengali Folktale.*** *Roaring Brook, 2013.* On her way to visit her daughter on the other side of the jungle, Grandma encounters a hungry fox, a black bear, and a tiger, all of whom want to eat her. Compare this version with Jessica Souhami's *No Dinner! The Story of the Old Woman and the Pumpkin,* below. (P, I)

Garland, Sherry. *Children of the Dragon: Selected Tales from Vietnam.* *Illus. by Trina Schart Hyman. Harcourt, 2001.* An attractive collection of six Vietnamese folktales, accompanied by magnificent full-page ink and acrylic paintings. (I, A)

Ginsburg, Mirra. *The Chinese Mirror.* *Illus. by Margot Zemach. Harcourt, 1988.* A Korean man brings his family an unfamiliar treasure from China—a hand mirror that shows their faces. (P, I)

Hamilton, Martha, and Mitch Weiss. *The Ghost Catcher: A Bengali Folktale.* *Illus. by Kristen Balouch. August House, 2008.* In India, a young barber tricks a ghost into giving him a thousand gold coins. (P, I)

Lee, Jeanne M. *Toad Is the Uncle of Heaven.* *Illus. by the author. Henry Holt, 1985.* How Toad visited the King of Heaven and brought rain to Vietnam. (P, I)

MacDonald, Margaret Read. *The Singing Top: Tales from Malaysia, Singapore, and Brunei.* *Libraries Unlimited, 2008.* World Folklore series; includes more than fifty folktales, with historical background, proverbs, songs, games, and color photos. (Professional)

Ness, Caroline. *The Ocean of Story: Fairy Tales from India.* *Illus. by Jacqueline Mair. Lothrop, 1996.* Eighteen stories from India about kings and rajahs; poor children and Brahmans; and transformed princes, thieves, and tigers. (I)

Ramanujan, A. K. *Folktales from India.* *Pantheon, 1994.* Pantheon Fairy Tale and Folklore Library series; 105 tales of gods, humans, and animals. (Professional)

Shrestha, Kavita Ram, and Sarah Lamstein. *From the Mango Tree and Other Folktales from Nepal.* *Libraries Unlimited, 1997.* World Folklore series; includes fifteen folktales, plus historical background and color photos. (Professional)

Souhami, Jessica. *No Dinner! The Story of the Old Woman and the Pumpkin.* *Illus. by the author. Frances Lincoln, 2012, c2000.* In a folktale from India, an old woman, on her way through the forest to visit her granddaughter, tricks a wolf, a tiger, and a bear into not eating her. Compare this with *Grandma and the Great Gourd* by Chitra Banerjee Divakaruni, above. (P)

Spagnoli, Cathy. *Asian Tales and Tellers.* *August House, 1998.* Four dozen fascinating, little-known folktales from Japan, Indonesia, Vietnam, China, Pakistan, India, Korea, the Philippines, Tibet, Sri Lanka, Burma, Cambodia, Laos, Taiwan, Bangladesh, and Nepal. (Professional)

Spagnoli, Cathy. *Jasmine and Coconuts: South Indian Tales.* *Libraries Unlimited, 1999.* A World Folklore series volume including forty-two folktales, with background and color photos. (Professional)

Vathanaprida, Supaporn. *Thai Tales: Folktales of Thailand.* *Libraries Unlimited, 1994.* More from the World Folklore series—twenty-eight folktales, with background and color photos. (Professional)

Vuong, Lynette Dyer. *The Brocaded Slipper and Other Vietnamese Tales.* *Illus. by Vo-dinh Mai. Addison-Wesley, 1982.* Five Vietnamese fairy tales reminiscent of familiar European tales for comparison. (I)

Wayupha Thotsa. *Lao Folktales.* *Libraries Unlimited, 2008.* Fifty folktales, plus historical background on China's ethnic minorities, recipes, games, crafts, and color photos in this entry in the World Folklore series. (Professional)

Yep, Laurence. *The Khan's Daughter: A Mongolian Folktale.* *Illus. by Jean Tseng and Mou-sien Tseng. Scholastic, 1997.* Möngke, a shepherd, believes he will become rich someday and marry the khan's daughter—and, of course, he does. (P, I)

TALES FROM AUSTRALIA, NEW ZEALAND, AND OCEANIA

Would that there were more books of tales available in the United States about the folklore of Australia, New Zealand, and the rest of Oceania, including the Philippines and Indonesia. (We moved Hawaiian tales to the North American booklist, though, technically, it's part of Oceania, along with all the other small islands of Polynesia dotting the Pacific.) Stories from Australia include myths and legends told by the aboriginal people, who passed them down orally for tens of thousands of years; folklore brought by the settlers, among them thousands of convicts brought from the British Isles (beginning in 1788); and tales from the Chinese, who emigrated in 1852 at the start of the Australian gold rush.

Dreamtime stories are the oral and sacred history of the original, indigenous Australians. They include creation myths, tales about constellations and natural phenomena, stories about animals or creatures such as the mythical swamp creature called *bunyip,* and stories about the culture and how to conduct one's life. The tales often begin, "A long time ago, back in the Dreamtime . . ." or "Back in the Dreaming, when the world was young . . ."

New Zealand was settled by the Maori, who are thought to have arrived from eastern Polynesia between 1250 and 1300, and the British, who began emigrating there in the early nineteenth century. Maori folklore and legends from New Zealand and Polynesia start with creation tales about Rangi (Father Sky) and Papa (Mother Earth).

BOOKLIST: TALES FROM AUSTRALIA, NEW ZEALAND, AND OCEANIA

Bunanta, Murti, and Margaret Read MacDonald. ***Indonesian Folktales.*** *Illus. by G. M. Sudarta. Libraries Unlimited, 2003.* Twenty-nine folktales, plus historical background, recipes, games, crafts, and color photos comprise this volume in the World Folklore series. (Professional)

Kawana, Kiri Te. ***Land of the Long White Cloud: Maori Myths, Tales and Legends.*** *Illus. by Michael Foreman. Little, Brown, 1989.* The author introduces each of these nineteen tales from New Zealand with a personal note. (I, A)

McLeod, Pauline E., Francis Firebrace Jones, June E. Barker, and Helen F. McKay. ***Gadi Mirrabooka: Australian Aboriginal Tales from the Dreaming.*** *Libraries Unlimited, 2001.* A World Folklore series volume with thirty-three folktales, plus historical background and color photos. (Professional)

Marshall, James Vance. ***Stories from the Billabong.*** *Illus. by Francis Firebrace. Frances Lincoln, 2008.* Ten stories from Aboriginal Australian folklore about the Dreamtime, including creation and pourquoi tales. (P, I)

Roth, Susan. ***The Biggest Frog in Australia.*** *Illus. by the author. Simon & Schuster, 1996.* In the Dreamtime, Kangaroo, Koala, Wombat, and others try to get thirsty Frog—who just drank all the water in Australia—to open his mouth. (P)

TALES FROM THE AMERICAS

Many folktales told and read in Northern America are European in origin, but the Americas have their own rich tradition: Native American legends, African American folktales, and tales of American folk heroes (aka tall tales). Native American lore from North, Central, and South America, in which animals figure prominently, holds a never-ending fascination for children. Because we're all immigrants—from the Indian tribes that migrated from Asia thousands of years ago to the folks who just arrived from other places—we have an astounding, enriching array of stories from every ethnic group.

Native American Legends

Through the telling of creation tales, trickster tales, hero stories, teaching or cautionary tales, epics, tall tales, and how and why stories, Native Americans have passed on their values, beliefs, and history to each generation for thousands of years. As there was no written language, the oral tradition was vital in keeping traditions and tales alive. With its focus on stories of the relationship of people to animals and nature, Native American folklore is often deeply spiritual; stories reinforce religious and cultural beliefs as well as chronicle how one's life should be lived. Listeners and readers will find in these many myths, legends, and folktales a respect for the earth and a sense of responsibility to care for it.

BOOKLIST: NATIVE AMERICAN STORIES

Bierhorst, John. *Latin American Folktales: Stories from Hispanic and Indian Traditions.* *Pantheon, 2003.* This entry in the Pantheon Fairy Tale and Folklore Library series features more than one hundred tales from Europe, Mexico, Central America, the American Southwest, and South America. (Professional)

Bruchac, Joseph. *Between Earth & Sky: Legends of Native American Sacred Places.* *Illus. by Thomas Locker. Harcourt, 1996.* Old Bear, a Native American man, shares with his young nephew, Little Turtle, ten legends about the "sacred places all around us." (I)

Bruchac, Joseph. *The Boy Who Lived with the Bears, and Other Iroquois Stories.* *Illus. by Murv Jacob. HarperCollins, 1995.* These six exciting and mostly humorous Native American animal tales from the Iroquois tradition are about tricksters, warriors, and friends. (P, I)

Bruchac, Joseph. *Flying with the Eagle, Racing the Great Bear: Stories from Native North America.* *Fulcrum, 2011, c1993.* Sixteen stories, with four per geographic region—Northeast, Southeast, Northwest, Southwest—about the rituals and experiences boys undergo in their passage to manhood. (I, A)

Bruchac, Joseph. *Native American Animal Stories.* *Illus. by John Kahionhes Fadden and David Kanietakeron Fadden. Fulcrum, 1992.* Twenty-four stories, organized by theme, from tribes across North America. (P, I, A)

Bruchac, Joseph, and Gayle Ross. *The Girl Who Married the Moon: Tales from Native North America.* *Fulcrum, 2006, c1994.* Sixteen stories about Native American girls from the Northeast, Southeast, Southwest, and Northwest. (I, A)

Curry, Jane Louise. *Hold Up the Sky, and Other Native American Tales from Texas and the Southern Plains.* *Illus. by James Watts. McElderry, 2003.* Twenty-six Native American tales include creation legends, pourquoi tales, and trickster tales from fourteen different tribes. Other collections by Curry include *Turtle Island: Tales of the Algonquian Nations* (1999) and *The Wonderful Sky Boat, and Other Native American Tales of the Southeast* (2001). (I, A)

DePaola, Tomie. *The Legend of the Bluebonnet: An Old Tale of Texas.* *Illus. by the author. Putnam, 1983.* She-Who-Is-Alone appeases the great spirits who send rain and flowers to the drought-starved Comanche. (P, I)

DePaola, Tomie. *The Legend of the Indian Paintbrush.* *Illus. by the author. Putnam, 1988.* Little Gopher, a Plains Indian boy, searches to capture the colors of the sunset. (P, I)

Erdoes, Richard, and Alfonso Ortiz. *American Indian Myths and Legends.* *Pantheon, 1985.* This Pantheon Fairy Tale and Folklore Library series entry includes 166 stories from a wide range of Nations, including creation legends; ghost tales, animal and trickster tales; and stories of love, war, and the end of the world. (Professional)

Goble, Paul. *Buffalo Woman.* *Illus. by the author. Bradbury, 1984.* A young man follows his wife and child to live with her Buffalo Nation people. (P, I, A)

Goble, Paul. *Crow Chief: A Plains Indian Story.* *Illus. by the author. Orchard, 1992.* A young hunter named Falling Star comes up with a plan to capture Crow Chief, the white crow who has spoiled his buffalo hunting. (P, I)

Goble, Paul. *Dream Wolf.* *llus. by the author. Atheneum, 1990.* A wolf befriends two lost Plains Indian children. (P, I)

Goble, Paul. *Her Seven Brothers.* *Illus. by the author. Bradbury, 1988.* Cheyenne legend of how a girl and her adopted brothers became the stars of the Big Dipper. (P, I)

Goble, Paul. *Iktomi and the Boulder: A Plains Indian Story.* *Illus. by the author. Orchard, 1988.* Humorous Native American trickster and pourquoi tale explains why bats have flat noses. See also *Coyote Steals the Blanket* by Janet Stevens, below. (P, I)

Goble, Paul. *Love Flute.* *Illus. by the author. Bradbury, 1992.* Elk Men give a shy young man a gift of the first flute. (I, A)

Goble, Paul. *The Return of the Buffaloes: A Plains Indian Story about Famine and Renewal of the Earth.* *Illus. by the author. National Geographic, 1996.* In a time of hunger, a mysterious woman promises to send her Buffalo People to feed a village. (P, I)

Goldin, Barbara Diamond. *The Girl Who Lived with the Bears.* *Illus. by Andrew Plewes. Harcourt, 1997.* When the Raven clan chief's daughter speaks disrespectfully about bears, she is kidnapped by the Bear People and taken away to their village, where she marries the bear chief's nephew. (P, I, A)

Green, Thomas A., ed. *Native American Folktales.* *Greenwood, 2009.* From Green's excellent Stories from the American Mosaic series, thirty-one assorted tales, arranged into four sections: origins; heroes, heroines, villains, and fools; society and conflict; and the supernatural. (Professional)

Hausman, Gerald. *Coyote Walks on Two Legs: A Book of Navajo Myths and Legends.* *Illus. by Floyd Cooper. Philomel, 1995.* Coyote weaves in and out of mischief in this elegant collection of five poetic stories from the Navajo tradition. (P, I)

Lelooska. *Echoes of the Elders: The Stories and Paintings of Chief Lelooska.* *Illus. by the author. DK, 1997.* A storyteller and artist, Chief Lelooska recorded, wrote down, and illustrated two magnificent collections of his traditional Northwest Coast Indian tales. The companion volume is *Spirit of the Cedar People: More Stories and Paintings of Chief Lelooska* (1998). (P, I, A)

Marshall, Bonnie C. *Far North Tales: Stories from the Peoples of the Arctic Circle.* *Libraries Unlimited, 2011.* This collection of eighty folktales, with historical background and color photos, is an entry in the World Folklore series. (Professional)

Max, Jill. *Spider Spins a Story: Fourteen Legends from Native America.* *Illus. by Robert Annesley, Benjamin Harjo, and others. Rising Moon, 1997.* Creation legends and pourquoi tales about how the earth and spiders came to be. (I, A)

McDermott, Gerald. *Arrow to the Sun.* *Illus. by the author. Viking, 1974.* The solar fire as the source of life is presented in a stunning picture book, a Pueblo Indian legend. (P, I)

McDermott, Gerald. *Coyote: A Trickster Tale from the American Southwest.* *Illus. by the author. Harcourt, 1994.* In a comical Zuni legend, trickster Coyote attempts to fly with the crows. (P, I)

McDermott, Gerald. *Raven: A Trickster Tale from the Pacific Northwest.* *Illus. by the author. Harcourt, 1993.* Trickster Raven steals the sun that is kept hidden in a box in the Sky Chief's lodge and gives it to all the people. (P, I)

Norman, Howard. *The Girl Who Dreamed Only Geese and Other Tales of the Far North.* *Illus. by Leo and Diane Dillon. Harcourt, 1997.* Ten fascinating Inuit folktales of people and animals. (I, A)

Pelton, Mary Helen, and Jacqueline DiGennaro. *Images of a People: Tlingit Myths and Legends.* *Libraries Unlimited, 1992.* A World Folklore series volume with twenty-two folktales, historical background, and color photos. (Professional)

Rodanas, Kristina. *Dragonfly's Tale.* *Illus. by the author. Clarion, 1991.* In an Ashiwi tale, two Corn Maidens disguised as poor old women bring famine to a wasteful pueblo until two kind children appease them. (P, I)

Steptoe, John. *The Story of Jumping Mouse: A Native American Legend.* *Illus. by the author. Lothrop, 1984.* A young mouse sets off on a perilous journey, aided by Magic Frog, to fulfill his dream. (P, I)

Stevens, Janet. *Coyote Steals the Blanket: A Ute Tale.* *Illus. by the author. Holiday House, 1993.* Though Hummingbird warns him not to, Coyote runs off with a blanket he finds draped over a rock, and now the rock is rumbling after him. See also the variant *Iktomi and the Boulder* by Paul Goble, above. (P, I)

Taylor, Harriet Peck. ***Coyote Places the Stars.*** *Illus. by the author. Bradbury, 1993.* In this Wasco tale, Coyote climbs a ladder of arrows to the moon and moves the stars around to create new sky pictures. (P, I)

Thompson, Susan C., Keith S. Thompson, and Lidia López. ***Mayan Folktales: Cuentos Folklóricos Mayas.*** *Libraries Unlimited, 2007.* World Folklore series; twenty-five folktales, plus historical background and color photos. (Professional)

Tingle, Tim. ***When Turtle Grew Feathers: A Folktale from the Choctaw Nation.*** *Illus. by Stacey Schuett. August House Little Folk, 2007.* In his race against Rabbit, Turtle is helped by Turkey, who hides inside his shell. (P, I)

Van Laan, Nancy. ***In a Circle Long Ago: A Treasury of Native Lore from North America.*** *Illus. by Lisa Desimini. Knopf, 1995.* A beautiful collection of twenty-five Native American animal fables, pourquoi, and trickster tales, grouped by geographic region. (P, I, A)

Van Laan, Nancy. ***Shingebiss: An Ojibwe Legend.*** *Illus. by Betsy Bowen. Houghton Mifflin, 1997.* Winter Maker tries to freeze and starve Shingebiss the duck. (P, I)

WEBSITES: NATIVE AMERICAN STORIES

Encyclopedia Mythica: Americas *www.pantheon.org/areas/mythology/americas*
This encyclopedia of mythology, folklore, and religion includes an extensive section on Native American legends.

First People *www.native-languages.org/legends.htm*
"Dedicated to all First People of the Americas and Canada, better known as Turtle Island," this remarkable, child-friendly site includes texts of more than 1,300 Native American legends, listed alphabetically by tribe; Native American poems and prayers; and thousands of photos and other images.

Native Languages of the Americas: Native American Indian Legends and Folklore
www.native-languages.org/legends.htm
A collection of hundreds of Native American folktales and traditional stories, indexed by tribe.

African American Folktales

When Africans were brought to the Western world as slaves, they managed to keep one aspect of their lives intact—a rich tradition of storytelling and singing. Once in North America, enslaved Africans used those stories as a basis for a new type of storytelling. Forbidden to read and write, their stories evolved into tales of survival, rebellion, and triumph over their conditions. Many of the tales in the list below can be traced back to Africa. You'll find trickster tales with characters, both human and animal, who outwit their dimwitted masters or triumph over bigger and more-powerful animals. Also well represented in African American folklore are pourquoi tales, tall tales, and ghost stories.

JOEL CHANDLER HARRIS AND UNCLE REMUS

In 1879, a thirty-year-old Georgia journalist named Joel Chandler Harris published a story in the *Atlanta Constitution* entitled "The Story of Mr. Rabbit and Mr. Fox as told by Uncle Remus." It was later followed by *Uncle Remus, His Songs and Sayings*, published in 1881, which comprised folktales, many of them trickster tales about Brer (Brother) Rabbit, Brer Bear, Brer Fox and others, which Harris heard from African American slaves as a boy. Readers couldn't get enough of his stories, which were narrated by elderly slave Uncle Remus, who tells his stories to a young white boy on the plantation. In his introduction to the book, Harris states, "My purpose has been to preserve the legends themselves in their original simplicity, and to wed them permanently to the quaint dialect—if, indeed, it can be called a dialect—through the medium of which they have become a part of the domestic history of every Southern family; and I have endeavored to give to the whole a genuine flavor of the old plantation."

Although the stylized dialect of the tales was accepted as authentic in the nineteenth century, it was rejected as patronizing, even racist, in the twentieth. Praised or criticized, it is certainly over the top, as you can see from this brief example:

> "I'm gwine ter larn you how ter talk ter 'spectubble folks ef hit's de las' ack," sez Brer Rabbit, sezee. "Ef you don't take off dat hat en tell me howdy, I'm gwine ter bus' you wide open," sezee.

During the Civil Rights era, these stories were derided as politically incorrect, and Harris was scorned for passing on as his own the stories he heard from African American slaves. However, had Harris not recorded these tales, twenty-five years after the Civil War ended, would they have survived until today? All the stories are now available at Project Gutenberg, www.gutenberg.org, if you want to read the originals and better understand the controversy.

Harris's books languished for many decades, but in the 1980s, several writers—the most prominent being African American storyteller, writer, and scholar Julius Lester—resurrected them, toned down the dialect, and made them viable for children again. Alice McGill recorded some of the Bruh Rabbit stories she heard as a child in North Carolina in *Sure as Sunrise: Stories of Bruh Rabbit & His Walkin' Talkin' Friends*, and in *When Birds Could Talk & Bats Could Sing: The Adventures of Bruh Sparrow, Sis Wren, and Their Friends*. Virginia Hamilton republished the stories that folklorist Martha Young heard on her father's Alabama plantation after the Civil War.

For many years Judy has been telling the little nonsense story, "The Singing Geese." One day, as she was in the middle of telling it, she realized that she had long known another version of the tale, a song sung by Huddie Ledbetter (Lead Belly) called "The Grey Goose." Upon researching her version of the story in B. A. Botkin's *A Treasury of American Folklore: The Stories, Legends, Tall Tales, Traditions, Ballads, and Songs of the American People*, she was excited to discover that it was an African American folktale. In addition, she now understood that it was far more than just a funny tall tale about a goose; it was a parable about freedom and invincibility. Sometimes it takes a while to parse the meaning of even the simplest tales.

The Singing Geese

Retold by Judy Freeman

A farmer and his wife were awakened one morning by the sound of a great flock of geese flapping overhead. "My dear," said the farmer as he threw on his clothes and grabbed his shotgun, "get the oven ready. We're going to have us some roast goose for supper tonight!"

He raced out the door and, looking up, saw a dozen geese circling above. As they flew, they were singing this song:

"La-lee-lu, come quilla, come quilla, bung, bung, bung, quilla bung."

He lifted up his gun and BLAM, BLAM, fired off both barrels. The shot hit the lead goose and it started to fall. The whole time it was falling, it sang,

"La-lee-lu, come quilla, come quilla, bung, bung, bung, quilla bung."

The farmer picked up the goose by the neck, and the whole time he was carrying it inside, the goose kept singing,

"La-lee-lu, come quilla, come quilla, bung, bung, bung, quilla bung."

He took it in the house, held up the goose by the neck, and announced, "Look, my dear, just as I told you, we're having roast goose for supper tonight!"

The whole time he was holding it up by the neck, that goose kept singing,

"La-lee-lu, come quilla, come quilla, bung, bung, bung, quilla bung."

"Quiet, can't you!" ordered the farmer.

He handed the goose over to his wife to pluck it for roasting. She brought the goose into the kitchen, laid it on the big wooden table, and started to pull out the feathers. But as she plucked each feather, it flew out of her fingers and flew out the window. She thought that was mighty strange, but never mind. And the whole time she was plucking that goose and the feathers were flying off her fingers and flying out the window, that goose kept singing,

"La-lee-lu, come quilla, come quilla, bung, bung, bung, quilla bung."

"Quiet, can't you!" ordered the farmer's wife.

She put the plucked goose in a big roasting pan, slid it into the hot oven, and closed the over door with a BANG. But the whole time that goose was cooking, she could hear it singing, kinda muffled-like,

"La-lee-lu, come quilla, come quilla, bung, bung, bung, quilla bung."

When the goose was brown and cooked to a turn, the farmer's wife opened the oven door, and pulled out the big roasting pan. She lifted up the goose and set it on a big oval platter on the big wooden table, and the farmer started to sharpen his long, sharp carving knife. And the whole time he was sharpening it, that goose on the big oval serving platter on the big wooden table was singing,

"La-lee-lu, come quilla, come quilla, bung, bung, bung, quilla bung."

"Quiet, can't you!" ordered the farmer and the farmer's wife together.

But just as the farmer picked up his big fork and was about to stick the fork in the goose and cut the first slice, there came a tremendous noise from outside, and a whole flock of eleven geese flew through the open window singing, kinda muffled-like,

"La-lee-lu, come quilla, come quilla, bung, bung, bung, quilla bung."

And each one had its beak stuffed full of feathers. They landed on that big wooden table and they began to stick those feathers back into the roasted goose. When all the feathers had been put back into the goose, that goose stood up on the big oval serving platter. It shook its feathers and nodded its head at the other geese. Then all twelve geese flew out the window, singing,

"La-lee-lu, come quilla, come quilla, bung, bung, bung, quilla bung."
And that was the end of that.

The song, "The Grey Goose," was first recorded by folklorists John A. Lomax and his son Alan Lomax in 1934 at a prison in Sugarland, Texas. On the liner notes of the subsequent album, *Afro-American Spirituals, Work Songs, and Ballads*, it says,

> The folk have always loved humble heroes who were absolutely invincible, who could endure any hardship or torture without fear or harm. For the southern Negro, faced with the problem of sheer survival under slavery and later as the sub-standard economic group, this pattern has dominated his ballads and folk-tales. The ballad of the heroic goose, who, after being shot, picked, cooked, carved and run through the sawmill, was last seen with a large, derisively honking flock of goslings, flyin' over the ocean, epitomizes the Negro's belief in his own ability to endure any hardship.
>
> The design of the song is the African leader-chorus form, and this version is used on the Texas prison farms for hoeing—a whole gang moving forward together, their hoes flashing together in the sun, across an irrigation ditch.[1]

When you sing "The Grey Goose" with children, have them come in on the "Lord, Lord, Lord" of each verse, and introduce it as a type of tall tale. Go to www.youtube.com/watch?v=-1T2bPFXYZY and you can hear Lead Belly's version.

The Grey Goose

One Sunday morning, Lord, Lord, Lord!
The preacher went a-huntin', Lord, Lord, Lord!
He carried along his shotgun, Lord, Lord, Lord!
The gun went off alone, Lord, Lord, Lord!
Down come the grey goose, Lord, Lord, Lord!
He was six weeks a-rollin', Lord, Lord, Lord!
He was six weeks a-haulin', Lord, Lord, Lord!
Well, my wife an' your wife, Lord, Lord, Lord!
They give a feather-pickin', Lord, Lord, Lord!

They were six weeks a-pickin', Lord, Lord, Lord!
An' they put him on a parboil, Lord, Lord, Lord!
He was six weeks a-boilin', Lord, Lord, Lord!
And they put him on the table, Lord, Lord, Lord!
And the fork couldn't stick him, Lord, Lord, Lord!
And a knife couldn't cut him, Lord, Lord, Lord!
And they threw him in a hog pen, Lord, Lord, Lord!
The hogs couldn't eat him, Lord, Lord, Lord!
He broke the hog's teeth out, Lord, Lord, Lord!
So they took him to the sawmill, Lord, Lord, Lord!
And the saws couldn't cut him, Lord, Lord, Lord!
He broke the saw's teeth out, Lord, Lord, Lord!
An' the last time I seen him, Lord, Lord, Lord!
He was flyin' cross the ocean, Lord, Lord, Lord!
With a long trail of goslins, Lord, Lord, Lord!
And they're all goin' "quack quack," Lord, Lord, Lord!

BOOKLIST: AFRICAN AMERICAN FOLKTALES

Abrahams, Roger. ***African American Folktales: Stories from Black Traditions in the New World.*** *Pantheon, 1999.* An entry in the Pantheon Fairy Tale and Folklore Library, this volume offers more than one hundred stories from the South and the Caribbean, some collected by Joel Chandler Harris and Zora Neale Hurston, others recorded by Abrahams. (Professional)

Courlander, Harold. ***A Treasury of Afro-American Folklore: The Oral Literature, Traditions, Recollections, Legends, Tales, Songs, Religious Beliefs, Customs, Sayings and Humor of Peoples of African American Descent in the Americas.*** *Crown, 1976.* A wide-ranging compendium of tales and more. (Professional)

Green, Thomas A., ed. ***African American Folktales.*** *Greenwood, 2009.* From Green's excellent Stories from the American Mosaic series, these fifty assorted tales are arranged into four sections: origins; heroes, heroines, villains, and fools; society and conflict; and the supernatural. (Professional)

Hamilton, Virginia. ***Her Stories: African American Folktales, Fairy Tales, and True Tales.*** *Illus. by Leo and Diane Dillon. Scholastic/Blue Sky, 1995.* Nineteen stories about African American women include animal tales, pourquoi tales, legends, tall tales, and true accounts. (I, A)

Hamilton, Virginia. ***The People Could Fly: American Black Folk Tales.*** *Illus. by Leo and Diane Dillon. Knopf, 1985.* Trickster tales, ghost stories, and animal stories. (I, A)

Hamilton, Virginia. ***The People Could Fly: The Picture Book.*** *Illus. by Leo Dillon and Diane Dillon. Knopf, 2004.* In the land of slavery, Sarah and her baby escape the overseer's whip when she rises into the sky. Another version is *Way Up and Over Everything* by Alice McGill (Houghton Mifflin, 2008). (I, A)

Hamilton, Virginia. ***When Birds Could Talk & Bats Could Sing: The Adventures of Bruh Sparrow, Sis Wren, and Their Friends.*** *Illus. by Barry Moser. Blue Sky/Scholastic, 1996.* This is a delectable collection of eight folktales that were first retold by Martha Young, Alabama's foremost folklorist in the early part of the twentieth century. (I, A)

Hurston, Zora Neale, coll. ***Lies and Other Tall Tales.*** *Adapted and illustrated by Christopher Myers. HarperCollins, 2005.* Picture book with colloquial snippets of stories, insults, and lies collected by Harlem Renaissance folklorist, anthropologist, and author Hurston in the 1930s and illustrated with assertive collages. (I, A)

Lester, Julius. ***The Knee-High Man and Other Tales.*** *Illus. by Ralph Pinto. Dial, 1972.* Jaunty retellings of six African American folktales. (P, I)

Lester, Julius. ***Uncle Remus: The Complete Tales.*** *Illus. by Jerry Pinkney. Dial, 1999.* A compilation of all four of Lester's folksy books of Joel Chandler Harris's Brer Rabbit tales—traditional African American trickster tales from the American South—retold in Lester's informal, shoot-the-breeze style. (I, A)

McGill, Alice. ***Sure as Sunrise: Stories of Bruh Rabbit & His Walkin' Talkin' Friends.*** *Illus. by Don Tate. Houghton Mifflin, 2004.* Five crackling African American folktales about the crafty trickster Bruh Rabbit and his animal pals and rivals. (P, I)

McGill, Alice. ***Way Up and Over Everything.*** *Illus. by Jude Daly. Houghton Mifflin, 2008.* Five newly arrived African slaves on Ol' Man Deboreaux's cotton plantation take to the air and fly away. Compare with *The People Could Fly: The Picture Book* by Virginia Hamilton, above. (P, I, A)

McKissack, Patricia. ***The Dark-Thirty: Southern Tales of the Supernatural.*** *Illus. by Brian Pinkney. Knopf, 1992.* Ten "original stories rooted in African American history and the oral storytelling tradition," to be told in the dark-thirty, the half hour before darkness falls. (I, A)

McKissack, Patricia C. ***Porch Lies: Tales of Slicksters, Tricksters, and Other Wily Characters.*** *Illus. by André Carrilho. Schwartz & Wade, 2006.* Based on the tales the author heard as a child on her grandparents' porch in Nashville, Tennessee. (I, A)

San Souci, Robert D. ***The Faithful Friend.*** *Illus. by Brian Pinkney. Simon & Schuster, 1995.* On the island of Martinique, Hippolyte's best friend, Clement, falls in love with Pauline, the niece of a dangerous *quimboiseur*, or wizard. (I, A)

San Souci, Robert D. *Sukey and the Mermaid.* *Illus. by Brian Pinkney. Four Winds, 1992.* On a little island off the coast of South Carolina, a hardworking girl with a harsh new step-pa summons up a "beautiful, brown-skinned, black-eyed mermaid" who gives her gold. (P, I)

San Souci, Robert D. *The Talking Eggs.* *Illus. by Jerry Pinkney. Dial, 1989.* Blanche is rewarded for her kindness to an old woman, while mean sister Rose is punished. For a retelling of the original African tale, read *Chinye: A West African Folk Tale* by Obi Onyefulu (Frances Lincoln, 2007, c1994). (P, I, A)

Young, Richard Alan, and Judy Dockrey Young, coll. *African-American Folktales for Young Readers.* *August House, 1993.* Thirty-one tales, retold favorites of African American storytellers, about heroes and heroines, animals, tricksters, and tall-tale characters. (I, A)

WEBSITES: AFRICAN AMERICAN FOLKTALES

John Henry: The Steel Driving Man *www.ibiblio.org/john_henry*
Research by different scholars on the legend of John Henry, with links to song lyrics and recordings.

"The Trickster in African American Literature"
http://nationalhumanitiescenter.org/tserve/freedom/1865–1917/essays/trickster.htm
From the TeacherServe section of the National Humanities Center website, an informative essay by Trudier Harris, a professor emerita of English at the University of North Carolina at Chapel Hill.

Tall Tales

Tall tales are uniquely American yarns of larger-than-life working heroes, some based on actual people, like frontiersman Davy Crockett, riverboatman Mike Fink, and Johnny Appleseed (the early-nineteenth-century apple tree–planting guy whose real name was John Chapman), though their exploits are vastly exaggerated in the retelling. There's John Henry (the African American railroad man who went up against a steam engine and died with a hammer in his hand, Lord, Lord), and Big Mose (the New York City firefighter). Others, such as cowboy Pecos Bill and mighty logger Paul Bunyan, are most likely "fakelore." That term was coined in 1950 by American folklorist Richard M. Dorson, who argued that many of our revered American heroes were actually invented by various writers, and not told in mining and logging camps or around a Western campfire. The stories about Pecos Bill, for instance, were actually created by the writer Edward J. O'Reilly in 1923.

In his 1940 article "Paul Bunyan, Myth or Hoax?" historian Carleton C. Ames questioned the authenticity of the logger with the big blue ox; he could find no old-timer loggers who recalled stories about Bunyan in their lumber camps. The prodigious logger grew to prominence starting in 1914, when William B. Laughead, lumberjack-turned-advertising-man, wrote and illustrated a series of pamphlets of Paul Bunyan stories for the Red River Lumber Company, a lumber mill in California. In the stories, he invented the characters of Paul's blue ox, Babe; and Johnny Inkslinger, who, as Paul's headquarters clerk, invented bookkeeping.

Other literary (instead of folkloric) heroes include Pittsburgh steelworker Joe Magarac; Old Stormalong, the New England–based sailor Captain Alfred Bulltop Stormalong, who was a character in nineteenth-century sea shanties, but didn't appear in stories until the 1930s; Febold Feboldson, Swedish American clodbuster from Nebraska, whose exploits were first published in a 1923 newspaper; and Tony Beaver, Paul Bunyan's champion griddle-skating cousin.

Note that there aren't any females in that list. Sally Ann Thunder Ann Whirlwind Crockett, Davy's wife, gets a shout-out every now and then—as in the picture book listed below by Steven Kellogg—but you need to go to recent literature, written in the style of the old stories, to find heroines. Caldecott Honor Book *Swamp Angel* by Anne Isaacs or *Doña Flor* by Pat Mora are good examples.

Perhaps many of these stories are not true examples of the folk process—but then again, perhaps they are, since writers continue to embellish them and create new ones. Regardless of who first concocted these exaggerated tales, they have taken on a life of their own and are still great stories to tell and read. Forerunners to superhero comics, these stories, with their colorful characters and their hyperbolic deeds, continue to capture the hearts of school-age children.

BOOKLIST: TALL TALES

Isaacs, Anne. *Meanwhile, Back at the Ranch.* *Illus. by Kevin Hawkes. Schwartz & Wade, 2014.* After the wealthy young English widow, Tulip Jones, buys a ranch in By-Golly Gully, Texas—where vegetables grow to gargantuan size and tortoises can outgallop racehorses—prospective suitors vie for her hand. (I, A)

Isaacs, Anne. *Swamp Angel.* *Illus. by Paul O. Zelinsky. Dutton, 1994.* In a glorious literary tall tale, Angelica Longrider, Tennessee's greatest woodswoman, takes on Thundering Tarnation, a bear to end all bears, during a five-day wrestling match. In the sequel, *Dust Devil* (2010), she moves to Montana and gets a horse. (P, I)

Keats, Ezra Jack. ***John Henry: An American Legend.*** *Illus. by the author. Pantheon, 1965.* How the steel-driving man beat the steam drill and died with his hammer in his hand. (P, I)

Kellogg, Steven. ***Mike Fink.*** *Illus. by the author. Morrow, 1992.* "Cock-a-doodle-doo!" crows amiable riverman and champion wrestler Mike Fink, the King of the Keelboatmen, whom even a steamboat couldn't stop. (P, I)

Kellogg, Steven. ***Sally Ann Thunder Ann Whirlwind Crockett.*** *Illus. by the author. Morrow, 1995.* Sally Ann Thunder Ann Whirlwind falls for the handsome young man she rescues, the legendary Davy Crockett. (P, I)

Lester, Julius. ***John Henry.*** *Illus. by Jerry Pinkney. Dial, 1994.* A large-size picture book based on several versions of the folk song about John, the tenacious African American man who won a contest against a steam engine. (P, I)

Miller, Bobbi, retel. ***Miss Sally Ann and the Panther.*** *Illus. by Megan Lloyd. Holiday House, 2012.* Miss Sally Ann Thunder Ann Whirlwind matches strength with Fireeyes, a panther, "hugeceously smart and mean as tarnation." (P, I)

Mora, Pat. ***Doña Flor: A Tall Tale about a Giant Woman with a Great Big Heart.*** *Illus. by Raúl Colón. Knopf, 2005.* In this literary tall tale, a Hispanic heroine, the giantess Doña Flor, who speaks every animal language, befriends the roaring puma that has been circling the pueblo and frightening the people. (P, I)

Osborne, Mary Pope. ***American Tall Tales.*** *Illus. by Michael McCurdy. Knopf, 1991.* This book recounts the exploits of nine uniquely American folklore heroes. (I, A)

Osborne, Mary Pope. ***New York's Bravest.*** *Illus. by Steve Johnson and Lou Fancher. Knopf, 2002.* On the night of a big hotel fire, Mose, New York City's mythical nineteenth-century firefighter, rescues all the people inside. (P, I, A)

Rounds, Glen. ***Ol' Paul, the Mighty Logger.*** *Illus. by the author. Holiday House, 1976, c1936.* The subtitle says it all: "Being a True Account of the Seemingly Incredible Exploits and Inventions of the Great Paul Bunyan." (I, A)

San Souci, Robert D. ***Cut from the Same Cloth: American Women of Myth, Legend, and Tall Tale.*** *Illus. by Brian Pinkney. Philomel, 1993.* Arranged by geographical region, these fifteen tales introduce a wide range of gutsy females. (I, A)

Schanzer, Rosalyn. ***Davy Crockett Saves the World.*** *Illus. by the author. HarperCollins, 2001.* In this literary tall tale, the president enlists Tennessee frontiersman Davy Crockett, to pull the tail off Halley's Comet so it won't crash into Earth. (P, I)

Walker, Paul Robert. ***Big Men, Big Country: A Collection of American Tall Tales.*** *Illus. by James Bernardin. Harcourt, 1993.* Boisterous, good-natured yarns about nine hardworking guys, including Davy Crockett, Paul Bunyan, and John Henry. (I, A)

WEBSITES: TALL TALES

Forest History Society *www.foresthistory.org/ead/Laughead_William_B.html*
If you want to do some scholarly research, you'll find an interesting article about William B. Laughead's connection to Paul Bunyan, and a list of the contents of its archives of Laughead papers, including drawings, and pamphlets.

John Henry: The Steel Driving Man *www.ibiblio.org/john_henry*
Research by different scholars on the legend of John Henry, with links to song lyrics and recordings.

"Tall Tales and Lumber Sales"
http://fhsarchives.wordpress.com/2009/05/26/tall-tales-and-lumber-sales
Peeling Back the Bark, an online blog exploring "the collections, acquisitions, and treasures of the Forest History Society," published the 2009 article "Tall Tales and Lumber Sales" by Amanda T. Ross, detailing how Laughead popularized Paul Bunyan. It includes reproductions from the original pamphlets.

Other Tales from the Americas

Many American folktales are actually variants of European tales, imported and adapted to the American experience. For example, some of the tales collected by Richard Chase in the southern mountain regions of Appalachia in the 1940s for his *Grandfather Tales* and *The Jack Tales* are European stories transformed by the use of American settings and dialects. Tales in the Hispanic tradition, which came originally from Spain and Portugal, are now often set in Cuba, Latin and South America, Mexico, or the Old Southwest. Storyteller Diane Wolkstein went to Haiti in the 1970s and collected the stories people still told there, turning them into her classic collection, *The Magic Orange Tree and Other Haitian Folktales.* Are people still telling stories here in the United States? Ask your friends and relatives what stories they know that were passed down in their families. You may be surprised.

BOOKLIST: OTHER TALES FROM THE AMERICAS

Ada, Alma Flor. ***The Rooster Who Went to His Uncle's Wedding: A Latin American Folktale.*** *Illus. by Kathleen Kuchera. Putnam, 1993.* "What to do? Peck or not peck?" the hungry rooster ponders as he contemplates a perfect kernel of corn lying in a mud puddle. (P)

Almeida, Livia de, and Ana Portella. ***Brazilian Folktales.*** *Ed. by Margaret Read MacDonald. Libraries Unlimited, 2006.* World Folklore series; includes more than forty folktales, with historical background, recipes, games, and color photos. (Professional)

Andrews, Jan. ***When Apples Grew Noses and White Horses Flew: Tales of Ti-Jean.*** *Illus. by Dusan Petricic. Groundwood, 2011.* Three fairy tales about Ti-Jean, the French-Canadian counterpart to Jack in English and American tales, sometimes wise, sometimes not. (I, A)

Armstrong, Jennifer. ***The American Story: 100 True Tales from American History.*** *Illus. by Roger Roth. Knopf, 2006.* A rich source of one hundred true and uniquely American stories from our history, starting with the founding in 1565 of St. Augustine and ending with the 2000 election. (I, A)

Botkin, B. A. ***A Treasury of American Folklore: The Stories, Legends, Tall Tales, Traditions, Ballads, and Songs of the American People.*** *Crown, 1944.* A vast and fascinating compendium of collected stories from primary sources, but many are unvarnished and not suitable for children. (Professional)

Brunvand, Jan Harold. ***The Study of American Folklore: An Introduction.*** *Fourth edition. Norton, 1998.* Essays on verbal and nonverbal folklore. (Professional)

Brusca, María Cristina, and Toña Wilson. ***When Jaguar Ate the Moon, and Other Stories about Animals and Plants of the Americas.*** *Illus. by María Cristina Brusca. Henry Holt, 1995.* A well-chosen collection of thirty-one folktales from North and South America, arranged alphabetically by the names of plants and animals. (P, I, A)

Campoy, F. Isabel, and Alma Flor Ada. ***Tales Our Abuelitas Told: A Hispanic Folktale Collection.*** *Illus. by Felipe Dávalos, Viví Escrivá, Susan Guevara, and Leyla Torres. Atheneum, 2006.* A dozen sprightly folktales with roots in Spain and Latin America. (P, I)

Chase, Richard. ***Grandfather Tales.*** *Illus. by Berkeley Williams Jr. Houghton Mifflin, 1948.* Many of these twenty-five splendid American folktales—which emigrated with English settlers to North Carolina, Virginia, and Kentucky—will be familiar to you. An essential book for every collection. (P, I, A)

Chase, Richard. ***Jack Tales.*** *Illus. by Berkeley Williams Jr. Houghton Mifflin, 1943.* Southern Appalachian tales about that clever, lazy, always-lands-on-his-feet hero, Jack. (P, I, A)

Cohn, Amy L. ***From Sea to Shining Sea: A Treasury of American Folklore and Folk Songs.*** *Illus. by eleven Caldecott Medal and four Caldecott Honor book artists. Scholastic, 1993.* A handsome and masterful collection of more than 140 songs and stories from US folklore and history. (P, I, A)

Deedy, Carmen Agra. ***Martina the Beautiful Cockroach: A Cuban Folktale.*** *Illus. by Michael Austin. Peachtree, 2007.* Martina's grandmother gives her interesting advice in looking for a husband: to spill coffee on her suitors' shoes. This is a Cuban version of the story you may know as "Perez y Martina," the Puerto Rican variant told by Pura Belpre. (P, I)

DePaola, Tomie. ***Tomie dePaola's Front Porch Tales & North Country Whoppers.*** *Illus. by the author. Putnam, 2007.* Told in the North Country dialect of New Hampshire, this is a droll compilation of eleven tales, dialogues, and wry asides, sorted by season. (P, I, A)

Ehlert, Lois. ***Cuckoo: A Mexican Folktale / Cucú: Un cuento folklórico Mexicano.*** *Illus. by the author. Harcourt, 1997.* Beautiful, lazy Cuckoo saves the other birds from a fire that scorches her colorful feathers black and turns her beautiful voice hoarse. (P)

Ehlert, Lois. *Moon Rope: A Peruvian Folktale / Un lazo a la luna: una leyenda Peruana.* *Illus. by the author. Harcourt, 1992.* Fox wants Mole to climb to the moon on a woven-grass rope, but it's Fox who gets trapped up there. (P)

Goldman, Judy. *Whiskers, Tails & Wings: Animal Tales from Mexico.* *Illus. by Fabricio Vanden Broeck. Charlesbridge, 2013.* Five engaging tales originally told by different indigenous peoples, with background on both the tales and the regions of Mexico from which the tales originated. (P, I)

Gonzalez, Lucia M. *The Bossy Gallito: A Traditional Cuban Folktale.* *Illus. by Lulu Delacre Scholastic, 1994.* On his way to his uncle's wedding, a bossy little rooster tries to make the grass, a goat, a stick, fire, water, and the sun clean his dirty beak. (P)

González, Lucia M. *Señor Cat's Romance, and Other Favorite Stories from Latin America.* *Illus. by Lulu Delacre. Scholastic, 1997.* Six well-told and well-known favorite folktales, or cuentos favoritos, about animals, told throughout Latin America. (P, I)

Green, Thomas A., ed. *Latino American Folktales.* *Greenwood, 2009.* From Green's excellent Stories from the American Mosaic series, thirty-five assorted tales, some Native American, others European-based, arranged into four sections: origins; heroes, heroines, villains, and fools; society and conflict; and the supernatural. See also his *African American Folktales* (2008), *Asian American Folktales* (2009), and *Native American Folktales* (2009). (Professional)

Haley, Gail E. *Mountain Jack Tales.* *Illus. by the author. Dutton, 1992.* Old Poppyseed regales us with nine stories about that hero, Jack, "and the things he done when he was off adventurin'." (I, A)

Hamilton, Virginia. *The Girl Who Spun Gold.* *Illus. by Leo and Diane Dillon.* Scholastic, 2000. Young Quashiba's mother tells Big King that her daughter can spin the finest golden thread. Compare this West Indies variant to the German "Rapunzel" as told by the Brothers Grimm. (P, I, A)

Harper, Wilhelmina. *The Gunniwolf.* *Illus. by William Wiesner. Dutton, 1967.* Little Red Riding Hood story from the American South, with wonderful chantable refrains. (P)

Hayes, Joe. *The Coyote under the Table / El coyote debajo de la mesa: Folktales Told in Spanish and English.* *Illus. by Antonio Castro L. Cinco Puntos, 2011.* Ten rousing folktales from the Hispanic tradition of Northern Arizona, retold by a master storyteller. (I, A)

Hayes, Joe. *Juan Verdades: The Man Who Couldn't Tell a Lie.* *Illus. by Joseph Daniel Fiedler. Orchard, 2001.* Hoping to catch him in a lie and win a bet, lovely Araceli entices Juan to pick all the apples from his employer's treasured apple tree in this Hispanic folktale from the Southwest. (P, I, A)

Hayes, Joe. *A Spoon for Every Bite.* *Illus. by Rebecca Leer. Orchard, 1996.* In a Hispanic tale from the Old Southwest, a rich man boasts that he has so many spoons, he could use a different one every day for a year. (P, I, A)

Hicks, Ray, as told to Lynn Salsi. *The Jack Tales.* *Illus. by Owen Smith. Callaway, 2000.* Storyteller Ray Hicks regales us with three stories he learned from his grandfather about that trickster, Jack. (P, I, A)

Hooks, William. *Moss Gown.* *Illus. by Donald Carrick. Clarion, 1987.* In this American Cinderella story, Candace tells her father, "I love you more than meat loves salt," but, misunderstanding her meaning, he casts her out. (P, I, A)

Johnson, Paul Brett. *Fearless Jack.* *Illus. by the author. McElderry, 2001.* Country boy Jack calls himself Fearless Jack after he kills ten yellow jackets at one whack. Also look for *Jack Outwits the Giants* (2002) where Jack takes on a two-headed giant and his one-headed wife. (P, I, A)

Keding, Dan. *The United States of Storytelling: Folktales and True Stories from the Eastern States.* *Libraries Unlimited, 2010.* A volume in the World Folklore series, this contains an average of six folktales, legends, true stories, or songs for each state east of the Mississippi, plus historical background. You'll also want the companion book, *The United States of Storytelling: Folktales and True Stories from the Western States* (2010), which covers each state west of the Mississippi. (Professional)

Leeming, David, and Jake Page. *Myths, Legends, and Folktales of America: An Anthology.* *Oxford University Press, 2000.* A rich compilation of stories and analysis of stories told by Native Americans, African Americans, Asian Americans, and European Americans. (Professional)

Louis, Liliane Nerette. *When Night Falls, Kric! Krac! Haitian Folktales.* *Libraries Unlimited, 1999.* Twenty-eight folktales, with historical background, recipes, and color photos, as in other volumes of the World Folklore series. (Professional)

MacDonald, Margaret Read. *Conejito: A Folktale from Panama.* *Illus. by Geraldo Valério. August House Little Folk, 2006.* On his way up the mountain to see his Tía Mónica, who will feed him till he is fat, a little rabbit encounters Señor Zorro, Señor Tigre, and Señor León, all of whom want to eat him. (P)

Martin, Rafe. *The Shark God.* *Illus. by David Shannon. Scholastic, 2001.* When a Hawaiian brother and sister touch the king's forbidden drum and are sentenced to death, their parents ask the fearsome Shark God for help. (P, I)

Pérez, Elvia. *From the Winds of Manguito: Cuban Folktales in English and Spanish / Desde los vientos de Manguito: Cuentos folkloricos de Cuba, en Ingles y Espanol.* *Ed. by Margaret Read MacDonald. Trans. by Paula Martín. Illus. by Victor Francisco Hernandez Mora. Libraries Unlimited, 2004.* World Folklore series; includes twenty-one folktales with historical background, recipes, games, music, and color photos. (Professional)

Shepard, Aaron. ***The Baker's Dozen: A Saint Nicholas Tale.*** *Illus. by Wendy Edelson. Atheneum, 1995.* In colonial Albany, New York, an honest baker learns how to be more generous with his Saint Nicholas cookies, which is why we now expect a baker's dozen. (P, I, A)

Storace, Patricia. ***Sugar Cane: A Caribbean Rapunzel.*** *Illus. by Raúl Colón. Hyperion/ Jump at the Sun, 2007.* In the Caribbean, when a fisherman steals sugar cane from Madame Fate's fields for his pregnant wife, the sorceress claims their new child, Sugar Cane, as payment and locks her in a tower. (P, I)

Van Laan, Nancy. ***With a Whoop and a Holler: A Bushel of Lore from Way Down South.*** *Illus. by Scott Cook. Atheneum, 1998.* Thirteen lively stories, plus songs, chants, superstitions, and riddles. (P, I)

Wardlaw, Lee. ***Punia and the King of Sharks: A Hawaiian Folktale.*** *Illus. by Felipe Dávalos. Dial, 1997.* Punia, a clever young Hawaiian boy, tricks the King of Sharks by stealing his tasty lobsters. (P, I)

West, John O., ed. ***Mexican-American Folklore: Legends, Songs, Festivals, Proverbs, Crafts, Tales of Saints, of Revolutionaries, and More.*** *August House, 1988.* A rich compendium with good background material; part of the Amercan Folklore Series. (Professional)

Wolkstein, Diane. ***The Magic Orange Tree, and Other Haitian Folktales.*** *Illus. by Elsa Henriquez. Knopf, 1978.* Twenty-seven unforgettable tales, collected in Haiti by storyteller Wolkstein back in the day. A classic, filled with warmth and humor. (P, I, A)

Yee, Paul. ***Tales from Gold Mountain: Stories of the Chinese in the New World.*** *Illus. by Simon Ng. Groundwood, 1989.* Contemporary stories about Chinese immigrants to North America. (I, A)

WEBSITES: OTHER TALES FROM THE AMERICAS

The American Folklife Center *www.loc.gov/folklife*

Created in 1976 by the US Congress in Washington DC to "preserve and present" this great heritage of American folklife, the center includes the Archive of Folk Culture, one of the largest collections of ethnographic material from the United States. You will find everything from Native American songs and Bruh Rabbit tales to English ballads and documentation from the lives of cowboys, quilt makers, ex-slaves, and more.

American Folklore *http://americanfolklore.net/folklore*

Sandy Schlosser retells scores of US folktales, including dozens of Native American legends, African American folktales, trickster tales, and ghost and spooky stories, plus tales from Mexico and Canada.

"Fakelore, Multiculturalism, and the Ethics of Children's Literature"
www.msu.edu/user/singere/fakelore.html

Published on Michigan State University's website, Eliot A. Singer's essay posits that many folklore-based children's picture books, especially Native American tales, are inaccurate and distort oral tradition. Food for thought, but if one's standards are that unyielding, few folktales or legends retold for children would pass muster.

INTERNATIONAL FOLK AND FAIRY TALE COLLECTIONS

When searching out good storytelling material, you'll want to explore as many collections as possible. Unfortunately many of the old, classic collections are out of print, which is practically criminal. When we started to weed out-of-print collections from our lists we discovered that some were just too important to leave out—thank goodness for your library, which may have a rich retrospective collection or be able to locate books for you using interlibrary loan or online. Often, the older, dustier, and mustier these books are, the more treasures you'll find inside.

For these collections, editors, compilers, and retellers have gathered stories on a common theme, from a particular region or country, or that have proved popular. Leaf through as many collections as you can to find the stories most suited to you and your audiences.

When looking for comprehensive collections of folktales for all ages, there are three publishers of note. The first is Pantheon. Its folklore series for storytellers, the Pantheon Fairy Tale and Folklore Library, includes more than twenty-four volumes, each containing scores of stories. Most of the books were published in the 1980s and 1990s, and many are now out of print. The series includes such diverse collections as *African Folktales* and *African American Folktales* by Roger Abrahams, *American Indian Myths and Legends* by Richard Erdoes and Alfonso Ortiz, *Folktales from India* by A. K. Ramanujan, *Latin American Folktales: Stories from Hispanic and Indian Traditions* by John Bierhorst, and *Russian Fairy Tales* by Aleksandr Afanasev.

August House, which publishes the American Folklore series, specializes in books written by storytellers working in the field. Their list includes well-known tale spinners like Margaret Read MacDonald, Pleasant DeSpain, husband-and-wife Martha Hamilton and Mitch Weiss, cowriters David Holt and Bill Mooney, and Steve Sanfield. When you come across an August House book, chances are you are in for a real treat.

Last but not least is Libraries Unlimited, which continues to issue (and keep in print) its World Folklore series, which, as of now, boasts more than three dozen titles covering a truly impressive range. Each illustrated collection focuses on one country and includes dozens of stories, story notes, and essays about the culture, history, and customs of the people. This series is an obvious labor of love by the authors, many of whom are well-known storytellers or folklorists, like Anne Pellowski, Dan Keding, Norma J. Livo, and Margaret Read MacDonald. Kudos must also go to the editor of the series, Barbara Ittner. It's admirable to see a publisher continuing to support new volumes when many publishers have decided that folktales aren't selling.

BOOKLIST: INTERNATIONAL FOLK AND FAIRY TALE COLLECTIONS

Cole, Joanna. *Best-Loved Folktales of the World.* *Illus. by Jill Karla Schwarz. Anchor/Doubleday, 1983.* With two hundred tales, broken down by continent, this resource for adults (but readable by kids) provides scores of tried-and-true selections. (P, I, A)

DeSpain, Pleasant. *Tales of Tricksters.* *Illus. by Don Bell. August House, 2001.* A compact volume of nine brief, easy-to-learn, funny folktales from around the world. Other books in this tidy Books of Nine Lives series, all published in 2001, include: *Tales of Nonsense and Tomfoolery, Tales of Wisdom and Justice, Tales of Heroes, Tales of Holidays, Tales of Insects, Tales of Enchantment, Tales to Frighten and Delight,* and *Tales of Cats.* (P, I)

Ehrlich, Amy. *The Random House Book of Fairy Tales for Children.* *Illus. by Diane Goode. Random House, 1985.* An attractive collection of nineteen best-known tales, mostly from Andersen, Grimm, and Perrault. (P, I)

Hamilton, Martha, and Mitch Weiss. *Through the Grapevine: World Tales Kids Can Read & Tell.* *Illus. by Carol Lynn. August House, 2001.* Thirty-one easy-to-tell tales from North and South America, Europe, Asia, and Africa. (I)

Hoberman, Mary Ann. *You Read to Me, I'll Read to You: Very Short Fairy Tales to Read Together.* *Illus. by Michael Emberley. Little, Brown, 2004.* Eight well-known fairy tales have been adapted into witty, easy-to-read, rhyming dialogue for two voices. (P)

Lang, Andrew. *The Blue Fairy Book.* *Edited by Brian Alderson. Illus. by Antony Maitland. Dover, 1965, c1889.* The first of Lang's twelve classic nineteenth-century compendiums of fairy tales. The other colors, all still available, are: Blue, Brown, Crimson, Green, Grey, Lilac, Olive, Orange, Pink, Red, Violet, and Yellow. (P, I)

Lurie, Alison. ***Clever Gretchen and Other Forgotten Folktales.*** *Illus. by Margot Tomes. Crowell, 1980.* Tales of fifteen resourceful European heroines. (I)

Minard, Rosemary. ***Womenfolk and Fairy Tales.*** *Illus. by Suzanne Klein. Houghton Mifflin, 1975.* Minard was one of the first to uncover—in eighteen satisfying tales—feisty females who don't sit back and wait for their princes to rescue them. (I)

Oberman, Sheldon. ***Solomon and the Ant and Other Jewish Folktales.*** *Boyds Mills, 2006.* Forty-three tales from both Ashkenazi and Sephardic traditions, from Europe and northern Africa to Israel, from legends to trickster tales, and ranging from biblical to modern times. (I, A)

Schwartz, Alvin. ***Gold and Silver, Silver and Gold: Tales of Hidden Treasure.*** *Illus. by David Christiana. Farrar, 1988.* Thirty legends, true stories, and tall tales, all about treasure. (I, A)

Shannon, George. ***Stories to Solve: Folktales from Around the World.*** *Illus. by Peter Sís. Greenwillow, 1985.* Each brief story contains a problem or mystery; have your listeners puzzle out the solution. Continue with *More Stories to Solve: Fifteen Folktales from Around the World* (1991) and *Still More Stories to Solve: Fourteen Folktales from Around the World* (1996). (P, I)

Shannon, George. ***True Lies: 18 Tales for You to Judge.*** *Illus. by John O'Brien. Greenwillow, 1997.* After each of these eighteen brief and intriguing international folktales, listeners must answer the questions: "Where's the truth, the whole truth? And where's the lie?" Follow up with *More True Lies: 18 Tales for You to Judge* (2001). (I)

Sierra, Judy. ***Can You Guess My Name? Traditional Tales around the World.*** *Illus. by Stefano Vitale. Clarion, 2002.* For each of five well-known European folktales, there are three variants to compare and contrast, including "The Three Little Pigs," "The Bremen Town Musicians," "Rumpelstiltskin," "The Frog Prince," and "Hansel and Gretel." (P, I)

Sierra, Judy. ***Nursery Tales Around the World.*** *Illus. by Stefano Vitale. Clarion, 1996.* Compare and contrast eighteen easy-to-tell stories, with three each on the themes of Runaway Cookies; Incredible Appetites; Victory of the Smallest; Chain Tales; Slowpokes & Speedsters; and Fooling the Big Bad Wolf. (P)

Sierra, Judy. ***Silly & Sillier: Read-Aloud Tales from Around the World.*** *Illus. by Valeri Gorbachev. Knopf, 2002.* Twenty humorous stories just right for telling. (P, I)

Tashjian, Virginia A. ***Juba This and Juba That.*** *Illus. by Nadine Bernard Westcott. Little, Brown, 1969.* "Stories to tell, songs to sing, rhymes to chant, riddles to guess, and more!" One of the best storytime collections ever, along with the companion, *With a Deep Sea Smile: Story Hour Stretches for Large or Small Groups* (1974). (P, I)

Yolen, Jane, ed. *Favorite Folktales from Around the World.* *Pantheon, 1986.* Almost five hundred pages of folktales from many countries. Excellent for browsing, as are the others in the Pantheon Fairy Tale and Folklore Library series. (P, I, A)

Yolen, Jane. *Mightier than the Sword: World Folktales for Strong Boys.* *Illus. by Raúl Colón. Harcourt, 2003.* Fourteen folktales from as many countries introducing courageous, pragmatic, compassionate, and wise boy heroes. (I)

Yolen, Jane. *Not One Damsel in Distress: World Folktales for Strong Girls.* *Illus. by Susan Guevara. Harcourt, 2000.* Thirteen well-told tales about independent and resourceful heroines. (I)

Researching Folk and Fairy Tales

Many stories can be found online on the site of the Baldwin Online Children's Literature Project at www.mainlesson.com, which includes full texts of more than ten thousand stories, indexed by title, author, and genre. Another indispensable site is SurLaLune (www.surlalunefairytales.com), where you can find annotated fairy tales and their histories, similar tales across cultures, modern interpretations, and e-books of many folktale collections. Also essential is Folklore and Mythology Electronic Texts (www.pitt.edu/~dash/folktexts.html), which supplies links to hundreds of stories edited and/or translated by D. L. Ashliman at the University of Pittsburgh.

Go to www.books.google.com and search *fairy tales* or *folklore*, and you'll find the full texts of scores of classic collections published from the 1890s to the 1920s that are now in the public domain. Project Gutenberg (www.gutenberg.org) has more than thirty thousand books whose copyrights have expired. You can download these books to your computer or portable device or read them online. Under "Book Categories," click on "Children's Bookshelf," and then "Children's Myths, Fairy Tales, etc.," and you'll find a wide array of the Brothers Grimm, Hans Christian Andersen, Charles Perrault, all of the Andrew Lang series, and folktale collections from many countries.

Another marvelous site is Story Lovers World (www.story-lovers.com). Founded by storyteller Jackie Baldwin, it's a treasure trove of information on where to find thousands of stories plus a source of beautiful graphics storytellers can use. When you go on the Story Lovers site, scroll down and click on the "SOS Site Map." This will bring you to a feature called "Searching Out Stories," described as a "free archival library for finding stories/

sources." According to the site, "You'll find full stories, abridged stories, book references, and descriptions of actual experiences and helpful hints in telling these tales at an event or using them in the classroom or at home with your own children or grandchildren." People write in to contribute stories, links, and ideas, and each link takes you to an ever-widening list of tales.

And then there's the Aarne-Thompson Classification System, which is also useful. Stories are categorized by letter and number, similar to the decimal system Melvil Dewey used for library books. In 1910, Finnish folklorist Antti Aarne published an index to all the types of folktales, *The Types of the Folktale: A Classification and Bibliography*. Folklorist Stith Thompson (1885–1976), who worked at the University of Indiana, translated it from the German in 1928 and revised it in 1961. (German folklorist, Hans-Jorg Uther, updated it again in 2004, in his *The Types of International Folktales: A Classification and Bibliography Based on the System of Antti Aarne and Stith Thompson*, though it's mostly just available to scholars.) Thompson also compiled a more comprehensive work, indispensable for folklorists: the six-volume *Motif-Index of Folk-Literature* (Indiana University Press, 1955). This index assigns one of twenty-three alphabet letters to a general subject, and then adds decimal-style numbers to possible motifs (the small elements of a story) to help folklorists identify, organize, and trace recurring themes in stories. The letter *B* is for animals, for instance, and within that designated type, every possible motif is categorized, with literally thousands of subdivisions by subject. To get a taste of just how detailed this is, check out the excellent wiki at http://en.wikipedia.org/wiki/Aarne–Thompson_classification_system.

You can also look up any subject on Story Search (http://storysearch.symbolicstudies.org), a searchable version of Stith Thompson's *Motif-Index* that categorizes more than 46,000 patterns (motifs) from myth, folklore, and literature and lists all the possible motifs and numbers for any given subject. Type the word *cat* in the search bar, and you will get 974 motifs, including "#K722: Giant tricked into becoming mouse. Cat eats him up," a motif that would describe "Puss in Boots," but is also found, according to the appended notes, in Indian and Japanese stories.

In 1982, folklorist and storyteller Margaret Read MacDonald undertook her own master work, *The Storyteller's Sourcebook: A Subject, Title, and Motif Index to Folklore Collections for Children*, categorizing thousands of children's books, both single stories and collections, by tale type and motif, and then arranging them by Aarne-Thompson numbers. In 2001 she updated the book adding another thousand children's folktale books published from 1983–1999. If a story sounds familiar, you can look it up in both of MacDonald's books to see what older single story or collection contains that story element.

As you continue to hone your storyteller chops, you will covet the print and online resources that follow. Many of the books contain collections of stories to tell and advice on how to tell them; others are more scholarly. A few of these books are out of print, but you can find them at many public libraries. While these are considered professional books, there's no reason that older children looking for good stories won't enjoy some of the collections, too. Online resources can be so extensive as to make you dizzy, but when you dip in, you will always find something eye opening and unexpectedly useful.

BOOKLIST: PROFESSIONAL BOOKS ABOUT FOLKLORE AND STORYTELLING

Baltuck, Naomi. *Storytime Stretchers: Tongue Twisters, Choruses, Games, and Charades.* *August House, 2007.* Delightful schtick for your story hours, including poems, chants, audience-participation stories, songs, and riddles. Keep this on your desk along with the author's equally nonsense-packed *Crazy Gibberish and Other Storytime Stretchers* (Apple Boat Press/Wyatt-MacKenzie, 2007, c1997).

Barchers, Suzanne I. *Wise Women: Folk and Fairy Tales from Around the World.* *Libraries Unlimited, 1990.* World Folklore series; a collection of both popular and little-known tales featuring women from all over the world.

Bettelheim, Bruno. *The Uses of Enchantment: The Meaning and Importance of Fairy Tales.* *Random House, 1976.* A scholarly defense and analysis of folk literature by the famed twentieth-century child psychologist.

De Las Casas, Dianne. *Handmade Tales: Stories to Make and Take.* *Libraries Unlimited, 2008.* Twenty-seven delightful tales with accompanying crafts to wow your kids, shared by a storytelling dynamo. You'll also want *Handmade Tales 2: More Stories to Make and Take* (2013).

De Las Casas, Dianne. *The Story Biz: How to Manage Your Storytelling Career from the Desk to the Stage.* *Libraries Unlimited, 2008.* The bible of everything you need to know to be a pro, with practical wisdom on every possible aspect of performance and promotion—mainly from storytelling queen Dianne, but with additional commentary from more than seventy established storytellers.

De Las Casas, Dianne. *Tell Along Tales! Playing with Participation Stories.* *Illus. by Soleil Lisette. Libraries Unlimited, 2011.* How to involve children, from kindergarten to grade 6, in storytelling, along with a bouncy international collection of twenty-five stories to try.

Del Negro, Janice M. *Folktales Aloud: Practical Advice for Playful Storytelling.* *ALA Editions, 2013.* Mostly little-known, but sixteen very merry stories and how to tell them to grades 3 through 6, 6 through 9, 9 through 12, and 12 through 14.

DeSpain, Pleasant. *Thirty-Three Multicultural Tales to Tell.* *Illus. by Joe Shlichta. August House, 1993.* Simply told stories in an amiable round-the-world collection.

De Vos, Gail. *Storytelling for Young Adults: A Guide to Tales for Teens.* *Libraries Unlimited, 2003.* Techniques, an extensive booklist by tale type, and a selection of stories to present to a young adult audience.

Forest, Heather. *Wonder Tales from Around the World.* *August House, 1995.* Twenty-seven tales excellent for telling. Also explore *Wisdom Tales from Around the World* (1996).

Frazer, Sir James G. *The Golden Bough: A Study in Magic and Religion: A New Abridgement from the Second and Third Edition.* *Ed. by Theodor H. Gaster. Oxford University Press, 2009.* An abridged—but still lengthy—version of Frazer's 1890 work. Studies the history of civilization from the point of view of primitive magic, taboos, and superstition.

Freeman, Judy. *Once Upon a Time: Using Storytelling, Creative Drama, and Reader's Theater with Children in Grades PreK–6.* *Libraries Unlimited, 2007.* Stories, chants, songs, annotated booklists, ideas, and lots of fun and nonsense to share with children.

Gordh, Bill. *Stories in Action: Interactive Tales and Learning Activities to Promote Early Literacy.* *Libraries Unlimited, 2006.* Each of fourteen chapters (which take you thematically through all types of stories and tales from around the world) includes a fingerplay warm-up, two to four stories, skeletons (story outlines), activities, and a list of picture-book suggestions. An invaluable resource. To hear a few samplings from storyteller Gordh's recordings, go to www.lingonberrymusic.com.

Goss, Linda, and Marian E. Barnes. *Talk That Talk: An Anthology of African-American Storytelling.* *Simon & Schuster, 1989.* An extensive collection of short stories and folktales by African American storytellers. A good adult resource.

Greene, Ellin, and Janice del Negro. *Storytelling: Art and Technique.* *Libraries Unlimited, 2010.* Fourth revised edition of a vital text for all storytellers. This classic survey of traditional storytelling techniques was first cowritten by Ellin Greene and Augusta Baker in 1987.

Hamilton, Martha, and Mitch Weiss. *Children Tell Stories: A Teaching Guide.* *Richard C. Owen, 2005.* Offers exercises and, on accompanying DVD, provides twenty-five sample stories for children to try.

Haven, Kendall. ***Crash Course in Storytelling.*** *Libraries Unlimited, 2006.* The basics, but nicely laid out. Also see Haven's *Super Simple Storytelling: A Can-Do Guide for Every Classroom, Every Day* (2000).

Holt, David, and Bill Mooney. ***More Ready-to-Tell Tales from Around the World.*** *August House, 2000.* Forty-four tales from some of America's best storytellers. Companion to *Ready-to-Tell Tales: Sure-Fire Stories from America's Favorite Storytellers* (1994).

Ireland, Norma Olin, comp. ***Index to Fairy Tales, 1949 to 1972, Including Folklore, Legends, and Myths in Collections.*** *Scarecrow, 1973.* Analyzes over four hundred collections of stories. Continues with: *Index to Fairy Tales, 1978–1986* (Scarecrow, 1989).

Keding, Dan. ***Elder Tales: Stories of Wisdom and Courage from Around the World.*** *Libraries Unlimited, 2008.* World Folklore series; includes fifty-seven folktales featuring sagacious old folks as the heroes, plus historical background.

Krappe, Alexander H. ***The Science of Folklore.*** *Kessinger, 2010, c1930.* "A classic introduction to the origins, forms, and characteristics of folklore."

Leach, Maria, and Jerome Fried, eds. ***Funk & Wagnalls Standard Dictionary of Folklore, Mythology and Legend.*** *HarperCollins, 1984, c1949–1950.* A reference work that encompasses folklore around the world.

Lipman, Doug. ***Improving Your Storytelling: Beyond the Basics for All Who Tell Stories in Work and Play.*** *August House, 1999.* Pithy advice from a well-known storyteller.

Livo, Norma J. ***Tales to Tickle Your Funny Bone: Humorous Tales from Around the World.*** *Libraries Unlimited, 2007.* World Folklore series; includes more than seventy folktales to read aloud and/or tell, with background notes on each.

Livo, Norma J., and Sandra A. Rietz. ***Storytelling: Process and Practice.*** *Libraries Unlimited, 1986.* An academic approach to collecting sources, practicing your technique, and telling a story.

MacDonald, Margaret Read. ***Earth Care: World Folktales to Talk About.*** *August House, 2005.* Thirty-three tales from five continents, stressing ecological themes of conservation and responsibility for the planet.

MacDonald, Margaret Read. ***Look Back and See: Twenty Lively Tales for Gentle Tellers.*** *Illus. by Roxane Murphy. H. W. Wilson, 1991.* The master storyteller and folklorist provides a wealth of easy-to-tell stories.

MacDonald, Margaret Read. ***The Parent's Guide to Storytelling: How to Make Up New Stories and Retell Old Favorites.*** *August House, 2001.* A collection of twenty stories and how to tell them.

MacDonald, Margaret Read. ***Peace Tales: World Folktales to Talk About.*** *August House, 2005.* An international assortment of three-dozen insightful and provocative tales, divided by themes of war and peace, that will help all of us get along better.

MacDonald, Margaret Read. ***Shake-It-Up Tales! Stories to Sing, Dance, Drum, and Act Out.*** *August House, 2000.* Get your whole body into these twenty audience participation stories.

MacDonald, Margaret Read. ***The Storyteller's Start-Up Book: Finding, Learning, Performing, and Using Folktales.*** *August House, 2006.* Excellent advice for the novice, with techniques for finding, practicing, learning, and, of course, telling stories, plus texts for a dozen tales to tell.

MacDonald, Margaret Read. ***Three-Minute Tales: Stories from Around the World to Tell or Read When Time Is Short.*** *August House, 2004.* With eighty short tales to choose from, you'll always find a quick story to tell. Follow with another four dozen in *Five-Minute Tales: More Stories to Read and Tell When Time Is Short* (2007).

MacDonald, Margaret Read. ***Tuck-Me-in Tales: Bedtime Stories from Around the World.*** *Illus. by Yvonne Davis. August House Little Folk, 1996.* Five sleep-inducing stories from Siberia, Japan, Liberia, Chile, Argentina, and the British Isles.

MacDonald, Margaret Read. ***Twenty Tellable Tales: Audience Participation Folktales for the Beginning Storyteller.*** *Illus. by Roxane Murphy. American Library Association, 2005, c1986.* Stories are formatted with easy-to-follow instructions for beginning storytellers, but perfect for any teller.

MacDonald, Margaret Read, and Brian W. Sturm. ***The Storyteller's Sourcebook: A Subject, Title, and Motif Index to Folklore Collections for Children, 1983–1999.*** *Gale, 2001.* An essential listing of one thousand children's folklore books, both single titles and collections of stories, published between 1983 and 1999, enabling you to find variants using the same or similar motifs or plot elements. The first edition of this reference book—published in 1982 and now out of print (but may be in your library)—covered thousands of prior titles of the twentieth century.

MacDonald, Margaret Read, Jennifer MacDonald Whitman, and Nathaniel Forrest Whitman. ***Teaching with Story: Classroom Connections to Storytelling.*** *August House, 2013.* Practical applications for teachers and librarians using storytelling with their kids for building community, character, communication skills, curriculum and Common Core tie-ins, cultural connections, creativity, and confidence, with plenty of easy-to-tell stories everyone will love.

Maguire, Jack. *Creative Storytelling: Choosing, Inventing, and Sharing Tales for Children.* *Illus. by Dale Gottlieb. Yellow Moon Press, 1985.* A survey of traditional storytelling techniques, with emphasis on preparation and containing original story examples.

Norfolk, Sherry, Jane Stenson, and Diane Williams. *The Storytelling Classroom: Applications across the Curriculum.* *Libraries Unlimited, 2006.* Interesting and innovative lesson plans from teachers and storytellers in language arts, math, science, and social studies for pre-K through grade 8.

Pellowski, Anne. *Drawing Stories from Around the World, and a Sampling of European Handkerchief Stories.* *Libraries Unlimited, 2005.* Thirty delightful tales that you draw as you tell, with step-by-step instructions.

Pellowski, Anne. *The Family Storytelling Handbook: How to Use Stories, Anecdotes, Rhymes, Handkerchiefs, Paper, and Other Objects to Enrich Your Family Traditions.* *Macmillan, 1987.* Object stories your listeners will find magical.

Pellowski, Anne. *The Story Vine: A Source Book of Unusual and Easy-to-Tell Stories from Around the World.* *Macmillan, 1984.* A must-have collection of clever stories to share.

Pellowski, Anne. *The Storytelling Handbook: A Young People's Collection of Unusual Tales and Helpful Hints on How to Tell Them.* *Illus. by Martha Stoberock. Simon & Schuster, 1995.* Turn your children into storytellers with this easy-to-learn collection of international tales.

Pellowski, Anne. *The World of Storytelling.* *H. W. Wilson, 1990.* A classic text, expanded and revised.

Raglan, FitzRoy Richard Somerset, Baron (Lord Raglan). *The Hero: A Study in Tradition, Myth, and Drama.* *Dover, 2011, c1956.* An analysis of myths as fictional narrative.

Sawyer, Ruth. *The Way of the Storyteller.* *Viking, 1962, c1942.* A classic introduction to storytelling. The eleven stories in the appendix are a bonus for the advanced storyteller.

Schram, Peninnah. *Jewish Stories One Generation Tells Another.* *Jason Aronson, 1987.* Almost five hundred pages of stories perfect for reading aloud, collected by a professional storyteller and professor.

Seeger, Pete, and Paul DuBois Jacobs. *Pete Seeger's Storytelling Book.* *Harcourt, 2000.* A collection of stories and how to adapt, make up, and tell your own, by America's most iconic folksinger.

Shah, Idries. *World Tales: The Extraordinary Coincidence of Stories Told in All Times in All Places.* *Octagon, 2003, c1979.* These sixty-five tales include notes describing the appearance of similar stories found in other countries.

Shedlock, Marie L. ***The Art of the Story-Teller.*** *Dover, 1951, c1915.* Shedlock is considered responsible for bringing traditional storytelling to American libraries. Good background reading about storytelling techniques, plus a fine little collection of stories to tell. You can find the entire text at http://digital.library.upenn.edu/women/shedlock/story/story.html.

Spaulding, Amy E. ***The Art of Storytelling: Telling Truths through Telling Stories.*** *Scarecrow, 2011.* Thoughtful essays about how to choose, learn, and perform stories.

Thompson, Stith. ***The Folktale.*** *University of California Press, 2009, c1946.* The classic study of the folktale, including motif and tale-type index.

Zipes, Jack. ***Creative Storytelling: Building Community, Changing Lives.*** *Routledge, 1995.* How to use storytelling as a natural part of the curriculum in schools.

WEBSITES: FOLKLORE AND STORYTELLING

Aarne-Thompson Classification System
http://en.wikipedia.org/wiki/Aarne–Thompson_classification_system
Extensive wiki showing the main classifications of the Aarne-Thompson folktale index. Click on one of the main types—say, 5.1 Animals—and you can see all related subtypes and motifs.

Aaron Shepard *www.aaronshep.com*
Writer and storyteller Shepherd provides the complete texts of fifty of his retold folk and fairy tales, plus original stories, information on storytelling, and reproducible readers' theater scripts for forty tales.

Andrew Lang's Fairy Books *www.mythfolklore.net/andrewlang*
Find every story in the thirteen color Fairy Books, accessible by book, title, or place of origin.

Baldwin Online Children's Literature Project *www.mainlesson.com*
A comprehensive collection of children's literature in the public domain, published from 1880 through 1922, formatted with original illustrations and presented in a typeface that children can read easily. Categories include nursery rhymes, fables, folktales, myths, legends and hero stories, literary fairy tales, bible stories, nature stories, biography, history, fiction, poetry, storytelling, games, and craft activities.

Beauty and the Beast Storytellers
www.beautyandthebeaststorytellers.com/handouts.html
Husband-and-wife storytellers Mitch Weiss and Martha Hamilton offer a treasury of handouts, lesson plans, story maps, and teaching ideas for all types of tales, which you can print out to use with your students.

Best of Legends *http://bestoflegends.org*
Links to texts of King Arthur, Robin Hood, the Brothers Grimm, and Andrew Lang's Fairy Books series.

Encyclopedia Mythica *www.pantheon.org*
An extensive encyclopedia of mythology, folklore, and religion, with more than seven thousand entries, divided into six geographic regions, and by country or culture. Includes myths, heroes, Arthurian legends, creatures and characters from folklore, an image gallery, and an invaluable pronunciation guide for English speakers.

"Fakelore, Multiculturalism, and the Ethics of Children's Literature" *www.msu.edu/user/singere/fakelore.html*
See page 227.

Folklore and Mythology Electronic Texts *www.pitt.edu/~dash/folktexts.html*
Text and commentary on thousands of stories, arranged by theme, motif, and story title; compiled by D. L. Ashliman, a professor emeritus from the University of Pittsburgh.

Folktale.net *http://folktale.net*
Storytellers Jim Jennings and Leanne Ponder include a link on their site to more than a hundred folktale openers (http://folktale.net/openers.html) and a hundred-plus closers (http://folktale.net/endings.html).

International Storytelling Center *www.storytellingcenter.net*
See pages 19 and 24.

Internet Archive *archive.org*
Includes digitized content of more than three million books, more than one million free e-books, plus audio, moving images, and software as well as archived web pages. Looking for old collections of folklore? This is the place, along with Project Gutenberg, below. Use search key words like *folklore* or *fairy tales* and dig in.

KPR: Kids Public Radio *www.kidspublicradio.org*
An offshoot of NPR, this is an advertising-free network of web-based radio channels for kids. There's Jabberwocky, with storytelling, music, and comedy programs; Pipsqueaks, with "songs to sing, songs written by kids, songs sung by kids, songs loved by kids"; and Cosquillas, with songs and stories in Spanish for kids. Listening makes you want to be a kid again.

The Online Books Page *http://onlinebooks.library.upenn.edu*
Founded and edited by John Mark Ockerbloom, a digital library planner and researcher at the University of Pennsylvania, and hosted by the university, this index provides links to the texts of online books that are free to read on the Internet. Lots of children's folk and fairy tale books are included.

Project Gutenberg *www.gutenberg.org*

The site provides access to more than thirty thousand books whose copyrights have expired, including a huge amount of folk and fairy tales; you can download them to your computer or portable device or them read online.

Sacred Texts *www.sacred-texts.com*

This is "the largest freely available archive of online books about religion, mythology, folklore and the esoteric on the Internet." Look up any country, continent, culture, or religion and read complete texts of books of folklore and myths that are no longer protected by copyright.

Snow White
http://comminfo.rutgers.edu/professional-development/childlit/snowwhite.html

A comprehensive scholarly resource and teaching guide to the "Snow White" stories, from the late Kay Vandergrift, a Rutgers professor.

The Story Connection *www.storyconnection.net*

Storyteller and author Dianne de Las Casas includes book activities, games, and the full text of more than fifty of her folktale retellings.

Story Lovers World *www.story-lovers.com*

A free archival library of stories, sources, and advice from professional storytellers, teachers, librarians, parents, and grandparents. Look for the enormously helpful feature "SOS: Searching Out Stories," where people write in asking about stories they are trying to find.

Story Search *http://storysearch.symbolicstudies.org*

A "Search Engine for Motifs in Myth and Folklore," this database was created by and dedicated to the work of Stith Thompson. It is maintained by the Center for Symbolic Studies.

Story Arts *http://storyarts.org*

A useful site put together by Heather Forest, the well-known storyteller and writer. It offers loads of stories to download, as well as telling techniques, ideas, lesson plans, and activities.

Storynet *www.storynet.org*

The website of the National Storytelling Network, this provides a US calendar of events and links to resources for storytelling.

Storyteller.net *http://storyteller.net*

This features more than two hundred articles about storytelling and audios of tellers performing more than 125 stories plus a list of hundreds of professional storytellers by state, country, keyword, or last name.

Storytelling Workshop with Gerald Fierst
http://teacher.scholastic.com/writewit/storyteller
Maintained under the Scholastic publisher's umbrella, this online resource features Gerald Fierst telling a West African folktale, "How Monkey Stole the Drum," and presents his ideas on how to tell, write, and perform stories.

SurLaLune Fairy Tales *www.surlalunefairytales.com*
Annotated texts of thirty-five well-known fairy tales, with detailed analyses of illustrations, history, variants, and modern interpretations.

Tell a Tale *http://tellatale.eu*
English storyteller Richard Martin provides more than four-dozen delightful folktales from his repertoire, some to read, some to listen to, and best of all, some to watch.

World of Tales *http://worldoftales.com*
Complete texts of more than fifty vintage collections of folk and fairy tales, now in the public domain, with hundreds of stories from around the world.

Lessons from a Storyteller

You can never have too much chocolate or too many stories to share. All of us looking for ways to help our children lead moral, satisfying, and productive lives can start by simply sharing the abundant wisdom in the folk and fairy tales that have shaped the values and beliefs of our multicultural, interdependent world.

While reading "Note from the Author" in Lise Lunge-Larsen's marvelous story collection *The Troll with No Heart in His Body, and Other Tales of Trolls from Norway*, we were struck by the sage observations she gathered about the stories she has read, told, and written over the years. She kindly allowed us to share her thoughts with you. Lise writes:

> Here are fifteen of the most basic lessons I have found repeated over twenty years as a storyteller:
>
> - Remember who you are.
> - Be true to your own nature.
> - Follow your dreams.
> - Every action has consequences, so be attentive, be kind, and always do what is right.
> - Life is a journey; nobody else can do that journey for you.
> - Your journey will unfold according to a pattern. The pattern is a guide.

> - Use your gifts.
> - Help will be offered when you most need it and least expect it.
> - Despite the odds, good will triumph over evil, and love over hatred.
> - Don't ever give up.
> - Be careful in what you wish for.
> - Things are not always as they appear.
> - Everything you need can be found inside yourself; it is always there.
> - Miracles happen.
> - There is magic in the world.
>
> Over and over again, in wonderful, fanciful stories, these themes are repeated in a predictable formula that exactly mirrors the child's view of the world. Children, like the heroes and heroines in these stories, perceive their lives to be constantly threatened. Will I lose a tooth? Will I be invited to play? Will I learn to read? By living a life immersed in great stories and themes, children will see that they have the resources needed to solve life's struggles. And while listening to these stories, children can rest for a while in a world that mirrors their own, full of magic and the possibility of greatness that lies within the human heart.[2]

Ask your listeners which of these truisms apply to their own lives. What would they add to the list? Here's one more thing: the stories you tell and read have legs. When your kids hear you share these stories, they will retell these stories, and dream about them, and put themselves in the hero's role in their mind's eye as they relive them, and they will pass on those tales to the children in their lives when they grow up. That's a mighty powerful gift.

NOTES

1. Archive of American Folk Song, "The Grey Goose," *Afro-American Spirituals, Work Songs, and Ballads* (notes), Library of Congress, Music Division, p. 10, www.loc.gov/folklife/LP/AfroAmerSpirtualsL3_opt.pdf.

2. Lise Lunge-Larsen, *The Troll with No Heart in His Body, and Other Tales of Trolls from Norway* (Boston: Houghton Mifflin, 1999), 10–11.

chapter 7

More Stories to Tell

Deeper meaning resides in the fairy tales told to me in my childhood than in the truth that is taught by life.

—FRIEDRICH VON SCHILLER

In this chapter we offer a look at some splendid nontraditional and modern-day versions of folk and fairy tales that you will find worth telling, a few famous folks you should know about, and a sampling of other great sources for storytelling material.

Stories Reworked, Reimagined, Reinvented, Parodied, Satirized, or Re-created from Folk and Fairy Tales

In these types of stories, authors play around with tradition. They might switch the gender of the protagonist, tell the story from another character's point of view, move the tale to different time or place, extend the plot, or give the story an all-new explanation.

Many modern-day authors have written clever, usually humorous tales patterned after familiar folktales like "The Three Little Pigs," "Goldilocks and the Three Bears," "The Little Red Hen," and "The Three Bears." These are not necessarily parodies per se, but rather homages to the original story. The plot and structure stay much the same. For example, in Jan Brett's handsome picture book *The 3 Little Dassies,* three brown-furred female dassies (rodents from Namibia, also called rock hyraxes) leave their family and look for a place where they will be safe from eagles. Each sister builds a house—one of grasses, one of sticks, and one of rock. An eagle comes flapping by and screeches, "I see you, dassie. I'll flap and I'll clap and I'll blow your house in." Sound familiar? Brett has taken the original "The Three Little Pigs," reset it in the Namib Desert of southern Africa, changed the animals, and retold it, changing the details but not the basic storyline. In another reworking, Eric Kimmel employs tasty Mexican food as protagonists in *The Three Little Tamales.* The villain in his story is Señor Lobo, who says, "I'll huff and I'll puff like a Texas tornado, and blow your casita from here to Laredo."

Take another old favorite, "The Three Billy Goats Gruff." Rebecca Emberley's *Three Cool Kids* is the story set in the inner city with a nasty, big rat instead of a troll as the villain, while *The Three Triceratops Tuff,* by Stephen Shaskan, is set in prehistoric times with a fierce *T. rex* as the bad guy. In *The Three Cabritos,* Eric A. Kimmel's goats reside by the border of the Southwest United States and northern Mexico. Then there's Kevin O'Malley's *Animal Crackers Fly the Coop,* which reimagines "The Bremen Town Musicians" by Jacob and Wilhelm Grimm. Instead of scaring off three robbers with their not-so-beautiful voices, O'Malley's animals, who dream of performing in a comedy club, roust the bad guys by telling jokes. Pair the tale with Jan Huling's *Ol' Bloo's Boogie-Woogie Band and Blues Ensemble,* in which Ol' Bloo Donkey and his new friends get waylaid on their way to launch singing careers in a New Orleans honky-tonk.

In order to fully understand these reworkings, your audience needs to know the original tale. If you tell Tony Johnston's *The Cowboy and the Black-Eyed Pea,* in which Farethee Well, the daughter of a wealthy Texas rancher, hopes to find a real cowboy by putting a pea under the saddle of each suitor, the humor will be lost on children who have never heard Hans Christian Andersen's "The Princess and the Pea." What works well is to use the two stories together—perhaps telling the original tale and reading aloud the updated version. After you have finished the stories, ask your group to compare and contrast them. See if they can tell you what changes the author made in the original story.

Other stories on the list are literary folktales, written by a modern-day author in the style of once-upon-a-time, but not handed down from the ages, like Hudson Talbott's *O'Sullivan Stew: A Tale Cooked Up in Ireland,* Tynia

Thomassie's *Feliciana Feydra LeRoux: A Cajun Tall Tale*, and David Wisniewski's Mayan story, *Rain Player.* Still others are societal satires or parodies of existing folktales, like *The Stinky Cheese Man* by Jon Scieszka, a riotous send-up of nine traditional tales. Scieszka and illustrator Lane Smith pretty much reignited a passion for spoofing folk and fairy tales, which had waned since the marvelous "Fractured Fairy Tale" segments, narrated by the great Edward Everett Horton, on *The Bullwinkle Show*, on TV in the early 1960s. Their now-classic picture book, *The True Story of the 3 Little Pigs*, brought the trend back into the spotlight. Narrated by the wolf, the book begins, "I'm the wolf. Alexander T. Wolf. You can call me Al. I don't know how this whole Big Bad Wolf thing got started, but it's all wrong."

James Thurber may have started the trend a generation or two before with his book of short, satirical stories for adults, *Fables for Our Time & Famous Poems Illustrated* (1940), which was followed by *Further Fables for Our Time* (1956). Thurber wasn't actually restructuring existing fables; he was creating comical new ones in the style of Aesop for a modern audience. In "The Little Girl and the Wolf," Thurber took the story of "Red Riding Hood" and turned it on its ear, with the little girl taking an automatic from her basket of goodies and shooting the wolf dead. You'll find the story easy to access online. Just Google the words *girl wolf Thurber* for the complete text, which is all of eighty-two words.

The picture books in the list that follows are all eminently tellable, though, because they have distinguished or unique artwork, you may want to consider reading them aloud at some point. As they aren't folktales in the traditional sense, they are usually shelved in the picture-book section of your library. Depending on how you plan to use them, the books can be very effective with children older than the suggested grade level. However you choose to use the stories, they promise a treat for your audience.

Before you jump into the booklist, here's a call-and-response retelling of "The Three Bears." Everyone seems to know a version of the story, and you can find many different ones online. This hipster telling has been tweaked, expanded, and fooled with. You can snap your fingers as you tell it, use a singsong voice, or give it a jazzlike beat. It's infectious. And of course, have your audience repeat the refrains (in parentheses below). Kids of all ages will love this version; it's so fast and funny, with three voices for the bears. *The 3 Little Dassies* by Jan Brett and *Goldilocks and the Three Dinosaurs* by Mo Willems are fitting read-aloud companions. What would Joseph Jacobs think?

Three Bears

Revised, Rewritten, and Retold by Judy Freeman, Based on Many Other Versions and Then Some.

Once upon a time in a nursery rhyme, there were three bears (three bears).

One was a Mama Bear, and one was a Papa Bear, and one was a Wee Bear (Wee Bear).

They all went a-walkin' in the woods and a-talkin'

When along came a girl with long curly hair. (*Use hand action for curls.*)

Her name was Goldilocks; upon the door she knocked.

She didn't care that no one was there.

She walked right in with a great big grin,

Checking out the place, a big smile on her face.

Home came the three bears. (*Sing* "Dum-da-dum-dum" *for suspense.*)

With the door open wide, was there someone inside?

"Someone's been eating my porridge!" said the Papa Bear (said the Papa Bear).

"Someone's been eating my porridge!" said the Mama Bear (said the Mama Bear).

"Hey, Mama Ree Bear," said the little Wee Bear, "someone has broken my bowl. *AAH!*" (*Throw arms up on* "AAH!")

"Someone's been sitting in my chair!" said the Papa Bear (said the Papa Bear).

"Someone's been sitting in my chair!" said the Mama Bear (said the Mama Bear).

"Hey, Papa Ree Bear," said the little Wee Bear, "someone has broken my chair. *OH!*"

(*Throw arms up on* "OH!")

"Someone's been sleeping in my bed," said the Papa Bear (said the Papa Bear).

"Someone's been sleeping in my bed," said the Mama Bear (said the Mama Bear).

"Hey, Mama Ree Bear," said the little Wee Bear, "someone is sleeping in mine. *YEAH!*"

(*Throw arms up on* "YEAH!")

Goldilocks, she woke up, and then the party broke up;

She beat it out of there (She beat it out of there).

"Bye, bye, bye, bye; bye, bye," said the Papa Bear (said the Papa Bear). (*Wave.*)

"Bye, bye, bye; bye, bye, bye," said the Mama Bear (said the Mama Bear). (*Wave.*)

"Hey, Papa Ree Bear," said the little Wee Bear,

"BYE, BYE, BYE, BYE, BYE, BYE, BYE! YEAH!" (*Throw arms up on* "YEAH!")

So ends the story, now that everything's hunky-dory, of the three bears (three bears).

Goldilocks is history; why she came's a mystery.

"BYE, BYE, BYE, BYE, BYE, BYE, BYE! YEAH!" (*Throw arms up on* "YEAH!")

BOOKLIST: STORIES REWORKED, REIMAGINED, REINVENTED, PARODIED, SATIRIZED, OR RE-CREATED FROM FOLK AND FAIRY TALES

Bang, Molly. ***Dawn.*** *Illus. by the author. Morrow, 1983.* Dawn's father tells her the story of the wounded goose he aided and of the beautiful dark-eyed woman who then appeared at his shipyard to help weave his sails. Compare this with the Japanese folktale on which it is based, *The Crane Wife* retold by Odds Bodkin (Harcourt, 1998). (P, I)

Bar-el, Dan. ***Such a Prince.*** *Illus. by John Manders. Clarion, 2007.* As related by Libby Gaborchick, fairy extraordinaire, Marvin seeks three magic peaches to cure love-starved Princess Vera. Based on the French fairy tale "The Three Peaches." (P, I)

Brett, Jan. ***The 3 Little Dassies.*** *Illus. by the author. Putnam, 2010.* It's the "Three Little Pigs" go to Namibia when Mimbi, Pimbi, and Timbi, three little rodents, build three houses, but are threatened by an eagle. (P)

Brett, Jan. ***The Three Snow Bears.*** *Illus. by the authors. Putnam, 2007.* Aloo-ki, an Inuit girl, enters the igloo of three polar bears, out for a walk. (P)

Briggs, Raymond. ***Jim and the Beanstalk.*** *Illus. by the author.* Coward-McCann, 1970. Jack's son, Jim, climbs the beanstalk and finds the now old, toothless, and bald son of the giant. (P, I)

Byrd, Robert. ***Brave Chicken Little.*** *Illus. by the author. Viking, 2014.* In this riotous rewrite of the old tale, resourceful Chicken Little prevails. (P)

Christelow, Eileen. ***Where's the Big Bad Wolf?*** *Illus. by the author. Clarion, 2002.* Police Detective Phineas T. Doggedly takes on the Big Bad Wolf. (P)

Claflin, Willy. ***The Uglified Ducky: A Maynard Moose Tale.*** *Illus. by James Stinson. August House Little Folk, 2008.* In this Moosified version of "The Ugly Duckling," narrated by Maynard Moose, Mommy Ducky thinks the baby moose she finds sleeping by her five unhatched eggs is a "large and distremely uglified ducky," one of her new offspring. If you like this kind of mangled language, also read Claflin's *Rapunzel and the Seven Dwarfs* (2011). (P, I)

Daly, Niki. ***Pretty Salma: A Little Red Riding Hood Story from Africa.*** *Illus. by the authors. Clarion, 2007.* At the market in urban Ghana, Salma talks to bad Mr. Dog, who tricks her out of her basket, her clothes, and even her song. (P)

Elya, Susan Middleton. ***Fairy Trails: A Story Told in English and Spanish.*** *Illus. by Mercedes McDonald. Bloomsbury, 2005.* Miguel and María take the wrong path through the woods and encounter an old brujita (witch), a talking lobo (wolf), and three osos (bears) on a walk, and even Humpty Huevo. (P)

Elya, Susan Middleton. ***Rubia and the Three Osos.*** *Illus. by Melissa Sweet. Hyperion, 2010.* In a charming Spanish language–laden and rhyming retelling of "The Three Bears," the family Oso heads out for a walk—and Little Miss Rubia comes in for a look around their casita. Elya takes on another tale, Spanish style, with *Little Roja Riding Hood* (Putnam, 2014). (P)

Emberley, Rebecca. ***Three Cool Kids.*** *Illus. by the author. Little, Brown, 1995.* Needing a taste of lovely grass and weeds, the three Cool Kids—Big, Middle, and Little—set out for the vacant lot down the street, but are threatened by a sewer rat. Compare with a traditional version, like the picture book *The Three Billy Goats Gruff* by either Marcia Brown or Paul Galdone. (P)

Ernst, Lisa Campbell. ***Goldilocks Returns.*** *Illus. by the author. Simon & Schuster, 2000.* A now middle-aged Goldilocks returns to the scene of her crime. (P)

Ernst, Lisa Campbell. ***Little Red Riding Hood: A Newfangled Prairie Tale.*** *Illus. by the author. Simon & Schuster, 1995.* Red meets up with a muffin-craving wolf. (P)

Gaiman, Neil. ***Instructions.*** *Illus. by Charles Vess. HarperCollins, 2010.* Journey with Puss in Boots as he follows this list of instructions on how to navigate and negotiate a fairy-tale landscape. (P, I)

Hartman, Bob. *The Wolf Who Cried Boy.* *Illus. by Tim Raglin. Putnam, 2002.* Little Wolf sets out to catch a nice boy so he can have a decent meal for once. (P)

Heapy, Teresa. *Very Little Red Riding Hood.* *Illus. by Sue Heap.* Houghton Mifflin Harcourt, 2014. On her way to Grandmama's for a sleepover, a very little and very assertive red-coated toddler meets up with a wolf and—much to the wolf's chagrin—she thinks he's a "foxie." (P)

Hodgkinson, Leigh. *Goldilocks and Just One Bear.* *Illus. by the author. Candlewick/ Noisy Crow, 2012.* Lost in the big city, a bear from the woods takes the elevator to the penthouse apartment of Snooty Towers where he tastes some porridge, sits in a just-right beanbag chair, and finally settles into a dreamy nap on a just-right bed. (P)

Huling, Jan. *Ol' Bloo's Boogie-Woogie Band and Blues Ensemble.* *Illus. by Henri Sorensen. Peachtree, 2010.* When Ol' Bloo Donkey overhears the farmer planning to kill him, he lights out for New Orleans, planning to sing in a honky-tonk. (P, I)

Isadora, Rachel. *The Fisherman and His Wife.* *Illus. by the author. Putnam, 2008.* In this traditional Grimm story reset in Africa, a greedy wife finds herself living back in her pigsty after she has her husband ask a talking flounder for one too many wishes. (P, I)

Jackson, Ellen. *Cinder Edna.* *Illus. by Kevin O'Malley. Lothrop, 1994.* Cinderella's next-door neighbor—take-charge Edna—has a ball at the ball with Prince Rupert, the fun younger brother of boring Prince Charming. (P, I)

Johnston, Tony. *Bigfoot Cinderrrrrella.* *Illus. by James Warhola. Putnam, 1998.* A nature-loving Bigfoot prince finds the stinking beauty of his dreams. (P)

Johnston, Tony. *The Cowboy and the Black-Eyed Pea.* *Illus. by Warren Ludwig. Putnam, 1992.* In this literary reworking of "The Princess and the Pea," Texas heiress Farethee Well is looking for a real cowboy who will love her and not her money. (P, I)

Ketteman, Helen. *Armadilly Chili.* *Illus. by Will Terry. Albert Whitman, 2004.* With a blue norther a-blowin', Miss Billie Armadilly asks her pals, tarantula Tex, bluebird Mackie, and horned toad Taffy to help her make a pot of hot armadilly chili, but they're all too busy to help. (P)

Ketteman, Helen. *Bubba the Cowboy Prince: A Fractured Texas Tale.* *Illus. by James Warhola. Scholastic, 1997.* With the help of a fairy godcow, Bubba— a hardworking Texas ranch hand—sets his sights on Miz Lurleen, the purtiest and richest gal in the county. (P, I)

Kimmel, Eric A. *The Three Cabritos.* *Illus. by Stephen Gilpin. Marshall Cavendish, 2007.* In a Southwestern version of "The Three Billy Goats Gruff," three music-loving cabritos head across the border to a Mexican fiesta, but are stopped by Señor Chupacabra. (P)

Kimmel, Eric A. ***The Three Little Tamales.*** *Illus. by Valeria Docampo. Marshall Cavendish, 2009.* Three newly made tamales run away from their taqueria and build their own casitas, when along comes Señor Lobo to blow them down. (P)

Lester, Julius. ***Sam and the Tigers: A New Telling of Little Black Sambo.*** *Illus. by Jerry Pinkney. Dial, 1996.* In the land of Sam-sam-sa-mara, where everyone is named Sam, Sam encounters five tigers on his way to school—and they want his new clothes. Other updates on the now controversial "Little Black Sambo" tale include *The Story of Little Babaji* by Helen Bannerman, illustrated by Fred Marcellino (HarperCollins, 1996) and *Pancakes for Supper* by Anne Isaacs (Scholastic, 2006). (P)

Lowell, Susan. ***Little Red Cowboy Hat.*** *Illus. by Randy Cecil. Henry Holt, 1997.* Little Red and her ax-wielding grandma drive off that varmint of a wolf from their ranch. (P)

Lowell, Susan. ***The Tortoise and the Jackrabbit.*** *Illus. by Jim Harris. Northland, 1994.* Out in the desert, patient Tortoise challenges bragging Jackrabbit to a race. You know who wins. (P)

McClements, George. ***Jake Gander, Storyville Detective.*** *Illus. by the author. Hyperion, 2002.* None-too-smart detective Jake Gander knows there's something strange about Red R. Hood's Granny but can't figure out what. (P)

Minters, Frances. ***Cinder-Elly.*** *Illus. by G. Brian Karas. Viking, 1993.* At a basketball game, Cinder-Elly meets star player Prince Charming. (P, I)

Muth, Jon J ***Zen Shorts.*** *Illus. by the author. Scholastic, 2005.* Karl, Michael, and Addy meet their new neighbor, Stillwater, a giant panda, who tells them three stories taken from traditional Buddhist and Taoist tales. (P, I)

O'Malley, Kevin. ***Animal Crackers Fly the Coop.*** *Illus. by the author. Walker, 2010.* Aspiring comedians Hen, Dog, Cat, and Cow run away from the farm and set off to open a comedy club. A modern-day update on "The Bremen Town Musicians" by the Brothers Grimm. (P, I)

O'Malley, Kevin. ***Gimme Cracked Corn and I Will Share.*** *Illus. by the author. Walker, 2007.* Chicken dreams of treasure buried under a pink pig in a beautiful barn, and sets off to find it. A punster's retelling of find-your-treasure-at-home stories like *The Treasure* by Uri Shulevitz (Farrar, 1978). (P, I)

O'Malley, Kevin. ***Once Upon a Cool Motorcycle Dude.*** *Illus. by Kevin O'Malley, Carol Heyer, and Scott Goto. Walker, 2005.* A boy and girl compete to tell their own versions of the fairy tale they made up; hers features a weeping princess, and his stars a "really cool muscle dude." (P, I)

Osborne, Mary Pope. *The Brave Little Seamstress.* *Illus. by Giselle Potter. Atheneum, 2002.* First, the little seamstress kills seven at one blow (seven flies, that is), and then takes on one giant, then two giants, a vicious wild unicorn, a wild boar, and finally, an ungrateful king. (P, I)

Osborne, Mary Pope. *Kate and the Beanstalk.* *Illus. by Giselle Potter. Atheneum, 2000.* In place of Jack, try the classic story with plucky Kate meeting the giant, who chants, "FEE, FI, FO, FUM'UN, I SMELL THE BLOOD OF AN ENGLISHWOMAN." (P, I)

Palatini, Margie. *The Cheese.* *Illus. by Steve Johnson and Lou Fancher. HarperCollins, 2007.* Rat decides he's going to go down to the dell and eat that big chunk of cheddar that's just standing there alone on the grass. (P)

Palatini, Margie. *Earthquack!* *Illus. by Barry Moser. Simon & Schuster, 2002.* Little Chucky Ducky feels the ground rumble and concludes that the earth is crumbling. (P)

Palatini, Margie. *Lousy Rotten Stinkin' Grapes.* *Illus. by Barry Moser. Simon & Schuster, 2009.* In a savvy retelling of Aesop's "The Fox and the Grapes," Fox makes a plan to reach the grapes high in a tree, with the help of Bear and other animals. (P, I)

Paul, Ann Whitford. *Tortuga in Trouble.* *Illus. by Ethan Long. Holiday House, 2009.* Iguana, Conejo (Rabbit), and Culebra (Snake) follow their pal, Tortuga (Tortoise), who is taking a basket supper to Abuela (Grandmother). This humorous Southwest, Spanish-infused take on "Little Red Riding Hood" features Coyote as the bad guy. Another comical retelling with these characters is *Mañana, Iguana* (2004), a reworking of "The Little Red Hen." (P)

Peck, Jan. *The Giant Carrot.* *Illus. by Barry Root. Dial, 1998.* Just like in the Russian folktale "The Turnip," on which the story is based, it sure takes some doing for Papa Joe, Mama Bess, Brother Abel, and sweet Little Isabelle to pull up their overgrown carrot. (P)

Ransom, Jeanie Franz. *What Really Happened to Humpty? (From the Files of a Hard-Boiled Detective).* *Illus. by Stephen Axelsen. Charlesbridge, 2009.* When that good egg, Humpty Dumpty, falls off the wall, his brother, ace detective Joe Dumpty, investigates what he thinks is a crime. (P, I)

Root, Phyllis. *Paula Bunyan.* *Illus. by Kevin O'Malley. Farrar, 2009.* Paul Bunyan's tall, strong, tree-loving little sister moves to the North Woods where she comes up against some tree-felling lumberjacks. (P, I)

Schwartz, Corey Rosen. *The Three Ninja Pigs.* *Illus. by Dan Santat. Putnam, 2012.* In a narrative poem told in galloping rhyme, three little pigs—disgusted with a wolf bully who blows down houses all over town—decide to train at the new ninja school to get strong enough to stop him. In the sequel, *Ninja Red*

Riding Hood (2014), the wolf sneaks into ninja school to get strong enough to catch a good meal, which he thinks he's found in a girl named Riding Hood. (P)

Scieszka, Jon. ***The Frog Prince Continued.*** *Illus. by Steve Johnson. Viking, 1991.* Not content with his happily-ever-after life with his princess, the prince decides he'd like to be a frog again, and seeks out a witch to help him. (P, I)

Scieszka, Jon. ***The Stinky Cheese Man, and Other Fairy Stupid Tales.*** *Illus. by Lane Smith. Viking, 1992.* Funniest fairy tale parody ever, and a Caldecott Honor winner, too. (P, I, A)

Scieszka, Jon. ***The True Story of the 3 Little Pigs.*** *Illus. by Lane Smith. Viking Kestrel, 1989.* Alexander T. Wolf defends his actions toward the three little pigs, insisting he was framed. (P, I)

Shaskan, Stephen. ***The Three Triceratops Tuff.*** *Illus. by the author. Beach Lane, 2013.* One by one, the three dino brothers Tuff—Stanley, Rufus, and Bob—set out to get some grub in the valley where a hungry T. rex awaits. (P)

Singer, Marilyn. ***Mirror, Mirror: A Book of Reversible Verse.*** *Illus. by Josée Masse. Dutton, 2010.* Fourteen reverso poems (two identical, side-by-side poems, with all the lines in the second one re-sorted upside down)—take on the double-sided nature of fairy tales. Continue with the companion book, *Follow Follow: A Book of Reverso Poems* (2013). (P, I, A)

Stanley, Diane. ***Rumpelstiltskin's Daughter.*** *Illus. by the author. Morrow, 1997.* The now sixteen-year-old daughter of the miller's daughter from the story "Rumpelstiltskin" decides it's time to teach the gold-loving king a lesson. (P, I)

Sturges, Philemon. ***The Little Red Hen (Makes a Pizza).*** *Illus. by Amy Walrod. Dutton, 1999.* The duck, the dog, and the cat all say, "Not I" when the little Red Hen needs help whipping up a pizza, until it comes time to eat it. (P)

Sylvester, Kevin. ***Splinters.*** *Illus. by the author. Tundra, 2010.* Made to clean the uniforms and tape the hockey sticks by mean Coach Blister (who favors her own two daughters), a poor, aspiring skater, Cindy Winters, is at last aided by her fairy goaltender. (P, I)

Talbott, Hudson. ***O'Sullivan Stew: A Tale Cooked Up in Ireland.*** *Illus. by the author. Putnam, 1999.* Red-haired Kate O'Sullivan makes a bargain with the king: if she can tell him a story about being in a worse spot than she is now, he will let her and her father and brothers go free. (P, I)

Thomassie, Tynia. ***Feliciana Feydra LeRoux: A Cajun Tall Tale.*** *Illus. by Cat Bowman Smith. Pelican, 2005, c1995.* Feliciana Feydra runs off to go alligator hunting in the Louisiana bayou, and, using her pecan-wood baby doll, outsmarts an ol' halligator. (P)

Trivizas, Eugene. *The Three Little Wolves and the Big Bad Pig.* *Illus. by Helen Oxenbury. McElderry, 1993.* A turnabout parody version of "The Three Little Pigs." (P)

Whipple, Laura. *If the Shoe Fits: Voices from Cinderella.* *Illus. by Laura Beingessner. McElderry, 2002.* Cinderella's big night is retold in thirty-three free-verse poems from many points of view. (I, A)

Wilcox, Leah. *Falling for Rapunzel.* *Illus. by Lydia Monks. Putnam, 2003.* When the prince says, " . . . throw down your hair," Rapunzel, up in her tower, can't quite hear him, and throws down her underwear. (P)

Willems, Mo. *Goldilocks and the Three Dinosaurs.* *Illus. by the author. Balzer + Bray, 2012.* Papa Dinosaur, Mama Dinosaur, and some other Dinosaur who happens to be visiting from Norway, claim they are not hiding in the woods waiting for Goldilocks to come traipsing along, but she shows up at their house just the same. (P)

Wisniewski, David. *Rain Player.* *Illus. by the author. Clarion, 1991.* In an original tale set in ancient Mayan times, Pik plays the ball game Pok-atok with the rain god to relieve the drought. (P, I)

Yolen, Jane, and Rebecca Kai Dotlich. *Grumbles from the Forest: Fairy-Tale Voices with a Twist.* *Illus. by Matt Mahurin. WordSong, 2013.* Fifteen pairs of poems, one by each of the authors, revisit beloved fairy tales. (I)

Young, Ed. *Seven Blind Mice.* *Illus. by the author. Philomel, 1992.* In a retelling of the classic folktale from India "The Blind Men and the Elephant," seven different-colored blind mice set out over the seven days of the week to discover the identity of a large, mysterious creature. (P)

WEBSITES: STORIES REWORKED, REIMAGINED, REINVENTED, PARODIED, SATIRIZED, OR RE-CREATED FROM FOLK AND FAIRY TALES

Fractured Fairy Tales and Fables with Jon Scieszka

http://teacher.scholastic.com/writewit/mff/fractured_fairy.htm

By children's book author Jon Scieszka and based on his own crazy picture books, this site is designed to help individuals write fractured fairy tales and fables and publish them online.

Fractured Thoughts Workshop

http://marilynkinsella.org/Workshop%20papers/Fractured_Thoughts_workshop.htm

Storyteller Marilyn Kinsella's workshop includes ideas for "fractured folk tales including fractured fairy tales, fables, myths," ways to fracture a tale, and links to other storyteller's fractured tales.

Literary Tales and Short Stories

Many modern authors have been much influenced by folktales and have attempted to write their own, some quite successfully. These original short stories, written with elements reminiscent of folklore, are sometimes referred to as "literary folktales." The stories of Hans Christian Andersen, Rudyard Kipling, Eleanor Farjeon, and Laurence Housman all fall into this category. After you feel comfortable telling more complex folktales, you may want to attempt to learn a literary tale. These stories are more appropriate for advanced storytellers because, to retain the beauty of the language, you need to memorize the entire story and concentrate on giving an expressive presentation. The booklist below suggests titles by the authors mentioned below as well as titles and collections of literary tales by a wide variety of contemporary authors in the style of once-upon-a-time, such as Hudson Talbott's *O'Sullivan Stew: A Tale Cooked Up in Ireland,* Tynia Thomassie's *Feliciana Feydra LeRoux: A Cajun Tall Tale,* and David Wisniewski's Mayan story, *Rain Player.*

HANS CHRISTIAN ANDERSEN

Danish author and storyteller Hans Christian Andersen published his first book of fairy tales in 1835 and is often considered the father of modern storytelling. Although his greatest desire was to be well thought of as a playwright and serious writer, his fairy tales were an instant success and are still read with great enjoyment today. Some of his first stories can be traced to folk sources—probably the stories he learned as a child—but his later work is entirely original. Since Andersen wrote in Danish, the works you read will be translations. For that reason, find an edition that retains the original flavor of Andersen's work. Erik Haugaard's translation, *Hans Christian Andersen: The Complete Fairy Tales and Stories,* is an excellent one, but unfortunately, it has no pictures.

The fantasy of Andersen's world is suitable for a wide age range. His satirical comments on human nature are universally accessible, and his stories have a worldwide audience. Andersen often told his stories while performing intricate paper cuttings, but for the rest of us mortals, just telling an Andersen story requires a good bit of concentration. Andersen's birthday, April 2, is a good time to plan an Andersen storytelling presentation. This date also happens to commemorate International Children's Book Day, so you might want to also feature stories from a range of countries around the globe.

The Andersen museum in Odense, Denmark, is housed in the cottage where Andersen was born. The collection contains memorabilia as well as Andersen books that have been translated and illustrated around the world. If flying to Denmark is not an option, you can visit the Hans Christian Andersen Museum at http://museum.odense.dk/en/museums/hans-christian-andersen-museum/exhibitions/the-art. You can examine eleven of his paper cuttings, hundreds of his drawings, photographs and painted portraits of Andersen, and take a virtual tour of his study.

BOOKS AND WEBSITES ABOUT HANS CHRISTIAN ANDERSEN

Brust, Beth Wagner. ***The Amazing Paper Cuttings of Hans Christian Andersen.*** *Houghton Mifflin, 1994.* Illustrated with more than twenty existing paper cuttings made by Andersen, this combination biography-and-art book will make you eager to get out your scissors and paper. (I, A)

Varmer, Hjordis. ***Hans Christian Andersen: His Fairy Tale Life.*** *Illus. by Lilian Brogger Groundwood, 2005.* Beautifully written and designed biography, illustrated with paintings, drawings, cut paper, prints, and photographs. (I, A)

Hans Christian Andersen Center
www.andersen.sdu.dk/liv/index_e.html
This extensive website from the University of Southern Denmark, which specializes in "research and information on matters related to Hans Christian Andersen," includes biographical information, Andersen's complete works, research about him, and extensive links.

Hans Christian Andersen Museum
http://museum.odense.dk/en/museums/hans-christian-andersen-museum/exhibitions/the-art
An online look at the museum in Andersen's hometown of Odense, which covers the life and work of its most famous hometown guy.

RUTH SAWYER

Ruth Sawyer, an American storyteller and author of children's books, wrote a classic on traditional storytelling, *The Way of the Storyteller* (Viking, 1962, c1942), which should be required background reading for every serious storyteller. The stories she has collected and those stories she wrote herself are as robust, humorous, and thoughtful as any you will find. "The Princess and the Vagabond," which appears in the appendix of Sawyer's book, is an Irish version of *The Taming of the Shrew* and is suitable for both young adults and adults. Sawyer's stories are long, so be prepared to take some time to learn them.

ELEANOR FARJEON

Eleanor Farjeon's *The Little Bookroom*, a short-story collection and a storyteller's dream, is still with us. In the best fairy-tale tradition, these stories transport us to a delicate world of poets and princesses. The theme of personal freedom is beautifully portrayed in "The Seventh Princess," while the quickly learned "The Lady's Room" is reminiscent of "The Fisherman and His Wife." Our favorite Farjeon, "Elsie Piddock Skips in Her Sleep," is perfect for a spring presentation because the plot revolves around skipping rope. It takes nearly half an hour to tell, so you can imagine the time and effort it takes to learn. Consider it worth it, though, since once you have learned it, you will have it forever. Every story you learn can be told over and over again for years of good telling and listening. And with such a long story as this one, you won't tell any others for that session.

HOWARD PYLE

Howard Pyle's stories are still funny. Many are lengthy, but they should be learned just as Pyle wrote them. *Pepper and Salt*, first published in 1885, and *The Wonder Clock*, published in 1887, provide humorous stories, written in a folktale style that is suitable for storytellers as well as for those who feel Pyle's tales are best read aloud. "How the Good Gifts Were Used by Two" makes an excellent Christmas story. The beginning of Pyle's Cinderella story, "The Apple of Contentment," will give you an idea of Pyle's style: "There was a woman once, and she had three daughters. The first daughter squinted with both eyes, yet the woman loved her as she loved salt, for she herself squinted with both eyes." If you'd like to share pictures with your group, Pyle's own wry illustrations are most appropriate to his stories.

RUDYARD KIPLING

Rudyard Kipling's longer works are somewhat out of fashion these days: many are too wordy, and a few seem decidedly racist to modern readers. However, two of his works, *The Jungle Book* and the *Just So Stories*, are treasure troves for the storyteller. By learning excerpts of *The Jungle Book* you can introduce potential readers to the book as a whole. (Note that Neil Gaiman modeled his novel *The Graveyard Book* (HarperCollins, 2008), which won the Newbery Medal in 2009, on Kipling's *The Jungle Book*, so they will make an interesting pairing.) The *Just So Stories*, which are original pourquoi stories, have great child appeal. Kipling imaginatively explains "How the Leopard Got His Spots" and "How the Camel Got His Hump." "The Elephant's Child," relates why an elephant has a trunk instead of "a blackish, bulgy nose as big as a boot." The wonderfully imaginative language of these stories is what makes them so delightful, and the texts of the stories are easy to find online.

CARL SANDBURG

Carl Sandburg is well known for his poetry and works for adults, but he wrote successfully for children as well. His *Rootabaga Stories*, which abound in nonsense phrasing and bizarre situations, will either enchant or baffle you. (Caroline loved these; Judy does not.) It takes a skilled storyteller, however, to offer these stories with just the right amount of tongue-in-cheek gravity. As with the tales of Andersen, many of Sandburg's *Rootabaga Stories* feature inanimate objects: umbrellas, rag dolls, and even skyscrapers. If you are fascinated by interesting names, Sandburg supplies them in abundance. His "How Bozo the Button Buster Busted All His Buttons When a Mouse Came" is told to three girls named Deep Red Roses, The Beans Are Burning, and Sweeter than the Bees Humming. Not as elaborate but just as delightfully descriptive is the Rootabaga story of Shush Shush, the big, buff banty hen who rings the doorbell when she lays an egg.

BOOKLIST: LITERARY TALES

Andersen, Hans Christian. *The Complete Fairy Tales and Stories.* *Trans. by Erik Christian Haugaard. Doubleday, 1974.* Unabridged, with all 156 tales faithfully translated and arranged as in the original 1874 Danish edition. (Professional)

Andersen, Hans Christian. ***Hans Christian Andersen's Fairy Tales.*** *Sel. and illus. by Lisbeth Zwerger, translated by Anthea Bell. Simon & Schuster, 1991.* Attractive watercolors light up eleven tales, most of them familiar. (P, I)

Andersen, Hans Christian. ***The Nightingale.*** *Retold and illus. by Jerry Pinkney. Putnam, 2002.* With the setting relocated from China to Northwest Africa, Andersen's classic tale about an emperor who loves and then forsakes a nightingale is a visual feast (P, I).

Andersen, Hans Christian. ***The Nightingale.*** *Retold by Stephen Mitchell. Illus. by Bagram Ibatoulline. Candlewick, 2002.* The emperor of China demands to have a nightingale presented to sing for him. Compare the magnificent paintings with Pinkney's artwork, above. (P, I)

Andersen, Hans Christian. ***Tales of Hans Christian Andersen.*** *Trans. and introduced by Naomi Lewis. Illus. by Joel Stewart. Candlewick, 2004.* Attractively illustrated, with stellar translations of thirteen best-known tales. (I, A)

Demi. ***The Emperor's New Clothes: A Tale Set in China.*** *Illus. by the author. McElderry, 2000.* You'll love the final four-page foldout of the underwear-clad emperor's final walk past his bemused subjects in this reworking of Hans Christian Andersen's classic tale. (P, I)

Farjeon, Eleanor. ***Elsie Piddock Skips in Her Sleep.*** *Illus. by Charlotte Voake. Candlewick, 2008.* Young Elsie Piddock, a born skipper, is given a magic skipping rope by the fairies, which she uses at age 109 to save her English village. (P, I)

Farjeon, Eleanor. ***The Little Bookroom: Eleanor Farjeon's Short Stories for Children Chosen by Herself.*** *Illus. by Edward Ardizzone. New York Review Books, 2003, c1955.* A charming collection of twenty-seven stories includes "The Lady's Room" and "The Seventh Princess," mentioned above. (I)

Kipling, Rudyard. ***A Collection of Rudyard Kipling's Just So Stories.*** *Illus. by Peter Sís and others. Candlewick, 2004.* An attractive collection of eight Kipling pourquoi tales, each illustrated by a different children's book illustrator, including Peter Sís, Jane Ray, and Louise Voce. (P, I, A)

Kipling, Rudyard. ***The Jungle Book.*** *Random House, 2012.* Originally published in 1894, this collection includes short stories set in India about jungle boy Mowgli, plus the whole text of "Rikki-Tikki-Tavi." (I, A)

Kipling, Rudyard. ***Just So Stories.*** *Illus. by Barry Moser. Morrow, 1996.* A dozen of Kipling's literary pourquoi tales. (P, I, A)

Kipling, Rudyard. *Just So Stories, Volume 1.* *Illus. by Ian Wallace.* Groundwood, 2013. Tenderly illustrated in watercolor, pencil, pastel, and chalk, this is one mighty attractive collection of six Kipling tales, written back in 1902. See *Just So Stories, Volume 2* (2014) for the other six. (P, I, A)

Kipling, Rudyard. *Rikki-Tikki-Tavi.* *Adapted and illus. by Jerry Pinkney. Morrow, 1997.* Classic Kipling tale of a pet mongoose in India that saves Teddy, a little English boy, from the deadly cobras Nag and Nagina. (P, I)

Peretz, I. L. *The Seven Good Years and Other Stories of I. L. Peretz.* *Trans. and adapted by Esther Hautzig. Illus. by Deborah Kogan Ray. Jewish Publication Society, 1984.* Ten stories by the Yiddish writer. (I, A)

Poe, Edgar Allan. *Tales of Edgar Allan Poe.* *Illus. by Barry Moser. Morrow, 1991.* The classics "The Tell-Tale Heart," "The Pit and the Pendulum," and "The Gold Bug" are among the macabre tales by the inventor of this genre. (A)

Pyle, Howard. *Pepper and Salt, or Seasoning for Young Folk.* *Illus. by the author. Echo Library, 2007, c1885.* Online, you can read facsimiles of the twenty-four literary fairy tales and poems both in this book and in *The Wonder Clock* (Starscape, 2003, c1915), with its one story for each of the twenty-four hours in a day, at www.mainlesson.com/displayauthor.php?author=pyle. (I, A)

Sandburg, Carl. *The Rootabaga Stories.* *Illus. by Maud and Miska Petersham. Harcourt, 1922.* These original nonsense stories have retained their charm, though they can be an acquired taste. (P, I, A)

Tatar, Maria, ed. *The Annotated Hans Christian Andersen.* *Trans. by Maria Tatar and Julie K. Allen. Illus. with paintings and reprods. W. W. Norton, 2007.* Translations in two sections—twelve of Andersen's Tales for Children and twelve Tales for Adults—illustrated with magnificent period paintings. (Professional)

Wilde, Oscar. *Oscar Wilde: Stories for Children.* *Illus. by P. J. Lynch. Hodder, 2000.* A lushly illustrated edition of Wilde's stories for children, including his most famous ones, "The Selfish Giant" and "The Happy Prince." (I, A)

Zipes, Jack, ed. *Spells of Enchantment: The Wondrous Fairy Tales of Western Culture.* *Viking, 1991.* Eight hundred pages of literary fairy tales collected for adults. (Professional)

Other Literary Sources for Storytelling

Don't confine your search for the perfect story to folklore. Consider picture books and easy readers, chapters in novels, short stories, anthologies, narrative nonfiction, biographies, and other informational books. Storytellers should look everywhere for sources of material, even to their own family stories.

PICTURE BOOKS AND BEGINNING READERS

Over the semester of Judy's 2012 graduate storytelling class at Pratt Institute, students selected, learned, and told three stories to the class. There were the usual retellings of folk and fairy tales, but there were also some surprising story choices. One student, Ashley Landry, selected a vintage picture book she found in the library. The book was *Anatole* by Eve Titus, about the bicycle-riding, cheese-tasting French mouse, whose anonymous nightly cheese reviews in the tasting room at the Duval Cheese Factory helped make Duval cheeses the best in all of Paris. The book had won Paul Galdone, the illustrator, a Caldecott Honor more than half a century before, but the story was spot on for telling even without the pictures. The young woman's oral rendition was *très charmante*, as *magnifique* as the mouse himself. She even brought in little rounds of brie so the class could do their own mouse-inspired tastings.

It's tricky to use picture books with memorable illustrations when they are essential to the story. If the telling loses effectiveness without the images, perhaps the book is not something you want to add to your storytelling repertoire. Many times, though, you'll find that a great story, like *Anatole*, can transcend the picture-book format and be just as effective told as read aloud. The pictures will help you, the storyteller, visualize the story as you learn it and practice telling it.

Even if you are working with high school students or adults, don't let the picture-book format deter you; many of these books are also appropriate for older audiences. Also keep in mind that you will sometimes find picture-book versions of folk and fairy tales shelved in the easy fiction section of the library. (You will also discover many more of our favorite tellable picture books listed in this chapter, in chapter 8, "Our Favorite Stories to Tell," and in the subject booklists in previous chapters.) Some books you read aloud so many times, you memorize them without even trying, such as classic titles including Maurice Sendak's *Where the Wild Things Are*, Harry Allard's *Miss Nelson Is Missing*, Jill Murphy's *Peace at Last*, and Doreen Cronin's *Click, Clack, Moo: Cows That Type.* If you love them that much, they will be good candidates for telling. If children know these stories, they will envision the illustrations as you tell each tale; if they don't, they'll simply create all new images based on the wonderful words.

Beginning readers can also be good sources for storytelling. Even though they use controlled vocabulary to help young readers achieve fluency, don't discount their tellability. Individual chapters in Arnold Lobel's brilliant Frog and Toad books—which are really short stories in miniature—are ideal to tell as quick but delectable fillers. Shelley Moore Thomas's easy readers about a knight and his three little dragon friends—*Get Well, Good Knight* and *Good Night, Good Knight* among them—also work wonderfully as stories to tell aloud. Slightly more challenging to learn are Kate DiCamillo's gloriously wacky Mercy Watson books about a free-spirited, toast-loving pig, starting with *Mercy Watson to the Rescue.*

NOVELS AND SHORT STORIES

Don't rule out novels and short stories as a source for material. When you're rereading a favorite middle-grade or young-adult novel, you may come across a self-contained section or chapter that lends itself easily to storytelling. After all, what better way to promote a title than to give your audience a hint of what it offers? Look for exciting, dramatic, and/or humorous chapters that wrap up at the end instead of trailing into the next chapter. It's probably easier to find good selections from books with an omniscient narrator rather than those told in first person.

The first chapter in Ann Cameron's *The Stories Julian Tells,* "Pudding Like a Night on the Sea," is an endearing short story just made for telling. Julian and his little brother, Huey, devour the entire lemon pudding their father has concocted for their mother. How can you blame them for wanting to taste a pudding about which their father has said, "It will taste like a whole raft of lemons, it will taste like a night on the sea"? The boys hide under the bed, fearing the repercussions of disobeying their dad. He thunders into their bedroom, promising a whipping and a beating. He follows through on the threat by having the boys help him whip up a new batch of pudding, beating it until it is light and fluffy and tastes "like a whole raft of lemons, like a night on the sea." It is a delicious chapter for telling aloud, though you will crave lemon pudding evermore. (Not to worry—you can find the recipe on the author's website, www.anncameronbooks.com/pudding-recipe.html.)

Short stories are often easy to adapt for oral presentation. In Patricia Santos Marcantonio's *Red Ridin' in the Hood, and Other Cuentos*, you'll be intrigued by the reworking of eleven traditional fairy tales reset in the barrios of the United States. They have an utterly original Latino flavor, including Spanish words and contemporary plot twists. In "Jaime and Gabriela," the children of a poor adobe maker are left in the desert by their parents. There they find a house made of *pan dulce* and tamales. Of course, it's the house of a *viejita*, or old woman, who plans to eat them. Sound familiar? In the title story, a girl named Roja is supposed to take the bus to see her *abuelita*, but decides to walk instead and save the bus fare for a cool new shirt. As she walks down Forest Street, she encounters Lobo Chávez in his glossy-brown low-rider Chevy. Listeners can compare and contrast these sassy updated tales with their European originals; they may even want to rewrite a traditional fairy tale with details from their own modern lives.

INFORMATIONAL BOOKS AND BIOGRAPHIES

Biography and informational books also offer intriguing material. You can excerpt a chapter, or pull out a selection of relevant, interestingly told anecdotes and weave them into a story.

Sometimes, though not often enough, you'll come across a narrative nonfiction picture book just ripe for telling, like *Elizabeth, Queen of the Seas* by Lynne Cox. Narrative nonfiction (which is simply a fancy term for a true book that tells a good story) should be every bit as compelling and involving as fiction. Take this affable, true account about Elizabeth, the elephant seal that made her home in and on the banks of the Avon River, which flows through the center of Christchurch, New Zealand. Visiting the city, the

author heard the story of Elizabeth firsthand from a boy named Michael and his sister, Maggie. Incorporating Michael into her account, Cox describes how the seal—eight feet long and 1,200 pounds—would haul herself out of the river and stretch out across the middle of the two-lane road, causing danger to both herself and car traffic. A group of townspeople volunteered to tow her into the ocean and to a beach far away where other elephant seals lived, but Elizabeth swam right back to town. Your children will cheer for the resilient Elizabeth and take as a rallying cry, "Welcome home, Queen of the Seas!"

Speaking of swimming, did you know that Ben Franklin's first invention—at age eleven in 1717—was a pair of swim fins that he tested out in the Charles River in Boston? Barbara Rosenstock's charmingly alliterative "mostly true" account of how Ben crafted his innovative creation is detailed in *Ben Franklin's Big Splash*, a narrative picture book that makes for a fine story to tell for a science-based story hour. Cut a pair of swim fins out of cardboard like the ones Ben made and talk about other inventions that he and others have undertaken. Ask children what still needs to be invented. End with a make-and-take activity where children draw or create with assorted materials—paper-towel and toilet tubes, aluminum foil, scraps of wood and the like—a brand-new prototype for an invention.

Listeners can learn much history from true stories. Take the account of how Matthew Perry persuaded Japan to open its borders to US ships in the 1850s, masterfully detailed in Rhoda Blumberg's Newbery Honor Book, *Commodore Perry in the Land of the Shogun.* The chapter "The Grand Banquet" is a fascinating oral presentation, filled with details about the feast given by Perry for the Japanese dignitaries and their retainers. Blumberg's companion book, *Shipwrecked! The True Adventures of a Japanese Boy,* is also rich with stories that can be told aloud. In January 1841, fourteen-year-old Manjiro and four fishermen were shipwrecked and marooned on an island for five months until they were rescued by an American whaler. Manjiro ultimately became the first Japanese person to come to the United States. Upon his return home, years later, he was jailed and could have been executed for the crime of traveling to a foreign country, but was ultimately released, became a samurai, and was one of the behind-the-scenes men who negotiated with Admiral Perry in 1853. Using the book as your source, pull together an overview of Manjiro's extraordinary story and then booktalk Margi Preus's riveting Newbery Honor Book *Heart of a Samurai: Based on the True Story of Nakahama Manjiro* (based on his life, though fictionalized).

Russell Freedman, one of the best biographers writing for children anywhere, provides in all of his books a treasure chest of anecdotes so deftly written, you could collect several from one of his books and tell them as an introduction to that extraordinary person's life. "Growing Up Rich," from *Franklin Delano Roosevelt*, tells about the privileged childhood of one man who grew up to be president of the United States. Then introduce another whose circumstances couldn't have been more different. The first five pages of *Lincoln: A Photobiography*, for which Freedman won the Newbery Medal in 1988, are a masterful summing-up of our thirteenth commander-in-chief, who during the Civil War was considered the most unpopular president ever: "His critics called him a tyrant, a hick, a baboon who was unfit for his office." Hark back to his childhood and his self-schooling, starting on page 12, and then recount, from page 38, how Lincoln the lawyer, in his most famous murder trial, defended Duff Armstrong and won an acquittal by using the 1857 almanac to contradict a witness's testimony.

Look to picture-book biographies for inspirational life stories compressed into thirty-two pages, often ideal for telling. During her 2012 storytelling class, another one of Judy's graduate students, Josephine Evans, chose Kathleen Krull's *Wilma Unlimited: How Wilma Rudolph Became the World's Fastest Woman*, a biography about African American role model and athlete Wilma Rudolph. Rudolph, who was born in 1940 in Tennessee, was the youngest of twenty children. Always a sickly child, she contracted polio and scarlet fever at age five and was told she would never walk again. How she fought against her illnesses and how, at the 1960 Rome Olympics, she became the first American woman to win three gold medals, makes a gripping story. Josephine's masterful telling was poignant, inspiring, stunning, and unforgettable.

Another book about a courageous women comes immediately to mind. *Who Says Women Can't Be Doctors?: The Story of Elizabeth Blackwell* by Tanya Lee Stone is the startling and thrilling account of how, in 1849, Elizabeth Blackwell became first American woman to graduate from medical school and practice medicine.

Jennifer Armstrong's *The American Story: 100 True Tales from American History* is a dazzling chronology of fascinating anecdotes, starting with the founding, in 1565, of St. Augustine, the oldest continuously occupied city in the United States, and concluding with the contested 2000 presidential election. Each boisterous and beguiling two- to five-page account is sumptuously illustrated with cheerful, colorful, carefully researched watercolors, ensuring this handsome and hefty volume will be one that that children and adults will pore over and reread. Here's an example of one chapter just right for telling.

1805: THE GREAT DIVIDE

Sacajawea and the Corps of Discovery

From The American Story: 100 True Tales from American History
by Jennifer Armstrong (Knopf, 2006)

The Corps of Discovery had been traveling for a year, finding a way up the Missouri River and searching for a water route through the Rockies. President Thomas Jefferson had sent them on their quest. He had advised the leaders, Captains Meriwether Lewis and William Clark, to make note of everything they saw as they explored this newly acquired Louisiana Purchase—animals, plants, native people, weather conditions, rivers, mountains. He also suggested they make use of native guides and translators if the chance arose.

Chance arose in the form of a teenage girl named Sacagawea.

Lewis and Clark had met up with Sacagawea during the first winter of their journey. She was a Shoshone, a Snake Indian from west of the mountains who had been kidnapped as a child by a raiding party of Minnetarees. The unhappy girl had been traded as a captive and ended up the wife of a French fur trapper, Toussaint Charbonneau. When Lewis and Clark and their company of explorers reached the Mandan villages on the upper Missouri in the winter of 1804, Sacagawea was there, awaiting the birth of her first child.

They were astonished at their good fortune. Here, right before them, was a girl who could possibly lead them to the country of her own native people, the Shoshone. In the long winter wait, Sacagawea gave birth to her son, Jean-Baptiste, and in the spring, the Corps of Discovery pressed westward. Sacagawea did not know if she would remember the path back to her people, but she remembered her own language and would be able to speak for the explorers when they finally met the Snake Indians. Lewis also felt sure that the presence of a young woman and an infant in their group would be an obvious sign that their purpose was a peaceful one.

In August, they struggled up the icy headwaters of the Missouri, dragging their boats against the current and portaging up and around chattering waterfalls. Vivid patches of wildflowers bloomed on the banks, and eagles drew great circles in the sky. In the distance was a tall rock silhouetted against the brilliant blue. With a flash of excitement, Sacagawea told Lewis and Clark that she recognized that rock, called Beaverhead, and that it was close to where her people had always made their summer camp.

Lewis was thrilled. They were close to the Shoshone, who could direct them to the Pacific Ocean. They hurried onward, looking for any sign of people. The air grew thin as they hurried on to Lemhi Pass and reached the Continental Divide, where water must choose to travel either east to the Atlantic or west to the Pacific. Sacagawea, with her baby strapped to her back, continued to scan the horizon for familiar landmarks.

At last, on August 17, the Corps of Discovery came within sight of a Shoshone camp. A young woman came rushing toward them with open arms. Her heart filled with joy, Sacagawea recognized her childhood friend, the playmate she had last seen on the day of her capture by the Minnetarees. The two Shoshone girls wept and held each other close and tried to tell one another all the years' worth of news as the white explorers went forward to meet with the chief.

Reluctantly Sacagawea separated herself from her friend, knowing that her job as translator was vital to the success of the mission. She ducked her head to enter the tent where the Shoshone sat in a council with Meriwether Lewis and made her way quietly to the captain's side.

When she raised her eyes to address the chief, she found herself looking into the eyes of her own brother. Lewis wrote in his journal, "She instantly jumped up, and ran and embraced him, throwing over him her blanket and weeping profusely." Again her tears were tears of happiness. Chief Cameahwait was astonished to find his sister among these pale-skinned men, the first white men the Shoshone had ever seen.

With Sacagawea's help, Meriwether Lewis told Cameahwait what their needs were and where they wished to go, bargaining for horses and guides to the westward-flowing river that would take them to the sea. Sacagawea relayed all these things to her brother, although she frequently broke down in tears as she spoke.

When she had been kidnapped, she had had no chance to say goodbye to her friends and family. She had not expected to see them again. Now her heart was full almost to breaking.

The Corps of Discovery stayed with the Shoshone several days before continuing westward. This time Sacagawea was able to say her goodbyes, and then she traveled with Lewis and Clark all the way to the Pacific shore.

Author Jennifer Armstrong's note: Like the Spanish conquistadors, French voyageurs, and so many others, President Jefferson and Lewis and Clark were sure there must be a river passage across the enormous continent that would link the Atlantic and Pacific oceans. Although they went all the way to the Pacific and came home again, Lewis and Clark had to tell Jefferson that no river passage existed. The only way boats could get from one ocean to the other was to go all the way around North and South America.

BOOKLIST: OTHER LITERARY SOURCES FOR STORYTELLING

Allard, Harry. *Miss Nelson Is Missing.* *Illus. by James Marshall. Houghton Mifflin, 1977.* The worst-behaved class in the whole school gets a substitute, the wicked Miss Viola Swamp. (P)

Blumberg, Rhoda. *Commodore Perry in the Land of the Shogun.* *Illustrated with reprods. Lothrop, 1985.* How Matthew Perry sailed to isolationist Japan in 1853 to persuade the authorities to open its borders and allow American trade. (I, A)

Blumberg, Rhoda. *Shipwrecked! The True Adventures of a Japanese Boy.* *Illustrated with reprods. HarperCollins, 2001.* Rescued by an American whaling ship in 1841 after being stranded for five months on an uninhabited island with his four other fisherman companions, Manjiro was brought to America by the ship's captain. (I, A)

Cameron, Ann. *The Stories Julian Tells.* *Illus. by Ann Strugnell. Pantheon, 1981.* Charming vignettes about a young African American boy and his family, with self-contained chapters just right to read aloud or tell. (P, I)

Cox, Lynne. *Elizabeth, Queen of the Seas. Illus. by Brian Floca. Schwartz & Wade, 2014.* A true account of Elizabeth, an elephant seal that made her home in and on the banks of the Avon River, which flows through the center of Christchurch, New Zealand. (P, I)

Cronin, Doreen. *Click, Clack, Moo: Cows That Type.* *Illus. by Betsy Lewin. Simon & Schuster, 2000.* Farmer Brown's cows go on strike. (P)

DiCamillo, Kate. *Mercy Watson to the Rescue.* *Illus. by Chris Van Dusen. Candlewick, 2005.* Toast-loving pet pig Mercy Watson saves the day when Mr. and Mrs. Watson's bed falls through the floor. (P)

Freedman, Russell. *Franklin Delano Roosevelt.* *Clarion, 1990.* From his privileged upbringing to the presidency, this is a revealing portrait of Roosevelt. For more about his indefatigable wife, follow up with *Eleanor Roosevelt: A Life of Discovery* (1997). (I, A)

Freedman, Russell. *Lincoln: A Photobiography.* *Clarion, 1987.* This Newbery Medal biography—filled with photographs and revealing insights into Lincoln's life—revolutionized the genre. (I, A)

Krull, Kathleen. ***Wilma Unlimited: How Wilma Rudolph Became the World's Fastest Woman.*** *Illus. by David Diaz. Harcourt, 1996.* A stirring picture-book biography describes how Wilma Rudolph overcame childhood polio, became a runner, and, at the 1960 Rome Olympics, was the first American woman to win three gold medals. (P, I)

Lobel, Arnold. ***Frog and Toad Are Friends.*** *HarperCollins, 1970.* Whimsical, easy-to-read vignettes about two best friends; others in the series include *Frog and Toad Together* (1971), *Frog and Toad All Year* (1976), and *Days with Frog and Toad* (1979). (P)

Marcantonio, Patricia Santos. ***Red Ridin' in the Hood, and Other Cuentos.*** *Illus. by Renato Alarcão. Farrar, 2005.* Eleven traditional fairy tales are reset in the barrio and given contemporary plot twists with Latino flavor. (I, A)

Murphy, Jill. ***Peace at Last.*** *Illus. by the author. Dial, 1980.* Mr. Bear can't sleep. (P)

Preus, Margi. ***Heart of a Samurai: Based on the True Story of Nakahama Manjiro.*** *Abrams/Amulet, 2010.* In January of 1841, after spending five months shipwrecked on an island, fourteen-year-old Nakahama Manjiro and four other Japanese fishermen were rescued by an American whaling ship. This masterful novelization of Manjiro's remarkable life won the author a Newbery Honor. (I, A)

Rosenstock, Barbara. ***Ben Franklin's Big Splash: The Mostly True Story of His First Invention.*** *Illus. by S. D. Schindler. Calkins Creek, 2014.* Taking a swim in Boston's Charles River, young Ben Franklin wonders why he can't swim like a fish and invents swim fins out of wood to help him try. (P, I, A)

Sendak, Maurice. ***Where the Wild Things Are.*** *Illus. by the author. HarperCollins, 1963.* Starts with that immortal first line, "The night Max wore his wolf suit and made mischief of one kind and another his mother called him 'WILD THING!' and Max said 'I'LL EAT YOU UP!' so he was sent to bed without eating anything." (P, I, A)

Stone, Tanya Lee. ***Who Says Women Can't Be Doctors? The Story of Elizabeth Blackwell.*** *Illus. by Marjorie Priceman. Henry Holt, 2013.* How Elizabeth Blackwell became the first female physician, graduating at the top of her otherwise all-male class in 1849. (P, I)

Thomas, Shelley Moore. Get Well, Good Knight. *Illus. by Jennifer Plecas. Dutton, 2002.* After the Good Knight's three little dragon friends come down with sneezes, coughs, and fevers, he seeks a cure from an old wizard, but finds that his own mother has the best soup recipe to heal them. Also cute to tell: *Good Night, Good Knight* (2000), where the Good Knight helps the three lonely little dragons get ready for bed in their deep, dark cave. (P)

Titus, Eve. *Anatole.* *Illus. by Paul Galdone. Knopf, 2006, c1956.* Appalled to learn of the low opinion humans have of mice, a principled French mouse earns the cheese to feed his family each night by secretly evaluating the cheeses at the Duval Cheese Factory in Paris. (P)

Family Stories

At every storytelling festival, there is sure to be at least one session devoted to family storytelling. Telling stories that feature an incident from personal experience or that describe an eccentric relative have become appealing for both amateur and professional storytellers, as evidenced by the extraordinarily popular programs of The Moth, live at cafes and venues across the United States and on The Moth Radio Hour. (Check it out at http://themoth.org.)

Should you make family stories a part of your tradition, too? At first Caroline was reluctant to participate in this movement. She had been so indoctrinated by the traditions of the New York Public Library she didn't see how this sort of storytelling could possibly help further her interests in promoting reading. She made a private rule that if a story wasn't published somewhere, she wouldn't tell it. After all, how could she recommend reading something that didn't exist?

Still, she was intrigued. It seemed as though anyone could tell this sort of story. She heard one woman tell a funny story about how her best dress was ruined while she hastily polished her nails, and another storyteller relate her first experience in spelunking. Caroline had dozens of wonderful travel stories, but none were from books. At a story session in Louisiana she heard the wonderful Donald Davis tell some of his famous family stories. Again, she thought about telling family stories. One day, she had a revelation: she could tell her family stories and recommend related books that her audience might enjoy reading. In fact, she could create an entire program around Feller Bauer family stories!

"Grandma and the Birds" is one of her family stories. It is about Caroline's grandmother, and it really happened.

Grandma and the Birds

By Caroline Feller Bauer

My Grandma was a very friendly person. She spoke to everyone: the clerk at the post office, the butcher, the bus driver, and the little girls who jumped rope in front of her apartment. We were always told not to talk to strangers, but I guess Grandma didn't think that at eighty-seven anyone was going to spirit her away.

Grandma loved animals and always had an assortment of dogs, cats, and birds, and an occasional rabbit in her apartment. Naturally, we were always excited to visit Grandma and play with her creatures.

When Grandma broke her hip, she could no longer manage the three flights of stairs to her apartment. So she gave her current dog to me, her two cats to her next-door neighbor, and her rabbit to my cousin Stevie. Then she moved into the Towers Nursing Home in Manhattan.

Since she was no longer as mobile as she had once been, my mother and I were constantly running errands for Grandma. I hated chores like buying shoes for her. They rarely fit, which meant a trip back to the store to return or exchange them. But I never minded bringing the birdseed. Grandma missed her own animals, but she said that New York City provided free birds to anyone who cared to have them.

"All you do," she said, "is put out a handful of birdseed on the windowsill and you'll have all the pigeons you could want flying around your window."

For three months I brought a bag of birdseed every Friday.

"They sure do eat a lot," I exclaimed.

"They can have as much as they want," said Grandma. "If they fly all the way up to the fourth floor, the least I can do is make it worth their effort!"

One Friday I was met at the door of the nursing home by the director, Mr. Crufts. He was furious. "Have you seen the front of our building? There is no way we can keep it clean when your grandmother attracts hundreds of pigeons every day. Please don't bring her any more birdseed or she will have to leave the facility."

When I entered my grandmother's room with the news, she was writing letters to her friends. She had friends and acquaintances all over town. Many of them she had met at church, or temple, or mosque. Grandma went to different services and the after-service potlucks all weekend. "I like the music at St. Mary's, I like the sermons at the cathedral, and I like the women's group at the synagogue," she'd say. "And those potlucks are always so delicious!"

"Hi, Grandma. Who are you writing to?" I asked.

"I got a lot done today," she answered. "Remember that lovely man who owns that car company? And I know you liked that actress I met. They've both read the new Jon Hassler book. We're comparing notes."

My Grandma was far more impressed if people had read the same book than if they owned "that car company."

"I have some bad news for you, Grandma. Mr. Crufts says that I can't bring you birdseed anymore. He says that you have to stop feeding the birds."

"That young man will never own a car company," my Grandma said indignantly. "He thinks small."

I thought that was the end of it, but I should have realized that my Grandma would find another way to feed her birds. "I'm so happy," she said one day. "The birds really love it here now. It turns out that they don't like birdseed all that much. I've been feeding them gourmet meals instead, just like the brochure for this place advertises."

"What do you mean?" I asked.

"They give you much too much food here. There's really plenty for the pigeons. For breakfast they get a little leftover egg and toast. For lunch they seem to like sandwich bread and lettuce. For dinner I give them chocolate cake or sometimes a bit of potato."

When I left after my visit, Mr. Crufts was standing in the entryway. "I am sorry. I am going to have to ask you to find another facility for your grandmother. I have repeatedly asked her not to feed the birds. The situation is really quite intolerable. Now, in addition to bird droppings, the building front is spotted with leftover food!"

I argued, of course, but Mr. Crufts was adamant. I returned to Grandma's room and explained the situation. She was already writing to "that man who has the theatrical agency who helped me get tickets to the play *M. Butterfly*."

"That silly man," was her reaction. "I guess I'll have to do something. I'll call one of my friends. I met that nice Mr. Restow the time they had the father/daughter dinner at Temple Emanuel. I'll call him."

Mr. Restow was a reporter for the *New York Times*. I probably don't need to tell you that there were headlines in the newspaper the next day. It was just a little article that appeared in section C, all about the little old lady in the nursing home who was forbidden to feed the birds. Mr. Crufts received many indignant phone calls and letters.

After that, if you were driving past the Towers Nursing Home on Central Park West in New York City around noon and you happened to look up at the fourth floor, at the window in the center, you'd see a flock of birds flying in the vicinity and perched on the window ledge. If you did, I hope you waved. If you did, I'm sure Grandma waved back. She was very friendly.

CREATING A FAMILY STORY

Here's what Anne Lamott, author of *Bird by Bird: Some Instructions on Writing and Life* (one of Judy's favorite books on writing), once tweeted: "You own everything that happened to you. Tell your stories. If people wanted you to write warmly about them, they should've behaved better."[1] Yes, everyone tells family stories; we are all storytellers, even if we don't always recognize it. But do stories like "Grandma and the Birds" count as "real" storytelling? Of course they do! Perhaps you would like to try telling your own family stories. Mine the memories of the elders in your family, friends, and neighbors for anecdotes, stories, and personal remembrances that can add a special, individualized touch to your storytelling repertoire.

Some people like to start by writing down their ideas, but Caroline preferred to begin by telling her story aloud. If you are more comfortable writing something down, try a simple outline to refer to as you relate your story. The best personal stories are those that you may have told already—perhaps at a party, at a family gathering, or in the staff lounge.

After you have told the story informally the first time, find another place to tell it. With each subsequent telling, you will tweak and perfect the narrative. For instance, a common fault of personal telling is the inclusion of too many details. If you are telling about the time that you got lost in a department store, it isn't necessary—and probably doesn't add to the story—to tell how you got to the store, why you went, and what you had purchased the day before. Another fault of the beginning teller is to drag the story out until it becomes too lengthy. If you are describing your first attempt at windsurfing, for example, it's not necessary to describe each and every time that you and your boat capsized! As you tell the story, notice where your listeners laugh, where they seem touched, and, most important, where they seem bored, and then edit accordingly.

What will be the subject of your story? There are certainly some experiences that many people have shared. A popular subject for personal stories, often used as an exercise to teach storytelling, is "how I got my scar." Amazingly, nearly everyone has a childhood scar, along with crystal clear memories of how they got it. You might use the suggested topics that follow to jog your memory or to get your children writing down and telling their own family stories.

- How I got my childhood scar
- A memorable birthday party
- The first day of school
- The first day on my new job
- The piano recital/talent show/school play
- My weird family and/or most eccentric relative
- The best/worst holiday or vacation ever
- My dog/cat/snake/tarantula/pet and other animal adventures
- The death of a pet
- The camping trip
- The sleepover
- The grade I got and how I did (or didn't) deserve it
- The report card
- The student I was
- The students I teach
- The high school prom
- My best/worst date
- The wedding
- The new brother/sister
- How my parents met
- The prize I didn't win
- Clothing fiascos and wardrobe malfunctions
- My favorite place
- The sick day
- The accident
- The hospital
- The day I got lost
- The county fair
- A crazy trip and/or vacation
- The worst/best thing I ever ate
- The time I got in big trouble
- The bad-hair day
- The most embarrassing/terrifying/hilarious (or all three) thing ever
- The weirdest dream
- The big snow/flood/fire/earthquake/tornado/disaster
- The big game: I lost! I won!
- My sports fiascos
- My college roommate or other weird friends

- My first job
- My first girlfriend or boyfriend
- The family car or my first car
- The argument
- How I got my name/nickname

As a case in point on the power of family stories, read aloud or booktalk *The Year of the Dog* by Grace Lin. Her winsome, autobiographical middle grade novel is based on her own experiences growing up as a Taiwanese American girl in a mainly Caucasian small New York town. She says in the author's note, "I wrote it because it was the book I wished I had had when I was growing up, a book that had someone like me in it."

The main character in Pacy's narrative, told in brief episodic chapters, takes us through the year, starting with her family's delicious Chinese New Year celebration. According to the Chinese zodiac, during the Year of the Dog, because dogs are faithful, honest, and sincere, you find best friends, decide what your values are, and maybe even figure out what you want to do when you grow up. All these things come to pass for Pacy, who bonds with a new girl, Melody, gets a crush on the cutest boy in school, doesn't win the school science fair, is a munchkin in the class play, and finds her true talent as a writer and artist. Sprinkled throughout Grace/Pacy's amiable first person narrative are her little black pen-and-ink sketches, as are humorous and instructive family stories her mom tells her about growing up in Taiwan and coming to America. Check out the author's website for activities and information at www.gracelin.com.

Every family has stories. Send your children to their elders to ask for them, record them—as Pacy does—and perhaps start their own story-filled autobiographies that they can share aloud.

BOOKLIST: FAMILY STORYTELLING

Fletcher, William. ***Recording Your Family History: A Guide to Preserving Oral History with Video Tape or Audio Tape.*** *Penguin, 1986.* Useful advice about questions to ask and how to interview the elders in your own family. (Professional)

Perl, Lila. ***The Great Ancestor Hunt: The Fun of Finding Out Who You Are.*** *Clarion, 1989.* How to do genealogical research for the beginner. (I, A)

Stock, Gregory. ***The Kid's Book of Questions: Revised for the New Century.*** *Rev. ed. Workman, 2004.* Interesting questions that can be discussion starters, useful for kids examining their own opinions and telling personal stories. (I, A)

Weitzman, David. ***Brown Paper School Book: My Backyard History Book.*** *Rev. ed. Little, 2006, c1973.* How to take oral histories and collect local and family stories. (I, A)

BOOKLIST: CHILDREN'S BOOKS WITH FAMILY REMINISCENCES

Bridges, Shirin Yim. ***Ruby's Wish.*** *Illus. by Sophie Blackall. Chronicle, 2002.* One of the one hundred children living in her family compound in China, Ruby writes a poem: "Alas, bad luck to be born a girl; worse luck to be born into this house where only boys are cared for." A story about the author's grandmother. (P, I)

Diakité, Penda. ***I Lost My Tooth in Africa.*** *Illus. by Baba Wagué Diakité. Scholastic, 2006.* On a trip to Mali with her family to visit relatives, young Amina loses a tooth and gets a chicken from the African tooth fairy. Written by Amina's twelve-year-old sister, Penda, and illustrated by their dad. (P)

Feiffer, Kate. ***My Side of the Car.*** *Illus. by Jules Feiffer. Candlewick, 2011.* Heading to the zoo with her dad when it starts to pour, Sophie says, "It's not raining on my side of the car." Based on a car trip Kate Feiffer took with her own dad, the cartoonist Jules Feiffer, when she was young. (P)

Houston, Gloria. ***My Great-Aunt Arizona.*** *Illus. by Susan Conde Lamb. HarperCollins, 1992.* The author's great-aunt was a beloved teacher in a one-room schoolhouse for fifty-seven years. (P, I)

Levinson, Riki. ***Watch the Stars Come Out.*** *Illus. by Diane Goode. Dutton, 1985.* A grandmother shares with her young granddaughter how her own mother, the girl's great-grandmother, sailed across the ocean to America as an immigrant a long time ago. (P)

Lin, Grace. ***The Year of the Dog.*** *Little, Brown, 2006.* In an autobiographical chapter book based on the author's childhood, growing up as a Taiwanese American girl in rural New York town, Pacy hopes to find herself and makes a new friend. (I)

Medina, Meg. ***Tía Isa Wants a Car.*** *Illus. by Claudio Muñoz. Candlewick, 2011.* A girl earns money on her own to help her aunt buy an old green clunker to take them to the beach. Loosely based on a true story about the author's aunt. (P, I)

Perkins, Lynne Rae. ***The Broken Cat.*** *Illus. by the author. Greenwillow, 2002.* In the vet's waiting room with their injured gray tabby cat, Andy's mom, Aunt

Cookie, and Grandma tell him the story of how his mother broke her arm in third grade. Their collaborative story can be a jumping-off place for looking at a story from more than one point of view, perhaps by asking each person in your family to recall the same family event, and then comparing their responses with your own. (P)

Polacco, Patricia. *Chicken Sunday.* *Illus. by the author. Philomel, 1992.* Even though Patricia and her friends, brothers Stewart and Winston, are falsely accused by Russian Jewish shopkeeper Mr. Kodinski of throwing eggs at his hat shop, the three kids feel obligated to make amends. Based on an incident from the author's childhood, as are so many of Polacco's picture books. (P, I)

Polacco, Patricia. *An Orange for Frankie.* *Illus. by the author. Philomel, 2004.* How Frankie gave his best sweater to a hobo passing through town at Christmastime. Based on a true story about Polacco's great-uncle. (P, I)

Polacco, Patricia. *Thank You, Mr. Falker.* *Illus. by the author. Philomel, 1998.* Trish suffers in reading class all through school until fifth grade when she encounters the patient and dedicated teacher Mr. Falker, who finally teaches her to read. Trish is actually the author, Patricia Polacco. She continues her school experiences with *The Junkyard Wonders* (2010), *The Art of Miss Chew* (2012), and *Mr. Wayne's Masterpiece* (2014). (P, I)

Rylant, Cynthia. *When I Was Young in the Mountains.* *Illus. by Diane Goode. Dutton, 1982.* A poetic remembrance of the author's childhood in the rural Appalachian Mountains of West Virginia. (P)

Warhola, James. *Uncle Andy's.* *Illus. by the author. Putnam, 2003.* Warhola looks back on the trip his family made in 1962 from western Pennsylvania to New York City to visit his famous uncle, the artist Andy Warhol. (P, I)

Woodson, Jacqueline. *Show Way.* *Illus. by Hudson Talbott. Putnam, 2005.* This stunning picture book traces seven generations of the women in author Jacqueline Woodson's family, from slavery times to now. (P, I)

NOTE

1. Anne Lamott, Twitter post, April 23, 2012, https://twitter.com/ANNELAMOTT/status/194580559962439681.

chapter 8

Our Favorite Stories to Tell

Unsung, the noblest deed will die.

—PINDAR, 500 BC

WE HAVE PREVIOUSLY TALKED A LITTLE ABOUT HOW TO FIND stories to tell. You can read like mad through hundreds of books—especially in the folk and fairy tale section (398.2) of your library—but you can also accept a helping hand from other storytellers. That's what we give you in this chapter. We've made a little list. Okay, a big, beautiful annotated list of hundreds of our personal favorites, arranged by subject or theme.

You will find stories that do more than entertain. We include tales with thoughtful themes that will tuck handily into a curriculum on ethics, values, virtues, and character education, including tales about compassion, conflict resolution, cooperation, courage, fairness, friendship, generosity, honesty, kindness, love, perseverance, resourcefulness, respect, responsibility, trustworthiness, and wisdom. Leading children to measure themselves against so many attributes is a tall order. That's where storytelling can help. It gives children a vicarious look at our shared humanity and the way we could lead our lives.

Most stories embody many intrinsic messages. Look under the entries "Greed" and "Laziness" below, for example, and you'll see how greedy or lazy characters are often (though not always, as in trickster tales) held accountable for their dreadful behavior, or learn better behavior, while inspiring us to mend our ways. Strength of character routinely helps heroes in fairy tales to overcome evil and obstacles. They experience temptation, tragedy, loss, danger, fear, and sorrow, and come out all the better for it.

Unfortunately, publishers are putting out fewer folk and fairy tales than ever before, and those being published seem to have a publication life of about two years—unless they win a big award. While a few of our choices may be out of print, they remain classics in the field, and are worth a little extra effort to find. If a story can be located online, we give you the URL.

If you are a librarian, treasure these books. Be careful about weeding them from your collection, and pray that no one ever loses them. Many used editions in perfectly reasonable condition can be found for ridiculously low prices on Amazon—often just pennies, though you'll pay a few dollars for shipping. Some of the books and stories listed in the last edition of this book are now so obscure as to be almost unfindable; we had to let them go. Most storytellers don't have weeks or months to search for a single story, though you can always find out what libraries have the book you need by visiting OCLC's WorldCat at www.worldcat.org and doing an interlibrary loan.

After you have learned a story or three, you will notice that many stories have common elements: the same theme, a similar background, or characters with the same desires. Of course, you don't need to have a theme to make a good storytelling program—just good stories. It is fun, though, to group stories together and create a session around a particular theme. Advertise your storytelling by announcing the subject: "Wishes" or "Tales from Japan." You can mix and match, too. A story that fits into a wishes theme one week might be used with tales about honesty or kindness another time.

Here, then, gleaned from the thousands of books and stories we've read, is our own selected, select, and delicious list of stories to tell (in addition to the eminently tellable texts of all the many delectable stories and splendid bibliographies we've scattered willy-nilly in previous chapters). We've found treasures in collections of folktales, single stories, picture book texts, and more.

Will you and your listeners love every one of our chosen tales? Of course not—but we bet you will find many plums here, old and new, which you can use to build up your story repertoire.

Favorite Stories to Tell, Listed by Subject

To give you an indication of the general interest and maturity level, we've added the following letters to each single story and book, which you can use as a loose guideline. However, if you think your sixth-grade audience will like "Henny Penny" or your preschoolers can appreciate "Cinderella," by all means, trust your judgment. Happy discovering.

P: Primary (preschool through grade 3; toddlers to age 8)
I: Intermediate (grades 3 through 6; ages 8 to 11)
A: Advanced (grade 6 and up; ages 11 to 111)

AFRICAN AMERICANS

(*See also* Freedom; Kwanzaa; and "Booklist: African American Folktales" on page 216)

Aunt Flossie's Hats (and Crab Cakes Later) by Elizabeth Fitzgerald Howard, illus. by James Ransome (Clarion, 1991). Tell one or all of Aunt Flossie's hat stories. (P, I)

Henry's Freedom Box: A True Story by Ellen Levine, illus. by Kadir Nelson (Scholastic, 2007). How Henry "Box" Brown became known as the slave who mailed himself to freedom in 1849. (I, A)

Sojourner Truth's Step-Stomp Stride by Andrea Davis Pinkney, illus. by Brian Pinkney. (Hyperion/Jump at the Sun, 2009). A robust overview of the extraordinary life of Sojourner Truth, ex-slave, abolitionist, and feminist. (I, A)

Wilma Unlimited: How Wilma Rudolph Became the World's Fastest Woman by Kathleen Krull, illus. by David Diaz (Harcourt, 1996). A stirring picture-book biography describes how Wilma Rudolph overcame childhood polio and went on to become the first American woman to win three gold medals in the 1960 Rome Olympics. (I, A)

ALLIGATORS AND CROCODILES

Counting Crocodiles by Judy Sierra, illus. by Will Hillenbrand (Harcourt, 1997). To reach the banana tree on an island across the water, Monkey crosses on the backs of crocodiles, who have lined up to be counted. (P)

The Gift of the Crocodile: A Cinderella Story by Judy Sierra, illus. by Reynold Ruffins (Simon & Schuster, 2000). In an Indonesian Cinderella story, Damura is protected by Grandmother Crocodile who repays her kindness with a silver sarong. (P, I)

How the Ostrich Got Its Long Neck: A Tale from the Akamba of Kenya by Verna Aardema, illus. by Marcia Brown (Scholastic, 1995). A sympathetic ostrich who heeds wily crocodile's pleas to pull out a bad tooth learns the hard way not to be so trusting. (P)

Mrs. Chicken and the Hungry Crocodile by Won-Ldy Paye and Margaret H. Lippert, illus. by Julie Paschkis (Henry Holt, 2003). Mrs. Chicken talks Crocodile out of eating her, insisting that they are really sisters. (P)

ANANSI STORIES

Anansi is a folk character that figures in African and Jamaican lore. A trickster, he is sometimes a man, but most often an actual spider. Once you start reading and telling Anansi stories to your listeners, they won't want you to stop. They love the irredeemable scamp. For more books about Anansi and other tricksters, see "Booklist: Trickster Tales" on page 135.

Ananse and the Lizard: A West African Tale by Pat Cummings, illus. by the author (Henry Holt, 2002). In this comical tale from Ghana, Ananse the Spider plans to win the hand of the human chief's daughter by guessing her name. (P, I)

Ananse's Feast: An Ashanti Tale by Tololwa M. Mollel, illus. by Andrew Glass (Clarion, 1997). Planning to devour dinner all by himself, Ananse the Spider sends his dinner guest, Akye the Turtle, down to the river again and again to wash his four hands. Another version of this story is "Anansi and His Visitor, Turtle" by Edna Mason Kaula in *Best-Loved Folktales of the World,* ed. by Joanna Cole (Anchor/Doubleday, 1983). (P)

Anansi and the Magic Stick by Eric A. Kimmel, illus. by Janet Stevens (Holiday House, 2001). That lazy Anansi steals Hyena's magic stick, planning to make it clean up his house. (P)

Anansi and the Moss-Covered Rock by Eric A. Kimmel, illus. by Janet Stevens (Holiday House, 1988). A classic read-aloud, tell-it, act-it-out picture book of how Anansi tries to trick all the animals out of their food. Janet Stevens's illustrations in this series are sublime. (P)

Anansi and the Talking Melon by Eric A. Kimmel, illus. by Janet Stevens (Holiday House, 1994). The greedy spider is too fat to emerge from the melon he's eaten his way into, so he has to trick his way out. (P)

Anansi Does the Impossible! An Ashanti Tale by Verna Aardema, illus. by Lisa Desimini (Atheneum, 1997). To buy the Sky God's stories, Anansi the Spider must complete three impossible tasks. (P)

Anansi Finds a Fool by Verna Aardema, illus. by Bryna Waldman (Dial, 1992). Seeking a fool for a fishing partner, Anansi teams up with Bonsu, who is savvier than Anansi realizes. In this version, Anansi is a man, not a spider.

Compare the retelling with Eric A. Kimmel's more slapstick version, *Anansi Goes Fishing* (Holiday House, 1992), where Anansi the Spider and Turtle divide the work: Anansi does all the fishing, while Turtle gets tired. (P, I)

Anansi the Spider: A Tale from the Ashanti by Gerald McDermott, illus. by the author (Henry Holt, 1972). West African story from Ghana about Anansi's six talented sons and of how the moon came to be. (P)

"The Hat-Shaking Dance," the title story in *The Hat-Shaking Dance and Other Ashanti Tales from Ghana* by Harold Courlander (Harcourt, 1957). This story explains why spiders are bald. The dance can be acted out. Start slowly and build up to zany movements in the climax. (P, I)

"Kisander" in *Anansi, the Spider Man: Jamaican Folk Tales* by Philip M. Sherlock, illus. by Marcia Brown (Crowell, 1954). Anansi and Mouse steal from Cat. (P)

A Story, A Story by Gail E. Haley, illus. by the author (Atheneum, 1970). Caldecott-winning picture book about how Anansi the Spider spread the world's first stories. (P, I)

ANTS

(*See also* Insects)

"Ants Live Everywhere" in *Tales of Insects* by Pleasant DeSpain, illus. by Don Bell (August House, 2001). In a beast tale from Burma, Ant finds a way to fight back when Lion orders all ants to leave the jungle. (P)

"The Goat from the Hills and Mountains" in *Tales Our Abuelitas Told: A Hispanic Folktale Collection* by F. Isabel Campoy and Alma Flor Ada, illus. by Felipe Davalos and others (Atheneum, 2006). While harvesting vegetables in a garden, a girl is frightened by a goat that tells her, "I'm the goat from the hills and mountains and I love to eat girls for dessert." An ant saves the day. (P)

The Little Red Ant and the Great Big Crumb: A Mexican Fable by Shirley Climo, illus. by Francisco X. Mora (Clarion, 1995). A little red ant sets out to find someone who is strong enough to carry her big crumb of torta (cake). (P)

Night Visitors by Ed Young, illus. by the author (Philomel, 1995). A young scholar, Ho Kuan, pleads with his father not to drown the ants that have stolen the grain from his family's storehouse. (P, I)

APPLES

(*See* Fruit)

APRIL FOOL'S DAY

April Foolishness by Teresa Bateman, illus. by Nadine Bernard Westcott (Albert Whitman, 2004) On April Fool's Day, Grandpa doesn't believe his two grandkids when they tell him the farm animals have all gotten out. (P)

The Chicken of the Family by Mary Amato, illus. by Delphine Durand (Putnam, 2008). Henrietta, the smallest of three sisters, doesn't want to believe Kim and Clare when they tell her she is really a chicken. (P, I)

Serious Farm by Tim Egan, illus. by the author (Houghton Mifflin, 2003). Edna the cow helps the animals plan to make the farm more fun and get Farmer Fred to smile. See if you can keep a straight face when you tell this. (P)

ARITHMETIC (*See* Counting; Mathematics; Multiplication)

ART AND ARTISTS

"The Boy Who Drew Cats" by Lafcadio Hearn. Brought to the temple to be educated, a young Japanese boy cannot stop drawing cats on the temple walls. Look for Hearn's original retelling of the story at www.horrormasters.com/Text/a0537.pdf and Aaron Shepard's simplified retelling at www.aaronshep.com/stories/045.html. This spooky Japanese story has also been retold in two splendid picture books: *The Boy Who Drew Cats* by Margaret Hodges (Holiday House, 2002) and *The Boy Who Drew Cats* by Arthur A. Levine (Dial, 1993). (P, I)

The Jade Stone: A Chinese Folktale by Caryn Yacowitz, illus. by Ju-Hong Chen (Holiday House, 1992). Though the emperor wants to see a dragon carved out of a perfect piece of jade, stone carver Chan Lo carves what he hears in the rock. (P, I)

"Tyl Eulenspiegel and the Marvelous Portrait" in *Trickster Tales: Forty Folk Stories from Around the World* by Josepha Sherman, illus. by David Boston (August House, 1996). In this version from the Netherlands, Tyl offers to paint the portraits of the noble folk at the palace of the Landgrave. Find Caroline Feller Bauer's version of this story from Germany, "Tyll Paints the Duke's Portrait," on page 104. (I, A)

ASTRONOMY (*See* Sun, Moon, Stars, and Sky)

AUTHORS

"The Peterkins Try to Become Wise" in *The Peterkin Papers* by Lucretia Hale (New York Review of Books, 2006, c1880). The members of the foolish Peterkin family attempt to write a book. (I, A)

Sholom's Treasure: How Sholom Aleichem Became a Writer by Erica Silverman, illus. by Mordicai Gerstein (Farrar, 2005). An anecdote-filled biography of a Yiddish writer and humorist who grew up poor in Russia in the mid-1800s. (I, A)

BABA YAGA

(*See also* Witches)

Baba Yaga, the famed and often fearsome witch from Russian and Slavic folklore has iron teeth, lives in a house on chicken legs, and rides through the skies in her mortar. Be polite and careful when you meet up with her.

Baba Yaga and the Stolen Baby by Alison Lurie, illus. by Jessica Souhami (Frances Lincoln, 2007). Elena must rescue her baby brother, who has been stolen by the Russian witch. (P, I)

Baba Yaga and Vasilisa the Brave by Marianna Mayer, illus. by K. Y. Craft (Morrow, 1994). Vasilisa is sent by her wicked stepmother to fetch a light from the sharp-toothed witch. (I)

Bony-Legs by Joanna Cole, illus. by Dirk Zimmer (Scholastic, 1983). Sasha's aunt sends her to a witch's house to fetch a needle and thread. (P, I)

BABIES

Curse in Reverse by Tom Coppinger, illus. by Dirk Zimmer (Atheneum, 2003). Even though poor, childless Mr. and Mrs. Trotter share their hospitality and food with old Agnezza, the witch woman still gives them the Curse of the One-Armed Man. (P, I)

Granite Baby by Lynne Bertrand, illus. by Kevin Hawkes (Farrar, 2005). Five giant sisters from New Hampshire don't know how to care for the caterwauling baby, Lil Fella, that one sister has carved from a tiny piece of pink granite. (P, I)

Tasty Baby Belly Buttons: A Japanese Folktale by Judy Sierra, illus. by Meilo So (Knopf, 1999). When the wicked *oni* kidnap the babies of the village, Urikohime (the melon princess) sets out to rescue them. (P, I)

BAKERS AND BAKING

(*See* Food)

BATHS

The Biggest Soap by Carole Lexa Schaefer, illus. by Stacey Dressen-McQueen (Farrar, 2004). On laundry day at the washing pool in a South Pacific island community, Mama sends her foolish son, Kessey, to the store to get the biggest bar of soap he can find. (P)

"A Fair Reward" in *The Wise Fool: Fables from the Islamic World* by Shahrukh Hussain and Mucha Archer (Barefoot, 2011). Two bathhouse attendants treat Mulla Nasruddin with disdain until he gives them an undeserved gold coin for a tip. (I, A)

The Piggy in the Puddle by Charlotte Pomerantz, illus. by James Marshall (Macmillan, 1974). In a narrative, tongue-twisty rhyme, Piggy refuses to jump in the muddy, muddy puddle. (P)

Soap! Soap! Don't Forget the Soap! An Appalachian Folktale by Tom Birdseye, illus. by Andrew Glass (Holiday House, 1993). The day Plug Honeycut's mama sends him to the store for soap, his forgetfulness gets him in a heap of trouble. (P, I)

BATS

The Elephant's Wrestling Match by Judy Sierra, illus. by Brian Pinkney (Dutton, 1992). When a mighty elephant challenges all the animals to a wrestling match, a little bat brings the boastful giant to his knees. (P, I)

Iktomi and the Boulder: A Plains Indian Story by Paul Goble, illus. by the author (Orchard, 1988). A humorous Native American trickster and pourquoi tale explains why bats have flat noses. (P, I)

A Promise to the Sun: An African Story by Tololwa M. Mollel, illus. by Beatriz Vidal (Little, Brown, 1992). In a pourquoi tale about why bats hide from the sun, Bat makes a bargain with the Sun but then breaks her promise. (P, I)

"When Miss Bat Could Sing" in *When Birds Could Talk & Bats Could Sing: The Adventures of Bruh Sparrow, Sis Wren, and Their Friends* by Virginia Hamilton, illus. by Barry Moser (Scholastic/Blue Sky, 1996). Meet Miss Bat back in the days when she still had a long tail and seven coats of multicolored feathers. (P, I)

BEARS

The Bear That Heard Crying by Natalie Kinsey-Warnock, illus. by Ted Rand (Dutton, 1993). Based on a true account of three-year-old Sarah Whitcher, who, in 1783, got lost in the New Hampshire woods and was cared for by a large black bear. (P, I)

The Girl Who Lived with the Bears by Barbara Diamond Goldin, illus. by Andrew Plewes (Harcourt, 1997). When the Raven clan chief's daughter speaks disrespectfully about bears, she is kidnapped by the Bear People and taken away to their village, where she marries the bear chief's nephew. (I, A)

Goldilocks and the Three Bears by Jim Aylesworth, illus. by Barbara McClintock (Scholastic, 2003). A saucy, impetuous Goldilocks disregards her mother's warnings about going into houses uninvited. Another good version is Paul Galdone's *The Three Bears* (Houghton Mifflin, 1972). (P)

"In Which Pooh Goes Visiting and Gets into a Tight Place," in *Winnie-the-Pooh* by A. A. Milne, illus. by Ernest H. Shepard (Dutton, 1926). Pooh gets stuck in Rabbit's hole and must stay for a week. (P, I)

"Miz Goose Deceives Mistah Bear" in *Sister Tricksters: Rollicking Tales of Clever Females* by Robert D. San Souci, illus. by Daniel San Souci (August House, 2006). Mistah Bear believes Miz Goose when she tells him he can hatch a nest of big orange eggs (actually pumpkins) to get the family he wants. (P, I)

"Sody Sallyratus" in *Grandfather Tales* by Richard Chase, illus. by Berkeley Williams Jr. (Houghton Mifflin, 1948). Off to the store to buy some sody sallyratus (baking soda), a little boy, his sister, an old man, and an old woman are eaten by a mean old bear. For a real treat, you can watch Richard Chase himself tell this story to an audience of children at www.professionalstoryteller.ning.com/video/1984817:Video:23341. You'll find a funny variant, "Cheese and Crackers," in Margaret Read MacDonald's *The Parent's Guide to Storytelling* (August House, 2001). (P, I)

BEDTIME

Bearsie Bear and the Surprise Sleepover Party by Bernard Waber, illus. by the author (Houghton Mifflin, 1997). On a cold snowy night, as Bearsie Bear is dozing off in his big warm bed, Moosie Moose and other animals knock on the door, wanting to spend the night. (P)

"The Bed Just So" by Jeanne B. Hardendorff, in Caroline Feller Bauer's *Halloween: Stories and Poems* (HarperCollins, 1989). A tailor can't sleep because there's a hudgin in his house. (P, I)

Good Night, Good Knight by Shelley Moore, illus. by Jennifer Plecas (Dutton, 2000). The Good Knight helps three lonely little dragons get ready for bed in their deep, dark cave. (P)

Peace at Last by Jill Murphy, illus. by the author (Dial, 1980). Mr. Bear can't sleep. (P)

The Squeaky, Creaky Bed by Pat Thomson, illus. by Niki Daly (Doubleday, 2003). Every night, when the little boy's bed goes "squeak, squeak, creak!," he cries until his grandfather brings in a cat, a dog, a pig, and a parrot to keep him company. (P)

The Squeaky Door by Margaret Read MacDonald, illus. by Mary Newell DePalma (HarperCollins, 2006). "Are you going to be scared?" Grandma asks before she closes his bedroom door. The little boy says, "No. Not me!" but he is. Our favorite version of this Puerto Rican folktale is Laura Simms *The Squeaky Door* (Crown, 1991). (P)

Too Much Noise by Ann McGovern, illus. by Simms Taback (Houghton Mifflin, 1967). When an old man can't sleep, he is told to bring his animals into his house. Two other great picture-book versions are *Could Anything Be Worse?* by Marilyn Hirsch (Holiday House, 1974) and *It Could Always Be Worse* by Margot Zemach (Farrar, 1976). Michael Bania transformed the story into

Kumak's House. (Alaska Northwest, 2002), in which an Alaskan fisherman's house seems too small until he invites his animals inside. (P, I)

What! Cried Granny: An Almost Bedtime Story by Kate Lum, illus. by Adrian Johnson (Dial, 1999). At bedtime, Patrick's Granny plucks chickens for his pillow, shears sheep to weave him a blanket, and sews him a giant teddy. (P)

BEES

(*See* Insects)

BEHAVIOR

Little Bunny Foo Foo by Paul Brett Johnson, illus. by the author (Scholastic, 2004). The Good Fairy narrates this cautionary story-song about a bad bunny who bops field mice on the head. See Judy Freeman's version on page 4 in this book. (P)

"Little Eight John" in *The People Could Fly: American Black Folk Tales* by Virginia Hamilton, illus. by Leo and Diane Dillon (Knopf, 1985). A contrary little boy disobeys his mama when she warns him about Old Raw Head Bloody Bones. A perfect poem to recite with this is James Whitcomb Riley's classic, "Little Orphant Annie," also known as "The Gobble-Uns'll Git You Ef You Don't Watch Out." You can find the full text at numerous sites online, including Wikipedia.

Toads and Diamonds by Charlotte Huck, illus. by Anita Lobel (Greenwillow, 1996). An old woman rewards helpful Renée with diamonds that fall from the girl's lips and punishes her rude stepsister with toads and snakes. You can find the full text online at www.accuracyproject.org/t-Perrault-Toads-andDiamonds.html. (I, A)

BIRDS

Honey, Honey—Lion! A Story from Africa by Jan Brett, illus. by the author (Putnam, 2005). Honeyguide, a honey-finding bird, leads Badger across the African landscape to what Badger thinks will be a beehive—but is really a lion's den. The call-and-response text is similar to "I'm Going on a Bear Hunt" (or "I'm Going on a Lion Hunt," if you prefer). (P)

"Jorinda and Joringel" by the Brothers Grimm. A witch turns children into birds. There are no picture-book versions of this story in print now, but you'll find the full text at www.grimmstories.com. (I)

"Owl's Paint Shop" in *Folktales from the Japanese Countryside* by Hiroko Fujita, edited by Fran Stallings with Harold Wright and Miki Sakurai (Libraries Unlimited, 2008). In a whimsical pourquoi tale, Crow can't decide what color he'd like to be, but he seals his fate when he trips over a jar of black paint. (P, I)

"The Trickster's Revenge" in *Trickster Tales: Forty Folk Stories from Around the World* by Josepha Sherman, illus. by David Boston (August House, 1996). In a tale told by the Minnesota's Menominee Indians, Manaboho, trickster and shape shifter, becomes angry when beautiful Buzzard takes him flying and allows him to fall to the ground. (I)

"Why Parrots Only Repeat What People Say" in *How & Why Stories: World Tales Kids Can Read & Tell* by Martha Hamilton and Mitch Weiss, illus. by Carol Lyon (August House, 1999). A pourquoi tale from Thailand about a lorikeet that told the truth. (P, I)

"The Wisdom of a Bird" in *Solomon and the Ant and Other Jewish Folktales* by Sheldon Oberman (Boyds Mills, 2006). A bird gives a hunter three pieces of wisdom. (I)

BIRTHDAYS

Big Red Lollipop by Rukhsana Khan, illus. by Sophie Blackall (Viking, 2010). Rubina's mother won't let her go to a birthday party unless she takes her little sister along. (P, I)

Clever Jack Takes the Cake by Candace Fleming, illus. by G. Brian Karas (Schwartz & Wade, 2010). When Jack, a poor boy, receives an invitation to the princess's tenth birthday party, he bakes a cake as his gift. (P, I)

Sleeping Bobby by Will Osborne and Mary Pope Osborne, illus. by Giselle Potter (Atheneum, 2005). On his eighteenth birthday, Prince Bob pricks his finger on a spindle and falls into a hundred-year snooze. (P, I)

BLACK HISTORY MONTH

(*See* African Americans; Freedom; and "Booklist: African American Folktales" on page 216)

BOOKS AND READING

Dream Peddler by Gail E. Haley, illus. by the author (Dutton, 1993). Based on an English folktale, "The Peddler of Swaffham," this literary tale introduces an eighteenth-century chapbook peddler who dreams he will hear joyful news if he travels to London—only to find his treasure is back home. Similarly themed tales include *Patrick and the Peddler* by Margaret Hodges (Orchard, 1993); *The Treasure* by Uri Shulevitz (Farrar, 1978); *Fortune* by Diane Stanley (HarperCollins, 1990); and "The Poor Man's Dream" in *Tenggren's Golden Tales from the Arabian Nights* by Margaret Soifer and Irwin Shapiro (Golden Books, 2003, c1957). (P, I, A)

More Than Anything Else by Marie Bradby, illus. by Chris K. Soentpiet (Orchard, 1995). Nine-year-old Booker T. Washington, who works from sunup to sundown packing salt in barrels, burns with the desire to learn to read "the song—the sounds the marks make." (I)

Stella Louella's Runaway Book by Lisa Campbell Ernst, illus. by the author (Simon & Schuster, 1998). Distraught when her library book disappears, book lover Stella spends a frantic day trying to track it down. (P)

BROTHERS

(*See* Siblings)

CATS

(*See also* Mice and Rats)

Chin Yu Min and the Ginger Cat by Jennifer Armstrong, illus. by Mary Grandpré (Crown, 1993). Proud but now poor, a haughty woman encounters a talking cat. (P, I, A)

Dick Whittington and His Cat by Marcia Brown, illus. by the author (Scribner, 1950). A poor boy becomes lord mayor of London, thanks to his cat. (P, I, A)

How the Cat Swallowed Thunder by Lloyd Alexander, illus. by Judith Byron Schachner (Dutton, 2000). A rascally cat tries out Mother Holly's forbidden magic weather-making objects. (P, I)

King o' the Cats by Aaron Shepard, illus. by Kristin Sorra (Atheneum, 2004). Father Allen refuses to believe his young sexton's yarn about a feline coronation in the church. *King of the Cats: A Ghost Story* by Paul Galdone, illus. by the author (Clarion, 1980) is a classic version of this slightly scary English folktale. You can find Joseph Jacobs's version at www.sacred-texts.com. (I)

Millions of Cats by Wanda Gág, illus. by the author (Coward, 1928). The classic tale of an old man who can't pick just one cat. (P)

Puss in Boots by Charles Perrault, illus. by Fred Marcellino (Farrar, 1990). A smart cat helps a poor young man defeat an ogre and win a princess. (I, A)

"The Spoiled Little Kitten" in *Indonesian Folktales* by Murti Bunanta and Margaret Read MacDonald (Libraries Unlimited, 2003). Seeking a better mother who will spoil him, a Siamese kitten asks the sun, the mist, the wind, and others to be his new mother. (P)

Three Samurai Cats: A Story from Japan by Eric A. Kimmel, illus. by Mordicai Gerstein (Holiday House, 2003). Unable to rid his castle of a savage, rampaging rat, the daimyo, a powerful Japanese lord, seeks a tough samurai cat to help. (I)

"Why the Cat Falls on Her Feet" in *Meow: Cat Stories from Around the World* by Jane Yolen, illus. by Hala Wittwer (HarperCollins, 2005). In a Chippewa legend, Manabozho saves a little cat from a poisonous snake and the cat returns the favor. (P, I)

CHICKENS

The Bossy Gallito: A Traditional Cuban Folktale by Lucia M. Gonzalez, illus. by Lulu Delacre (Scholastic, 1994). On his way to his uncle's wedding, a bossy little rooster tries to make the grass, a goat, a stick, fire, water, and the sun clean his dirty beak. Another good version is *The Rooster Who Went to His Uncle's Wedding: A Latin American Folktale* by Alma Flor Ada (Putnam, 1993). Both versions are circular stories, like "The Old Woman and Her Pig" (see page 100). (P)

Brave Chicken Little by Robert Byrd, illus. by the author (Viking, 2014). On his way to tell the king the sky is falling, Chicken Little and his friends are waylaid by Foxy Loxy, who plans on boiling them up into an extraordinary stew. In this riotous rewrite of the old tale, plucky Chicken Little prevails. (P)

Henny Penny by Paul Galdone, illus. by the author (Clarion, 1968). "The sky is falling!" cries the simple hen. (P)

Little Rooster's Diamond Button by Margaret Read MacDonald, illus. by Will Terry (Albert Whitman, 2007). In this Hungarian folktale, Little Rooster wants the king to return his diamond button. Other good renditions include *The Valiant Red Rooster: A Story from Hungary* by Eric A. Kimmel (Henry Holt, 1995), and, from Romania, *The Impudent Rooster* by Sabina I. Rascol (Dutton, 2004). (P)

The Red Hen by Rebecca Emberley and Ed Emberley, illus. by the authors (Roaring Brook, 2009). No one will help the Red Hen prepare her new recipe for a "Simply Splendid Cake." Just one of the many retellings out there, including *The Little Red Hen* by Jerry Pinkney (Dial, 2006). (P)

CHINESE NEW YEAR

Cat and Rat: The Legend of the Chinese Zodiac by Ed Young, illus. by the author (Henry Holt, 1995). Cat and Rat hope to win the emperor's race and have a year in the Chinese calendar named after them. A good companion story is *The Rooster's Antlers: A Story of the Chinese Zodiac* by Eric A. Kimmel (Holiday House, 1999), below. (P, I, A)

The Rooster's Antlers: A Story of the Chinese Zodiac by Eric A. Kimmel, illus. by YongShen Xuan (Holiday House, 1999). Rooster lends his beautiful antlers to Centipede, who gives them to Dragon as the animals jockey to be chosen to be in the Jade Emperor's new calendar. (P, I)

The Runaway Rice Cake by Ying Chang Compestine, illus. by Tungwai Chau (Simon & Schuster, 2001). "Ai yo! I don't think so!" cries the Chang family's rice cake as it pops out of the steamer and runs away. (P, I)

CHINESE STORIES (*See also* "Booklist: Tales from China" *on page 201*)

"Ah Tcha the Sleeper" in *Shen of the Sea: Chinese Stories for Children* by Arthur Bowie Chrisman, illus. by Else Hasselriis (Dutton, 1925). Ah Tcha can't seem to stay awake in this story about the origin of tea. (I, A)

The Greatest Treasure by Demi, illus. by the author (Scholastic, 1998). Wealthy Pang tries to destroy the happiness of Li, a poor farmer, by giving him a bag of gold. (P, I, A)

How the Ox Star Fell from Heaven by Lily Toy Hong, illus. by the author (Albert Whitman, 1991). This pourquoi tale explains why we eat three times a day, and why oxen are now beasts of burden. (P, I, A)

The Hunter: A Chinese Folktale by Mary Casanova, illus. by Ed Young (Atheneum, 2000). Hearing the birds talk of an impending flood that will destroy the village, Hai Li Bu is warned that he will be turned to stone if he tells his neighbors. (I, A)

The Seven Chinese Brothers by Margaret Mahy, illus. by Jean and Mou-sien Tseng (Scholastic, 1990). Seven siblings, each with a unique, magical talent, mend a hole in the Great Wall of China. (P, I)

The Seven Chinese Sisters by Kathy Tucker, illus. by Grace Lin (Albert Whitman, 2003). In this feminist reworking of the traditional tale about identical Chinese brothers, seven sisters, each with a special talent, jump into action when baby Seventh Sister is snatched by a hungry red dragon. (P)

Two of Everything: A Chinese Folktale by Lily Toy Hong, illus. by the author (Albert Whitman, 1993). After digging up a large pot in his garden, poor old Mr. Haktak is astonished to find whatever he throws in the pot automatically doubles. (P, I, A)

CHRISTMAS

The Baker's Dozen: A Saint Nicholas Tale by Aaron Shepard, illus. by Wendy Edelson (Atheneum, 1995). In colonial Albany, an honest baker learns how to be more generous with his Saint Nicholas cookies, which explains the legendary origin of the baker's dozen. (P, I, A)

A Child's Christmas in Wales by Dylan Thomas, illus. by Trina Schart Hyman (Holiday House, 1985). Parts or all of Thomas's boyhood memories are worth sharing. (A)

"The Christmas Apple" by Ruth Sawyer in *Celebrations* by Caroline Feller Bauer, illus. by Lynn Gates Bredeson (H. W. Wilson, 1985). The story of a kind clockmaker and a miracle. (I, A)

"The Christmas Roast" by Margret Rettich in *Celebrations* by Caroline Feller Bauer, illus. by Lynn Gates Bredeson (H. W. Wilson, 1985). How can you eat a goose that has become a friend? (P, I)

The Clown of God: An Old Story by Tomie dePaola, illus. by the author (Harcourt, 1978). A street urchin becomes a juggler but finds fulfillment only when he performs for a statue of the Holy Child on Christmas. (P, I, A)

The Gift of the Magi by O. Henry, illus. by P. J. Lynch (Candlewick, 2008). The classic short story of love and Christmas sacrifice, first published in 1906, is best appreciated by grades 6 and up. You can also find the full text online at www.accuracyproject.org/t-Henry,O-Magi.html. (I, A)

The Legend of Old Befana: An Italian Christmas Story by Tomie dePaola, illus. by the author (Harcourt, 1980). An old woman sets out to find the Child King, and visits sleeping children, leaving them gifts from her basket. (P, I)

The Legend of the Poinsettia by Tomie dePaola, illus. by the author (Putnam, 1994). With no other gift to offer Baby Jesus for Christmas, young Lucida brings to church an armful of weeds that transform into the first poinsettias. (P, I)

"The Night before Christmas," aka "A Visit from St. Nicholas" and "'Twas the Night Before Christmas," was first published in 1823 and attributed to Clement C. Moore. Many handsome versions of the classic are in print, including those with illustrations by Jan Brett (Putnam, 1998), Tomie dePaola (Holiday House, 1980), Robert Ingpen (Sterling, 2010), Will Moses (Philomel, 2006), Robert Sabuda (Little Simon, 2002), and Gennady Spirin (Marshall Cavendish, 2006). (P, I, A)

"The Peterkins' Christmas Tree" in *The Peterkin Papers* by Lucretia Hale (New York Review of Books, 2006, c1880). How can a too-tall tree fit into the Peterkins' house? (I, A)

The Remarkable Christmas of the Cobbler's Sons by Ruth Sawyer, illus. by Barbara Cooney (Viking, 1994). In a magical Austrian folktale, a poor cobbler warns his sons not to open the door to strangers on Christmas Eve. (P, I)

"The White Cat in the Dovre Mountains" in *The Troll with No Heart in His Body, and Other Tales of Trolls from Norway* by Lise Lunge-Larsen, illus. by Betsy Bowen (Houghton Mifflin, 1999). Thanks to a stranger's big white bear, Halvor gets a pack of rampaging trolls to leave him alone on Christmas Eve. Tomie dePaola's charming picture-book version is called *The Cat on the Dovrefell: A Christmas Tale* (Putnam, 1979), while Jane Yolen retold the tale with a girl protagonist in *Sister Bear: A Norse Tale* (Marshall Cavendish, 2011). (P, I)

CLOTHING AND DRESS

(*See also* Shoes)

The Emperor's New Clothes: A Fairy Tale by Hans Christian Andersen, retold by Anthea Bell, illus. by Dorothée Duntze (North-South, 1986). One of the best loved of all stories, this is one of our favorite versions. To find the original in translation, go to www.bartleby.com/17/3/3.html. The political implications of this story continue to be as relevant today as ever. (P, I, A)

"The Girl Who Wore Too Much" in *Shake-It-Up Tales! Stories to Sing, Dance, Drum, and Act Out* by Margaret Read MacDonald (August House, 2000). In a tale from Thailand, Aree wants to be The Most Beautiful Girl at the Dance. (P, I)

The Hungry Coat: A Tale from Turkey by Demi, illus. by the author (McElderry, 2004). Ostracized for wearing an old, smelly coat to a rich friend's banquet, Nasrettin Hoca changes into a fine silk coat and feeds his dinner to it. Meet Hoca's Egyptian counterpart in *Goha the Wise Fool* by Denys Johnson-Davies (Philomel, 2005) and in *Joha Makes a Wish* by Eric A. Kimmel (Marshall Cavendish, 2010). (P, I, A)

Joseph Had a Little Overcoat by Simms Taback, illus. by the author (Viking, 1999). Joseph turns his old and worn overcoat into a succession of lesser garments, ending up with a button. *Something from Nothing* by Phoebe Gilman (Scholastic, 1993) is another delightful version of the old Yiddish song and folktale, as is *Bit by Bit* by Steve Sanfield (Philomel, 1995) and *My Grandfather's Coat* by Jim Aylesworth (Scholastic, 2014). For a cowboy-based rendition, see *'Til the Cows Come Home* by Jodi Icenoggle (Boyds Mills, 2004). (P, I)

Little Britches and the Rattlers by Eric A. Kimmel, illus. by Vincent Nguyen (Marshall Cavendish, 2008). On her way to the rodeo, Little Britches encounters rattlers who want to eat her—till she offers them her new hat, vest, chaps, and boots. A plucky New England version, *Pancakes for Supper* by Anne

Isaacs (Scholastic, 2006), makes a good companion to this western-themed reworking of the "Little Black Sambo" tale. (P)

The Mitten by Jim Aylesworth, illus. by Barbara McClintock (Scholastic, 2009). A little boy loses his hand-knitted red mitten in the snow, but the animals find it and use it to stay warm. Two other wonderful picture book versions are *The Mitten: A Ukrainian Folktale* by Jan Brett (Putnam, 2009, c1989) and *The Mitten: An Old Ukrainian Folktale* by Alvin Tresselt (Lothrop, 1964). (P)

Nabeel's New Pants: An Eid Tale by Fawzia Gilani-Williams, illus. by Proiti Roy (Marshall Cavendish, 2010). Nabeel's new pants are four fingers too long, but everyone is too busy getting ready for the Muslim holiday of Eid (which comes after Ramadan) to help him shorten them. (P, I, A)

Sam and the Tigers: A New Telling of Little Black Sambo by Julius Lester, illus. by Jerry Pinkney (Dial, 1996). Helen Bannerman's "The Tale of Little Black Sambo," long a source of controversy, has been recast in this reworked retelling of the story about a boy who outsmarts tigers. In Sam-sam-sa-mara, where everyone is named Sam, Sam appeases menacing tigers with items of his colorful new school clothes. Also try Fred Marcellino's retelling, *The Story of Little Babaji* by Helen Bannerman (HarperCollins, 1996), set in India. (P)

Trouble with Trolls by Jan Brett, illus. by the author (Putnam, 1992). On her way to visit her cousin, Treva is waylaid by trolls who want to take her shepherd dog, but settle instead for pieces of her warm winter clothing. (P)

The Wonderful Shrinking Shirt by Leone Castell Anderson, illus. by Irene Trivas (Albert Whitman, 1983). Each time Elbert's new shirt is washed, it shrinks and must be handed down to a smaller family member. (P)

COATS

(*See* Clothing and Dress)

COLOR

"The Lady's Room" in Eleanor Farjeon's *The Little Bookroom* (New York Review of Books, 2003, c1955). Tired of her all-white room, a lady asks a fairy to turn everything green, and then pink—but she's still not satisfied. You can also find the full text online at www.eldrbarry.net/rabb/farj/ladyroom.htm. (I)

Pete the Cat: I Love My White Shoes by Eric Litwin, illus. by James Dean (HarperCollins, 2010). Pete the Cat steps in strawberries, blueberries, and mud, each of which turns his new shoes a new color. Does Pete cry? "Goodness, no!" (P)

COMPASSION

The Hunterman and the Crocodile: A West African Folktale by Baba Wagué Diakité, illus. by the author (Scholastic, 1997). Donso the Hunterman helps Bamba the crocodile across the river and then looks for a way out when the croc wants to eat him. There are many versions of this "ungrateful beast" story. Among them are "The Crocodile, the Boy, and the Kind Deed" from *Tales from the African Plains* by Anne Gatti (Dutton, 1995) and *Shadow Dance* by Tololwa M. Mollel (Clarion, 1998), set in Tanzania and with a girl protagonist. Snakes are the bad guys in the Mexican story, "Señor Coyote, the Judge," in *Tales of Tricksters* by Pleasant DeSpain (August House, 2001); and in the African American variants, "Rattlesnake's Word" from *Bo Rabbit Smart for True: Folktales from the Gullah* by Priscilla Jaquith (Philomel, 1981), and the "The Farmer and the Snake" in *The Knee-High Man and Other Tales* by Julius Lester (Dial, 1972). In a Korean version, *The Rabbit's Judgment* by Suzanne Crowder, a man must outwit a tiger; in a Polish one, "The Righteous Rabbit" in *Polish Folktales and Folklore* by Michael Malinowski and Anne Pellowski (Libraries Unlimited, 2009), a kind man saves a bear. And from China, there's "Bagged Wolf," about a man who saves a wolf from a hunting party, in *Sweet and Sour: Tales from China,* retold by Carol Kendall and Yao-wen Li (Seabury, 1978). (P, I, A)

"Slops" in *Peace Tales: World Folktales to Talk About* by Margaret Read MacDonald (August House, 1995). Every time an old man throws his slops bucket of dirty water and peelings over the garden wall, he hears a little voice yelling, "I wish you would stop doing that!" (P, I)

CONFLICT RESOLUTION

(*See also* War and Peace)

"A Dispute in Sign Language" in *Wisdom Tales from Around the World* by Heather Forest (August House, 1995). In a Japanese tale, a wandering monk and a Zen master's student have different ways of interpreting their interaction in sign language. Pair this with the hilarious Jewish version of the story, "A Debate in Sign Language," from Amy L. Cohn's *From Sea to Shining Sea: A Treasury of American Folklore and Folk Songs* (Scholastic, 1993). Since this essential book is now out of print, you can find the story online at: http://tinyurl.com/205794. (I, A)

"Old Joe and the Carpenter" by Pleasant DeSpain in *Peace Tales: World Folktales to Talk About* by Margaret Read MacDonald (August House, 1995). When Old Joe and his neighbor have a falling out, Joe asks an itinerant carpenter to build a fence between their properties. (I, A)

"The Roof of Leaves: A Tale of Anger and Forgiveness from the Congo" in *A Pride of African Tales* by Donna L. Washington, illus. by James Ransome (Harper-

Collins, 2004). After a terrible argument with his wife, a husband pulls the leaves off the roof of the house, signifying he wants a divorce, and neither party knows how to save face. (A)

"Two Goats on the Bridge" in *Peace Tales: World Folktales to Talk About* by Margaret Read MacDonald (August House, 1995). Two stories from Russia with the same title and the same first paragraph (one on page 5, under the heading "Stubbornness," and the other on page 53, with the heading "Cooperation") show different approaches and solutions to the same problem: two goats meet in the middle of a bridge—how will they cross? A good discussion starter for when your kids get into a tussle. (P, I, A)

COOKS AND COOKING

(*See* Food)

COOPERATION

Head, Body, Legs: A Story from Liberia by Won-Ldy Paye and Margaret H. Lippert, illus. by Julie Paschkis (Henry Holt, 2002). Head, Arms, Body, and Legs assemble themselves so they can work together to pick and eat mangoes. (P, I)

"Heaven and Hell" in *Stories to Solve: Folktales from Around the World* by George Shannon, illus. by Peter Sís (Greenwillow, 1985). In a Chinese folktale, a man discovers the difference between hell and heaven. (I, A)

The Little Red Hen by Jerry Pinkney, illus. by the author (Dial, 2006). The little red hen's neighbor won't help her plant her wheat seeds. There's also *The Red Hen* by Rebecca Emberley and Ed Emberley (illus. by the authors; Roaring Brook, 2009), where no one will help the Red Hen prepare her new recipe for a "Simply Splendid Cake." For a change of venue, tell "Pancake Party" from Siberia, where Little Mouse makes pancakes and Raven and Ptarmigan won't help, in *Three-Minute Tales: Stories from Around the World to Tell or Read When Time Is Short* by Margaret Read MacDonald (August House, 2004). (P)

Mañana, Iguana by Ann Whitford Paul, illus. by Ethan Long (Holiday House, 2004). Iguana is planning a fiesta on sábado (Saturday), but Conejo (rabbit), Tortuga (turtle), and Culebra (snake) say "Yo no," ("Not I") each time Iguana asks for help. Compare this comical reworking with your favorite version of "The Little Red Hen," above.

Too Many Fairies: A Celtic Tale by Margaret Read MacDonald, illus. by Susan Mitchell (Marshall Cavendish, 2010). An old woman who hates housework lets the fairies do it for her. (P, I)

COUNTING

(*See also* Mathematics; Multiplication)

Counting Crocodiles by Judy Sierra, illus. by Will Hillenbrand (Harcourt, 1997). To reach the banana tree on an island across the water, Monkey crosses on the backs of crocodiles that have lined up to be counted. (P)

How Many Donkeys? An Arabic Counting Tale by Margaret Read MacDonald and Nadia Jameel Taibah, illus. by Carol Liddiment (Albert Whitman, 2009). Jouha (whom you might know as Goha from Egyptian folklore or Nasreddin Hodja in Turkey), the well-meaning fool, brings his ten donkeys to market, but every time he climbs on one of them, he can only count nine. In this comical picture-book version, you and your listeners will learn to count to ten in Arabic. (In her notes, MacDonald cites it as listed in Stith Thompson's Motif Index of Folk Literature as "Motif J222, Numskull cannot find ass he is sitting on.") To hear the Arabic pronunciation of the numbers, play Taibah's audio clip at www.margaretreadmacdonald.com/Activity_Files/ArabicDigits.wav. Compare the story with "Goha Counts His Donkeys" in *Goha the Wise Fool* by Denys Johnson-Davies, illustrated by Hany El Saed Ahmed from drawings by Hag Hamdy Mohamed Fattouh (Philomel, 2005). (P, I)

Six Foolish Fisherman by Robert D. San Souci, illus. by Doug Kennedy (Hyperion, 2000). When six friends try to count each other, they come up with five fishermen instead of six, which, they conclude, means one of them must have drowned. For six other stories about foolish men who can't count themselves, go to www.pitt.edu/~dash/type1287.html. (P, I)

Two Ways to Count to Ten: A Liberian Folktale by Ruby Dee, illus. by Susan Meddaugh (Henry Holt, 1988). "I will be king. I can do this thing!" the animals say, but only one can win. (P, I)

COURAGE

The Legend of the Lady Slipper: An Ojibwe Tale by Lise Lunge-Larsen and Margi Preus, illus. by Andrea Arroyo (Houghton Mifflin, 1999). A courageous young girl braves a snowstorm to fetch healing herbs for the people in her village. (P, I)

COWBOYS

Bubba the Cowboy Prince: A Fractured Texas Tale by Helen Ketteman, illus. by James Warhola (Scholastic, 1997). With the help of his fairy godcow, Bubba—a hardworking Texas ranch hand—tries to win Miz Lurleen, the purtiest and richest gal in the county. (P, I, A)

Cindy Ellen: A Wild Western Cinderella by Susan Lowell, illus. by Jane Manning (Orchard, 1997). Thanks to assistance from her pistol-totin' fairy godmother, Cindy Ellen heads to the rodeo where she meets Joe Prince. (P, I, A)

The Cowboy and the Black-Eyed Pea by Tony Johnston, illus. by Warren Ludwig (Putnam, 1992). Texas heiress Farethee Well is looking for a real cowboy to love her and not her money. (P, I, A)

"Montana Tex" in *Storytime Stretchers: Tongue Twisters, Choruses, Games, and Charades* by Naomi Baltuck (August House, 2007). In an interactive story with a different sound effect for each character, good-guy cowboy Montana Tex and mountain woman Trapper Sue capture outlaw Big Bogue Bill.

'Til the Cows Come Home by Jodi Icenoggle, illus. by Normand Chartier (Boyds Mills, 2004). A young cowboy stitches a fine piece of leather into chaps, which he plans to wear "'til the cows come home." You'll recognize this as a western version of the Yiddish song and folktale that Simms Taback retold as *Joseph Had a Little Overcoat* (Viking, 1999). (P)

COWS

Click, Clack, Moo: Cows That Type by Doreen Cronin, illus. by Betsy Lewin (Simon & Schuster, 2000). Farmer Brown's cows demand a typewriter in exchange for their milk. (P, I, A)

The Irish Cinderlad by Shirley Climo, illus. by Loretta Krupinski (HarperCollins, 1996). After his magic bull dies, its tail helps to protect Becan from danger. (I, A)

COYOTES

Coyote: A Trickster Tale from the American Southwest by Gerald McDermott, illus. by the author (Harcourt, 1994). In a comical Zuni legend, trickster Coyote attempts to fly with the crows. (P, I)

Coyote Steals the Blanket: A Ute Tale by Janet Stevens, illus. by the author (Holiday House, 1993). Though Hummingbird warns him not to, Coyote runs off with a blanket he finds draped over a rock, and now the rock is rumbling after him. See also the variant *Iktomi and the Boulder* by Paul Galdone, illus. by the author (Orchard, 1988). (P, I)

Fire Race: A Karuk Coyote Tale about How Fire Came to the People by Jonathan London and Lanny Pinola, illus. by Sylvia Long (Chronicle, 1993). Wise Old Coyote plans to steal fire from the Yellow Jacket sisters. (P, I)

CREATION STORIES

"The Great Flood: A Kiowa Legend" from *Spider Spins a Story: Fourteen Legends from Native America* by Jill Max (Rising Moon, 1997). When only Grandmother Spider and Grandfather Snake survive the great flood, they plant a garden from which all living plants still come. (I)

"Mosni's Search" in *Whiskers, Tails & Wings: Animal Tales from Mexico* by Judy Goldman, illus. by Fabricio Vanden Broeck (Charlesbridge, 2013). Hant Caai, god of creation, needs sand from the bottom of the sea he just created and asks the sea creatures to fetch some. Mosni the sea turtle is the one who succeeds. (P, I)

CROCODILES

(*See* Alligators and Crocodiles)

CUMULATIVE STORIES

(*See* "Booklist: Beast Tales, including Cumulative and Repetitive Tales, and Swallowing Stories" on page 129)

CURIOSITY

Pandora by Robert Burleigh, illus. by Raúl Colón (Harcourt, 2002). Pandora is warned not to open the mysterious jar that Zeus gave to her husband. Does she listen? You'll find another elegant retelling in *Greek Myths* by Ann Turnbull (Candlewick, 2010), and a more hopeful one, "Pandora's Box" in *The McElderry Book of Greek Myths* by Eric A. Kimmel (McElderry, 2008). (I, A)

Two Bad Boys: A Very Old Cherokee Tale by Gail E. Haley, illus. by the author (Dutton, 1996). Boy becomes the brother of Wild Boy, and the two spy on Corn Mother and learn her secret. (P, I)

DANCE

"Bouki Dances the Kokioko" in *The Magic Orange Tree and Other Haitian Folktales* by Diane Wolkstein (Knopf, 1978). Making up his own samba song and dance he calls the kokioko, the king of Haiti announces he will pay five thousand gourdes to anyone who can guess all the steps to his new dance. (I, A)

"Cinderella." *The Blue Fairy Book* by Andrew Lang, ed. by Brian Alderson (Dover, 1965, c1889) and *The Complete Fairy Tales of Charles Perrault*, tr. by Neil Philip and Nicoletta Simborowski, illus. by Sally Holmes (Clarion, 1993). The English version is "Cap o' Rushes," in *English Fairy Tales* by Joseph Jacobs, illus. by John Batten (Knopf, 1993), but there are hundreds—some say thousands—of variants worldwide. See some listed on page 151. (P, I)

"The Goat Well" in *Fire on the Mountain* by Harold Courlander and Wolf Leslau (Henry Holt, 1950). An African trader is tricked into believing that a well produces living goats. The book is long out of print, but the story is well worth getting from your library or from interlibrary loan in *The Anthology of Children's Literature,* fifth edition, compiled by Edna Johnson and others

(Houghton Mifflin, 1969). The full text of the story is also online; you'll find it at www.archive.org/stream/anthologyofchild00horoarch/anthologyofchild00horoarch_djvu.txt. You can also find it in this book's companion volume, *The Handbook for Storytime Programs* (ALA Editions, 2015).

Ming Lo Moves the Mountain by Arnold Lobel, illus. by the author (Greenwillow, 1982). In a literary folk tale set in China, an old man's wife wants him to ask a wise man how to move a mountain away from their house. (P)

The Twelve Dancing Princesses by Jacob and Wilhelm Grimm, illus. by Rachel Isadora (Putnam, 2007). In a Brothers Grimm tale reset in Africa, a soldier outwits twelve princesses who dance each night. For a more traditional setting, see the versions by Ruth Sanderson (Crocodile Books, 2012, c1990) and Marianna Mayer (Morrow, 1989). Find the original Grimm story, translated from the German, at www.surlalunefairytales.com/twelvedancing/index.html. (P, I, A)

"Wee Meg Barnileg and the Fairies" in *The Way of the Storyteller* by Ruth Sawyer (Penguin, 1977, c1962). Meg dances with the fairies after a year of penance for her naughty manners. This story should be told in Sawyer's words and, if possible, with a slight Irish brogue. (P, I)

DEVIL

"The Devil In a Bottle" in *Brazilian Folktales* by Livia de Almeida and Ana Portella, ed. by Margaret Read MacDonald (Libraries Unlimited, 2006). A jealous husband asks the Devil to look after his wife when he leaves home on a business trip. (I, A)

"Nuts" in *The Devil's Storybook* by Natalie Babbitt (Farrar, 1974). A not-so-greedy farm wife tricks the Devil, giving him a stomachache as well. (I, A)

Ouch! A Tale from Grimm by Natalie Babbitt, illus. by Fred Marcellino (HarperCollins, 1998). The king sends Marco off on an errand to Hell, where the Devil's own grandmother helps him collect three golden hairs from the Devil's head. (I, A)

DISASTERS

(*See also* Earthquakes; Fire; Floods; Volcanoes)

The Hunter: A Chinese Folktale by Mary Casanova, illus. by Ed Young (Atheneum, 2000). Hearing the birds talk of an impending flood that will destroy the village, Hai Li Bu, a hunter who understands the language of the animals, knows he will be turned to stone if he warns his neighbors. (I, A)

New York's Bravest by Mary Pope Osborne, illus. by Steve Johnson and Lou Fancher (Knopf, 2002). On the night of a big hotel fire, Mose, New York City's mythical nineteenth-century firefighter, rescues all of the people inside. (I, A)

Tsunami! by Kimiko Kajikawa, illus. by Ed Young (Philomel, 2009). A wise and wealthy old rice farmer called Ojiisan ("Grandfather") sets his own rice fields ablaze to warn villagers of an impending tsunami. (I, A)

The Village of Round and Square Houses by Ann Grifalconi, illus. by the author (Little, Brown, 1986). After a volcanic eruption near a village in Central Africa, the men move to square houses and the women to round ones. (I)

DOGS

The Great Smelly, Slobbery, Small-Tooth Dog: A Folktale from Great Britain by Margaret Read MacDonald, illus. by Julie Paschkis (August House Little Folk, 2007). In this "Beauty and the Beast" variant, the dog who saves a wealthy man's life wants as a reward the hand of the man's beautiful daughter. (P, I)

"Greyfriar's Bobby" in *Animal Stories: Heartwarming True Tales from the Animal Kingdom* by Jane Yolen, Heidi E. Y. Stemple, Adam Stemple, and Jason Stemple, illus. by Jui Ishida (National Geographic, 2014). True account of a nineteenth-century constable's faithful dog who, after his master, Auld Jock, died in Edinburgh, sat by the man's grave every night from 1857 to 1872. (P, I, A)

"The Poor Old Dog" in *Fables* by Arnold Lobel, illus. by the author (HarperCollins, 1980). A one-page story about a dog who gets his wish. (P, I, A)

The Tinderbox by Hans Christian Andersen, retold by Stephen Mitchell, illus. by Bagram Ibatoulline (Candlewick, 2007). With the help of three huge-eyed dogs and a witch's tinderbox, a young soldier falls in love with a sleeping princess. Find the full text of the original story at www.bartleby.com/17/3/18.html. For a compelling American version of the story, see if you can find a copy of *The Tinderbox* by Barry Moser, illus. by the author (Little, Brown, 1990), about Yoder Ott, a Confederate soldier, on his way home from the Civil War. (I, A)

DONKEYS

(*See* Goats and Donkeys)

DRAGONS

"The Emperor's Dragon" in *Handmade Tales: Stories to Make and Take* by Dianne de Las Casas (Libraries Unlimited, 2008). Draw-and-tell story about a Chinese emperor looking for a dragon. Kids will adore this. (P, I)

The Loathsome Dragon by David Wiesner and Kim Kahng, illus. by David Wiesner (Putnam, 1987). Princess Margaret is turned into a dragon by her stepmother, the wicked queen. (I, A)

The Sons of the Dragon King: A Chinese Legend by Ed Young, illus. by the author (Atheneum, 2004). Pondering the singular talents of his nine dragon sons, the Dragon King finds a new job or role for which each is best suited. (I, A)

"Stan Bolovan and the Dragon" in *Tales of Heroes* by Pleasant DeSpain, illus. by Don Bell (August House, 2001). With one hundred children to feed, Stan Bolovan—who calls himself "the bravest, strongest, smartest, and finest-looking man in Europe"—takes on the job of deterring a sheep-eating dragon. A picture-book version of the story, though sadly long out of print, is *Alexandra the Rock-Eater: An Old Rumanian Tale* retold by Dorothy Van Woerkom (Knopf, 1978), which features a stalwart girl as the heroine with a hundred children. Two US variants are *Clever Beatrice: An Upper Peninsula Conte* by Margaret Willey (Atheneum, 2001), in which Beatrice outsmarts a rich giant; and *Jack Outwits the Giants, a Jack Tale from Appalachia,* by Paul Brett Johnson (McElderry, 2002). (I, A)

DREAMS AND DAYDREAMS

"The Hunter of Java" in *Noodlehead Stories: World Tales Kids Can Read & Tell* by Martha Hamilton and Mitch Weiss, illus. by Ariane Elsammak (August House, 2000). When hunter Ali bin Bavah comes upon a sleeping deer, he daydreams about how he will parlay the deer's meat into a fortune and become the "greatest hunter in all of Java." A lighthearted male version of the Aesop fable about the milkmaid who counts her chicks before they hatch. (P, I)

"The Poor Man's Dream" in *Tenggren's Golden Tales from the Arabian Nights* by Margaret Soifer and Irwin Shapiro, illus. by Gustaf Tenggren (Golden Books, 2003, c1957). A poor man from Baghdad dreams he will find his fortune in Cairo, but finds it at home. See also the category "Books and Reading," above (page 287). (P, I, A)

DUCKS AND GEESE

Lucky Ducklings by Eva Moore, illus. by Nancy Carpenter (Orchard, 2013). Firemen come to the rescue when Mama Duck's five ducklings fall through the grate of a storm drain. (P)

"The Singing Geese" retold by Judy Freeman on page 213. A farmer shoots a goose for dinner, but it won't stop singing. (P, I)

The Tale of the Mandarin Ducks by Katherine Paterson, illus. by Leo and Diane Dillon (Dutton, 1990). In this Japanese tale, Yasuko, a kitchen maid, and one-eyed former samurai, Shozu, are condemned to death for freeing a captive drake. (I, A)

Why Ducks Sleep on One Leg by Sherry Garland, illus. by Jean and Mou-sien Tseng (Scholastic, 1993). In this Vietnamese pourquoi tale, three ducks, dissatisfied with having only a single leg each, petition the Jade Emperor for more legs. (P, I, A)

EARTHQUAKES (*See* Disasters)

ELDERLY

"The King Who Hated the Old" in *Asian Tales and Tellers* by Cathy Spagnoli (August House, 1998). The newly crowned king of Laos decrees that all the elders in the kingdom should be banished, but one advisor can't bear to part with his elderly father. The theme of the elderly being shunted aside until they demonstrate their wisdom is also explored in the story "Plowing Up the Road," a Romanian folktale in *Earth Care: World Folktales to Talk About* by Margaret Read MacDonald (August House, 2005) and *The Wise Old Woman* by Yoshiko Uchida (McElderry, 1994), a tale from Japan. (I, A)

Tsunami! by Kimiko Kajikawa, illus. by Ed Young (Philomel, 2009). See under "Disasters," page 299.

ELEPHANTS

"The Blind Men and the Elephant" in *Wisdom Tales from Around the World* by Heather Forest (August House, 1995). Three blind men from India investigate the elephant in the garden, each perceiving it differently depending on the part of its body they feel. Pair this with a reading of Ed Young's picture book, *Seven Blind Mice* (Illus. by the author; Philomel, 1992. (I, A)

The Elephant's Wrestling Match by Judy Sierra, illus. by Brian Pinkney (Dutton, 1992). When a mighty elephant challenges the other animals to a wrestling match, a little bat brings the boastful giant to his knees. (P, I)

EMPERORS (*See* Kings, Queens, and Rulers)

FABLES (*See* "Booklist: Fables" on page 157)

FAIRIES

"The Changeling Child" in *The Celtic Breeze: Stories of the Otherworld from Scotland, Ireland, and Wales* by Heather McNeil, illus. by Nancy Chien-Eriksen (Libraries Unlimited, 2001). Brave of heart, Mairead ventures to the world of the faeries to rescue her baby. (I, A)

Too Many Fairies: A Celtic Tale by Margaret Read MacDonald, illus. by Susan Mitchell (Marshall Cavendish, 2010). An old woman who hates housework lets the fairies do it for her. (P, I)

"Wee Meg Barnileg and the Fairies" in *The Way of the Storyteller* by Ruth Sawyer (Penguin, 1977, c1962). Meg dances with the fairies after a year of penance for her naughty manners. This story should be told in Sawyer's words and, if possible, with a slight Irish brogue. (I)

"The Woman Who Flummoxed the Fairies" in *Heather and Broom* by Sorche Nic Leodhas (Henry Holt, 1969). In this Scottish story, the fairies are relieved to send a master baker back to her own home. Heather Forest wrote a lovely picture-book version with the same title (Harcourt, 1990). Both of these books are out of print, though you can still find copies on Amazon and other websites. (P, I, A)

FAIRNESS

"Dividing the Property" in *Asian Tales and Tellers* by Cathy Spagnoli (August House, 1998). In a story from Bangladesh, Selim's tricky older brother, Ali, says they will share things but Selim keeps getting the worst of everything. (I, A)

"The Theft of a Smell" from *Tales of Wisdom and Justice* by Pleasant DeSpain, illus. by Don Bell (August House, 2001). A stingy baker from Peru wants to charge his neighbor for stealing the smell of his fresh-baked goods and takes the case to a judge. Also see *Yoshi's Feast,* below. (I, A)

Yoshi's Feast by Kimiko Kajikawa, illus. by Yumi Heo (DK, 2000). Sabu wants to charge Yoshi money for enjoying the aroma of Sabu's broiled eels. For a Jewish variant, look for *In the Month of Kislev: A Story for Hanukkah* by Nina Jaffe (Viking, 1992), in which a wealthy merchant insists on being paid for the "theft" by three hungry daughters who enjoy the aroma of his latkes (potato pancakes). (I, A)

FALL

(*See* Seasons)

FARMS AND FARMERS

Click, Clack, Moo: Cows That Type by Doreen Cronin, illus. by Betsy Lewin (Simon & Schuster, 2000). Farmer Brown's cows demand a typewriter in exchange for their milk. (P, I, A)

Mary's Penny by Tanya Landmann, illus. by Richard Holland (Candlewick, 2010). A farmer's two sons compete to take over their father's farm, though it's the smart daughter who proves that brains are better than brawn.

Rooster Can't Cock-a-Doodle-Doo by Karen Rostaker-Gruber, illus. by Paul Rátz de Tagyos (Dial, 2004). The farm animals come up with a plan to wake Farmer Ted when Rooster comes down with a sore throat.

Serious Farm by Tim Egan, illus. by the author (Houghton Mifflin, 2003). "Farmin' is serious business," says Farmer Fred, but his animals, led by Edna, the cow, are thinking up ways to get Fred to lighten up. (P)

FIRE

Fire Race: A Karuk Coyote Tale about How Fire Came to the People by Jonathan London and Lanny Pinola, illus. by Sylvia Long (Chronicle, 1993). Wise Old Coyote plans to steal fire from the Yellow Jacket sisters. (P, I)

"The First Fire" in *Tales of Insects* by Pleasant DeSpain, illus. by Don Bell (August House, 2001). In a Cherokee myth, it's Water Spider who succeeds in bringing home fire after the other animals try and fail. (P, I)

"Promethius" in *The McElderry Book of Greek Myths* by Eric A. Kimmel, illus. by Pep Montserrat (McElderry, 2008). How Prometheus brought the gift of fire to humans and was punished by Zeus for doing it. (I, A)

"The Theft of Fire" in *Trickster Tales: Forty Folk Stories from Around the World* by Josepha Sherman, illus. by David Boston (August House, 1996). From the Philippines comes the story of how the animals worked together to steal fire for the people from two greedy giants. (P, I)

"Tlacuache's Tail" in *Whiskers, Tails & Wings: Animal Tales from Mexico* by Judy Goldman, illus. by Fabricio Vanden Broeck (Charlesbridge, 2013). Opossum's bushy tail is his pride and joy unt il he helps people by bringing them Bright Thing (aka fire), which Old Woman has been hiding in her hut. (P, I)

FISH

Kumak's Fish: A Tall Tale from the Far North by Michael Bania, illus. by the author (Alaska Northwest, 2004). "Good day for fish," says Kumak, his wife, his wife's mother, his sons, and his daughters, who help him pull in a huge fish. An Alaskan version of "The Enormous Turnip." (P, I)

"Tossing Starfish" in *Three-Minute Tales: Stories from Around the World to Tell or Read When Time Is Short* by Margaret Read MacDonald (August House, 2004). A man throws a starfish stranded on the beach back into the water. (P, I, A)

FLOODS

(*See* Disasters)

FLOWERS

(*See* Plants)

FOOD

(*See also* Fruit)

Armadilly Chili by Helen Ketteman, illus. by Will Terry (Albert Whitman, 2004). With a blue norther a-blowin', Miss Billie Armadilly asks her pals to help her make a pot of armadilly chili, but they're all too busy. Another cheeky Southwest version of "The Little Red Hen" is *Mañana, Iguana* by Ann Whitford (Holiday House, 2009). Meet the Little Red Hen's grandson in *Cook-a-Doodle-Doo!* by Janet Stevens and Susan Stevens Crummel (Harcourt, 1999), and cook up another treat in *The Little Red Hen (Makes a Pizza)* by Philemon Sturges (Dutton, 1999). (P)

The Bake Shop Ghost by Jacqueline K. Ogburn, illus. by Marjorie Priceman (Houghton Mifflin, 2005). After master baker Cora Lee Merriweather dies, she haunts her bake shop in an effort to run off Annie, the shop's new owner. (P, I, A)

The Baker's Dozen: A Saint Nicholas Tale by Aaron Shepard, illus. by Wendy Edelson (Atheneum, 1995). In colonial Albany, an honest baker learns how to be more generous with his Saint Nicholas cookies, which is why we now expect a baker's dozen. (P, I, A)

Cactus Soup by Eric A. Kimmel, illus. by Phil Huling (Marshall Cavendish, 2004). In this reworking of "Stone Soup," set in old Mexico, a troop of soldiers claim they can make soup from a cactus thorn, to which the townsfolk eagerly contribute ingredients. Compare it with other versions including Marcia Brown's classic French version, *Stone Soup: An Old Tale* (Atheneum, 1977, c1947). Jon J Muth's *Stone Soup* (Scholastic, 2003) is reset in China, and, though long out of print, Harve Zemach's *Nail Soup: A Swedish Folk Tale* (Follett, 1944, c1964) is well worth searching out. Go to the "Stone Soup" section of D. L. Ashliman's extraordinary folklore website, www.pitt.edu/~dash/type1548.html, to find the text of seven stone-soup stories, including the delectable "The Old Woman and the Tramp," a Swedish variant in which a tramp uses a four-inch nail to make a grand soup, fit for royalty. Eric Maddern based his *Nail Soup* (Frances Lincoln, 2009) on this version. You can also find "Nail Soup" from Croatia in *Stories of Hope and Spirit: Folktales from Eastern Europe* by Dan Keding (August House, 2004).

"Clever Gretel" in *The Seven Swabians, and Other German Folktales* by Anna E. Altmann (Libraries Unlimited, 2006). Gretel eats both of the tasty chickens she cooked for her master and his dinner guest. (I, A)

Fandango Stew by David Davis, illus. by Ben Galbraith (Sterling, 2011). In an Old West version of "Stone Soup," Slim and his grandson, Luis, ride into the town of Skinflint singing, "Chili's good, so is barbecue, but nothing's finer than fandango stew," which they claim they can make from a single fandango bean.

The Funny Little Woman by Arlene Mosel, illus. by Blair Lent (Dutton, 1972). A laughing old woman is captured underground by three-eyed *oni,* traditional Japanese monsters. (P, I)

The Gingerbread Man by Jim Aylesworth, illus. by Barbara McClintock (Scholastic, 1998). He runs, and everyone chases him. Other dandy versions include Richard Egielski's *The Gingerbread Boy* (HarperCollins, 1997); Paul Galdone's classic, *The Gingerbread Boy* (Clarion, 1975); and Eric A. Kimmel's *The Gingerbread Man* (Holiday House, 1993). With a few alterations you can turn this into a story for any holiday. For Hanukkah, for example, try *Runaway Dreidel!* by Lesléa Newman (Henry Holt, 2002); for Passover, *The Matzo Ball Boy* by Lisa Shulman (Dutton, 2005); and, for Chinese New Year, *The Runaway Rice Cake* by Ying Chang Compestine (Simon & Schuster, 2001). (P)

"The Goose with One Leg" in *Polish Folktales and Folklore* by Michael Malinowski and Anne Pellowski (Libraries Unlimited, 2009). A nobleman's cook eats one of the legs from a roasted goose, and then claims it only had one leg to start with. (I, A)

"The Graveyard Voice" by Betty Lehrman in *Scared Witless: Thirteen Eerie Tales to Tell* by Martha Hamilton and Mitch Weiss, illus. by Kevin Pope (August House, 2006). Walking through the graveyard, John hears a strange voice calling, "TURN ME OVER." (P, I)

"The Lady Who Put Salt in Her Coffee" in *The Peterkin Papers* by Lucretia Hale (New York Review of Books, 2006, c1880). The Peterkins try to change salt to sugar. (I, A)

The Princess and the Pizza by Mary Jane Auch, illus. by Mary Jane Auch and Herm Auch (Holiday House, 2002). Competing against eleven other princesses to become the royal bride to drippy Prince Drupert, Princess Paulina invents a recipe for something she calls "pizza." (P, I)

Stone Soup by Jon J Muth, illus. by the author (Scholastic, 2003). Three Chinese monks arrive in an inhospitable village and help show the people the way to happiness by making soup from a stone. Compare and contrast this reset version with other more authentic folktale variants such as Marcia Brown's *Stone Soup: An Old Tale* (Scribner, 1947). (P, I, A)

Strega Nona: An Original Version of an Old Tale by Tomie dePaola, illus. by the author (Prentice-Hall, 1975). Italian tale of Big Anthony, who does not listen; Strega Nona, or Grandmother Witch; and lotsa pasta. Other overflowing pots that need magic words to stop cooking include *The Magic Porridge Pot* by Paul Galdone (Clarion, 1976) and "The Oatmeal Pot" in *Pete Seeger's Storytelling Book* (Harcourt, 2000). (P, I)

Ugly Pie by Lisa Wheeler, illus. by Heather Solomon (Harcourt, 2010). Ol' Bear wakes up one morning with a hankering for Ugly Pie, which he makes with apples, walnuts, and raisins (recipe appended). (P)

Why the Sky Is Far Away: A Nigerian Folktale by Mary-Joan Gerson, illus. by Carla Golembe (Little, Brown, 1992). The people are punished after Adese eats too much of the delicious sky. See a simpler version of the story, "Too Much Sky," in *Earth Care: World Folktales to Talk About* by Margaret Read MacDonald (August House, 2005). (P, I, A)

FOOLS

(*See also* "Booklist: Drolls and Humorous Stories (Sillies, Fools, and Noodleheads)" on page 139)

"Bastianello" in *Best-Loved Folktales of the World,* ed. by Joanna Cole (Anchor/ Doubleday, 1983). Before a young man will agree to marry the gardener's foolish daughter, he roams the world to find three fools greater than the girl and her parents. While this tale hails from Italy, "Clever Elsie" in *Tales from Grimm,* translated and illustrated by Wanda Gág (University of Minnesota Press, 2006, c1936), is from Germany. Elsie isn't clever at all, but neither is her family, which her husband-to-be, Hans, doesn't seem to mind. Find an online translation of this comical Grimm tale at www.bartleby.com/ 17/2/18.html. (I, A)

"Bouki Cuts Wood" from *The Piece of Fire and Other Haitian Tales,* retold by Harold Courlander (Harcourt, 1964). Bouki believes a stranger who tells him he will die when his donkey brays three times.

"Doctor Know-It-All" in *Tales from Grimm,* translated and illustrated by Wanda Gág (University of Minnesota Press, 2006, c1936). A peasant named Fish, who declares himself to be a doctor, is approached by a wealthy lord who asks him to catch a thief. You can look up and read the story online at www .books.google.com. (I)

Epossumondas by Coleen Salley, illus. by Janet Stevens (Harcourt, 2002). Each time the foolish little possum, Epossumondas, attempts to carry home gifts from his auntie, his exasperated Mama says, "Epossumondas, you don't have the sense you were born with." (P)

"The First Shlemiel" in *Zlateh the Goat and Other Stories* by Isaac Bashevis Singer, illus. by Maurice Sendak (HarperCollins, 1966). When Mrs. Shlemiel leaves her lazy, inept husband at home while she heads off to work, she tells him to take care of the baby, keep the rooster in the house, and be careful not to eat the potful of poison (actually delicious jam she's made) on the shelf. Uh, oh. (I, A)

Goha the Wise Fool by Denys Johnson-Davies, illus. by Hany El Saed Ahmed from drawings by Hag Hamdy Mohamed Fattouh (Philomel, 2005). Fifteen short, droll tales about Goha, the well-meaning fool, trickster, and sage from Egyptian folklore, all of which are eminently tellable and funny. Also see *Joha Makes a Wish: A Middle Eastern Tale* by Eric A. Kimmel (Marshall Cavendish, 2010). In Turkey, he is known as Nasrettin Hoca, whom you'll meet in *The Hungry Coat: A Tale from Turkey* by Demi (McElderry, 2004) and in *Nearly Nonsense: Hoja Tales from Turkey* by Rina Singh (Tundra, 2011). (I, A)

"How Boots Befooled the King" in *The Wonder Clock* by Howard Pyle (Dover, 1965). Considered the foolish one of three brothers, Boots is nevertheless the lad who manages to fool the king and win the hand of the princess. You can read the whole book online and/or download it free at www.archive.org/details/wonderclockorf000pylegoog. (I, A)

Juan Bobo Goes to Work: A Puerto Rican Folktale by Marisa Montes, illus. by Joe Cepeda (HarperCollins, 2000). Juan Bobo goes to work on Don Pepe's farm, but the foolish boy does everything wrong. Also try "Juan Bobo," another hilarious tale of this Hispanic fool and folk hero, in *Tales Our Abuelitas Told* by F. Isabel Campoy and Alma Flor Ada (Atheneum, 2006). (P, I)

"The Lost Half Hour" in *The Firelight Fairy Book* by Henry Beston (BiblioBazaar, 2007, c1919). Bobo may be a simpleton sent on a fool's errand, but he manages to find old Father Time and marry a princess in this imaginative literary fairy tale. You can find the full text at www.tonightsbedtimestory.com/the-lost-half-hour and at www.gutenberg.org/ebooks/9313. (I, A)

FORGETTING AND FORGETFULNESS

The Name of the Tree: A Bantu Tale by Celia Barker Lottridge, illus. by Ian Wallace (Groundwood, 2002, c1989). The animals won't be able to reach the tantalizing fruit hanging from a tall tree unless they can remember its name.

"Soap, Soap, Soap" in *Grandfather Tales* by Richard Chase, illus. by Berkeley Williams Jr. (Houghton Mifflin, 1948). A boy can't remember what he's been sent to buy. There's a Turkish version of this story called "Hic! Hic! Hic!" in Margaret Read MacDonald's *Twenty Tellable Tales* (American Library Association, 2005, c1986), in which a young servant boy is sent to the market to buy salt (hic, pronounced heech, in Turkish). Tie it in to a reading of the picture book *Don't Forget the Bacon* by Pat Hutchins (Greenwillow, 1976). (P, I)

FOXES

"El Enano" in *Tales from Silver Lands* by Charles Finger (Doubleday, 1924). The terrible, ever-hungry El Enano is outwitted by a fox. (I)

Flossie & the Fox by Patricia C. McKissack, illus. by Rachel Isadora (Dial, 1986). A little girl chooses not to believe the creature she meets in the woods is a fox. (P, I)

"The Fox and the Bear" in *The Magic Listening Cap* by Yoshiko Uchida (Harcourt, 1955). A Japanese story in which the bear finally outwits the fox. (P)

"Mighty Mikko" in *Mighty Mikko: A Book of Finnish Fairy Tales and Folk Tales* by Parker Fillmore (Harcourt, 1922). In a Finnish variant of "Puss in Boots," a lovable fox finds a princess and a suitable castle for his master. Find the whole book online to read and/or download at: www.archive.org/details/mightymikkobook000fill. (I)

The Tale of Tricky Fox: A New England Trickster Tale by Jim Aylesworth, illus. by Barbara McClintock (Scholastic, 2001). Tricky Fox boasts to Brother Fox that he can fool a human into putting a fat pig into his sack. Compare and contrast this retelling with Bill Harley's "Fox's Sack," in *Ready-to-Tell Tales from Around the World* by David Holt and Bill Mooney (August House, 2000).

FREEDOM

"The Hen and the Dove" in *Misoso: Once upon a Time Tales from Africa* by Verna Aardema, illus. by Reynold Ruffins (Knopf, 1994). In an Ashanti tale, a hen goes to the village of men where she is tied to a tree but fed every day, while her friend, the dove, goes to the tall grass country, where she must scratch to find food but is free. (P, I)

Henry's Freedom Box: A True Story by Ellen Levine, illus. by Kadir Nelson (Scholastic, 2007). Based on the life of Henry "Box" Brown, the slave who mailed himself to freedom in 1849. (I, A)

"The People Could Fly" in *The People Could Fly: American Black Folk Tales* by Virginia Hamilton, illus. by Leo Dillon and Diane Dillon (Knopf, 1985). In the land of slavery, Sarah and her baby escape the overseer's whip by rising into the sky and flying to Free-dom. Hamilton and the Dillons also published a beautiful picture-book version of the story, *The People Could Fly: The Picture Book* (Knopf, 2004). (I, A)

The Secret Message by Mina Javaherbin, illus. by Bruce Whatley (Disney/Hyperion, 2010). A parrot from India, now kept in a large golden cage, asks his master, a wealthy Persian merchant planning a trip to India, to give the wild parrots there a special greeting. Based on a poem written in the thirteenth century by the poet Jalaledin Rumi. (P, I, A)

FROGS

The Foolish Frog by Pete Seeger and Charles Seeger. Illus. by Miloslav Jagr (Macmillan, 1973). Pete Seeger's effervescent story-song about a frog who gets all puffed up with his own importance. Can also be found in *Pete Seeger's Storytelling Book* (Harcourt, 2000). (P, I)

"The Frog-King, or Iron Henry" by Wilhelm and Jacob Grimm. Also known as "The Frog Prince." A princess breaks her promise to the talking frog who retrieved her golden ball. See page 109 for the text of the tale. (P, I)

"Nyame's Well" in *The Hat-Shaking Dance and Other Ashanti Tales from Ghana* by Harold Courlander with Albert Kofi Prempeh (Harcourt, 1957). Why frogs have tails. (P, I)

"The Prince Who Married a Frog" in *Stories of Hope and Spirit: Folktales from Eastern Europe* by Dan Keding (August House, 2004). In a tale from Croatia, a wicked king marries off his tenderhearted youngest son to a frog (who, you will not be surprised to discover, is really a beautiful maiden). An appealing companion to "The Frog King," above.

FRUIT

(*See also* Food; Plants)

Atalanta's Race: A Greek Myth by Shirley Climo, illus. by Alexander Koshkin (Clarion, 1995). Atalanta agrees to wed the man who can outrun her in a race, but is sidetracked by a golden apple. (I, A)

Down the Road by Alice Schertle, illus. by E. B. Lewis (Harcourt, 1995). On her way home from the store, Hetty stops to pick apples and breaks all the eggs she is carrying. (P)

The First Strawberries: A Cherokee Story by Joseph Bruchac, illus. by Anna Vojtech (Dial, 1993). When the first man on earth hurts his wife's feelings and she leaves him, the sun creates the first strawberries as the man's apology. (I, A)

Juan Verdades: The Man Who Couldn't Tell a Lie by Joe Hayes, illus. by Joseph Daniel Fiedler (Orchard, 2001). Hoping to catch him in a lie and win a bet, lovely Araceli entices Juan to pick all the apples from his employer's treasured apple tree. (I, A)

"The Magic Orange Tree" in *The Magic Orange Tree and Other Haitian Folktales* by Diane Wolkstein (Knopf, 1978). Afraid of her cruel stepmother, a girl prays for help at her mother's grave and plants there a tiny orange pit that grows instantly into a full-sized, fruit-covered orange tree. (I, A)

GARDENS AND GARDENING

(*See* Plants)

GENEROSITY

Fandango Stew by David Davis, illus. by Ben Galbraith (Sterling, 2011). In an Old West version of "Stone Soup," Slim and his grandson, Luis, claim they can make fandango stew from a single bean. See more versions under "Food" on page 305. (P, I)

"The Living Kuan-yin" in *Sweet and Sour: Tales from China*, retold by Carol Kendall and Yao-wen Li, illus. by Shirley Felts (Seabury, 1978). Po-wan, whose name means "million," gives all of his money to people poorer than he is and sets off to ask an all-merciful goddess why he is so poor. (I, A)

The Magic Gourd by Baba Wagué Diakité, illus. by the author (Scholastic, 2003). Dogo Zan (Brother Rabbit) is given a gourd that fills itself with food and water, and greedy Mansa Jugu, the king, wants it. (P, I)

Stone Soup by Jon J Muth, illus. by the author (Scholastic, 2003). Three Chinese monks arrive in an inhospitable village and help show the people the way to happiness by making soup from a stone. Find more versions of stone soup-like stories under "Food" on page 305. (P, I, A)

GHOSTS

(*See also* Halloween; Scary Stories)

The Bake Shop Ghost by Jacqueline K. Ogburn, illus. by Marjorie Priceman (Houghton Mifflin, 2005). See under "Food," page 305. (P, I, A)

The Ghost Catcher: A Bengali Folktale by Martha Hamilton and Mitch Weiss, illus. by Kristen Balouch (August House, 2008). A young barber tricks a ghost into giving him a thousand gold coins. (P, I, A)

"The Ghost of Mable Gable" in *Scared Silly: 25 Tales to Tickle and Thrill* by Dianne de Las Casas (Libraries Unlimited, 2009). Papa, Mama, Brother, Sister, and Baby move to an old house with a ghost in the attic. (P, I)

Hubknuckles by Emily Herman, illus. by Deborah Kogan Ray (Crown, 1985). Lee dances with a ghost in her yard on Halloween, thinking it is her own father. (P, I)

GIANTS

Clever Beatrice: An Upper Peninsula Conte by Margaret Willey, illus. by Heather Solomon (Atheneum, 2001). Sharp-as-a-tack little Beatrice outwits a rich giant who lives in the Michigan woods. Another American version of this tale is *Jack Outwits the Giants* by Paul Brett Johnson (McElderry, 2002). Still another delightful picture-book version, if you can find a copy, is *Alexandra the Rock-Eater: An Old Rumanian Tale* retold by Dorothy Van Woerkom (Knopf, 1978). A variant of that one is "Stan Bolovan and the Dragon" in *Tales of Heroes* by Pleasant DeSpain (August House, 2001). (P, I, A)

Fin M'Coul, the Giant of Knockmany Hill by Tomie dePaola, illus. by the author (Holiday House, 1981). The Irish giant and his clever wife, Oonah, outsmart the giant bully Cucullin. Other picture-book retellings of the story include *Finn MacCoul and His Fearless Wife: A Giant of a Tale from Ireland* by Robert Byrd (Dutton, 1999) and *Mrs. McCool and the Giant Cuhullin: An Irish Tale* by Jessica Souhami (Henry Holt, 2002). (P, I, A)

The Giant of Seville: A "Tall" Tale Based on a True Story by Dan Andreasen, illus. by the author (Abrams, 2007). Martin Van Buren Bates and his wife—retired circus folk and each nearly eight feet in height—move to the little town of Seville, Ohio, where their new neighbors go out of their way to make them feel at home. Essentially, the story is true; the couple moved to Seville in the 1870s. You can find more, including a photo, at http://en.wikipedia.org/wiki/Martin_Van_Buren_Bates. (P, I, A)

"The Little Boy's Secret" in *The Book of Giant Stories* by David L. Harrison, illus. by Philippe Fix (Boyds Mills, 2001, c1972). A little boy scares off three mean, ugly giants when he finally agrees to reveal his secret. (P)

"Pedro Urdemales and the Giant" in *Once Upon a Time: Traditional Latin American Tales* by Reuben Martínez, illus. by Raúl Colón (HarperCollins/Rayo, 2010). The rogue Pedro Urdemale accepts a giant's challenge to compete in four contests, with the winner going away with one thousand pesos. Compare this Spanish folktale with the similarly themed *Clever Beatrice: An Upper Peninsula Conte* by Margaret Willey (Atheneum, 2001), above, and *Jack Outwits the Giants* by Paul Brett Johnson (McElderry, 2002). (I)

GIFTS AND PRESENTS

The Gifts of Wali Dad: A Tale of India and Pakistan by Aaron Shepard, illus. by Daniel San Souci (Atheneum, 1995). Wali Dad, an elderly grass cutter, sends a generous gift to the young queen of Khaistan. (I, A)

"The Most Precious Gift" in *Stories of Hope and Spirit: Folktales from Eastern Europe* by Dan Keding (August House, 2004). In a tale from Turkey and Croatia, three prince brothers each find a most precious gift that saves the life of a princess, but only one can win her hand. Try to locate a copy of Eric A. Kimmel's Arab variant, *The Three Princes: A Tale from the Middle East* (Holiday House, 1994). Peninna Schram retold a Jewish version, "The Magic Pomegranate," which you can find in *Ready-to-Tell Tales from Around the World* by David Holt and Bill Mooney (August House, 2000). (I, A)

Priceless Gifts: A Folktale from Italy by Martha Hamilton and Mitch Weiss, illus. by John Kanzler (August House Little Folk, 2007). Antonio the merchant presents an island king with two rat-catching cats. (P, I)

Silver Packages: An Appalachian Christmas Story by Cynthia Rylant, illus. by Chris K. Soentpiet (Orchard, 1997). Frankie dreams of getting a toy doctor's kit as he waits each year for the Christmas Train to appear. (P, I, A)

"The Swineherd" by Hans Christian Andersen. An ungrateful princess fails to appreciate a prince's thoughtful gifts. Two good picture-book versions—one translated by Naomi Lewis (North-South, 1987) and the other translated by Anthea Bell (North-South, 1982)—are out of print but still findable. For the full text of the story, go to www.hca.gilead.org.il/swineher.html. (I, A)

GOATS AND DONKEYS

(*See also* Counting)

"The Goat from the Hills and Mountains" in *Tales Our Abuelitas Told: A Hispanic Folktale Collection* by F. Isabel Campoy and Alma Flor Ada, illus. by Felipe Davalos and others (Atheneum, 2006). See under "Ants," page 281. (P)

"The Goat Well" in *Fire on the Mountain* by Harold Courlander (Henry Holt, 1950). See under "Dance," page 298.

"The Hairy, Horned Goat" in *Polish Folktales and Folklore* by Michael Malinowski and Anne Pellowski (Libraries Unlimited, 2009). An angry goat hides in Mr. and Mrs. Fox's den, threatening anyone who tries to enter, saying, "If you touch me you will regret it. I will stamp you with my feet, butt you with my horns, eat you up to the last bit." Pair this with Caldecott Medal–winner, *Who's in Rabbit's House?* an African variant by Verna Aardema (Dial, 1977), in which Rabbit and his friends are afraid of The Long One. (P, I)

How Many Donkeys? An Arabic Counting Tale by Margaret Read MacDonald and Nadia Jameel Taibah, illus. by Carol Liddiment (Albert Whitman, 2009). See under "Counting," page 296.

Ol' Bloo's Boogie-Woogie Band and Blues Ensemble by Jan Huling, illus. by Henri Sorensen (Peachtree, 2010). When Ol' Bloo Donkey overhears the farmer planning to kill him, he sets out for New Orleans where folks might appreciate his "beee-yoooo-ti-ful singin' voice." You'll recognize this reworked story as "The Bremen Town Musicians" by Jacob and Wilhelm Grimm, which you'll find in *The Seven Swabians, and Other German Folktales* by Anna E. Altmann (Libraries Unlimited, 2006). You can find the text online at www.pitt.edu/~dash/grimm027.html. An Americanized parody is *Animal Crackers Fly the Coop* by Kevin O'Malley (Walker, 2010). (P, I, A)

The Three Billy Goats Gruff by Peter C. Asbjørnsen and Jorgen E. Moe, illus. by Marcia Brown (Harcourt, 1957). "Who's that tripping over my bridge?" (P)

"Ticky-Picky Boom-Boom" in *Anansi, the Spider Man: Jamaican Folk Tales* by Philip M. Sherlock, illus. by Marcia Brown (Crowell, 1954). A goat saves Tiger from Anansi's rampaging yams. (P, I)

"The Wolf and the Seven Young Kids" by Jacob and Wilhelm Grimm. "Never open the door to strangers" is the moral that Mother Goat's kids learn the hard way. There are no picture books in print of this classic tale, but you can find an excellent translation at www.pitt.edu/~dash/grimm005.htm and another text version, "The Wolf and the Seven Little Kids," in *Best-Loved Folktales of the World*, ed. by Joanna Cole (Anchor/Doubleday, 1983). (P)

GRATITUDE

The Boy from the Dragon Palace: A Folktale from Japan by Margaret Read MacDonald, illus. by Sachiko Yoshikawa (Albert Whitman, 2011). When a flower seller casts his unsold flowers into the sea as a gift to the Dragon King who lives there, he is given in return a snot-nosed little boy to bring him luck. A story that will remind listeners of the importance of always saying thank you. (P, I)

GREED

"The Fisherman and His Wife" in *Tales from Grimm,* tr. and illus. by Wanda Gág (University of Minnesota Press, 2006, c1936). The discontented wife of a fisherman finally wishes for too much. In her picture-book version, *The Fisherman and His Wife* (Putnam, 2008), Rachel Isadora gives the story an African setting and characters. Compare it with an English variant, *The Old Woman Who Lived in a Vinegar Bottle* by Margaret Read MacDonald (August House, 1995), and with Demi's version of the Aleksandr Pushkin tale from Russia, *The Magic Gold Fish* (Henry Holt, 1995). (P, I, A)

The Greedy Sparrow by Lucine Kasbarian, illus. by Maria Zaikina (Marshall Cavendish, 2011). A sparrow parlays the thorn in his foot into a loaf of bread, a sheep, a bride, and a lute, in a circular tale from Armenia. (P, I)

"King Midas and the Golden Touch" in *Greek Myths* by Ann Turnbull, illus. by Sarah Young (Candlewick, 2010). When Dionysus, the god of wine and revelry, offers to grant King Midas his heart's desire, Midas asks for anything he touches to turn to gold. One of the original "be careful what you wish for" stories. (I, A)

"The Pointing Finger" in *Sweet and Sour: Tales from China,* retold by Carol Kendall and Yao-wen Li, illus. by Shirley Felts (Seabury, 1978). One of the eight Immortals comes to Earth in search of a person who is not greedy. You'll find the story here on page 199. (I, A)

"Shrewd Todie and Lyzer the Miser" in *When Shlemiel Went to Warsaw* by Isaac Bashevis Singer, illus. by Maurice Sendak (Farrar, 1969). Todie tricks Lyzer into believing that his silver tablespoon gave birth to teaspoons. (I, A)

"The Werewolf in the Forest" in *More Bones: Scary Stories from Around the World* by Arielle N. Olson and Howard Schwartz, illus. by E. M. Gist (Viking,

2008). When a poor man finds a wish-giving magic ring, his greedy wife takes it and wishes for him to be transformed into a werewolf living in the forest. (I, A)

HALLOWEEN

(*See also* Ghosts; Scary Stories)

Cinderella Skeleton by Robert D. San Souci, illus. by David Catrow (Harcourt, 2000). As explained in wonderfully ghoulish rhymes, Cinderella Skeleton loses her slippered foot at Prince Charnel's Halloween Ball. (P, I)

"The Jigsaw Puzzle" by J. B. Stamper in *Halloween: Stories and Poems*, edited by Caroline Feller Bauer, illus. by Peter Sís (HarperCollins, 1989). Lisa puts together a strange and increasingly terrifying jigsaw puzzle. You can find the full text of the short story at http://home.earthlink.net/~halloween_magenta/puzzle.html. (I, A)

The Little Old Lady Who Was Not Afraid of Anything by Linda Williams, illus. by Megan Lloyd (HarperCollins, 1986). Heading home, a little old lady encounters two clomping shoes, a wiggling pair of pants, a shaking shirt, two clapping gloves, a nodding hat, and one scary pumpkin head that says, "Boo!" (P)

Not Very Scary by Carol Brendler, illus. by Greg Pizzoli (Farrar, 2014). In a jolly cumulative tale, little green monster girl Melly, on her way to her ghouly cousin's on Halloween night, is followed by a line of slightly scary creatures. (P)

The Pumpkin Giant by Mary E. Wilkins, retold by Ellin Greene, illus. by Trina Schart Hyman (Scholastic, 1970). This story about the origin of pumpkin pie can be told for Halloween or Thanksgiving. A meaty and amusing story, it is long out of print, but you can find the full text at www.soupsong.com/fpumpki2.html. (I)

HANUKKAH

(*See also* Jewish Holidays and Celebrations)

The Hanukkah Bear by Eric A. Kimmel, illus. by Mike Wohnoutka (Holiday House, 2013). Old Bubba Brayna, who doesn't hear or see as well as she once did, mistakes Old Bear for the village rabbi and invites him in for latkes. (P, I)

Hershel and the Hanukkah Goblins by Eric A. Kimmel, illus. by Trina Schart Hyman (Holiday House, 1989). The beggar, Hershel of Ostropol, volunteers to help a village rid its synagogue of terrifying goblins. (P, I)

In the Month of Kislev: A Story for Hanukkah by Nina Jaffe, illus. by Louise August (Viking, 1992). The three hungry daughters of a penniless peddler spend Hanukkah inhaling the luscious aroma of latkes outside the house of wealthy merchant Feivel, who insists on being paid for their "theft." (P, I)

The Magic Dreidels: A Hanukkah Story by Eric A. Kimmel, illus. by Katya Krenina (Holiday House, 1996). The goblin in the well gives Jacob a magic dreidel that spins out latkes. (P, I)

"The Magic Spoon" in *The Jar of Fools: Eight Hanukkah Stories from Chelm* by Eric A. Kimmel, illus. by Mordicai Gerstein (Holiday House, 2000). In the Polish village of Chelm, a stranger gets the villagers to contribute ingredients to make potato pancakes with the help of his magic latke spoon. (P, I)

Runaway Dreidel! by Lesléa Newman, illus. by Kyrsten Brooker (Henry Holt, 2002). On the first night of Chanukah, a city boy and his relatives pursue a shiny new dreidel as it spins out of the apartment, into the countryside, and up to the sky, where it shines like a star. (P, I)

"The Snow in Chelm" in *Zlateh the Goat, and Other Stories* by Isaac Bashevis Singer, illus. by Maurice Sendak (HarperCollins, 1966). On Hanukkah, when the fallen snow shimmers like pearls and diamonds, the Elders of Chelm, convinced a treasure has fallen from the sky, must devise a plan so the people won't trample on it. (I, A)

"Zlateh the Goat" in *Zlateh the Goat, and Other Stories* by Isaac Bashevis Singer, illus. by Maurice Sendak (HarperCollins, 1966). On his way to take Zlateh, an old goat, to the butcher's at Hanukkah time, Aaron loses his way in a blizzard. (I, A)

HAPPINESS

The Greatest Treasure by Demi, illus. by the author (Scholastic, 1998). In this Chinese folktale, wealthy Pang tries to destroy the happiness of Li, a poor farmer, by giving him a bag of gold. (I, A)

"Kertong" in *Sweet and Sour: Tales from China,* retold by Carol Kendall and Yao-wen Li, illus. by Shirley Felts (Seabury, 1978). A lonely farmer's life changes when a beautiful maiden appears in his house to cook and clean and keep him company, as long as he keeps silent about her existence. (I, A)

HARES

(*See* Rabbits and Hares)

HEROES AND HEROINES

The Brave Little Seamstress by Mary Pope Osborne, illus. by Giselle Potter (Atheneum, 2002). First, the little seamstress kills seven at one blow (seven flies, that is), and then takes on one giant, then two giants, a vicious wild unicorn, a wild boar, and finally, an ungrateful king. A picture-book version of the original Brother's Grimm story, "The Valiant Little Tailor," is *Seven at One Blow: A Tale from the Brothers Grimm,* retold by Eric A Kimmel (Holiday House, 1998). (I, A)

"Clever Manka" in *Tatterhood and Other Tales: Stories of Magic and Adventure* by Ethel Johnston Phelps, illus. by Pamela Baldwin Ford (Feminist Press,

1978). Manka outwits her husband. Find the full text from the book at www.books.google.com. (I, A)

Elsie Piddock Skips in Her Sleep by Eleanor Farjeon, illus. by Charlotte Voake (Candlewick, 2000). A long and beautiful story, first published in 1937, in which a girl with a singular talent for jumping rope is given a magical skipping rope by the fairies. (I)

"Molly Whuppie" in *English Fairy Tales* by Joseph Jacobs, illus. by John Batten (Knopf, 1993). A girl outwits a giant. Find all of Joseph Jacobs's collected tales online at www.sacred-texts.com. A retold version can be found in *English Folktales* by Dan Keding and Amy Douglas (Libraries Unlimited, 2005). (I, A)

Robin Hood and the Golden Arrow by Robert D. San Souci, illus. by E. B. Lewis (Orchard, 2010). Disguised as a beggar, Robin enters the Sheriff of Nottingham's archery contest. (I, A)

Three Strong Women: A Tall Tale from Japan by Claus Stamm, illus. by Jean Tseng and Mou-sien Tseng (Viking, 1990). On his way to compete before the emperor, a wrestler encounters three women—a girl, her mother, and her grandmother—who are far stronger than he. You can also find the text in *Tatterhood and Other Tales: Stories of Magic and Adventure* by Ethel Johnston Phelps (Feminist Press, 1978), which you'll find online at www.books.google.com. (I, A)

HISPANIC/LATINO STORIES

(*See also* "Booklist: Other Tales from the Americas" on page 222)

"The Goat from the Hills and Mountains" in *Tales Our Abuelitas Told: A Hispanic Folktale Collection* by F. Isabel Campoy and Alma Flor Ada, illus. by Felipe Davalos and others (Atheneum, 2006). See under "Ants," page 281.

Juan Verdades: The Man Who Couldn't Tell a Lie by Joe Hayes, illus. by Joseph Daniel Fiedler (Orchard, 2001). See under "Fruit," page 310.

Martina the Beautiful Cockroach: A Cuban Folktale by Carmen Agra Deedy, illus. by Michael Austin (Peachtree, 2007). Grandmother gives Martina good advice about finding a husband; she tells her to spill coffee on her suitors' shoes. This is a Cuban version of the story you may know as "Perez and Martina," the Puerto Rican tale made popular by Pura Belpré. Compare it with "Martina Martínez and Pérez the Mouse" in *Tales Our Abuelitas Told* by F. Isabel Campoy and Alma Flor Ada (Atheneum, 2006) or "Martina the Cockroach and Pérez the Mouse" in *Once Upon a Time: Traditional Latin American Tales* by Reuben Martínez (HarperCollins/Rayo, 2010). (P, I, A)

The Three Little Tamales by Eric A. Kimmel, illus. by Valeria Docampo (Marshall Cavendish, 2009). Three newly made tamales run away from their taqueria and build their own casitas—then along comes Señor Lobo to blow them down. (P)

HOLIDAYS AND CELEBRATIONS

(*See* Black History Month; Christmas; Halloween; Hanukkah; Jewish Holidays and Celebrations; Kwanzaa; Valentine's Day)

HONESTY

"The Bell That Knew the Truth" in *Through the Grapevine: World Tales Kids Can Read and Tell* by Martha Hamilton and Mitch Weiss, illus. by Carol Lynn (August House, 2001). In China, Judge Chen determines the identity of a thief with the help of a temple bell that the judge claims has magical powers. (I, A)

The Empty Pot by Demi, illus. by the author (Henry Holt, 1990). To choose a worthy successor, the Emperor gives his youngest subjects seeds to grow. (P, I)

Juan Verdades: The Man Who Couldn't Tell a Lie by Joe Hayes, illus. by Joseph Daniel Fiedler (Orchard, 2001). See under "Fruit," page 310.

"The Silent Witness" in *Through the Grapevine: World Tales Kids Can Read and Tell* by Martha Hamilton and Mitch Weiss, illus. by Carol Lynn (August House, 2001). In Iran, a poor man must defend himself in court when his horse kills a rich man's horse. (I, A)

"The Sticks of Truth" in *Stories to Solve: Folktales from Around the World* by George Shannon, illus. by Peter Sís (Greenwillow, 1985). In India, a judge catches a thief with magic sticks. (I, A)

"The Talking Skull" in *Wonder Tales from Around the World* by Heather Forest, illus. by David Boston (August House, 1995). A West African man in search of food comes upon a talking skull that warns him to tell no one what he has seen. Unfortunately, the man doesn't heed the skull's warning. (I, A)

"The Wise Master" in *Wisdom Tales from Around the World* by Heather Forest (August House, 1995). In this Jataka tale, a wise teacher instructs his students to steal in order to make money to repair their run-down temple. (I, A)

HORSES

Are You a Horse? by Andy Rash, illus. by the author (Scholastic, 2009). Roy may be dressed like a cowboy, but he doesn't even know what a horse is. (P)

Rocking-Horse Land by Laurence Housman, illus. by Kristina Rodanas (Lothrop, 1990). Prince Freedling's rocking horse turns into a dashing steed who wishes to be set free. You can find the text of this evocative short story at http://equiki.wikidot.com/rocking-horse-land. (I)

"The Squire's Bride" in *East o' the Sun and West o' the Moon* by George Webbe Dasent (Dover, 1970). In the old Norwegian folktale, a wealthy squire insists he will marry a poor young girl who won't have him, even if he has to trick her into it. The laugh's on him. See the full text on page 186. (I, A)

HOUSES

"How to Make a Small House into a Large One" retold by Caroline Feller Bauer in *The Handbook for Storytime Programs* by Judy Freeman and Caroline Feller Bauer (ALA Editions, 2015). A man asks the rabbi for advice about his too-small one-room cottage. See also *Too Much Noise* by Ann McGovern, illus. by Simms Taback (Houghton Mifflin, 1967). Two other great picture-book versions are *Could Anything Be Worse?* by Marilyn Hirsch (Holiday House, 1974) and *It Could Always Be Worse* by Margot Zemach (Farrar, 1976). (P)

Kumak's House: A Tale of the Far North by Michael Bania, illus. by the author (Alaska Northwest, 2002). In an Alaskan-style variant of the "appreciate what you've got" theme above, Kumak invites animals into his too-small house. (P)

The Old Woman Who Lived in a Vinegar Bottle by Margaret Read MacDonald, illus. by Nancy Dunaway Fowlkes (August House, 1995). An old woman is too busy complaining to be thankful after a fairy rewards her with a succession of bigger and better houses. An English variant of Grimm's "The Fisherman and His Wife"; for a Russian version based on an Aleksandr Pushkin tale, read Demi's *The Magic Gold Fish* (Henry Holt, 1995). (P, I)

The Village of Round and Square Houses by Ann Grifalconi, illus. by the author (Little, Brown, 1986). See under "Disasters," page 300.

INSECTS

King Solomon and the Bee by Dalia Hardof Renberg, illus. by Ruth Heller (HarperCollins, 1994). Stung on the nose by a bee, King Solomon forgives the repentant insect that then helps him when the Queen of Sheba comes to visit. (P, I, A)

Martina the Beautiful Cockroach: A Cuban Folktale by Carmen Agra Deedy, illus. by Michael Austin (Peachtree, 2007). See under "Hispanic and Latino Stories," page 317.

"Ouch" in *Whiskers, Tails & Wings: Animal Tales from Mexico* by Judy Goldman, illus. by Fabricio Vanden Broeck (Charlesbridge, 2013). After making Man and Woman, the God of Creation makes insects to get the lazy couple to do some work. (P, I)

"When Señor Grillo Met Señor Puma" in *Whiskers, Tails & Wings: Animal Tales from Mexico* by Judy Goldman, illus. by Fabricio Vanden Broeck (Charlesbridge, 2013). Puma and Cricket prepare for war against each other. With the help of the other insects, Cricket wins. (P, I)

Why Mosquitoes Buzz in People's Ears by Verna Aardema, illus. by Leo and Diane Dillon (Dial, 1975). A cumulative pourquoi tale that ends with a good slap. A perfect companion tale is *Zzzng! Zzzng! Zzzng!* by Phillis Gershator, below. (P)

Zzzng! Zzzng! Zzzng! A Yoruba Tale by Phillis Gershator, illus. by Theresa Smith (Orchard, 1998). Mosquito offers to marry Ear, Arm, and Leg, and is angered to learn that they're planning to marry Head, Chest, and Hips instead. Another classic mosquito pourquoi tale is the Caldecott winner *Why Mosquitoes Buzz in People's Ears* by Verna Aardema (Dial, 1975). (P)

JEWISH HOLIDAYS AND CELEBRATIONS

(*See also* Hanukkah)

Cakes and Miracles: A Purim Tale by Barbara Diamond Goldin, illus. by Jaime Zollars (Marshall Cavendish, 2010, c1991). A blind boy, Hershel finds a way to celebrate Purim with the baking of the traditional cookie, the hamentaschen. (P)

"A Celebration" in *The Feather Merchants and Other Tales of the Fools of Chelm* by Steve Sanfield, illus. by Mikhail Magaril (Orchard, 1991). A proud father ends up serving water to celebrate his daughter's birth. A similar noodlehead story featuring a wedding celebration is *Simon Boom Gives a Wedding* by Yuri Suhl (Four Winds, 1972). (I, A)

The Little Red Hen and the Passover Matzah by Leslie Kimmelman, illus. by Paul Meisel (Holiday House, 2010). Little Red Hen kvetches that those lazy no-goodniks Sheep, Horse, and Dog won't help her get ready for the Passover seder. (P)

The Matzah Man: A Passover Story by Naomi Howland, illus. by the author (Clarion, 2002). On Passover, a little matzah man jumps out of Mr. Cohen's oven and races through the village, chased by everybody. Another Passover take on "The Gingerbread Man" is *The Matzo Ball Boy* by Lisa Shulman, illus. by Rosanne Litzinger (Dutton, 2005). Filled with Yiddishisms, this features an old *bubbe* (grandmother) whose matzo ball jumps out of the chicken soup and leads everyone on a merry chase. (P)

KINDNESS

Cloud Tea Monkeys by Mal Peet and Elspeth Graham, illus. by Juan Wijngaard (Candlewick, 2010). When her mother falls ill, young Tashi tries to take her place at the tea plantation picking tea leaves, and is aided by the wild monkeys she has befriended. (I)

"The Girl and the Chenoo" in *The Girl Who Married the Moon: Tales from Native North America* by Joseph Bruchac and Gayle Ross (Fulcrum, 2006, c1994). A tale of the Passamaquoddy about Little Listener who welcomes as a guest and transforms the Chenoo, the great cannibal monster who comes to her lodge. (I, A)

"Hold Tight and Stick Tight" in *Earth Care: World Folktales to Talk About* by Margaret Read MacDonald (August House, 2005). In Japan, the Kind Old Man is rewarded with gold coins for helping a pine tree; the Mean Old Man is punished with sticky sap for not helping. (P, I)

"The Old Traveler" in *Stories of Hope and Spirit: Folktales from Eastern Europe* by Dan Keding (August House, 2004). In a tale from Estonia, a poor man seeking shelter for the night is scorned by a rich woman but treated with hospitality by a poor one. (I, A)

"The Wish-Fulfiller Shell" in *From the Mango Tree, and Other Folktales from Nepal* by Kavita Ram Shrestha and Sarah Lamstein (Libraries Unlimited, 1997). Because of his great kindness to a cat, a dog, and a mouse, Kaude is given a magic wishing shell by the serpent god of the Underworld. (I)

"The Woodcutter and the Bird" in *Asian Tales and Tellers* by Cathy Spagnoli (August House, 1998). A Korean woodcutter who saves a mother pheasant and her babies from a snake is later captured by the spirit of that snake and threatened with death. (I)

KINGS, QUEENS, AND RULERS

"Bujang Permai" in *Indonesian Folktales* by Murti Bunanta and Margaret Read MacDonald (Libraries Unlimited, 2003). Bujang Permai sets out with his two older brothers to seek their fortunes and tells them his deepest wish: to become a king. (I)

The Emperor's New Clothes: A Fairy Tale by Hans Christian Andersen, retold by Anthea Bell, illus. by Dorothée Duntze (North-South, 1986). One of the best loved of all stories, this is an excellent version. To find an original version in translation, go to www.bartleby.com/17/3/3.html. (P, I, A)

King Solomon and the Bee by Dalia Hardof Renberg, illus. by Ruth Heller (HarperCollins, 1994). See under "Insects," page 319. (P, I, A)

Merlin and the Making of the King by Margaret Hodges, illus. by Trina Schart Hyman (Holiday House, 2004). Three of the best-known tales of King Arthur—"The Sword in the Stone," "Excalibur," and "The Lady of the Lake"—describe his crowning, marriage, and death. (I, A)

The Well at the End of the World by Robert D. San Souci, illus. by Rebecca Walsh (Chronicle, 2004). Plain but practical Princess Rosamond runs the kingdom for her father, the king of Colchester, until he weds the beautiful Lady Zantippa, who loots the treasury and causes her husband to become ill. (I, A)

KWANZAA

(*See also* African Americans and "Booklist: African American Folktales" on page 216)

Seven Spools of Thread: A Kwanzaa Story by Angela Shelf Medearis, illus. by Daniel Minter (Albert Whitman, 2000). Seven quarreling sons must learn to work together in this literary pourquoi tale about how multicolored kente cloth came to be. (P, I, A)

LAZINESS

"Ah Tcha the Sleeper" in *Shen of the Sea: Chinese Stories for Children* by Arthur Bowie Chrisman, illus. by Else Hasselriis (Dutton, 1925). Lazy Ah Tcha can't seem to stay awake in this story about the origin of tea. (I)

The Boy of the Three-Year Nap by Dianne Snyder, illus. by Allen Say (Houghton Mifflin, 1988). Taro, a lazy Japanese boy who has never had a real job, tricks a rich merchant into arranging a marriage with his daughter. (P, I)

"Fool's Paradise" in *Zlateh the Goat and Other Stories* by Isaac Bashevis Singer, illus. by Maurice Sendak (HarperCollins, 1966). Atzel, a lazy man, wishes to die because he hears that there is no work in Paradise. (I, A)

Jamie O'Rourke and the Pooka by Tomie dePaola, illus. by the author (Putnam, 2000). With his wife away for a week, Jamie, the laziest man in Ireland, is grateful for the help of a donkey-like creature, a pooka, who cleans the cottage. Also take a look at *Jamie O'Rourke and the Big Potato: An Irish Folktale* by Tomie dePaola (Putnam, 1992), in which the lazy fellow gets a wish from a leprechaun. (P, I, A)

"Lazy as an Ox: A Korean Tale" retold by Caroline Feller Bauer in *The Handbook for Storytime Programs* by Judy Freeman and Caroline Feller Bauer (ALA Editions, 2015). Wan Le, lazy apprentice to a mask maker, thinks it would be easier to be an ox and nap all day than to work for his master. (P, I, A)

"Lazy Jack" in *English Folktales* by Dan Keding and Amy Douglas (Libraries Unlimited, 2005). Jack's mother sends her lazy son to get a job, which results in his making a bored princess laugh. This will put you in mind of "The Princess Who Would Not Laugh" in *Polish Folktales and Folklore* by Michael Malinowski and Anne Pellowski (Libraries Unlimited, 2009), as well as the Brothers Grimm tale "The Golden Goose," where the boy is known as Dummling, and which can be found at www.authorama.com/grimms-fairy-tales-50.html. (I, A)

Lazy Lion by Mwenye Hadithi, illus. by Adrienne Kennaway (Little, Brown, 1990). Lion is too lazy to build his own house.

LEPRECHAUNS

Jamie O'Rourke and the Big Potato: An Irish Folktale by Tomie dePaola, illus. by the author (Putnam, 1992). See under "Laziness," page 322.

The Leprechaun's Gold by Pamela Duncan Edwards, illus. by Henry Cole (HarperCollins, 2004). Humble Old Pat and Young Tom, a braggart, plan to enter the king's harping contest. (P, I)

"The Leprechaun's Gold" in *Trickster Tales: Forty Folk Stories from Around the World* by Josepha Sherman, illus. by David Boston (August House, 1996). Tom, a young farmer, catches a leprechaun and demands the little man's treasure. (I, A)

Leprechauns Never Lie by Lorna Balian, illus. by the author (Star Bright, 2004, c1980). Lazy young Ninny Nanny captures a wee fairy man. (P, I)

Tim O'Toole and the Wee Folk: An Irish Tale by Gerald McDermott, illus. by the author (Viking, 1990). The wee folk give Tim marvelous gifts, but he keeps squandering them. (P, I)

LIONS AND TIGERS

Auntie Tiger by Laurence Yep, illus. by Insu Lee (HarperCollins, 2009). Two squabbling sisters must work together to defeat the tiger disguised as an old woman. Pair this Chinese version of "Little Red Riding Hood" with the darker *Lon Po Po: A Red-Riding Hood Story from China* by Ed Young (Philomel, 1989). (P, I)

Lazy Lion by Mwenye Hadithi, illus. by Adrienne Kennaway (Little, Brown, 1990). See under "Laziness," this page.

Sam and the Tigers: A New Telling of Little Black Sambo by Julius Lester, illus. by Jerry Pinkney (Dial, 1996). See under "Clothing and Dress," page 293.

Subira, Subira by Tololwa M. Mollel, illus. by Linda Saport (Clarion, 2000). After Mother dies and Tatu cannot get her little brother to obey her, she seeks help from a spirit woman who tells her to pluck three whiskers from a lion.

Two Ethiopian versions of this affecting story are "The Lion's Whiskers" in *Peace Tales: World Folktales to Talk About* by Margaret Read MacDonald (August House, 1995) and *Pulling the Lion's Tail* by Jane Kurtz (Simon & Schuster, 1995). The "The Tiger's Whisker" in *Wisdom Tales from Around the World* by Heather Forest (August House, 1995), from Korea, is about a wife who searches for a love potion that will make her soldier husband love her again. (I, A)

LOVE

East o' the Sun and West o' the Moon by Sir George Webbe Dasent, illus. by P. J. Lynch (Candlewick, 1992). In this Norwegian fairy tale, a man gives his youngest daughter to the White Bear, who carries her off to his castle. (I, A)

"The Kelpie and the Girl" in *The Celtic Breeze: Stories of the Otherworld from Scotland, Ireland, and Wales* by Heather McNeil (Libraries Unlimited, 2001). A kelpie who takes the form of a selfish young man decides he wants to marry the prettiest girl on the Isle of Barra. (I, A)

"The Pottle of Brains" in *English Folktales* by Dan Keding and Amy Douglas (Libraries Unlimited, 2005). Jack's mother sends her lazy son to see the Henwife to ask her if she has a pottle of brains to spare for him. (I, A)

The Steadfast Tin Soldier by Hans Christian Andersen, illus. by P. J. Lynch (Andersen Press, 2005). A tin soldier falls in love with a ballet dancer made of paper. Find an annotated version of the classic at www.surlalunefairytales.com/steadfasttinsoldier. (I)

"The Very Pretty Lady" from *The Devil's Storybook* by Natalie Babbitt, illus. by the author (Farrar, 1974). The Devil offers a lady the chance to be beautiful forever, but she turns it down for love.

"The Yellow Ribbon" in *Juba This and Juba That* by Virginia Tashjian, illus. by Nadine Bernard Westcott (Little, Brown, 1969). John and Jane love each other, but Jane won't tell John why she wears a yellow ribbon around her neck. (P, I)

LUCK

The House Gobbaleen by Lloyd Alexander, illus. by Diane Goode (Dutton, 1995). Down on his luck, Dooley thinks the surly little man Hook—one of the Friendly Folk—will bring him good fortune, so he lets him move in. (P, I)

"The Most Unfortunate Man" in *English Folktales* by Dan Keding and Amy Douglas (Libraries Unlimited, 2005). A man sets off to find God and ask why he has never had any luck in his life. You'll find another version, "The Edge of the World," in David Holt and Bill Mooney's *More Ready-to-Tell Tales from Around the World* (August House, 2000). (I, A)

MAGIC, MAGICIANS, AND MAGICAL OBJECTS

"Aladdin and the Wonderful Lamp" in *Tenggren's Golden Tales from the Arabian Nights* by Margaret Soifer and Irwin Shapiro, illus. by Gustaf Tenggren (Golden Books, 2003, c1957). When he outwits an evil magician, Aladdin becomes the master of a magic lamp from which a genie emerges to do the boy's bidding. (I, A)

"Ti-Jean and the Princess of Tomboso" in *When Apples Grew Noses and White Horses Flew: Tales of Ti-Jean* by Jan Andrews, illus. by Dusan Petricic (Groundwood, 2011). In this humorous French Canadian tale, a princess steals Ti-Jean's magical items, but he finds a magic apple that makes her nose grow until she gives them back. Interestingly, Harve and Margot Zemach did a wonderfully comic picture book of a similar Italian story, *Too Much Nose* (Holt, Reinhart, & Winston, 1967), now long out of print. (I, A)

MARRIAGE

"Goha Refuses to Say a Word" in *Goha the Wise Fool* by Denys Johnson-Davies, illus. by Hany El Saed Ahmed from drawings by Hag Hamdy Mohamed Fattouh (Philomel, 2005). Goha and his wife agree that the first one of them to speak aloud will have to go feed the donkey. (I, A)

Gone Is Gone; Or, The Story of a Man Who Wanted to Do Housework by Wanda Gág, illus. by the author (University of Minnesota Press, 2006, c1935). A man changes places with his wife—with disastrous results. (P, I)

"Gudbrand on the Hill-side" in *Popular Tales from the Norse* by Peter C. Asbjørnsen (Book Jungle, 2009, c1904). A loving Norwegian wife thinks her foolish husband, Gudbrand, can do no wrong, even after he trades his cow for a shilling. Find the story online at www.sacred-texts.com/neu/ptn/ptn31.htm and in print as "Gudbrand on the Hillside; Or, What the Good Man Does Is Always Right" in *Best-Loved Folktales of the World*, edited by Joanna Cole (Anchor/Doubleday, 1983). (I, A)

"The Husband Who Was to Mind the House" in *Popular Tales from the Norse* by Peter C. Asbjørnsen (Book Jungle, 2009, c1904). A farmer who thinks his wife has an easy job of it at home trades places with her, staying to care for the house while she spends the day in the fields. Find the story online at www.sacred-texts.com/neu/ptn/ptn49.htm. You may want to dig up the picture-book version of the story, *The Man Who Kept House,* retold by Kathleen and Michael Hague (Harcourt, 1981) or access a readers' theater script of the tale at www.saskschools.ca/~gregory/plays/man_house.html. (I)

MATHEMATICS

(*See* Counting; Multiplication)

MICE AND RATS

(*See also* Cats)

The Barking Mouse by Antonio Sacre, illus. by Alfredo Aguirre (Albert Whitman, 2003). On a picnic with Mamá and Papá Ratón, two mouse siblings, Hermano and Hermana, tease a ferocious cat. (P, I)

Cat and Rat: The Legend of the Chinese Zodiac by Ed Young, illus. by the author (Henry Holt, 1995). Cat and Rat hope to win the emperor's race and have a year in the Chinese calendar named after them. A good companion story is *The Rooster's Antlers: A Story of the Chinese Zodiac* by Eric A. Kimmel, illus. by YongShen Xuan (Holiday House, 1999). (P, I)

Mabela the Clever by Margaret Read MacDonald, illus. by Tim Coffey (Albert Whitman, 2001). In this sweet picture-book story from Sierra Leone, Mabela is the only mouse who pays attention when the big orange cat entreats the mice to follow it into the forest. There's a marvelous chantable refrain: "When we are marching, / we never look back! / The cat is at the end, / Fo Feng! / Fo Feng!" For a variant of this tale, see the Tibetan story "Rambé and Ambé" from Jane Yolen's *Meow: Cat Stories from Around the World* (HarperCollins, 2005). (P)

MONEY

"Bouqui Rents a Horse" in *The Piece of Fire and Other Haitian Tales,* retold by Harold Courlander (Harcourt, 1964). When Haitian trickster Bouqui rents a horse from greedy Toussaint, he needs his friend Ti Malice's help to get his money back. You can also find the story reprinted in *Best-Loved Folktales of the World,* edited by Joanna Cole (Anchor/Doubleday, 1983). (I, A)

"Dirt for Sale: A Story from Mexico" retold by Caroline Feller Bauer in *The Handbook for Storytime Programs* by Judy Freeman and Caroline Feller Bauer (ALA Editions, 2015). Ortego, a simple man, believes the man who tells him he can get rich from selling dirt. (P, I)

The Greatest Treasure by Demi, illus. by the author (Scholastic, 1998). In this Chinese folktale, wealthy Pang tries to destroy the happiness of Li, a poor farmer, by giving him a bag of gold. You'll love the farmer's wife's adage: "He who has heaven in his heart is never poor." Compare with the Ukrainian tale "Singing Together" in *Five-Minute Tales: More Stories to Read and Tell When Time Is Short* by Margaret Read MacDonald (August House, 2007), in which a rich man gives a poor family a bag of gold to stop them from singing together every evening. (P, I, A)

"The Tale of the Spotted Cat" in *The Coyote under the Table / El coyote debajo de la mesa: Folktales Told in Spanish and English* by Joe Hayes, illus. by Antonio Castro L. (Cinco Puntos, 2011). Juan, the poor youngest of three brothers, finds his fortune thanks to a resourceful cat he names Gato Pinto. (I, A)

MONKEYS

Caps for Sale by Esphyr Slobodkina, illus. by the author (HarperCollins, 2008, c1947). "You monkeys, you. Give me back my caps!" demands the cap-selling peddler. (P)

The Hatseller and the Monkeys: A West African Folktale by Baba Wagué Diakité, illus. by the author (Scholastic, 1999). BaMusa is horrified when he wakes from his nap and finds all his hats are gone, stolen by monkeys up in the mango tree. Compare this with the classic *Caps for Sale* by Esphyr Slobodkina, above. (P)

Itching and Twitching: A Nigerian Folktale by Patricia C. McKissack and Robert L. McKissack, illus. by Laura Freeman (Scholastic, 2003). When Rabbit and Monkey have dinner together, itchy Monkey and twitchy Rabbit agree that the first to scratch or twitch must do the dishes. (P)

"Ms. Monkey" in *From the Winds of Manguito: Cuban Folktales in English and Spanish / Desde los vientos de Manguito: Cuentos folkloricos de Cuba, en Ingles y Espanol* by Elvia Pérez, trans. by Paula Martín, illus. by Víctor Francisco Hernández Mora (Libraries Unlimited, 2004). A cute lady monkey covers her hairless head with a scarf, winds her tail around her waist, and dons a dress to go dancing with her handsome human sweetheart. (I, A)

MONSTERS

"The Bellybutton Monster" in *More Ready-to-Tell Tales from Around the World* by David Holt and Bill Mooney (August House, 2000). Jimmy's mother warns him that if he doesn't keep his blankets on, the Belly Button Monster will take away his belly button. This will be fun to pair with Judy Sierra's *Tasty Baby Belly Buttons: A Japanese Folktale,* below. (P)

Liza Lou and the Yeller Belly Swamp by Mercer Mayer, illus. by the author (Aladdin, 1997, c1976). A fearless little girl outsmarts all the fearsome critters she meets in the swamp. (P, I)

"Oniroku" in *Can You Guess My Name? Traditional Tales Around the World* by Judy Sierra, illus. by Stefano Vitale (Clarion, 2002). After a terrifying *oni* helps the finest builder in Japan build a bridge, it demands the builder's eyes as payment—unless the man can guess the *oni*'s name. (P, I)

Tasty Baby Belly Buttons: A Japanese Folktale by Judy Sierra, illus. by Meilo So (Knopf, 1999). When wicked *oni* kidnap all the babies of a village, a brave baby, Uriko-hime (the melon princess) sets out to rescue them. (P, I)

"The Terrible Nung Gwama" in *Shake-It-Up Tales: Stories to Sing, Dance, Drum, and Act Out* by Margaret Read MacDonald (August House, 2000). In China, an old woman gets advice from others on how to deter a terrible monster from eating her up. Search out the marvelous (though long out-of-print) picture-book version, *The Terrible Nung Gwama: A Chinese Folktale*, by Ed Young (Collins-World, 1978). (I, A)

MOON

(*See* Sun, Moon, Stars, and Sky)

MOSQUITOES

(*See* Insects)

MOUNTAINS

Ming Lo Moves the Mountain by Arnold Lobel, illus. by the author (Greenwillow, 1982). See under "Dance," page 299.

Yonder Mountain: A Cherokee Legend by Robert H. Bushyhead and Kay Thorpe Bannon, illus. by Kristina Rodanas (Marshall Cavendish, 2002). Only Soaring Eagle follows his chief's instructions to bring back what he finds on the mountaintop, though he finds nothing but a story. (I, A)

MULTIPLICATION

"The Doughnuts" in *Homer Price* by Robert McCloskey, illus. by the author (Viking, 1943). A doughnut machine run amok produces doughnuts until an entire luncheonette is crowded with them. This chapter in a book of small-town adventures can easily be shortened for telling aloud. (I)

Millions of Cats by Wanda Gág, illus. by the author (Coward, 1928). The classic picture book in which a man finds "hundreds of cats, thousands of cats, millions and billions and trillions of cats." (P)

One Grain of Rice: A Mathematical Folktale by Demi, illus. by the author (Scholastic, 1997). Offered a reward from a greedy raja for a good deed, Rani, a clever village girl, asks for a single grain of rice to be doubled each day for thirty days. Do the math—that's a lotta rice! (I)

Two of Everything: A Chinese Folktale by Lily Toy Hong, illus. by the author (Albert Whitman, 1993). After digging up a large pot in his garden, poor old Mr. Haktak is astonished to find whatever he throws in it automatically doubles. *One Potato, Two Potato* by Cynthia DeFelice (Farrar, 2006) also features a doubling pot. (P, I, A)

NAMES

"How Ijapa the Tortoise Tricked the Hippopotamus" in *Can You Guess My Name? Traditional Tales Around the World* by Judy Sierra, illus. by Stefano Vitale (Clarion, 2002). In a Yoruba pourquoi tale from Nigeria, the hippopotamus promises to leave the land and live in the water if anyone can guess his name. (P, I)

"I'm Tipingee, She's Tipingee, We're Tipingee, Too" in *The Magic Orange Tree and Other Haitian Folktales* by Diane Wolkstein (Knopf, 1978). When Tipingee's stepmother tries to give her away to an old man, the little girl gets her friends to dress like her so he won't know who she is. You can watch Diane Wolkstein tell this story to children when you look up *Tipingee* at www.youtube.com. (I)

Rumpelstiltskin by Paul Galdone, illus. by the author (Clarion, 1985). A splendid rendering of the Grimm brothers' tale. (P, I)

"The Silly Farmer" from *Tales of Nonsense & Tomfoolery* by Pleasant DeSpain, illus. by Don Bell (August House, 2001). A foolish farmer from Ethiopia consults a wise old woman to find out what kind of baby his wife is having and what its name will be. (I, A)

Tikki Tikki Tembo by Arlene Mosel, illus. by Blair Lent (Henry Holt, 1968). Mosel's picture-book version of the cautionary nonsense story has become a bit controversial. Some storytellers who love leading their audiences in reciting the boy's long name; others find it culturally insensitive, as the story is set in China but has no realistic Chinese components. In fact, the original versions of the tale came from Japan, where it is known as a *rakugo*, a traditional form of comedic monologue. (P)

"Tom Tit Tot" in *English Fairy Tales* by Joseph Jacobs, illus. by John Batten (Knopf, 1993). "Nimmy nimmy not, my name's Tom Tit Tot." Though hard to find, there's a delightful picture-book version of this Rumpelstiltskin variant called *Tom Tit Tot: An English Folk Tale* by Evaline Ness (Scribner, 1965). (P, I)

"Yung-Kyung-Pyung" in *Anansi, the Spider Man: Jamaican Folk Tales* by Philip M. Sherlock, illus. by Marcia Brown (Crowell, 1954). Anansi and his friends discover the names of the king's three daughters. (I)

NONSENSE WORDS AND WORDPLAY

"Abasement" from *The Weighty Word Book* by Paul M. Levitt, Douglas A. Burger, and Elissa S. Guralnick, illus. by Janet Stevens (Court Wayne, 2000). Because of his incompetence, Benjamin Van Der Bellows is demoted from his fortieth-floor office to the basement.

"Master of All Masters" in *English Fairy Tales* by Joseph Jacobs, illus. by John Batten (Knopf, 1993). A short, funny story in which a master insists on calling things by names he has invented. Find the text at www.authorama

.com/english-fairy-tales-45.html, or see page 182 in this book. Cynthia DeFelice's *Nelly May Has Her Say* (Farrar/Margaret Ferguson, 2013) is a zippy reworking of this comical story. (I, A)

"Ticky-Picky Boom-Boom" in *Anansi, the Spider Man: Jamaican Folk Tales* by Philip M. Sherlock, illus. by Marcia Brown (Crowell, 1954). A goat saves Tiger from Anansi's rampaging yams. You can also find the story in *Twice upon a Time: Stories to Tell, Retell, Act Out, and Write About* by Judy Sierra and Robert Kaminski (H. W. Wilson, 1989). There's another charming version of it printed online by storyteller Marilyn Kinsella at www.marilyn kinsella.org. Click on "Fabulous Folktales" and you'll find it. (P, I)

OBEDIENCE

"The Boogey Man's Wife" in *Misoso: Once upon a Time Tales from Africa* by Verna Aardema, illus. by Reynold Ruffins (Knopf, 1994). When Da is taken in for the night by a man so ugly people call him the Boogey Man, Da promises him the hand of Goma, his beautiful, usually obedient daughter, who does not like the Boogey Man one little bit. There's a wonderful refrain the Boogey Man recites, which is fun to sing in a complaining voice, and a very satisfying "No!" Goma says to everything he asks her to do. (I, A)

Chinye: A West African Folk Tale by Obi Onyefulu, illus. by Evie Safarewicz (Frances Lincoln, 2007, c1994). In a good sister/bad sister story, Chinye, sent by her stepmother to fetch water, is taken home by an old woman who tests her obedience. The African American version of this tale is the gorgeous Caldecott Honor Book, *The Talking Eggs,* by Robert D. San Souci (Dial, 1989). Find, too, a Haitian variant, "Mother of the Waters," in *The Magic Orange Tree and Other Haitian Folktales* by Diane Wolkstein (Knopf, 1978), in which an orphaned servant girl is taken in by an old woman who rewards the girl for her faithful assistance. (I)

OCEANS AND SEAS

"Sam the Whaler" in *Pete Seeger's Storytelling Book* by Pete Seeger and Paul DuBois Jacobs (Harcourt, 2000). Young Sam goes to sea on a whaling ship as a cabin boy. (P, I)

"Urashima Taro" retold by Rafe Martin in *Ready-to-Tell Tales from around the World* by David Holt and Bill Mooney (August House, 2000). A famous Japanese folktale about a kind fisherman who marries a princess from under the sea and returns home only to find that three hundred years have passed. Another retelling, "Urashima the Fisherman," can be found in *Wisdom Tales from Around the World* by Heather Forest (August House, 1995). Pair the tales with a retelling of Washington Irving's New England–based short story, "Rip Van Winkle." (I, A)

PAPER

The Paper Dragon by Marguerite W. Davol, illus. by Robert Sabuda (Atheneum, 1997). Humble scroll-painting artist Mi Fei must answer three difficult questions about paper when he volunteers to face the dragon Sui Jen.

"The Rainhat" in *Once Upon a Time: Using Storytelling, Creative Drama, and Reader's Theater with Children in Grades PreK–6* by Judy Freeman (Libraries Unlimited, 2007). In this paperfolding story about a little girl who doesn't have a rain hat, you'll make a pilgrim hat, a firefighter's hat, a pirate hat, and even a boat out of a simple piece of paper. (P, I)

The Story of Paper by Ying Chang Compestine, illus. by YongSheng Xuan (Holiday House, 2003). In a literary folktale, the three clever Kang brothers invent paper making. (P, I)

PARODIES

(*See* "Stories Reworked, Reimagined, Reinvented, Parodied, Satirized or Re-created from Folk and Fairy Tales" on page 247)

PARTICIPATION STORIES

"Bandana Man" in *Handmade Tales: Stories to Make and Take* by Dianne de Las Casas (Libraries Unlimited, 2008). An old woman who wants a baby makes a little man out of a bandana, but he runs away. As in all the stories in this delightful book, there are clear instructions for related crafts—in this case, for making an adorable Bandana Man. (P)

The Gunniwolf by Wilhelmina Harper, illus. by William Wiesner (Dutton, 1967). This is an American "Little Red Riding Hood" with wonderful, chantable refrains for children to sing and then act out in pairs. The original picture book was re-illustrated by Barbara Upton in 2003, but in the revised text, the refrain was changed to "The Alphabet Song," which was not an improvement. Look for the original text at http://teachers.net/lessons/posts/123.html. Margaret Read MacDonald also has a good version, "The Gunny Wolf," in *Twenty Tellable Tales: Audience Participation Folktales for the Beginning Storyteller* (American Library Association, 2005, c1986). (P)

"The Stubborn Turnip" in *Handmade Tales: Stories to Make and Take* by Dianne de Las Casas (Libraries Unlimited, 2008). String-story version of Russian tale, with a cheerful, clapping, chantable refrain. (P)

PEACE (*See* Conflict Resolution; War and Peace)

PERSEVERANCE

Don't Spill the Milk by Stephen Davies, illus. by Christopher Corr (Andersen, 2013). Carefully balancing a bowl of milk on her head, Penda walks through her West African village and into the grasslands to bring the bowl to Daddy, who is tending the sheep. (P)

The Little Red Hen by Jerry Pinkney, illus. by the author (Dial, 2006). See under "Cooperation," page 295.

Splinters by Kevin Sylvester, illus. by the author (Tundra, 2010). Cindy Winters works hard to earn enough money to join a hockey team, but Coach Blister's two daughters, the Blister Sisters, make her look bad on the ice. Thank goodness for her fairy goaltender. See under "Sports," page 345. (I)

Subira, Subira by Tololwa M. Mollel, illus. by Linda Saport (Clarion, 2000). See under "Lions and Tigers," page 323.

"The Two Frogs" in *Pete Seeger's Storytelling Book* by Pete Seeger and Paul DuBois Jacobs (Harcourt, 2000). Trapped in a tall can of fresh milk, the so-be-it frog says, "There's no hope"; the why-is-it frog says, "There must be some other way." (P, I)

PIGS

Aunt Pitty Patty's Piggy by Jim Aylesworth, illus. by Barbara McClintock (Scholastic, 1999). Aunt Pitty Patty's niece enlists everyone and everything she meets to make the stubborn new piggy enter the gate—but they refuse to help. The chantable refrain goes like this: "It's gettin' late, and piggy's by the gate sayin,' 'No, no, no, I will not go!'" For the original text of the English cumulative tale, "The Old Woman and Her Pig," on which this delightful version is based, see page 100. Also look for Margaret Read MacDonald's take on the story *The Old Woman and Her Pig* (HarperCollins, 2007), about an old woman who can't get her new pig to cross the bridge. (P)

The Pig Who Went Home on Sunday: An Appalachian Folktale by Donald Davis, illus. by Jennifer Mazzucco (August House Little Folk, 2004). In an Appalachian variant of "The Three Little Pigs," Tommy and Willie Pig don't listen to Mama Pig's advice about building their new houses, but Jackie Pig does—and he tricks Mr. Fox, too. Another Southern US picture-book version of the story is *The Three Little Pigs and the Fox* by William H. Hooks (Macmillan, 1989). (P)

"The Tamworth Two" in *Animal Stories: Heartwarming True Tales from the Animal Kingdom* by Jane Yolen, Heidi E. Y. Stemple, Adam Stemple, and Jason Stemple, illus. by Jui Ishida. (National Geographic, 2014). In 1998, two five-month-old pigs being driven by truck to a slaughterhouse in England, escaped and evaded their captors, earning the nicknames "Butch" and "Sundance" from the media. A true story where the fugitive pigs prevailed. (P, I, A)

Teeny Weeny Bop by Margaret Read MacDonald, illus. by Diane Greenseid (Albert Whitman, 2006). Teeny Weeny Bop, a feisty old lady, finds a gold coin and heads to the market to buy a pig. (P)

The True Story of the 3 Little Pigs by Jon Scieszka, illus. by Lane Smith (Viking Kestrel, 1989). Alexander T. Wolf defends his actions towards the three little pigs, insisting he was framed. (P, I, A)

PLANTS

"Echo and Narcissus" in *The McElderry Book of Greek Myths* by Eric A. Kimmel, illus. by Pep Montserrat (McElderry, 2008). Punished by the goddess Artemis for talking too much, forest nymph Echo is rejected by handsome, heartless Narcissus, who falls in love with his own reflection. Bring in a daffodil to show what Narcissus became. (I, A)

"Mikku and the Trees" in *Earth Care: World Folktales to Talk About* by Margaret Read MacDonald (August House, 2005). In a folktale from Estonia, Mikku is gathering firewood in the forest when the trees implore him not to cut them, saying, "You care for us and we will care for you." (P, I)

Muncha! Muncha! Muncha! by Candace Fleming, illus. by G. Brian Karas (Simon & Schuster, 2002). Mr. McGreely builds bigger and better fences to keep three little bunnies from getting into his just-planted garden. (P)

"Pickin' Peas" in *Shake-It-Up Tales: Stories to Sing, Dance, Drum, and Act Out* by Margaret Read MacDonald (August House, 2000). While Little Girl picks the peas in her garden, a brazen rabbit eats up all the ones she's left behind. MacDonald wrote a darling picture-book version of the story, illustrated by Pat Cummings (HarperCollins, 1998), though it's now out of print. (P)

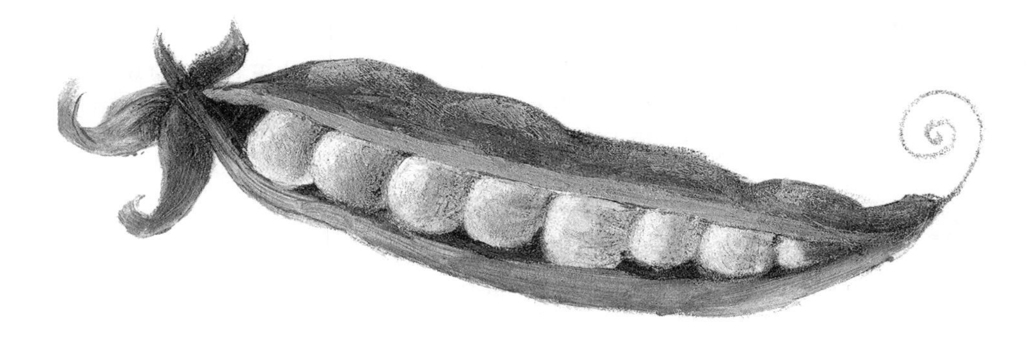

"Talk" in *The Cow-Tail Switch and Other West African Stories,* retold by Harold Courlander and George Herzog (Henry Holt, 1947). A farmer, digging up yams in his garden, is flummoxed when one of the yams speaks to him. (P, I, A)

Tops & Bottoms by Janet Stevens, illus. by the author (Harcourt, 1995). Hare offers to plant and harvest crops for Bear and split the veggies down the middle, which *seems* like a good idea . . . Find a Cajun variant in the title story of *Lapin Plays Possum: Trickster Tales from the Louisiana Bayou* (Farrar, 2002). For older audiences, tell "Tops and Bottoms" from *The Adventures of High John the Conqueror* by Steve Sanfield (Orchard, 1989), about the formerly enslaved High John, who offers to farm a piece of land for Old Boss and split the crops half and half. (P, I, A)

"Yop Up Peas" in *Pete Seeger's Storytelling Book* by Pete Seeger and Paul DuBois Jacobs (Harcourt, 2000). Young Johnny can't stop saying "Yop" instead of "Yes," and now all the peas in his garden are saying "Yop," too. (P, I)

POTS AND PANS AND OTHER KITCHEN IMPLEMENTS

The Empty Pot by Demi, illus. by the author (Henry Holt, 1990). See under "Honesty," page 318.

One Potato, Two Potato by Cynthia DeFelice, illus. Andrea U'Ren (Farrar, 2006). When Mr. O'Grady digs up a huge black pot from his garden, he soon discovers that it is a doubling pot. *Two of Everything: A Chinese Folktale* by Lily Toy Hong (Albert Whitman, 1993) also features a doubling pot. (P, I, A)

The Runaway Wok by Ying Chang Compestine, illus. by Sebastia Serra (Dutton, 2011). Sent to the market by his mother to trade eggs for rice for their New Year's dinner, Ming meets an old man who owns a remarkable singing wok. (P, I)

The Story of Chopsticks by Ying Chang Compestine, illus. by YongSheng Xuan (Holiday House, 2001). In a literary folktale, Kùai, the youngest of three boys in the Kang family, invents chopsticks. (P, I)

Tunjur! Tunjur! Tunjur! A Palestinian Folktale by Margaret Read MacDonald, illus. by Alik Arzoumanian (Marshall Cavendish, 2006). Wishing for a child to love, "even if it is nothing more than a cooking pot," a woman's wish comes true in the guise of a naughty Little Pot. (P)

POURQUOI TALES

(*See also* "Booklist: Pourquoi Tales" on page 143)

"How Animals Got Their Tails" in *Ashley Bryan's African Tales, Uh-Huh* by Ashley Bryan, illus. by the author (Atheneum, 1998). After the god Raluvhimba creates tailless animals, Spider takes a message to him from the animals asking him to remove the flies that won't stop biting them. The tale explains why spiders catch flies and why rabbits have such short tails. (P, I)

"Leelee Goro" in *Misoso: Once upon a Time Tales from Africa* by Verna Aardema, illus. by Reynold Ruffins (Knopf, 1994). To get fire, the animals must first fight a little girl named Leelee Goro who defeats Antelope, Leopard, Elephant, and Spider, but can't best Conk the snail. This intriguing story with a singable refrain explains the origins of eight different traits and behaviors, including why people cry and how they stop crying. (P, I)

PRINCES AND PRINCESSES

"The Princess and the Pea" in *Hans Christian Andersen's Fairy Tales* by Hans Christian Andersen, illus. by Lisbeth Zwerger, translated by Anthea Bell (Simon & Schuster, 1991). Is she a true princess? Of course she is. Read an original translation online at www.hca.gilead.org.il/princess.html. (P, I)

"The Princess Who Would Not Laugh" in *Polish Folktales and Folklore* by Michael Malinowski and Anne Pellowski (Libraries Unlimited, 2009). The youngest of three princes, considered a simpleton, is the one who finally cracks her up. A variant of the German tale by Grimm, "The Golden Goose," with a boy known as Dummling, can be found at www.authorama.com/grimms-fairy-tales-50.html. (I)

"Tattercoats" in *English Folktales* by Dan Keding and Amy Douglas (Libraries Unlimited, 2005). In an English variant of "Cinderella," the mistreated granddaughter of an old lord is persuaded by her only friend, the gooseherd boy, to attend the prince's ball dressed in her tattered clothes. (I, A)

QUEENS

(*See* Kings, Queens, and Rulers)

RABBITS AND HARES

Brother Rabbit: A Cambodian Tale by Minfong Ho and Saphan Ros, illus. by Jennifer Hewitson (Lothrop, 1997). Brother Rabbit promises to cure crocodile of his rough skin in exchange for a ride across the river. (P, I)

Conejito: A Folktale from Panama by Margaret Read MacDonald, illus. by Geraldo Valério (August House Little Folk, 2006). On his way to see his Tía Mónica, who will feed him till he is fat, a little rabbit encounters Señor Zorro, Señor Tigre, and Señor León, all of whom want to eat him. The chantable refrains, saucy song, and Spanish vocabulary sprinkled throughout make this a dream to tell. (P)

Rabbit Makes a Monkey of Lion by Verna Aardema, illus. by Jerry Pinkney (Dial, 1989). Rabbit and his friends Bush-rat and Turtle raid Lion's beehive high up in a calabash tree. (P, I)

The Rumor: A Jataka Tale from India by Jan Thornhill, illus. by the author (Maple Tree, 2002). Upon hearing a falling mango, a hare is convinced the world is breaking up and she warns the other animals to run. Compare this telling of the ancient story with "The Lion King" in *Buddha Stories* by Demi (Henry Holt, 1997) and with *Foolish Rabbit's Big Mistake* by Rafe Martin (Putnam, 1985). Make a connection with *Henny Penny* by Paul Galdone (Clarion, 1968) and *Chicken Little* by Rebecca Emberley and Ed Emberley (Roaring Brook, 2009). (P, I)

Who's in Rabbit's House? by Verna Aardema, illus. by Leo and Diane Dillon (Dial, 1977). Rabbit and his friends are afraid of The Long One inside the house. Compare this with the Polish version, "The Hairy Horned Goat," in *Polish Folktales and Folklore* by Michael Malinowski and Anne Pellowski (Libraries Unlimited, 2009), about a fierce-sounding goat that hides in Mr. And Mrs. Fox's den. (P, I)

RACES

"Ambecco and Aguatí" in *From the Winds of Manguito: Cuban Folktales in English and Spanish* by Elvia Pérez, trans. by Paula Martín, illus. by Víctor Francisco Hernández Mora (Libraries Unlimited, 2004). When Ambecco, the long-legged deer, challenges the animals to a race, Aguatí, the turtle, accepts and wins. Compare this with your favorite version of Aesop's "The Tortoise and the Hare." (P, I)

"Peace and Quiet" by Heather McNeil in *Hyena and the Moon: Stories to Tell from Kenya* (Libraries Unlimited, 1994). Aggravated with Tai the Vulture's constant bragging, Kinyonga the Chameleon challenges him to a race. (P, I)

Raccoon's Last Race: A Traditional Abenaki Story by Joseph Bruchac and James Bruchac, illus. by Jose Aruego and Ariane Dewey (Dial, 2004). Long-legged Azban the Raccoon pushes Grandfather Rock off a mountain and races it downhill. (P, I)

"The Wish-Fulfiller Shell" in *From the Mango Tree and Other Folktales from Nepal* by Kavita Ram Shrestha and Sarah Lamstein (Libraries Unlimited, 1997). See under "Kindness," page 321.

RAIN

Bringing the Rain to Kapiti Plain by Verna Aardema, illus. by Beatriz Vidal (Dial, 1981) An African cumulative tale in rhyming "This Is the House That Jack Built" style, which explains how Ki-Pat shot an arrow into the clouds to end the drought. (P)

"The Jolly Tailor" by Lucia Mercka Borski and Kate B. Miller in *Rainy Day,* ed. by Caroline Feller Bauer (HarperCollins, 1986). The tailor and his friend Scarecrow repair a hole in the sky. (P)

"Rainbow Makers: An Achomawi Legend" from *Spider Spins a Story: Fourteen Legends from Native America* by Jill Max (Rising Moon, 1997). The Spider Brothers climb up to the clouds to ask Old Man Above to stop the rain. (I)

RATS

(*See* Mice and Rats)

REPETITIVE, CUMULATIVE, AND SWALLOWING STORIES

(*See also* "Booklist: Beast Tales, including Cumulative and Repetitive Tales and Swallowing Stories" on page 129)

The End by David LaRochelle, illus. by Richard Egielski (Scholastic/Arthur A. Levine, 2007). A cumulative story of a princess and a knight, told backwards, starting with, "And they all lived happily ever after."

"Hoimie the Woim" by Judy Freeman in *Once Upon a Time: Using Storytelling, Creative Drama, and Reader's Theater with Children in Grades PreK–6* (Libraries Unlimited, 2007). A ravenous worm explains how he ate a rat, a cat, a dog, and a cow, getting fatter and fatter until he "boips." For a companion story, tell "Skippin' Home from School" in *Storytime Stretchers* by Naomi Baltuck (August House, 2007), in which Herbie, the family pet, swallows everyone until he burps. (P, I)

"The Pear Tree" in *Polish Folktales and Folklore* by Michael Malinowski and Anne Pellowski (Libraries Unlimited, 2009). A fine pear tree won't let go of its pears, the goat won't shake the tree, the dog won't bite the goat, and so on, with an infectious chantable refrain: "eye vye bim bom bom." (P)

"A Whale of a Tale" in *Twenty Tellable Tales: Audience Participation Folktales for the Beginning Storyteller* by Margaret Read MacDonald, illus. by Roxane Murphy (American Library Association, 2005, c1986). In the Far North, a hungry little boy swallows a codfish, a seal, a walrus, and even a whale before he feels full. (P)

REPTILES AND AMPHIBIANS (*See* Alligators and Crocodiles; Frogs; Snakes)

RESOURCEFULNESS

"Butterball" in *The Troll with No Heart in His Body, and Other Tales of Trolls from Norway* by Lise Lunge-Larsen, illus. by Betsy Bowen (Houghton Mifflin, 1999). Butterball, a young boy, is carried away by a troll hag in her sack, but he finds a way to get free. (P, I)

"The Magic Cap" by Johan Hart from *Picture Tales from Holland* (Lippincott, 1935) and reprinted in *The Buried Treasure, and Other Picture Tales,* selected by Eulalie Steinmetz Ross (Lippincott, 1958), both long out of print. Taking his cow to market to sell her, Willem is fleeced by three ne'er-do-wells, but his clever wife comes up with a plan to deal with them. Find the story in *The Handbook for Storytime Programs* by Judy Freeman and Caroline Feller Bauer (ALA Editions, 2015). (I, A)

Mary's Penny by Tanya Landmann, illus. by Richard Holland (Candlewick, 2010). A farmer's two sons compete to take over their father's farm, though it's the smart daughter who proves that brains are better than brawn. (P, I, A)

"What Herschel's Father Did" in *Five-Minute Tales: More Stories to Read and Tell When Time Is Short* by Margaret Read MacDonald (August House, 2007). When the innkeeper tells Herschel, a hungry traveler, that he can spare not a crumb or drop of food, Hershel says, "Then I will do what my father did!" (I)

RESPECT

"A Fair Reward" in *The Wise Fool: Fables from the Islamic World* by Shahrukh Hussain and Mucha Archer (Barefoot, 2011). Two bathhouse attendants treat Mulla Nasruddin with disdain until he gives them an undeserved gold coin for a tip. (I, A)

"Goha Gives His Son a Lesson about Life" in *Goha the Wise Fool* by Denys Johnson-Davies (Philomel, 2005). Goha, the Egyptian counterpart to Turkey's Nasreddin Hodja, takes his son—who always worries too much about what others think—for an instructive walk with his donkey. (I, A)

"Granny Squannit and the Bad Young Man" in *Flying with the Eagle, Racing the Great Bear: Stories from Native North America* by Joseph Bruchac (Fulcrum, 2011, c1993). In a Wampanoag tale, a disrespectful boy called Bad Young Man is taken by Granny Squannit, an old, old woman who knows how to deal with misbehaving children, into her cave. (I, A)

RESPONSIBILITY

"One, My Darling, Come to Mama" in *The Magic Orange Tree and Other Haitian Folktales* by Diane Wolkstein (Knopf, 1978). In a somber story, the rejected youngest daughter, Philamandré, is the only one left after the Devil takes her three sisters. (A)

"Papa God's Well" in *Earth Care: World Folktales to Talk About* by Margaret Read MacDonald (August House, 2005). In a Haitian tale about the abuse of power, Papa God gives the thirsty animals their own well, but Lizard—named its guardian—won't let anyone drink. (P, I)

"Tossing Starfish" in *Three-Minute Tales: Stories from Around the World to Tell or Read When Time Is Short* by Margaret Read MacDonald (August House, 2004). A man throws some of the starfish stranded on the beach back into the water. (P, I, A)

RIDDLES

"The Five Clever Girls" in *Polish Folktales and Folklore* by Michael Malinowski and Anne Pellowski (Libraries Unlimited, 2009). Gonella the trickster meets his match in five young sisters who outwit him with riddles about their family. (I, A)

"What Am I Thinking?" in *The Coyote under the Table / El coyote debajo de la mesa: Folktales told in Spanish and English* by Joe Hayes, illus. by Antonio Castro L. (Cinco Puntos, 2011). With the help of Pélon, a bald-headed man who can answer any riddle, the kind Padre Chiquito is able to answer three impossible questions posed by the greedy and cruel governor of the province. (I, A)

ROBBERS, THIEVES, AND OUTLAWS

"Ali Baba and the Forty Thieves" in *Tenggren's Golden Tales from the Arabian Nights* by Margaret Soifer and Irwin Shapiro, illus. by Gustaf Tenggren (Golden Books, 2003, c1957). A poor Persian woodcutter stumbles upon the loot-filled lair of forty robbers, who say "Open, sesame," to enter their magical cave. You'll also meet the levelheaded slave girl, Morgiana, who saves Ali Baba's life. (I, A)

"The Clever Thief" in *Best-Loved Folktales of the World,* edited by Joanna Cole (Anchor/Doubleday, 1983). In Korea, a thief gains an audience with the king to present him with a peach pit that he claims will grow golden peaches for any person who has never stolen or cheated. (I, A)

Meanwhile, Back at the Ranch by Anne Isaacs, illus. by Kevin Hawkes (Schwartz & Wade, 2014). After the wealthy young English widow Tulip Jones buys a ranch in By-Golly Gully, Texas, she must come up with a plan to outsmart crooked Sheriff Arroyo, leader of the infamous Hole in the Pants Gang, who intends to marry her. This original tall tale needs telling with a straight face and a bit of a Texas twang. (I, A)

"The Thief Who Kept His Hands Clean" in *Sweet and Sour: Tales from China,* retold by Carol Kendall and Yao-wen Li, illus. by Shirley Felts (Seabury, 1978). Magistrate Chen asks a group of robbery suspects to touch an old bronze bell, which he claims will peal when the real thief touches it. (I, A)

ROCKS AND STONES

Anansi and the Moss-Covered Rock by Eric A. Kimmel, illus. by Janet Stevens (Holiday House, 1988). A classic read-aloud, tell-it, act-it-out picture book of how Anansi tries to trick all of the animals out of their food. Janet Stevens's illustrations in this series are sublime. (P)

Coyote Steals the Blanket: A Ute Tale by Janet Stevens, illus. by the author (Holiday House, 1993). Though Hummingbird warns him not to, Coyote runs off with a blanket he finds draped over a rock, and now the rock is rumbling after him. See also a variant, *Iktomi and the Boulder* by Paul Galdone (Orchard, 1988). (P, I)

ROOSTERS

(*See* Chickens)

SCARY STORIES

(*See also* Ghosts; Halloween; and "Booklist: Jump Tales, Scary Stories, and Urban Legends" on page 145)

"The Coffin That Wouldn't Stop" in *Scared Witless: Thirteen Eerie Tales to Tell* by Martha Hamilton and Mitch Weiss, illus. by Kevin Pope (August House, 2006). Walking home alone, a man hears a "THUMP! THUMP! THUMP!" (The other twelve stories are perfect to tell as well.) (I)

The Dancing Skeleton by Cynthia C. DeFelice, illus. by Robert Andrew Parker (Macmillan, 1989). Aaron gets up out of his grave, sits in his rocker, and refuses to budge. (I, A)

Lucy Dove by Janice Del Negro, illus. by Leonid Gore (DK, 1998). In return for a sack of gold, seamstress Lucy Dove agrees to sew a pair of trousers in a haunted churchyard. Paul Galdone's picture-book version, *The Monster and the Tailor: A Ghost Story* (Clarion, 1982), is also nicely spooky. (I)

Precious and the Boo Hag by Patricia C. McKissack and Onawumi Jean Moss, illus. by Kyrsten Brooker (Atheneum, 2005). Precious is home alone when Pruella the Boo Hag comes calling. (P, I)

Scared Silly: 25 Tales to Tickle and Thrill by Dianne de Las Casas (Libraries Unlimited, 2009). These silly, scary jump tales—most of them peppy rewrites of ones you know—are just begging for a campfire or a darkened room. Bet you can't tell just one! (P, I)

The Tailypo: A Ghost Story by Joanna Galdone, illus. by Paul Galdone (Clarion, 1977). After an old man chops off, cooks, and eats the tail of a cat-like varmint, the critter returns, wanting his "tailypo" back. Find another version, "The Peculiar Thing," in *The People Could Fly: American Black Folk Tales* by Virginia Hamilton (Knopf, 1985). (I, A)

Wiley and the Hairy Man by Molly Garrett Bang, illus. by the author (Macmillan, 1976). An easy-reader version of an African American folktale about a boy and his quick-thinking mama and how they outwit the Hairy Man. Judy Sierra also told the story in a picture book of the same title (Dutton, 1996). (P, I)

"You Are Watched" in *Folktales from the Japanese Countryside* by Hiroko Fujita, edited by Fran Stallings with Harold Wright and Miki Sakurai (Libraries Unlimited, 2008). A hunter, about to shoot a pheasant, notices the bird staring at a snake that is staring at a frog that is staring at a worm, which makes him scared, thinking about what might be watching him. (I, A)

SEAS AND SEASHORE

(*See* Oceans and Seas)

SEASONS

Little Sister and the Month Brothers by Beatrice Schenk de Regniers, illus. by Margot Tomes (Marshall Cavendish, 2009, c1976). A Czechoslovakian story about a girl sent by her mean stepmother to find flowers and strawberries in a winter blizzard. You'll find another version of this story, "Strawberries in Winter," in Dan Keding's *Stories of Hope and Spirit: Folktales from Eastern Europe* (August House, 2004). (I)

Persephone by Sally Pomme Clayton, illus. by Virginia Lee (Eerdmans, 2009). After Hades abducts Persephone and brings her to the Underworld, her mother, Demeter—Goddess of Growth—curses the land so nothing will grow. (I, A)

SEEDS

(*See* Plants)

SHIPS AND SAILING

(*See* Oceans and Seas)

SHOES

(*See also* Clothing and Dress)

The Elves and the Shoemaker by Paul Galdone, illus. by the author (Clarion, 1984). A poor but honest shoemaker is aided by two selfless elves. You can find the original Grimm tale at www.authorama.com/grimms-fairy-tales-39.html. (P, I)

"The Golden Shoes" in *My Grandmother's Stories: A Collection of Jewish Folk Tales,* by Adèle Geras, illus. by Anita Lobel (Knopf, 1990). How do you show off your golden shoes when the streets are muddy? (P, I, A)

Pete the Cat: I Love My White Shoes by Eric Litwin, illus. by James Dean (HarperCollins, 2010). See under "Color," page 293. (P)

SHORT, SHORT STORIES

"The Gorilla That Escaped" in *Through the Grapevine: World Tales Kids Can Read and Tell* by Martha Hamilton and Mitch Weiss, illus. by Carol Lynn. (August House, 2001). In this shaggy dog story, Sarah is chased by a ferocious gorilla. "Tag, you're it!" he says when he reaches her. (P, I)

"A Nose for a Nose" in *Trick of the Tale: A Collection of Trickster Tales* by John Matthews and Caitlin Matthews, illus. by Tomislav Tomic (Candlewick, 2008). When Coyote plays a trick on Wildcat, giving him a short nose and a stubby tail, Wildcat returns the favor. (P, I)

"The Snooks Family" in Virginia Tashjian's *Juba This and Juba That,* illus. by Nadine Bernard Westcott (Little, Brown, 1969). No one can blow out the candle. This American folktale is also known as "The Twist-Mouth Family," which you can find online at www.story-lovers.com/liststwistmouthstory.html. (P, I)

"The Tail" in *More Celtic Fairy Tales* by Joseph Jacobs (Nabu, 2010, c1894). "If it had not been for that, this tale would have been a great deal longer." A really short story, available online at www.surlalunefairytales.com/authors/jacobs/moreceltic/tail.html. (P, I, A)

SIBLINGS

Anansi the Spider by Gerald McDermott, illus. by the author (Henry Holt, 1972). When Anansi disappears, his six sons use their singular talents to find him. (P, I)

The Chicken of the Family by Mary Amato, illus. by Delphine Durand (Putnam, 2008). "We have a secret to tell you. You're a chicken," Henrietta's two older sisters tell her. (P, I)

"The Cow-Tail Switch" in *The Cow-Tail Switch and Other West African Stories* by Harold Courlander and George Herzog (Henry Holt, 1947). To which of his seven sons should Ogaloussa the hunter bequeath his cow-tail switch, for helping to bring him back from the dead? (I, A)

Mufaro's Beautiful Daughters: An African Tale by John Steptoe, illus. by the author (Lothrop, 1987). One good sister and one bad; each hopes the king will choose her to be his queen. (P, I, A)

One-Eye! Two-Eyes! Three-Eyes! A Very Grimm Fairy Tale by Aaron Shepard, illus. by Gary Clement (Atheneum, 2007). Two-Eyes is mistreated by her sisters because she has two eyes instead of one or three, as they do. Go to www.aaronshep.com for a readers' theater script of the story. (P, I, A)

The Seven Chinese Brothers by Margaret Mahy, illus. by Jean and Mou-sien Tseng (Scholastic, 1990). Seven talented siblings mend a hole in the Great Wall of China. (P, I)

The Seven Chinese Sisters by Kathy Tucker, illus. by Grace Lin (Albert Whitman, 2003). In a feminist reworking of the traditional tale about those identical Chinese brothers, meet seven sisters, each with a special talent, who jump into action when the baby, Seventh Sister, is snatched away by a hungry red dragon. (P, I)

SINGING (*See* Songs and Music)

SISTERS (*See* Siblings)

SKELETONS (*See* Scary Stories)

SKY (*See* Sun, Moon, Stars, and Sky)

SLEEP (*See* Bedtime)

SNAKES

"Bruh Possum and the Snake" in *Sure as Sunrise: Stories of Bruh Rabbit & His Walkin' Talkin' Friends* by Alice McGill, illus. by Don Tate (Houghton Mifflin, 2004). Good-hearted Bruh Possum helps Bruh Snake three times, which is one time too many. From this story you'll learn, "No matter how good your heart, if you ever spot trouble, don't never trouble trouble if trouble don't trouble you." A jazzy Louisiana version of this story is "Elephant and Snake" in *Tell Along Tales!: Playing with Participation Stories* by Dianne De Las Casas (Libraries Unlimited, 2011). Another good one from Louisiana is "One Cold Day," also about Elephant and Snake, plus Compé Lapin (Rabbit) who comes to Eléphant's rescue. You will find it in Nancy Van Laan's *With a Whoop and a Holler: A Bushel of Lore from Way Down South* (Atheneum, 1998). (P, I)

"Delgadina and the Snake" by Laura Simms in *More Read-to-Tell Tales from Around the World,* edited by David Holt and Bill Mooney (August House, 2000). Delgadina cares for a magic red snake who gives her an unusual gift: when she washes her hands and shakes her fingers dry, gold coins fall from her hands. (I, A)

"The Terrible Black Snake's Revenge" from *The Sea of Gold and Other Tales from Japan* by Yoshiko Uchida (Scribner, 1965). A man named Badger encounters the man-eating, terrible black snake of the mountains. (I, A)

SONGS AND MUSIC

"The Bremen Town Musicians" in *The Seven Swabians, and Other German Folktales* by Anna E. Altmann (Libraries Unlimited, 2006). A warbling donkey, dog, cat, and rooster scare off robbers. An attractive picture-book version is *The Bremen-Town Musicians* by Ilse Plume (Doubleday, 1980), but you can find the text of the version by Jacob and Wilhelm Grimm online at: www.pitt.edu/~dash/grimm027.html. See how the story was transported to America in the literary folktale *Ol' Bloo's Boogie-Woogie Band and Blues Ensemble* by Jan Huling (Peachtree, 2010), below. (P, I, A)

"Mr. Benjamin Ram and His Wonderful Fiddle" in *Uncle Remus: The Complete Tales* by Julius Lester, illus. by Jerry Pinkney (Dial, 1999). Mr. Benjamin Ram's old-time fiddle playing gets him out of trouble with Brer Wolf. (I)

The Nightingale by Hans Christian Andersen, retold by Stephen Mitchell, illus. by Bagram Ibatoulline (Candlewick, 2002). The emperor discovers that a real bird is superior to a mechanical one. Compare this with Jerry Pinkney's picture-book version of the same title, reset from China to Northwest Africa (Putnam, 2002). (I, A)

Ol' Bloo's Boogie-Woogie Band and Blues Ensemble by Jan Huling, illus. by Henri Sorensen (Peachtree, 2010). On their way to New Orleans to sing in a honky-tonk, Ol' Bloo Donkey, Gnarly Dog, One-Eyed Lemony Cat, and Rusty Red Rooster stop off at a cabin to sing for their supper. A down-home retelling of "The Bremen-Town Musicians." (I)

"Playing the Fourth Part" in *The Hidden Folk: Stories of Fairies, Dwarves, Selkies, and Other Secret Beings* by Lise Lunge-Larson, illus. by Beth Krommes (Houghton Mifflin, 2004). At a Midsummer's Night dance, the fiddler plays "The River Sprite's Reel"—and can't stop. (I, A)

"Singing Together" in *Five-Minute Tales: More Stories to Read and Tell When Time Is Short* by Margaret Read MacDonald (August House, 2007). A rich man gives a poor family a bag of gold to stop them singing together every evening. (P, I, A)

SOUP

(*See* Food)

SPIDERS

(*See also* Anansi Stories)

"Arachne" in *The McElderry Book of Greek Myths* by Eric A. Kimmel, illus. by Pep Montserrat (McElderry, 2008). Arachne, a master weaver, accepts a challenge from Athena—goddess of wisdom, who invented weaving—to see who is more skilled in the craft. (I, A)

"How Animals Got Their Tails" in *Ashley Bryan's African Tales, Uh-Huh* by Ashley Bryan, illus. by the author (Atheneum, 1998). See under "Pourquoi Tales," page 335. (P, I)

"How Spider Got Its Web: A Wiyat Legend" from *Spider Spins a Story: Fourteen Legends from Native America* by Jill Max (Rising Moon, 1997). Spider asks the Old Man Above for a way to catch food. The other legends in this handsome collection, many spider-based, are also well worth telling, including "Swift Runner and Trickster Tarantula," a Zuni legend. (P, I)

"Two Feasts for Anansi" from *The Hat-Shaking Dance, and other Ashanti Tales from Ghana,* retold by Harold Courlander (Harcourt, 1957). How greedy Anansi got such a skinny waist. Find the story on page 193. (P, I, A)

SPORTS

The Princesses Have a Ball by Teresa Bateman, illus. by Lynne Cravath (Albert Whitman, 2002). In a modern rhyming update on the "The Twelve Dancing Princesses," the sisters wear out their shoes playing basketball. (P, I)

Splinters by Kevin Sylvester, illus. by the author (Tundra, 2010). See under "Perseverance," page 332.

SPRING

(*See* Seasons)

STARS

(*See* Sun, Moon, Stars, and Sky)

STORIES AND STORYTELLING

Interrupting Chicken by David Ezra Stein, illus. by the author (Candlewick, 2010). Little Red Chicken can't stop herself from interrupting Papa's bedtime book of fairy tales and giving life-saving advice to Hansel and Gretel, Little Red Riding, and Chicken Little. (P)

"Scheherazade or the Story of These Stories" in *Tenggren's Golden Tales from the Arabian Nights* by Margaret Soifer and Irwin Shapiro, illus. by Gustaf Tenggren (Golden Books, 2003, c1957). How the wise new wife of murderous woman-hater, King Shahryar, keeps her head by telling him bedtime stories for 1,001 nights. (I, A)

A Story, A Story by Gail E. Haley, illus. by the author (Atheneum, 1970). Caldecott winning picture book about how Anansi the Spider spread the world's first stories. (P, I)

SUMMER (*See* Seasons)

SUN, MOON, STARS, AND SKY

Anansi the Spider: A Tale from the Ashanti by Gerald McDermott, illus. by the author (Henry Holt, 1972). West African pourquoi tale from Ghana about Anansi's six talented sons and of how the moon came to be. (P, I)

"The Girl Who Married the Moon" in *The Girl Who Married the Moon: Tales from Native North America* by Joseph Bruchac and Gayle Ross (Fulcrum, 2006, c1994). On Kodiak Island (now part of Alaska), a girl marries the handsome Moon, who takes her to his house in the sky and warns her not to go in his storehouse. (I, A)

"Phaethon and Helios" in *Favorite Greek Myths* by Mary Pope Osborne, illus. by Troy Howell (Scholastic, 1989). Phaethon, son of Helios, loses control of his father's sun chariot and scorches the earth. (I, A)

"The Sack of Diamonds" by Helen Kronberg Olson in *Read for the Fun of It* by Caroline Feller Bauer (H. W. Wilson, 1992). A little old woman uses a slingshot to send diamonds up to the sky, where they become stars. (P, I)

Ten Suns: A Chinese Legend by Eric A. Kimmel, illus. by YongSheng Xuan (Holiday House, 1998). How the emperor's ten sons disobeyed him and why there is only one sun in the sky as a result. (I)

Why the Sky Is Far Away: A Nigerian Folktale by Mary-Joan Gerson, illus. by Carla Golembe (Little, Brown, 1992). The people are punished after Adese eats too much of the delicious sky. (P, I, A)

Why the Sun and the Moon Live in the Sky: An African Folktale by Elphinstone Dayrell, illus. by Blair Lent (Houghton Mifflin, 1968). African pourquoi tale explaining the creation of those two heavenly bodies. (P, I)

"The Wolverine's Secret" in *The Girl Who Dreamed Only Geese and Other Tales of the Far North* by Howard Norman, illus. by Leo and Diane Dillon (Harcourt, 1997). In the earliest Inuit times, an orphan boy sets out to rescue the sun and moon from the wolverine that has stolen them. (I, A)

TIGERS (*See* Lions and Tigers)

TREES (*See* Plants)

TRICKSTERS

(*See also* Anansi Stories; Coyotes; and "Booklist: Trickster Tales" on page 135)

"The Greedy Guest" by Cathy Spagnoli and Paramasivam Samanna in *Jasmine and Coconuts: South Indian Tales* (Libraries Unlimited, 1999). Afraid they will be accused of murder when a greedy soldier dies after swallowing a chicken bone at their house, a captain and his wife move the body to the doctor's house. "Old Dry Fry" from *Grandfather Tales* by Richard Chase (Houghton Mifflin, 1948) is an American variant of this amusing, slightly macabre story. (I, A)

"Mis Goose Deceives Mistah Bear" in *Sister Tricksters: Rollicking Tales of Clever Females* by Robert D. San Souci, illus. by Daniel San Souci (August House, 2006). See under "Bears," page 285. (P, I)

Sungura and Leopard: A Swahili Trickster Tale by Barbara Knutson, illus. by the author (Little, Brown, 1993). Sungura the rabbit looks for a sneaky way to get Leopard to leave the house they are sharing. (P, I)

TROLLS

(*See also* "Booklist: Tales from Scandinavia" *on* page 188)

D'Aulaires' Book of Trolls by Ingri and Edgar Parin D'Aulaire, illus. by the authors (Doubleday, 1972). Stories with all you need to know about forest trolls, mountain trolls, and bridge trolls. (I)

The Three Billy Goats Gruff by Peter C. Asbjørnsen and Jorgen E. Moe, illus. by Marcia Brown (Harcourt, 1957). Three goat brothers encounter a fierce troll guarding a bridge. You'll also love the version in *The Troll with No Heart in His Body, and Other Tales of Trolls from Norway* by Lise Lunge-Larsen, illus. by Betsy Bowen (Houghton Mifflin, 1999). (P, I)

Trouble with Trolls by Jan Brett, illus. by the author (Putnam, 1992). On her way to visit her cousin on the other side of Mount Baldy, Treva is waylaid by a succession of furry-tailed trolls who want to take her shepherd dog, Tuffi, but are satisfied when she gives them pieces of her warm winter clothing instead. (P)

TRUSTWORTHINESS

"Himsuka" in *Asian Tales and Tellers* by Cathy Spagnoli (August House, 1998). In a story-within-a-story from India, a king questions his three sons to decide which is the worthiest to succeed him; the third son tells him a story about a king who falsely accused a bird of betraying his trust. (I, A)

TRUTHFULNESS

(*See* Honesty)

TURTLES

"Anansi and His Visitor, Turtle" by Edna Mason Kaula in *Best-Loved Folktales of the World,* edited by Joanna Cole (Anchor/Doubleday, 1983). Anansi invites Turtle to share his dinner, but asks that he first go to the stream and wash his paws. There's also an amusing picture-book version of this story: *Ananse's Feast: An Ashanti Tale* by Tololwa M. Mollel (Clarion, 1997). (P, I)

Jabutí the Tortoise: A Trickster Tale from the Amazon by Gerald McDermott, illus. by the author (Harcourt, 2001). How Jabutí, a flute-playing trickster from the Amazon rain forest, cracked his smooth and shiny shell. Other pourquoi tales on the same subject are *The Flying Tortoise* by Tololwa M. Mollel (Clarion, 1994) and *How Turtle's Back Was Cracked: A Traditional Cherokee Tale* by Gayle Ross (Dial, 1995). Also read the title story, an Aesop's fable, in Margaret Mayo's collection *Tortoise's Flying Lesson: Animal Stories* (Harcourt, 1995). (P, I)

The Leopard's Drum: An Asante Tale from West Africa by Jessica Souhami, illus. by the author (Little, Brown, 1996). Achi-cheri, the tortoise—the "titchy little, weak little creature"—is the one who succeeds in bringing Leopard's drum to Nyame, the Sky-God. (P, I)

"The Singing Tortoise" in *The Cow-Tail Switch and Other West African Stories* by Harold Courlander and George Herzog (Henry Holt, 1947). A tortoise can't keep a secret. (P, I, A)

"The Singing Turtle" in *Look Back and See: Twenty Lively Tales for Gentle Tellers* by Margaret Read McDonald (H. W. Wilson, 1991). A turtle refuses to sing for a mean rich man. (P)

"Turtle of Koka" in *The Storyteller's Start-Up Book: Finding, Learning, Performing and Using Folktales* by Margaret Read MacDonald (August House, 1993). Threatened with being turned into turtle stew, Turtle of Koka fools the villagers into throwing him into the water. (P)

VALENTINE'S DAY

(*See* Love)

VEGETABLES

(*See* Food; Plants)

VILLAINS AND NOGOODNIKS

"Mr. Fox" in *English Fairy Tales* by Joseph Jacobs, illus. by John Batten (Knopf, 1993). Lady Mary has a most unsuitable suitor, whom she unmasks for what he is—a ladykiller. See the full text in this book on page 71. (A)

"Red Ridin' in the Hood" from *Red Ridin' in the Hood: And Other Cuentos* by Patricia Santos Marcantonio (Farrar, 2005). On her way to bring food to her ailing *abuelita,* Roja detours down sinister Forest Street and encounters Lobo Chávez in his low-rider Chevy. (I, A)

"What Am I Thinking?" in *The Coyote under the Table / El coyote debajo de la mesa: Folktales Told in Spanish and English* by Joe Hayes, illus. by Antonio Castro L. (Cinco Puntos, 2011). See under "Riddles," page 339.

VOLCANOES
(*See* Disasters)

WAR AND PEACE
(*See also* Conflict Resolution)

"Not Our Problem" in *Peace Tales: World Folktales to Talk About* by Margaret Read MacDonald (August House, 1995). How a simple drop of honey and a king who says, "It is not our problem," leads to war, in a thoughtful cautionary tale from Burma and Thailand. (I, A)

"The War between the Sandpipers and the Whales" in *Peace Tales: World Folktales to Talk About* by Margaret Read MacDonald (August House, 1995). Whale's warning to little Sandpiper to stay out of his water leads to a conflict of birds versus sea creatures, almost causing the destruction of all of them. MacDonald also put this out as a picture book, *Surf War! A Folktale from the Marshall Islands* (August House Little Folk, 2009). (P, I)

WEATHER
(*See* Disasters; Rain; Seasons; Wind)

WEDDINGS

"The Three Spinners" in *The Seven Swabians, and Other German Folktales* by Anna E. Altmann (Libraries Unlimited, 2006). Locked in a room filled with flax she must spin, a lazy girl accepts the help of three odd-looking women who ask to be invited to her upcoming wedding. For a Norwegian version, see "The Three Aunties" in *Tales of Enchantment* by Pleasant DeSpain (August House, 2001); from Ireland, there's "The Widow's Lazy Daughter" in *Favorite Fairy Tales Told in Ireland* by Virginia Haviland (Little, Brown, 1961). (I, A)

WIND

"The Boy and the North Wind" in *The Troll with No Heart in His Body, and Other Tales of Trolls from Norway* by Lise Lunge-Larsen, illus. by Betsy Bowen (Houghton Mifflin, 1999). Upset when the wind blows away the last of his mother's flour, young Per goes to see the North Wind, who gives him magical treasures. Other tales using similar themes or magic objects that get stolen and then retrieved include "The Lamb, the Tablecloth, and the Club" in *Polish Folktales and Folklore* by Michael Malinowski and Anne Pellowski (Libraries Unlimited, 2009); *The Table, the Donkey, and the Stick,* Paul Galdone's version of a story from the Brothers Grimm (McGraw-Hill, 1975); and *Willa and the Wind* by Janice M. Del Negro (Marshall Cavendish, 2005). (P, I)

WINTER
(*See* Seasons)

WISDOM

"The King Who Hated the Old" in *Asian Tales and Tellers* by Cathy Spagnoli (August House, 1998). See under "Elderly," page 302.

"This Too Shall Pass" in *Wisdom Tales from Around the World* by Heather Forest (August House, 1995). In ancient Israel, King Solomon asks his boastful captain of the guards to find him a ring that can make a happy person sad and a sad person happy. (I, A)

"Why Wisdom Is Found Everywhere" in *The Hat-Shaking Dance and Other Ashanti Tales from Ghana* by Harold Courlander with Albert Kofi Prempeh (Harcourt, 1957). Anansi collects the wisdom of the world in a big pot, but it's too hard to carry. You can also find the story online at www.archive.org/stream/anthologyofchild00horoarch, which will take you to the Internet Archive and the full text of the fifth edition of *The Anthology of Children's Literature*, compiled by Edna Johnson and others (Houghton Mifflin, 1969). (P, I, A)

WISHES

Joha Makes a Wish: A Middle Eastern Tale by Eric A. Kimmel, illus. by Omar Rayyam (Marshall Cavendish, 2010). On his way to Baghdad, Joha finds a wishing stick that grants the opposite of what he wishes for. (P, I, A)

"One Wish" in *More Ready-to-Tell Tales from Around the World* by David Holt and Bill Mooney (August House, 2000). In County Mayo, Ireland, a poor young man is about to kill a white deer to feed his family when it speaks to him, offering to grant him one wish. (P, I, A)

"The Three Wishes" in *More English Folk and Fairy Tales* by Joseph Jacobs (Flying Chipmunk, 2009). A man gets his wishes, but with ridiculous results, including a sausage on the end of his nose. Find this story and others like it at www.pitt.edu/~dash/type0750a.html#england. (I, A)

"Wishes" in *The Devil's Storybook* by Natalie Babbitt (Farrar, 1974). The Devil dresses as a fairy godmother and goes looking for someone to whom he can give a wish. (I, A)

WITCHES

(*See also* Baba Yaga)

Curse in Reverse by Tom Coppinger (Atheneum, 2003). Although poor childless Mr. and Mrs. Trotter offer to share their small house and supper with old witch named Agnezza, she still gives them the Curse of the One-Armed Man. (I, A)

Hansel and Gretel by Rika Lesser, illus. by Paul O. Zelinsky (Dodd, Mead, 1984). The classic Grimm tale. Also see *Hansel & Gretel*, another lovely version retold and illustrated by Susan Jeffers (Dutton, 2011, c1980). (I)

Heckedy Peg by Audrey Wood, illus. by Don Wood (Harcourt, 1987). An old witch turns seven children into seven types of food. (I)

Paco and the Witch: A Puerto Rican Folktale by Felix Pitre, illus. by Christy Hale (Dutton, 1995). La Bruja won't let Paco go unless he guesses her name. (I)

The Rabbi and the Twenty-Nine Witches by Marilyn Hirsch (Marshall Cavendish, 2009, c1976). A crafty rabbi finds a way for townsfolk to deal with a caveful of wicked witches. (P, I)

WOLVES

"Bagged Wolf" in *Sweet and Sour: Tales from China,* retold by Carol Kendall and Yao-wen Li, illus. by Shirley Felts (Seabury, 1978). A man saves a wolf from a hunting party but is dismayed to learn the wolf now plans to eat him. (I, A)

The Gunniwolf by Wilhelmina Harper, illus. by William Wiesner (Dutton, 1967). See under "Participation Stories," page 331.

The Three Little Wolves and the Big Bad Pig by Eugene Trivizas, illus. by Helen Oxenbury (McElderry, 1993). A turnabout parody version of "The Three Little Pigs." (P)

The True Story of the 3 Little Pigs by Jon Scieszka, illus. by Lane Smith (Viking Kestrel, 1989). See under "Pigs," page 333.

"The Wolf and the Seven Young Kids" by Jacob and Wilhelm Grimm. "Never open the door to strangers" is the moral that Mother Goat's kids learn the hard way. There are no picture books of this classic tale, but you can find an excellent translation at www.pitt.edu/~dash/grimm005.htm and another text version, "The Wolf and the Seven Little Kids," in *Best-Loved Folktales of the World,* edited by Joanna Cole (Anchor/Doubleday, 1983). (P)

WORDPLAY

(*See* Nonsense Words and Wordplay)

WRITERS

(*See* Authors)

Afterword: And, Finally . . .

JUDY FREEMAN TEACHES A GRADUATE COURSE IN STORYTELLING AT the School of Information and Library Science at Pratt Institute in New York City. At the end of the course, she asks her students to pair up and make a list—based on their experiences learning and telling stories for class—of their ten best reasons for telling stories. Here are some of the insightful responses from her class in 2009:

1. With every story you share, you will be carrying on an age-old tradition and making an impact on the lives of the children who listen to your tales.
2. It helps build and broaden the imagination, so you can see a story as you tell it, and your children can see the story as they listen to it.
3. Storytelling gives us the magic of language out loud.
4. Hearing stories helps us bond with the storytellers—whether it be a teacher or parent—when they look us in the eye and seem to be telling the story right into our brains.
5. Stories can form memories that will eventually be passed down to the next generation. With storytelling, a child can learn about his or her own heritage and develop new personal traditions.
6. Listening to stories provides us with vicarious life experiences and helps us feel empathy for people in our own lives and in the world at large. It can leave a lasting impression on children and even shape who they want to be and how they want to live their lives.
7. We learn about history and connect with other cultures around the world and see that we're more alike than different.

8. Hearing stories (and reading folktales) can help us deal with difficult situations in our own lives. If the hero of the story could surmount impossible odds, maybe we can, too.
9. It inspires other people to tell and share their own stories, which will inspire other people to tell and share their own stories, which will inspire other people to tell and share their own stories, into an endless story.
10. Because it's fun.

Can you ever hear too many stories? Here, in our final story of this volume, is one answer to that question.

The Endless Tale

From Fifty Famous Stories Retold *by James Baldwin (American Book Company, 1896)*

In the Far East there was a great king who had no work to do. Every day, and all day long, he sat on soft cushions and listened to stories. And no matter what the story was about, he never grew tired of hearing it, even though it was very long.

"There is only one fault that I find with your story," he often said. "It is too short."

All the storytellers in the world were invited to his palace; and some of them told tales that were very long indeed. But the king was always sad when a story was ended.

At last he sent word into every city and town and country place, offering a prize to any one who should tell him an endless tale. He said, "To the man that will tell me a story which shall last forever, I will give my fairest daughter for his wife; and I will make him my heir, and he shall be king after me."

But this was not all. He added a very hard condition. "If any man shall try to tell such a story and then fail, he shall have his head cut off."

The king's daughter was very pretty, and there were many young men in that country who were willing to do anything to win her. But none of them wanted to lose their heads, and so only a few tried for the prize.

One young man invented a story that lasted three months; but at the end of that time, he could think of nothing more. His fate was a warning to others, and it was a long time before another storyteller was so rash as to try the king's patience.

But one day a stranger from the south came into the palace.

"Great king," he said, "is it true that you offer a prize to the man who can tell a story that has no end?"

"It is true," said the king.

"And shall this man have your fairest daughter for his wife, and shall he be your heir?"

"Yes, if he succeeds," said the king. "But if he fails, he shall lose his head."

"Very well, then," said the stranger. "I have a pleasant story about locusts which I would like to relate."

"Tell it," said the king. "I will listen to you."

The storyteller began his tale.

"Once upon a time a certain king seized upon all the corn in his country, and stored it away in a strong granary. But a swarm of locusts came over the land and saw where the grain had been put. After searching for many days, they found on the east side of the granary a crevice that was just large enough for one locust to pass through at a time. So one locust went in and carried away a grain of corn; then another locust went in and carried away a grain of corn; then another locust went in and carried away a grain of corn."

Day after day, week after week, the man kept on saying, "Then another locust went in and carried away a grain of corn."

A month passed; a year passed. At the end of two years, the king said, "How much longer will the locusts be going in and carrying away corn?"

"O king!" said the storyteller, "they have as yet cleared only one cubit; and there are many thousand cubits in the granary."

"Man, man!" cried the king, "you will drive me mad. I can listen to it no longer. Take my daughter; be my heir; rule my kingdom. But do not let me hear another word about those horrible locusts!"

And so the storyteller married the king's daughter. And he lived happily in the land for many years. But his father-in-law, the king, did not care to listen to any more stories.

Here's something all grown-ups can be: social historians who can help children connect to their heritage and their humanity through stories. Nowadays, with so many forms of literature-based entertainment—TV, tablets, computer games and apps, e-books, videos, and the world of the Internet—we're not even sure if paper books will be around that much longer. Perhaps that's why it's so reassuring to connect with some of the old ways. No matter the medium, children need stories. And we're the ones who can deliver them, just like the griots and wandering troubadours of old. A storyteller is a kind of magician to children. "How did you do that," they ask in wonder. And we reply, "Once upon a time . . ."

Credits

From *The Hat Shaking Dance and Other Ashanti Tales from Ghana* by Harold Courlander with Albert Kofi Prempeh © 1957, 1985 by Harold Courlander. Reprinted by permission of the Emma Courlander Trust.

"The Pointing Finger" from *Sweet and Sour: Tales from China* by Carol Kendall and Yao-Wen Li. Text copyright © 1980 by Carol Kendall and Yao-Wen Li. Used by permission of Clarion Books, an imprint of Houghton Mifflin Harcourt Publishing Company. All rights reserved.

"1805: The Great Divide" from *The American Story: 100 True Tales from American History* by Jennifer Armstrong, text copyright © 2006 by Jennifer Armstrong. Used by permission of Alfred A. Knopf, an imprint of Random House Children's Books, a division of Random House LLC. All rights reserved.

"Note from the Author" from *The Troll with No Heart in His Body* by Lise Lunge-Larsen © 1999 by HMH Books for Young Readers. Used by permission of the author.

Subject Index

C

K

L

M

N

O

P

Q

R

S

T

U

V

W

X

Y

Z

Author Index

N

O

T

Title Index

Titles of books are shown in italic.
Titles of stories, articles, and chapters are shown in quotes.

A

C

D

E

F

G

H

L

N

O

P

R

S

U